Worlds Apart?

Worlds Apart?

Dualism and Transgression in Contemporary Female Dystopias

Dunja M. Mohr

CRITICAL EXPLORATIONS IN
SCIENCE FICTION AND FANTASY, 1
Donald Palumbo *and* C.W. Sullivan III, *series editors*

McFarland & Company, Inc., Publishers
Jefferson, North Carolina, and London

All quotations from *Walk to the End of the World, Motherlines, The Furies,* and *The Conqueror's Child*, by Suzy McKee Charnas, are used with the expressed permission of the author.

All quotes from the *Native Tongue* series are copyright 1984 by Suzette Haden Elgin. New York: The Feminist Press at CUNY, 2000. www.feministpress.org.

Margaret Atwood: *The Handmaid's Tale* © O.W. Toad Ltd., 1985. Used by permission of the author.

This book has originally been handed in as a doctoral thesis at the University of Trier in Germany.

Published with the support of the Hans-Böckler-Foundation, Düsseldorf, Germany.

LIBRARY OF CONGRESS CATALOGUING-IN-PUBLICATION DATA

Mohr, Dunja M., 1968–
  Worlds apart: dualism and transgression in contemporary female dystopias / Dunja M. Mohr.
    [Donald Palumbo and C.W. Sullivan III, series editors]
    p.   cm. — (Critical explorations in science fiction and fantasy ; 1)
  Includes bibliographical references and index.

  ISBN 0-7864-2142-8 (softcover : 50# alkaline paper) ∞

  1. American fiction—Women authors—History and criticism. 2. Dystopias in literature. 3. Women and literature—United States—History—20th century. 4. Women and literature—Canada—History—20th century.
  5. Atwood, Margaret Eleanor, 1939– Handmaid's tale.
  6. Fantasy fiction, American—History and criticism.
  7. Fantasy fiction, Canadian—History and criticism.
  8. Elgin, Suzette Haden. Native tongue trilogy. 9. Charnas, Suzy McKee. Holdfast chronicles. 10. Imaginary societies in literature. 11. Deviant behavior in literature.
  12. Dissenters in literature. 13. Dualism in literature.
  I. Title. II. Series.
  PS374.D96M64 2005
  813'.509372—dc22   2005000883

British Library cataloguing data are available

©2005 Dunja M. Mohr. All rights reserved

No part of this book may be reproduced or transmitted in any form or by any means, electronic or mechanical, including photocopying or recording, or by any information storage and retrieval system, without permission in writing from the publisher.

Cover illustration ©2005 Digital Vision

Manufactured in the United States of America

*McFarland & Company, Inc., Publishers
  Box 611, Jefferson, North Carolina 28640
  www.mcfarlandpub.com*

In memory of
Stéphane Doiron

Acknowledgments

Nothing appears out of thin air, and anything that is written is embedded in a web of support. With the greatest pleasure and gratitude I acknowledge the many people involved in the production of this work.

I would like to thank my doctoral thesis advisor, Prof. Dr. Horst Breuer, University of Trier, Germany, for wholeheartedly supporting this project and related endeavors in many ways, for allowing me to explore this field of study in my own manner, and also for providing me with the chance to teach utopian/dystopian literature. I am also indebted to Prof. Dr. Gerd Hurm, University of Trier, who agreed without further ado to be my second advisor.

It is a rare and valuable privilege to correspond with authors about their writing, and I am particularly grateful to Suzette Haden Elgin and Suzy McKee Charnas for allowing me to interview them, and for graciously offering to read, comment upon, and discuss the chapters dealing with their respective novels. While I was conducting an e-mail interview with Suzette for *Foundation*, an e-mail discussion about my approach ensued. As a result, Suzette provided me with invaluable comments on the chapter dealing with her novels.

With Suzy I conducted an "epic interview"—according to the editors of *The New York Review of Science Fiction*, which published the interview—at the 20th International Conference on the Fantastic in the Arts (ICFA) in Fort Lauderdale. The shorter, previously unpublished part of this interview is contained in the appendix. Suzy and I met again at WisCon 24 in Madison and at the 22nd ICFA, where Suzy proved to be a superb critic of my work. At WisCon Suzy generously contributed the manuscript of *The Conqueror's Child*, the concluding book of the *Holdfast* series, to the annual Tiptree Auction. I thank Margaret McBride for introducing me to Ron Larson, who had bought the manuscript and allowed me to pore over it.

Earlier versions of sections of this study have been published in *Selbst und Andere/s oder Von Begegnungen und Grenzziehungen*, edited by

Christina Strobel and Doris Eibl; in *Frauen in Kultur und Gesellschaft*, edited by Renate von Bardeleben; in *Foundation*; and in *Science Fiction Studies*. I would also like to acknowledge that the German academic journals *AAA—Arbeiten aus Anglistik und Amerikanistik* and *Referatedienst zur Literaturwissenschaft* allowed me to review and discuss Lucy Sargisson's notion of transgressive utopianism, which inspired the present study.

I presented earlier portions of this work on transgression and female utopian dystopias at the following conferences: 5. Workshop zur Frauen- und Genderforschung at the University of Trier; at the 2nd and the 3rd Fachtagung Frauen- und Genderforschung in Rheinland-Pfalz at the University of Mainz and at the University of Koblenz; at the German National Research Project "The Self and the Others" at the University of Trier; at WisCon 24 in Madison; at the 5th Internationales und Interdisziplinäres Symposion zur Geschlechterforschung at the University of Kiel; and at the 22nd ICFA in Fort Lauderdale. I have also presented an extended paper including Margaret Atwood's *Oryx and Crake* (2003) at the 120th MLA Convention in Philadelphia. I would like to thank the participants at those presentations (and the members of ICFA in particular) for their lively responses and suggestions, which helped me to develop my ideas.

I am indebted to the Hans-Böckler-Foundation in Düsseldorf, Germany, for granting me a doctoral scholarship and for generously providing the funds to attend numerous conferences at home and abroad. I especially want to thank Werner Fiedler for his encouragement and support.

Many people have assisted me in various ways to bring this study to fruition. I thank Karsten Domke for retrieving lost data from the matrix. He left this planet far too early. I would like to thank Dr. Silke Schlichtmann, Dr. Christina Strobel, and Dr. Astrid Swift for their reading of early drafts of various chapters and for their stimulating responses. My wonderful friend Nikki Jordan has helped with this project from its earliest stages: supplying me with an unceasing stream of related books (and some for diversion), locating and sending material from the United States that I could not access from Germany, and patiently and meticulously reading the manuscript. Prof. Dr. Bill Clemente provided essential succor through his encouragement, his enthusiasm, and his informed comments on the manuscript. I am further indebted to Bill, Anne Vasey, and Brian Attebery for making available to me their work on Suzy McKee Charnas. Don Palumbo has been a tremendous help in getting this study published, and Farah Mendlesohn asked me to do that Elgin interview just at the right time. Alain Brodeur and my Canadian family, Doiron-Richer, in Montréal, and my British family, Mary King and Peter Heard, in London always provided me with a home away from home during my research visits.

Finally, I would like to thank my sister Dr. Claudia Mohr for her ongoing support. My deepest thanks go to my parents, Brigitte and Alexander Mohr, who encouraged me to roam freely wherever I chose and to do so with an open mind, who taught me to question borders of various kinds, and who are my most loyal travelling companions on all roads past, present, and future. Above all, I thank my partner in life, Lucas Graßal, for steadfastly working with me on borderwalking utopia. Thank you all.

Dunja M. Mohr
Munich
May 2005

Table of Contents

Acknowledgments	vii
Introduction	1

PART I. LITERARY HISTORY AND THEORETICAL BACKGROUND

1 ~ The Classical Vision: Utopia, Dystopia, and Science Fiction	11
2 ~ Demanding the Possible? The Artificiality of Boundaries	49

PART II. TEXTUAL ANALYSES

3 ~ Rewriting the Colonization of Physical and Mental Space: Suzette Haden Elgin's *Native Tongue* Trilogy	71
4 ~ Beyond Separate Worlds and War: Suzy McKee Charnas's *Holdfast* Series	145
5 ~ The Poetic Discourse of the Split Self: Margaret Atwood's *The Handmaid's Tale*	229
Conclusion	270
Appendix: "First you are human": An Interview with Suzy McKee Charnas	281
Bibliography	287
Index	305

Introduction

> *Anyone who takes the either/or, light/dark, order/chaos dichotomy that feminism has embraced really, really seriously will end up in the same place, falling over the brink into the utter void where there are no more stories.*
> —Gwyneth Jones, *Deconstructing the Starships* [31]

The oracular voice of the British writer Gwyneth Jones cautions against stories that only rise from a pandemonium of opposites, exclusory dualisms, and neat compartmentalizations, because such tales remain in the realm of dualism and, eventually, evaporate into nothingness.[1] Yet there are stories, drawn from the abyss of polarizations, that have begun to move beyond the either/or dichotomy and that tell not of a void but of futures in the plural sense. The pandemonium from whence such unheard tales arise is a literature of subversion that speculates about the future, while desiring the transformation of the present, and that demands the (im)possible: the transgression of dualism.

Literature that relies on dualisms has been, and often still is, the rule rather than an exception. In fact, literary genres compose a meta-pandemonium of literary opposites. Ever since Aristotle's *Poetics*, genres have been hierarchized and boundaries and aesthetic categories have been constructed, producing limiting canons based on exclusion. Literary criticism has notoriously distinguished between high and low culture, between the canon of the chosen few for the chosen few and its paraliterary underdog for the masses.[2] Firmly established on binarisms, this

---

[1] *Jones refers here explicitly, among others, to Charnas's first two novels of the* Holdfast *series and to Atwood's* The Handmaid's Tale, *and critically asserts that these authors take "a proposition from their parent culture ... and run ... with it, far as they can go ... right up against the wall of the world," because these stories of "classic fall-of-patriarchy scenario[s] ... [have] nowhere to go" (31). Jones calls for feminist science fiction "to abandon ... its either/or stance" (33), but fails to notice that authors such as Charnas, Atwood, and Elgin have attempted exactly such a transgression.*

[2] *Although, it must be noted, the division into high and low art is hardly as traditional as often suggested. Terms like popular fiction and bestseller began appearing around the 1880s with the*

2 Introduction

ideology of generic purity and canon-building has practiced literary inclusion and exclusion, smugly keeping the same in while keeping the *other* out. Questioning such practices, postmoderism has questioned and dissolved the distinction into high and low literature, broadened the notions of canonicity, subverted, destabilized, and dissolved boundaries of various kinds, and it has collapsed the hierarchization of genres.[3]

At the same time the age of postmodernism has, as Chris Ferns so aptly enumerates, poured out a so far unprecedented list of obituaries, proclaiming the "[d]eath of the Novel, and of the Author, but also the End of Ideology, and even—in the aftermath of the collapse of the Soviet bloc—the End of History" (1999, 1). Without doubt, Russell Jacoby's provocative study *The End of Utopia* (1999), announcing that the "utopian spirit—a sense that the future could transcend the present—has vanished" (xi), can be added to this list of obituaries. Getting back at radical notions, above all at feminism, postcolonialism, and postmodernism, Jacoby notes a "collapsing [of] intellectual visions and ambitions" (xii) and concludes that the "belief that the future could fundamentally surpass the present ... is stone dead. Few envision the future as anything but a replica of today.... There are no alternatives. This is the wisdom of our times, an age of political exhaustion and retreat" (xi–xii). Inasmuch as Jacoby addresses literary utopia understood as the universal blueprint of perfection, his charge seems justified; yet it is equally justifiable to hesitate to include literary utopia in the list of postmodern obituaries. On the contrary, literary utopia (and dystopia) is very much alive. In his eagerness to debunk utopia, Jacoby gazes exclusively at classical and modern utopian texts and never once turns to look at contemporary literary utopia and dystopia, perhaps because these postmodern texts are to a large extent feminist.[4]

[continued] *emergence of a mass market, of the penny dreadful, and later of pulp fiction; they are largely connected with developments in the publishing industry and the social developments leading to a growing mass literacy and thus to a mass audience from the mid–nineteenth century on.*

[3]*Thus, today the academically more respectable utopian and dystopian literature and the fast growing field of science fiction (sf), once considered paraliterature and a newfangled genre of non-canonic popular literature, can look back on a long history of academic standing, as Tom Moylan outlines in* Scraps of the Untainted Sky *(2000) and as the 1999 special issue of* Science Fiction Studies, *one of the three leading academic journals in the field, proves. On the growing body of literary criticism on utopian/dystopian literature, see Gary K. Wolfe (1986) and Paul G. Haschak (1994). Various bibliographies and encyclopedias document the vast abundance of utopian/dystopian literature in English-speaking literatures; among the best known are those by Lyman Tower Sargent (1988) and by Mary Ellen Snodgrass (1995).*

[4]*Seminal works on feminist literary utopia/dystopia and science fiction such as works by Sarah Lefanu (1988), Nan Bowman Albinski (1988), Frances Bartkowski (1989), Marleen S. Barr (1992; 1993; 2000), and Jenny Wolmark (1994; 2000) have established women writers as important contributors to, and innovators of, the genre. Yet the inclusion of women writers' works is still not the rule, as another recent study proves. The Australian critic and science fiction writer*

Introduction

As this study shows, contemporary utopian narratives indeed abound, though in the disguise of dystopias that contest and disprove the notion that we live in a post-ideological age, where ideal societies are out of fashion. These works challenge the claim that this is an age devoid of imaginative hope and speculation, an age that "cannot picture ... a world that is *essentially* different from the present one, and at the same time better" (Fukuyama 46). What could be more radically different than imagining and creating from a world riven by binary logic an alternative world of transgressions, of new interstices and interrelations? These contemporary, predominantly feminist texts envision precisely such a world, demonstrating such transgressions on the generic, the formal narrative, and the content level.

While some critics have noticed a shift within the utopian/dystopian genre and have recognized the emergence of the critical utopia and recently of the critical dystopia, in her study *Contemporary Feminist Utopianism* (1996), the British political scientist Lucy Sargisson has identified the more radical shift towards transgression in select feminist literary, postmodern, and political theories and in a number of feminist utopian/dystopian narratives. Aiming at the establishment of and the call for a new transgressive utopianism, Sargisson, however, only fleetingly touches upon transgression in a number of feminist utopian/dystopian works to underline her interest in a political oppositional movement grounded in the transgression of dualistic thinking. Thus, while her findings provide the starting point and the theoretical groundwork for my literary analysis, this study analyzes in depth transgressive aspects of contemporary feminist utopian/dystopian literature and argues that these texts form a new subgenre: that of feminist "transgressive utopian dystopias." I suggest calling these hybrid texts transgressive utopian dystopias for two reasons. First, they incorporate within the dystopian narrative a utopian undercurrent. Second, these utopian strategies criticize, undermine, and transgress the established binary logic of dystopia. The objective of this study is therefore threefold. Apart from identifying generic mergings and hybridizations and examining transgressions on the formal narrative level, I investigate, on the one hand, the dualisms the dystopian narratives are grounded in and, on the other hand, trace the various transgressions therein that embody the utopian narrative strands.

From a number of feminist dystopian texts that propose utopian

---

[continued] *Damien Broderick (1995; the second part of his dissertation turned into an academic triptych) does largely not consider feminism(s) and women science fiction writers. Broderick's study, however, is otherwise valuable in terms of an analysis of postmodernism's influence on the science fiction narrative, though much of it, as David N. Samuelson has justly criticized, centers around and reads like an exclusive "homage" to and "apotheosis" (150) of Samuel R. Delaney.*

alternatives and/or suggest transgressions on various levels—for instance, Angela Carter's *Heroes and Villains* (1969) and her *Passion of New Eve* (1977), Joanna Russ's *The Female Man* (1975), Marge Piercy's *Woman on the Edge of Time* (1976) and her *He, She and It* (1991), to name just a few—I have chosen Suzette Haden Elgin's *Native Tongue* (1984), *The Judas Rose* (1987), and *Earthsong* (1994); Suzy McKee Charnas's *Walk to the End of the World* (1974), *Motherlines* (1978), *The Furies* (1994), and *The Conqueror's Child* (1999); and Margaret Atwood's *The Handmaid's Tale* (1985) for various reasons. On the one hand, the *Native Tongue* trilogy and the *Holdfast* tetralogy are like *The Handmaid's Tale* part of the internal canon building within feminist utopian and dystopian literature. In a recent interview with Suzy McKee Charnas, Joan Gordon, for instance, has claimed the *Holdfast* series as one of the "canonical texts of feminist science fiction" (447); yet only a handful of academics has focused on the first two books of each series in short articles. Sargisson's own study briefly refers to the first two books of Charnas's *Holdfast* tetralogy and completely ignores Elgin's trilogy and Atwood's dystopia. In fact, little secondary material has appeared on the works by Elgin and Charnas and virtually none on *Earthsong, The Furies*, and *The Conqueror's Child*. Even recently published studies on feminist utopian, dystopian, and science fiction ignore these last novels (although due to the publication date criticism on *The Conqueror's Child* must naturally be sparse). Both Jane Donawerth (1997) and David Sisk refer to *Earthsong* only in passing, whose publication Dagmar Priebe (1998) entirely omits, while Gwyneth Jones's collection of essays (1999) contains at least a review of *The Furies*. Surprisingly, neither series has been the subject of a detailed full-length study and precisely such a detailed analysis of both series— as dystopias *and* as utopias—the study on hand thus provides.

On the other hand, I have chosen this body of texts in particular because these works are highly instructive and very successful examples of the postmodern turn to the transgressive utopian dystopia.[5] Because the texts by Charnas and Elgin are series and have been written over a

---

[5]*Ursula K. Le Guin's* The Left Hand of Darkness *(1969), which invalidates dualistic human categorization into woman or man on the content level but fails to do so narratively, describes a good example of how very tricky the actual narrative representation of the envisioned transgression of bipolarity is. On the planet Winter, peopled by sexually altered human offspring, Gethenians alternate between sexually inactive periods of androgyny and "kemmer," an oestrus period during which a Gethenian develops through hormonal secretion into a sexually active female or male, depending on whether female or male hormonal dominance develops during that particular oestrus period. Gethenians have no control whatsoever over this process. Although it is an intriguing thought experiment on eliminating gender and dualism, Le Guin fails to address adequately this transgressive change in sex and sexuality on the narrative level, as readers and critics have repeatedly pointed out and as she notes herself: "the Gethenians seem like* men, *instead of menwomen" (Le Guin 1979b, 168). In defense of the central character Estraven, Le Guin claims that she perceives "him" "as man and woman, familiar and different, alien and utterly*

long span of time, they demonstrate exceptionally well the development of a utopian subtext within a narrative that starts out as a predominantly dystopian text. Contesting the reading of *The Handmaid's Tale* as a classical dystopia, I chose Atwood's novel to illustrate that, read from a fresh perspective, even in well-established classical feminist dystopian texts transgressive aspects and a utopian potential can be discerned. Focusing on the dystopian narrative, critics have tended to overlook this utopian subtext so far.

Part I of this study lays out the generic and the theoretical background for the close readings of the novels in the second part. To situate the new transgressive subgenre within the literary genre, the first chapter outlines the literary history of utopia, dystopia, and science fiction (sf) and pays specific attention to the definitions and classifications of each subgenre. I briefly delineate the generic developments and postmodern genre mergings within each subgenre—from classical utopia to modern, to socialist, and to feminist utopia; from classical dystopia to feminist dystopia; from scientific romance to space opera, to inner space fiction, and to cyberpunk—since a comprehensive literary history of the genre would definitely exceed the scope of this study.

Concentrating first on the shift from critical utopia and critical dystopia to transgressive utopia and transgressive utopian dystopia, the second chapter provides a theoretical discussion of Sargisson's concept of transgression and the postmodern, feminist, and poststructuralist theories she draws on. Additionally, I discuss the transgressive aspects of postcolonial theories, which Sargisson's study does not include, but which assume an important position in the *Native Tongue* and the *Holdfast* series. Moreover, just as the colonialist narrative drive of and the postcolonialist critique in utopian, dystopian, and science fiction have generally not been topicalized, both series have not yet been studied from or linked with a postcolonial perspective.

The second part of this study consists of close readings of each author's works. Rather than discussing themes, I purposely chose to devote a chapter to each body of texts, since such an approach avoids cumbersome cross-references and clarifying repetitions and facilitates the detailed textual analysis, particularly in the case of the *Native Tongue* and the *Holdfast* series. After a brief introduction of the relevant themes discussed in the respective chapter, each of the three chapters of the second part provides short plot summaries and then proceeds to examine the novels' generic hybridity, narrative structure, transgressive aspects of

[continued] *human" (ibid. 168). This failure of depicting the Gethenians as "menwomen" is partly due to the use of the generic pronoun "he," but more importantly to her failure of "showing the 'female' component of the Gethenian characters in action" (ibid. 168), as Le Guin admitted upon re-examination of her novel.*

form, postmodern narrative elements, and transgressive narration. Focusing my thematic analysis on the dualistic dystopian and on the transgressive utopian narrative strands, I approach the body of texts from a postcolonial and feminist perspective and pay particular attention to the interrelating categories of gender, race, and class. Although some aspects concerning the employed and transgressed binaries overlap, each author foregrounds other issues and, therefore, each chapter provides a slightly different focus.

In the third chapter I read Elgin's *Native Tongue* trilogy—among this body of dystopian texts Elgin's novels come decidedly the closest to sf—as a postcolonial counter-narrative within the context of the colonial discourse of sf. I argue that she repositions the colonial object (Aliens) as subject and the earth/center as peripheral to the universe. Furthermore, Elgin connects this postcolonial criticism of space imperialism/colonialism with a feminist critique of the way patriarchy exploits women and colonizes women's minds. Thematically, I first foreground the various dualistic patterns of the dystopian narrative and then turn to the utopian subtext. Postulating the decolonization of physical and mental space, of the mind and the body, Elgin suggests two transgressive utopian projects: Láadan, a women's language that represents female perceptions of reality, and Audiosynthesis, a form of active chanting that nourishes humans with soundwaves similar to the photosynthesis process for plants. Among the transgressions that Elgin advocates are the reconceptualization of the dualistic nature of our thinking, our approach to reality, and the reorganization of geographical and bodily space in terms of center/periphery, individual/community, inside/outside, human/alien or human/non-human perception, subject/object, body/mind, and spirit/matter. It is not my aim to enter or to elaborate on the linguistic debate that Láadan has sparked among critics, who have almost exclusively focused on Elgin's linguistics, discussing the probability and validity of Elgin's artificial women's language. Rather, in my endeavor to verify the transgressive potential of Láadan, I look at the women's language from a postcolonial perspective, connecting the Sapir-Whorf hypothesis with Homi K. Bhabha's "aesthetics of liberation" and code-switching. My investigation of language acquisition and the psychological nature of Láadan, however, is informed by Julia Kristeva's semiotics, Hélène Cixous's feminine libidinal economy, and Luce Irigaray's *le parler femme*.

Where Elgin draws on and rewrites the sf trope of aliens and the colonization of outer space, Charnas refers to the mythical/historical Amazon culture that in a redesigned fashion functions less as a utopian model than a utopian stimulus for the dystopian Holdfast society engaged in the reconstruction of their dysfunctional society. Unlike Elgin, Charnas does not propose specific utopian projects; rather, she suggests the individual experience of borderwalking,[6] of slipping in and out of different societies, cultures, and norms, so that all societal and personal aspects are involved in the transformation of society. Roughly divided into the sections past, present, and future, the fourth chapter on Charnas addresses first the narrative's move from the patriarchal/colonial monopolization of the representation of the past—the exclusive construction of truth as represented in the collective cultural and the personal memory stored in myths, religions, history, and stories—towards an exploration of the intersections of myth/history, the transgression of the spirit/matter, madness/sanity, and orality/literacy divide, and towards a plurality of truths, histories, religions, and perspectives. In the section on the reshaping of the present, I focus on the cultural, social, familial, generational, personal, and sexual relationships that are all characterized by a master/slave opposition. In contrast, the utopian redefinitions of interpersonal relationships hinge on the necessary shift from biological to psychological ties, from enforced sexual orientation towards transgressive polygendered sexualities, and with regard to intercultural relationships on the formation of a hybrid cultural identity. My discussion of the social transformation revolves around themes of neo-colonialism, rehumanization, and the necessity to experience *both* roles, that of master and slave. The last part of the fourth chapter deals with the shaping of the future and applies as well as extends Marie Louise Pratt's notion of the "contact zone" and of the ensuing process of "transculturation" to the aforementioned principle of borderwalking. Borderwalking involves here the transgression of a number of binary poles, including mind/body, masculine/feminine notions, human/animal, and cultural and sexual divides.

Contradicting the standard readings of *The Handmaid's Tale* as a classical dystopia, the fifth chapter traces—apart from ascertaining the various forms of fragmentation on the geographical (USA/Canada), the sociopolitical (male/female), and the psychological level (self/other)— the utopian subtext of Atwood's novel: the poetic discourse of the split subject. While the Australian critic Sonia Mycak (1996) has analyzed the recurrent motif of the split subject from a psychoanalytical and phenomenological angle in six novels by Atwood, her study leaves out *Surfacing* and *The Handmaid's Tale*. Moreover, Mycak follows the frequent interpretation of the female split subject as Atwood's dualistic view of the world. So far only Eleonora Rao (1993) has marginally touched the composite nature of Atwood's fiction. However, her study covers primarily

---

[6]*I coined the terms "borderwalking" and "borderwalker" to denote the ongoing process of walking along and invariably transgressing the various bipolar borderlines of the categories class, race, gender and age, to name just a few.*

the dialectics of oppositions, such as past/present, reality/fiction and the split functions/roles of women in the novel, and provides no detailed analysis of *The Handmaid's Tale*. Unlike these readings that reduce Atwood to a writer enmeshed in binary logic, I argue that the poetic discourse of the narrating split subject constitutes a form of resistance and allows psychological survival, because the split is multiple rather than dualistic (i.e., schizophrenic). From a Kristevan approach, I investigate the utopian potential of poetic language and the act of narrating that allows the decentered subject, juggling various perspectives, versions of truth/reality, and multiple meanings of language, to escape from the binary logic of either/or and instead to repattern the consciousness and to persist in a psychic state of plurality.

While the three close readings deal with the novels separately, the last chapter presents the combined findings of the textual analyses. This chapter compares the various suggested utopian transgressions, the interstitial spaces these transgressive utopian dystopias open up, and the moments of disruption of binaries on the levels of genre, narrative, and content, and then summarizes what similarities the novels share and what differentiates them. Turning to the very impetus dystopian and utopian literature is fueled by, namely the dissatisfaction with the sociopolitical status quo and the desire for change, the last chapter also deals with the relevancy of these utopian transgressions and asks how the imagination of the future, the telling of stories of the future, can shape the present. Neither dystopia nor utopia provide blueprints for political action; but as literary thought experiments, their very objective is the creation of fictional future scenarios that may induce transformational paradigm shifts in the present, or a momentarily altered perception of our present reality. It is perhaps this inherent hybridity of being located between fiction and reality, vision and action, of being situated between the envisioned possible in the future and what is perceived as yet impossible in the present, of speaking from beyond the suffocation of dualism that allows these stories to capture glimpses of an essentially different and better world.

PART I
LITERARY HISTORY AND THEORETICAL BACKGROUND

1
The Classical Vision
Utopia, Dystopia, and Science Fiction

> *The utopian impulse begins in the radical inadequacy of the present; it deconstructs our assumptions about social inevitability through representations that provoke a cognitive dissonance between the present as lived and the potentialities hidden within. Utopia tempts us as an evocation of political desire.*
> —Jean Pfaelzer, "What Happened to History?" [198–199]

> *In Paradise there are no stories, because there are no journeys. It's loss and regret and misery and yearning that drive the story forward, along its twisted road.*
> —Margaret Atwood, *The Blind Assassin* [518]

Popular usage of the highly ambiguous term utopia, always posited in the realm of aesthetic conflict between mimesis and the fantastic, is derogatory. Generally, when we talk about utopia, utopian thought or utopianism we mean something unattainable, an illusion that can never be realized. While Thomas More described *nowhere*, a non-existent (good) place, with his neologistic pun *utopia/eutopia*—derived from the Greek noun "topos" (place) and the prefixes "u"/"ou" (no/not) and "eu"/good)[1]—for most of us utopia nowadays carries a pejorative connotation and is colloquially used to denigrate all sorts of seemingly "unrealistic," overtly idealistic, absurd or foolish proposals. The usage of the general term utopia is very vague and can be found in all sorts of contexts: within political concepts and thought, philosophy, ideology, literature, architecture, even food. The field is wide and ever expanding. However, the labels "unrealistic" or "foolishly idealistic" that we sub-

---
[1] Though conscious of the frequent use of the term utopia as a generic term encompassing both utopia and dystopia, I will hereafter use the term utopia to denote eutopia, the good non-existent place, unless indicated otherwise.

consciously attach these days to utopia have not always been associated with it. Originally, the philosophical and political meaning of utopia was not only aligned with a more positive, though equally unattainable connotation—denoting a vision of an ideal, a "perfect" society, whereas utopia's alter ego dystopia connotes a much worse, bad society—but could also be pinpointed in a definite realm: that of literature and politics.

This chapter casts a brief glance at what differentiates literary utopia from other related concepts such as paradise, Cockaigne, Arcadia, and ideology or utopian thought, and then traces the definitional jungle of what constitutes the classical notion of literary utopia. After outlining the key narrative elements, a short and inevitably abbreviated and by no means comprehensive literary history of classical, social, modern, and feminist literary utopia is given. The next section explores the generic classifications of dystopia, anti-utopia, and utopian satire; and it then traces the literary development from classical to feminist dystopia, paying special attention to shifts in narrative content, form, and strategies. The last section examines the contradictory definitional and generic jungle, this time in relation to sf, and briefly delineates the assumed differences of sf and such concepts as fantasy, folk-tale, and fairy-tale, before turning to the historical development of sf, the newest, the third element of a literature concerned with the future. It is needless to stress that in such limited space, only a round-up of the usual literary suspects and identification of key elements, key epochs, and key definitions can be provided here where in similar endeavours others have filled excellent book-length studies.

1.1. The Blueprint: Classical, Social, Modern, and Feminist Utopia

What exactly *is* a literary utopia? There are probably as many contradictory definitions and classifications of utopia (dystopia, and sf) as there are critics who try to answer this question. Lacking critical consensus, definitions vary according to whether content, form or function is emphasized, and whether a broader view of utopia as utopianism or a more rigid view as literary genre is applied.[2] As Margaret Mead writes:

[2]*There is an abundance of works discussing the generic development, the literary history, and the various definitions of utopia and dystopia. Among these are Arthur Morton (1952), Lewis Mumford (1962), Robert C. Elliott (1970), George Kateb (1972), Darko Suvin (1973; 1979), Lyman Tower Sargent (1975), Frank E. and Fritzie P. Manuel (1979), Kenneth M. Roemer (1981), David Bleich (1984), Krishan Kumar (1987; 1991), Tom Moylan (1985; 2000), and Ruth Levitas (1990) to name just a few. Especially Kumar's knowledgeable study of astounding scope is an excellent source for the history of ideas and for the sociological, political, and philosophical back-*

1. The Classical Vision

> Utopias may be seen from many points of view—as projections from individual experience; as projections from individual experience stamped by the point of view of a particular period; as sterile blueprints, too narrow to confine the natural varieties of the human mind for very long, as when they are lived out by small cult groups.... Or they may be seen as those visions of future possibilities which lead the minds of men [sic] forward into the future [43].

In popular usage literary utopia is naturally lumped together with other imaginations of better worlds and ideal societies. Among these are religious concepts of a lost time and place or religious anticipations (paradise/Eden, Golden Age, millennium); fantastic fabulations, voyages, folktales and legends (Cockaigne, Arcadia, Robinsonades, Atlantis legends); political concepts (political treatise, manifestos, utopian thought, and ideology); and practiced communitarianism (e.g., the communitarian communities based on the theories of Robert Owen, Charles Fourier, and Étienne Cabet). Yet, although these concepts are often hard to distinguish and may overlap in certain aspects, or indeed may be part of the fictional world that a literary utopia describes, there are a number of factors that differentiate literary utopia from other utopian imaginings if we, first of all, take a closer look at the content.

Precisely for the purely religious connotation, we can refute the mistaken but prevailing presumption that utopia is a mere variation on Biblical paradise, whilst by analogy dystopias represent "the inverse fall from the paradise: the fall into nothingness" (Mihailescu 218), into the underworld of (modern) hell. Judaeo-Christian religion is central to the Western idea of paradise. Although classical utopia values religion as significant, while modern utopia devalues religion and any other transcendental ideas, literary utopia (and dystopia) concentrates on sociopolitical themes and changes, opting for solutions in the sociopolitical or economical realm and not for teleological adjustments to reform a fictitious future society. This belief in sociopolitical process, in the active engagement of humans rather than in salvational divine intervention, as a catalyst for change also distinguishes utopia from millennialism. A certain proximity of utopia to paradisiacal visions, however, is undeniable. Some utopias do employ pastoral elements: untouched nature, sexual innocence, and the absence of violence symbolize the concept of Eden.[3] Symbolically, the prohibited fruit of knowledge, in the form of technology,

---

[continued] *ground in relation to utopian literature. For German criticism on Anglo-American literary utopia, see Wolfgang Biesterfeld (1982), Manfred Pfister (1982), Klaus L. Berghahn and Hans Ulrich Seeber (1983), Hartmut Heuermann and Bernd-Peter Lange (1984), Arno Heller, Walter Hölbling and Waldemar Zacharasiewicz (1988), and Hiltrud Gnüg (1999).*

[3]*For instance, in* The Time Machine *(1895) H.G. Wells seemingly presents such a vision of Eden with the Eloi.*

is excluded or at least marginalized in such visions of a "pastoral equanimity" (Rabkin 1983, 3). Literary utopia and paradise also differ in their disparate time focus and their view of society. Whilst the former focuses on a future time and describes a fictional society constituting a state with politically mature citizens, the religious concept of paradise must look backwards, and evokes primordial time with politically immature members of a Rousseauian community. Considering the above, it is surprising that some critics, such as Fritzie and Frank Manuel, pin the persistence of utopia on the continuing prevalence of Christianity rather than on culture and the human mind's ongoing desire to dream. Other critics, for example, Krishan Kumar, consider religion—speci-fically "the paradisiac and millennial expectations that Christianity inspires"—an emotional undercurrent, the "unconscious of utopia" (1987, 421), and thus perceive utopia and religion as intrinsically linked.

Equally common is the mixed usage of utopia and Cockaigne, the land of milk and honey. As with the Greek's poetic vision of pastoral Arcadia, Cockaigne, however, is an utterly fantastic construct, whereas literary utopia is grounded in the historical and contemporary sociopolitical realities of the respective author. Cockaigne presents a hedonist's dream fulfilled: food and beverage in abundance and leisure at will. It is the tale of the body satisfied. Where literary utopia constructs a believable though fictional concept of alternate possibilities to change social reality, formulating an "alternative historical hypothesis" (Suvin 1979, 41), Cockaigne presents a soothing dreamland, unrelated to history and inappropriate as well as without the intention to alter the social present.[4]

Politics are generally seen as a distinct factor of a literary utopia. Yet, although the fictional politics stem from a dissatisfaction with the actual politics that they often satirize and aim to change,[5] the politics of utopia are not firmly grounded in reality but in the imaginary.[6] In Northrop Frye's words, "utopia is a *speculative* myth; it is designed to contain or provide a vision for one's social ideas, not to be a theory connecting social facts together" (1966, 25). This is what characteristically differentiates literary utopia from ideology and political concepts or utopian communities. Literary utopia "transcends reality and breaks the

---

[4]*On Cockaigne and Arcadia in contrast to utopia see also Frye (1966, 41).*

[5]*For example, Plato designed his ideal state in contrast to the Greek polis which underwent a crisis;Thomas More's utopia was kindled by unsatisfactory social conditions in his society, namely pauperism affecting especially peasants; and Edward Bellamy wrote* Looking Backward *(1888) during the great upheaval in the U.S.*

[6]*Cf. also A.L. Morton's early definition: "[Utopia is] an imaginary country described in a work of fiction with the object of criticising existing society" (10).*

bounds of existing order, as opposed to 'ideology,' which expresses the existing order" (ibid. 39). Whereas ideology either struggles for its expression in concrete political models or comprehends existing political orders, utopia remains in the fictional realm and, although referring to, commenting on, and envisioning the improvement of the present status quo, literary utopia neither claims realization nor depicts existing states.

The classic view of utopia exclusively favors form and rigidly defines utopia, in the words of Krishan Kumar, "being in the first place a piece of fiction" (1991, 20). From this perspective, literary utopia is commonly understood as a visionary reform, describing an imaginary, ideal commonwealth whose fictional inhabitants exist under perfect conditions in a perfect social, legal, and political system, although strictly speaking More's term u/eutopia does not necessarily connote the classical understanding of a "perfect" society but rather simply a "good" one. A second important defining characteristic of literary utopia is its historically oriented criticism of the sociopolitical status quo of the author's (in some cases also of the reader's) society, a criticism that is grounded in speculation and hypothesis as well as in the existing reality. The American literary critic Kenneth Roemer suggests that literary utopia is "a fairly detailed description of an imaginary community, society or world—a 'fiction' that encourages readers to experience vicariously a culture that represents a prescriptive, normative alternative to their own culture" (1981, 3). Although most critics are aware of the impossibility of providing a universally valid, single, and stable definition of utopia (cf. also Manuel 5), many critics consider valid the widely-known definition of literary utopia by the eminent Croatian-Canadian critic Darko Suvin, who subsumes literary utopia under sf[7]:

> Utopia is the verbal construction of a particular quasi-human community where sociopolitical institutions, norms, and individual relationships are organized according to a more perfect principle than in the author's community, this construction being based on estrangement arising out of an alternative historical hypothesis [1973, 132; also 1979, 49].[8]

---

[7]*Suvin posits sf as the genre name and subsumes utopia, dystopia,* romans scientifique, *and science romances under this umbrella term. For him, utopias are thus "sociological fictions or social-science-fiction" (1979, 14).*

[8]*Suvin's definition has not gone unchallenged. While Lyman Tower Sargent, for example, considers Suvin's definition of utopia "by far the best" (1975, 140)—despite his own quibbles with Suvin's use of the term "community" instead of "society" (cf. ibid. 142)—a judgment he later somewhat modifies (see my discussion of the broadening of utopia below), Dingbo Wu contests Suvin's phrasing of "verbal construction" that "fails to define the literary quality of the genre" (236) and challenges Suvin's preconception of utopia as perfect. The latter in particular is rejected by a number of critics and many contemporary authors of critical and transgressive utopias, as I will discuss in Chapter 2.*

The term utopia, however, remains flexible and is subject to changing definitions, in part due to its fragmentary occurrence in so many different forms, images, and modes, and in part as Roemer cautions, because "[d]ifferent types of studies call for different working definitions, and different historical eras and cultural and interpretative contexts influence how utopia is perceived" (1984, 320). Roemer then goes on to list as common denominators of utopian literature the defamiliarizing context, the location in the imaginary, and its embodiment of an alternative to the present as well as a better or ideal society (preferably with a sociopolitical system described in detail). Another structural characteristic of utopia is, one might add, its predominant appearance as prose fiction.

Form- and content-based approaches, however, restrict utopia either exclusively to the literary genre or inherently pre-define what exactly constitutes a perfect and good society and thus verge on the edge of essentialism and universalism. Especially in the twentieth century an emphasis on the utopian function—what Ernst Bloch has called the "utopian impulse" in *The Principle of Hope* (1986), the "utopian anticipation" or the "utopian desire" that can be located in a variety of (not necessarily literary) works and practices manifested in popular culture—has extended these originally narrow generic definitions of utopia as purely literary images to denote the much broader field of utopian studies.

For Bloch, all human actions and desires, the definition of human nature and the human subject as such, are directed at improving the human condition, and history is thus driven by utopian intentions, a view shared by philosophers and (religious) thinkers such as Karl Mannheim and Paul Tillich who both ascribe an inherent utopian mentality to humans.[9] This view rescues utopia from the predominantly individual and imaginary realm, and places it in the real context of human existence and a collective move towards social change. Informed by Bloch, Lyman Tower Sargent, for example, understands utopia(nism) as "social dreaming" (1994) in the sense of an umbrella term that includes utopian thought and theory, utopia, eutopia, and dystopia.

Approaching utopia from a sociological perspective, exploring the concepts and rejections of utopia by Marx, Engels, Mannheim, Sorel, Morris, Bloch, and Marcuse, Ruth Levitas argues for a broad definition of utopia not based on form or content, but rather on its primary function of articulating a "desire for a better way of being"

---

[9] *For Tillich, utopia is "rooted in the nature of man [sic] himself" (Tillich 296), while Mannheim aligns utopianism with a state of mind translating its desire into action "to burst the bounds of an existent order" (Mannheim 193). For both the future is conditional, depending on actions taken in the present, and utopianism is therefore not the solution but a guideline.*

(199). With reference to Sargent and Bloch, Levitas stresses the emancipatory role of utopianism in its various appearances—"depictions of the good society do not necessarily take the form of literary fictions—and indeed this form is only available under certain very specific historical conditions" (5)—and underlines its power of vision, initiating social change when at its best.

Although utopian literature in general intends to move readers to a new critical awareness—this consciousness-raising is facilitated by the reader's identification with the protagonist/narrator who is usually a member of the reader's society—as readers compare the defamiliarized literary construct with the social reality in which they live, there is a curious "absence of historical process in utopian fiction" (Pfaelzer 1983, 312). In classical utopia an account of the actual transformatory process of how a more desirable communal life could be achieved is mostly omitted or only referred to in retrospect. Consequently, there is little action in classical utopian novels. Despite critically reflecting on reality, classical utopia thus merely arrives at a juxtaposition of an imperfect present and a perfect future, whereby this future model that classical utopia depicts is predominantly a regulating, hierarchical state in a closed, rationalistic, and unchanging society: "a final or definitive social ideal, the utopia is a static society; and most utopias have built-in safeguards against radical alteration of the structure" (Frye 1966, 31). Indeed, utopia exists in an eternal, ahistoric present. Verging on the *roman à these*, the didactic, linear narrative structure underwrites this static nature of classical utopia.[10] In removing the time factor from society and from the narration, the utopian plot must verge on the uneventful and, consequently, lacks the notion of process and progress, and invariably precludes narrative representations of social and individual evolution (e.g. character development).

The narrative pattern conventionally starts with an explanatory framing device accounting for the protagonist's knowledge of and travel to utopia; for instance, in the form of a found manuscript that recounts the voyager's travels, or the narrator journeys in a prolonged sleep, in a dream vision or via time travel, to utopia. In both cases, the utopian

---

[10]*On the changing narrative pattern in utopia (and dystopia) and the correlation between aesthetics and politics, ideology and narration, see Chris Ferns's excellent and highly informative study* Narrating Utopia *(1999; esp. chap. 1) that traces the narrative development from the stasis and authoritarian lecturing of classical utopias to the influence of realism and the modern novel on sf to the self-reflexive "partial visions" of modern and contemporary utopias that require active reader responses. Ferns observes that, seen from within the respective historical contexts of social upheaval, the highly regimented societal order of classical utopia, "the notion of a sane, orderly, rational, and above all peaceful society must clearly have exerted an almost irresistible appeal" (1999, 14). His key argument is that the outmoded narrative structure of the classical utopia persists undercover in contemporary utopian fiction.*

traveller either describes in detailed passages the wondrous, new society and its social system, or alternatively questions the utopian guide in long philosophical dialogues about the laws and the construction of the new society before returning (awakening) to his or her own society at the novel's closure. The narrative structure of utopian literature thus copies the then contemporaneous narrative conventions of the travelogue in the Renaissance, the many factual accounts of exploratory voyages to unknown destinations. In fact, by imitating these equally incredible tales of the discovery of previously unknown continents, the utopian tale gained credibility at this time. Importantly, the utopian alternative and the fictional representation of the real world remain narratively connected, as Chris Ferns notes, "the *relation* between utopia and reality is always a crucial aspect of utopian fiction" (1999, 5).

Unsurprisingly, at the end of the nineteenth century and with the end of spatial exploration, this restrictive narrative pattern of the travelogue format and the classical dialogue partially changes as "the traveller gives way to ... the tourist: a cataloguer" and "while the *form* of the traveller's tale is preserved well into the twentieth century, the intrepid explorer of the Renaissance utopia is replaced by the more prosaic figure of the holiday-maker" (ibid. 19). Furthermore, Edward Bellamy's introduction of the popular sentimental romance pattern to the utopian genre changes the narrative pattern. The utopian guide is now also the traveller's or sleeper's love interest, and the retrospectively told utopian narrative extends to the account of the traveller's romantic experiences and the unfolding of events. Along with the rise of the novel and the shift in content from the description of the "perfect" society to a focus on the individual, the narrative strategy shifts from assertive dialogue to extended characterization and a foregrounding of plot and character interaction, and, therefore, from a static to a dynamic narration.[11]

While the beginning of utopian literature dates back to Plato's concept of an ideal state ruled by philosophers in *The Republic* (4th c.B.C.), the history of utopia in English literature indisputably begins in the Renaissance with Thomas More's coinage of the genre's name and his description of an imaginary ideal state on a fictive island in *De optimo reipublicae statu, deque nova insula Utopia*, published in Latin in 1516. More's isolated ideal island community thus prefigures the spatial locus utopists used as principal setting for alternative societies up to the beginning of the eighteenth century. These "space utopias," set in dislocated geographical space such as removed islands, lost continents, the inside of the earth or on other planets, are typical of the Renaissance era with its urge for the exploration of unknown parts of the earth and the

---

[11]*Chapter 2 discusses contemporary narrative changes in more detail.*

discovery of previously unknown continents such as America. The Italian philosopher and Dominican monk Tommaso Campanella, for instance, places his utopian novel *La Città del Sole* (1602) on the island of Tap-obrane (Cyprus) where Raphael Hythlodaeus, More's protagonist, incidentally resided before returning home; and Francis Bacon's posthumously published fragment *New Atlantis* (1629) draws on Plato's mythical island. Copernicus's heretic heliocentrism, as opposed to the prevailing ptolemaic, geocentric worldview, and Galileo's advocacy of the Copernican system triggered planetary utopias. The very first examples that take up outer space as a location are the two posthumously published lunar utopias *The Man in the Moone* (1638) by Francis Godwin and *L'autre Monde ou les Etats et Empires de la Lune* (1657) by Cyrano de Bergerac and Voltaire's planetary tale *Micromégas* (1752).

From More's *Utopia* on and up to the end of the eighteenth century, utopian literature expressed the *desire* for, but also the fictionality of, equality for (hu)mankind. With the French Revolution and its advocacy of the new freedom of liberté *and* egalité and with Western society's founding of a "new and better world" in America, the fictional models of egalitarian societies suddenly crystallized as grounded in reality. Utopia no longer merely expressed wishful thinking, but was conceived as an attainable, concrete political act. When the actual mapping of the earth had come to an end with the discovery of the last continent, the unknown future became the preferred setting at the end of the eighteenth century. This crucial shift from space to time as the locus of the utopian desire comprises a shift from the comparison between the better place and the author's actual society to the extrapolation into the future of the author's own but reformed society. The first example of a time utopia, what Frank and Fritzie Manuel have called "euchronia," is Louis Sébastien Mercier's *L'An 2440* (1770) where after a long sleep the narrator awakens to a changed and reformed Paris. Here, time in the form of human history is foregrounded as the tool for progress.

In the nineteenth century socialism and, especially in the twentieth century, individualism and the freedom of the individual supersede the state collectivism that earlier utopias promulgated. The heyday of literary utopia is fed by the tangibility of social improvement. As Kumar writes, America with its promise of freedom and the pursuit of happiness and later the Soviet Union as the "heir" to socialism are "the two great utopian experiments of modern times" (1987, 381) that inspire utopian literature. On the one hand, the new belief in individualism, capitalism, and an emerging anti-authoritarian way of thinking especially in the U.S. contrasts with the preceding fictionalized proposals for a collective subordination to the idea of the common good and to a centralized state. On the other hand, the recognition of the darker side of industrialism and the publication of socialist political thought such as *Die Entwicklung des Socialismus von der Utopia zur Wissenschaft* (1883) by Friederich Engels and *Das Kapital* (1885) by Karl Marx—and despite their own critical stance towards utopianism or, more precisely, social utopianism—triggered an enthusiasm for social utopias and a critique of capitalism, especially of the oppression, exploitation, and pauperism of the fast-growing industrial proletariat. Even in the U.S. a significant number of writers turned towards social utopia. In fact, during this time of transition—the numerous strikes, the Haymarket riot of 1886, and the economic crash in 1893, all contributed to an increasing frenzy in the U.S.—utopian fiction (and the founding of utopian communities following the social treatise and theories by Owen, Fourier, and Cabet) flourished in the U.S.: "Utopian fiction became a major genre of popular literature in the decades between the Civil War and World War I" (Pfaelzer 1983, 312).[12] Two socialist utopias with diametrically opposed stances towards industrialized technology were particularly popular. Undeniably, Edward Bellamy's *Looking Backward 2000–1887* (1888) with its industrial republic—a curious socialist version of the American Dream—was one of the bestsellers of the nineteenth century, and led to the foundation of a large number of utopian clubs set on implementing Bellamy's vision of an industrial army in a planned economy. Bellamy advocates an unshakeable belief in technological perfection for the good of mankind, whereas his British counterpart William Morris postulates in *News from Nowhere* (1890), an ecological Camelot, the renunciation of technology to achieve a pre-industrial, pastoral community of artisans and vehemently criticizes Bellamy for his unreflecting admiration of technical progress. This critique recalls Samuel Butler's earlier anti-technological stance in *Erewhon* (1872) and its sequel *Erewhon Revisited* (1901) where citizens ban machines for fear of being supplanted by them. Wells's "quintessential utopia" (Mumford 1962, 184) *A Modern Utopia* (1905) not only combines the social with the technophile perspective, celebrating the advantages of technological progress, but also represents a turning point in utopian literature. Wells is the first to envision the modern utopia: utopia as a concept for the whole world rather than only for a segment of it (as Plato or More did). However, Wells's projection of an international government and centralized bureaucracy of an ever-present and controlling World State contains the totalitarian seeds that the dystopias of the twentieth century attack.

The upheaval of the fin de siècle, the onset of communism and fascism at the beginning of the twentieth century are mirrored by the

---

[12]*For an extensive survey of the upsurge of American utopias at the end of the nineteenth century, see Roemer (1976).*

1. The Classical Vision 21

juxtaposition of positive and negative images within one utopian text, as, for instance, in H.G. Wells's *The Time Machine* (1895) or in Mark Twain's *A Connecticut Yankee in King Arthur's Court* (1889). These utopian novels of the turn of the century, however, "represent schizoid clashes between fears and hopes rather than true resolutions" (Roemer 1976, 6) and serve "the dual purpose of offering dramatic articulations of anxieties about historical conditions and of presenting hopeful future possibilities that promised escape from the present" (Roemer 1988, 8). As the anxieties of the historical present became more and more pressing, the utopian genre increasingly veered towards negative representations, projecting negative worlds (dystopia) or, in an enthusiastic belief in future technological developments, technologized worlds (sf). In fact, since the advent of sf and the emergence of a popular sf mass market, dystopia and utopia have "practically become a subcategory of science fiction" (Roemer 1981, 6). Disowning the literary historical perspective by which at least utopia is the older form, Suvin also claims that "strictly and precisely speaking, utopia [and in the same logic dystopia] is not a genre but the sociopolitical subgenre of science fiction" (1979, 61).[13]

The end of the nineteenth century also saw the burgeoning of a new body of thought, pushing the "woman question" into the limelight. A new group of authors with new thematical concerns stepped into the literary arena and turned to the hitherto male utopian genre, noting that Your-topia is not necessarily My-topia. Women authors began to recognize utopia's potential for feminist purposes, as both feminism and utopia share an interest in the (narrative) interstices and (narrative) function of space and time:

> Women's space: the gap, the rupture, the enclosure, the absence of female inscription in discourse and history. Utopian space: no place, the inversion, the hole in history which signifies and allows for the fantasy and the wish.... The author of the feminist utopia writes of spaces in which women cannot yet live [Pfaelzer 1988, 282].[14]

In fact, over the last, the twentieth, century feminism(s) has become one of the most lively if not the foremost or "the primary utopian movement in the West today and a primary influence on utopian thinking and speculative fiction" (Stimpson 2).

Apart from Christine de Pizan's early utopian novel of the late Mid-

---

[13]*Suvin understands science not in the more restrictive English sense but as "German Wissenschaft, French science, or Russian nauka, which include not only natural but also all the cultural or historical sciences and even scholarship" (1979, 13).*

[14]*In fact, today some critics equate feminism with utopia in the sense of externalizing the utopian vision into reality and vice versa: "Feminism, today, is the most utopian project around. That is, it demands the most radical and truly revolutionary transformation" (Patai 151).*

dle Ages, *Le Livre de la Cité des Dames* (1405), the first spate of female utopias occurred at the close of the nineteenth century, inspired by the suffragette movement, women's fight for political rights and for the vote in particular. Readopting earlier ideas about the liberation of women and equal rights postulated by the British novelist Mary Wollstonecraft in *A Vindication of the Rights of Women* (1792) in England and by the American journalist and critic Margaret Fuller in *Woman in the Nineteenth Century* (1845) and drawing on the debates about the "woman question," women's role and (sexual) nature, demands for improved property, and inheritance rights, and equal citizenship, female authors criticized the misogyny of male utopias.

Up to then the utopian genre had been a male-dominated genre. Furthermore, classical but also modern utopias, written by male authors, designed a Western, androcentric blueprint of perfection universally applicable for all cultures and both sexes. These utopias neglected issues of race and gender, leaving gender roles and the sexual division of labor (e.g. domestic servitude) basically the same in their projected futures, improving women's roles only marginally in comparison to the author's or the narrator's present. Male utopists criticized class antagonism and imagined the equality of all *men*, but assigned women once more to subordination, inferiority, and passivity. In male utopia, female characters are mostly restricted to the traditional role of housekeeper, child-bearer, and mother within the private sphere.[15] Above all, female characters remain flat, they are relegated to the margins and their domain is silence. In More's *Utopia*, for instance, despite the novelty of access to education, women are principally restricted to the roles of mother and servant and remain their husbands' subordinates. Likewise, the primary task of Bellamy's female characters is motherhood; and in Morris's *Nowhere* women are simply servants. In *A Modern Utopia* Wells even proposes that the state appoint women to men.

In the nineteenth century, women writers investigated exactly this sexual status quo and pushed women's position into the center of utopian literature, questioned gender roles, and created futures and utopian visions of non-patriarchal societies with free women.[16] Often they contrast the actual male-dominated world with a matriarchal or all-female utopia. Preceding the suffragette movement, Mary Bradley Lane's description of a single-sex female society in *Mizora: A Prophecy* (1880) is generally considered to be the first though less well-known English female utopia, whilst Charlotte Perkins Gilman's *Herland* (1915) and its sequel *With Her in Our Land* (1916) were probably the most prominent

---

[15]*For gender roles in male utopias, see Elaine Hoffman Baruch (1984).*
[16]*On utopian literature by American female writers, see Carol Farley Kessler (1984).*

female utopias of that time. In contrast to male utopias and turning away from the dominant utopian pattern of euchronia, Gilman envisions an all-female society set on a secluded island. Using spatial rather than temporal extrapolation also allows her to juxtapose her pastoral, matriarchal utopia with the gender inequality of the industrial U.S., a theme Gilman specifically explores in *With Her in Our Land*. As exceptional as *Herland* is for its time and, despite the emphasis on women's capability to organize a state system and the negation of marriage, it centers around motherhood as woman's ultimate fulfilment, and the Herlanders readily re-accept men, the three male travellers, into their society. As Frances Bartkowski states, the "all-female utopias produced in the nineteenth century ... were far from feminist, in that they tended to idealize the 'true' woman of the domestic sphere, not the 'new' woman" (9). Like their classical, patriarchal predecessors, these early female utopias remain curiously static.

An important change from static to dynamic utopia takes place with the introduction of the feminist perspective of the mid-twentieth century to utopian literature. Not only do women writers create active and strong female heroes, lending women a voice in utopia, they rewrite some stock characteristics of classical utopia. Although feminism connotes a concrete political utopia and utopia remains in the realm of literature, feminist utopia reveals and demonstrates their shared interest in transformational politics. Feminist utopian fiction, Sally Miller Gearhart writes,

> a. contrasts the present with an envisioned idealized society (separated from the present by time or space); b. offers a comprehensive critique of present values/conditions; c. sees men or male institutions as a major cause of present social ills; and d. presents women not only as at least the equals of men but also as the sole arbiters of their reproductive functions [296].

While politics is conventionally equated to institutionalized bureaucracy and, therefore, politics *cum* bureaucracy cease to exist in classical utopias, politics in feminism denotes the *distribution* of (sexual) power in society, groups, classes, and states, or gendered power relations of language, and thus politics *cum* distribution of power thrives in feminist utopias, often because these include parallel societies and hence allow fluidity and progress. Wells had already called for precisely such a shift towards a dynamic utopia in *A Modern Utopia*, although his re-evaluation of utopia is grounded in Darwin's evolutionary theory:

> The Utopia of a modern dreamer must needs differ ... from the Nowheres and utopias ... before Darwin.... Those were all perfect and static States, a balance of happiness won forever against the forces of unrest and disorder.... Change and development were

dammed back.... But the Modern Utopia must be not static but kinetic, must shape not as a permanent state but as a hopeful stage, leading to a long ascent of stages [5].

Reworking the generic form, feminist writers, in particular, of the 1970s and onward experiment with new narrative forms that often coalesce with postmodern narrative strategies. While Doris Lessing's *Canopus in Argos* series (1979–1983) has been noted for its moderate narrative inventiveness, Joanna Russ's *The Female Man* (1975) and Monique Wittig's *Les Guérillères* (1969) are among the most avant-garde writing, using multiperspectivism, polyphony, collage of various discourses, fragmented subjects, and a discontinuous structure. Ursula K. Le Guin's *Always Coming Home* (1985) is also a composition of "novels, stories, poems, maps, myths, histories, autobiographies, romances, drawings, music, meditations, plays, [and] jokes" (Cullen Khanna 131).

Feminist utopias significantly differ in terms of narrative content from male utopias. Thematically, feminist utopias shift the focus to female reality and to everyday life; they restructure the distribution of power within society *and* family and reject sex-segregated labor. They particularly emphasize gender equality, communitarian goals, decentralization, consensual decision-making, cooperation, education, and ecological issues, and they discard the classical utopian notion of growth and the domination of nature. These non-aggressive, non-hierarchical, and hence classless future societies challenge patriarchy: "Throughout its literary history, the feminist utopia has challenged the Lockean notion that patriarchy is a natural right" (Pfaelzer 1988, 283). For women utopists, a better society means not only the "transformation of political and economical structures, but the transformation, also, of the most basic social structures—those that determine gender identity" (Patai 150). Poignantly, feminist utopia distinguishes between the social construction of gender and biological sexual difference—often allowing an extensive sexual permissiveness to separate sexuality from questions of ownership, reproduction, and social structure—and, generally favoring basic living units or close-knit communities and communal childcare, abolishes the nuclear family. Taking an oppositional stance towards compulsory heterosexuality, some feminist utopias create lesbian societies or violate sexual taboos by daring to fuse aliens and humans; others create all-female societies and simply explore relations free from gender hierarchies. Criticizing natural reproduction as a mechanism of oppression, feminist utopian fiction often suggests artificial insemination, parthenogenesis, and in-vitro fertilization. In regard to these key issues, the importance of parenting and nurturing are emphasized. Frequently, the mothering function is separated from biology and is spread to several women, some-

1. The Classical Vision

times the parenting concept embraces men. In Elgin's *Native Tongue* series the community of women linguists raises the girls; the children in Sally Miller Gearhart's *The Wanderground: Stories of the Hill Women* (1980) have seven mothers; Charnas's Riding Women of *Motherlines* practice "sharemothering," a principle extended to include men in *The Conqueror's Child*, the concluding volume of the series; in *Woman on the Edge of Time* (1976) Marge Piercy suggests that children are taken care of by three "co-mothers," who can also be of the male sex.

Contrary to gloomy prognostications that announce the demise of utopia, "although the search for utopia, for the good life, continues, literary utopia is all but dead" (Elliott 1975, 37), literary utopia has been resuscitated in the twentieth century. Along with a strong and vociferous wave of feminist utopias that grew out of the women's liberation movement in the 1970s and intensified in the 1980s and 1990s in form of feminist dystopias and sf narratives,[17] ecological concerns, nourished by a growing concern about alternative technology and renewable energy sources, rejuvenated utopian literature. These ecological utopias, however, do not envision a pastoral, pre-industrial age but rather imagine an alternative technological utopia. Of this utopian strand of the twentieth century Ernest Callenbach's *Ecotopia* (1975) and its less popular sequel *Ecotopia Emerging* (1981) are the most prominent examples, although many feminist utopias take a strong ecological stand.[18] Even one of the great dystopian writers of the twentieth century, Aldous Huxley, surprised readers with his ecologically-minded people of Pala in his less than well received utopia *Island* (1962).

The projected feminist futures now present a more varied scope of imagined societies, utopian spaces that the Québec writer Louky

---

[17]Along with the female writers' renewed interest in the utopian, dystopian, and sf genre, feminist criticism turned to examine the propensity of feminism and feminist extrapolations. Today, the student of feminist literary utopia/dystopia and sf can consult an abundance of seminal works on the intersections of the genre and the various strands of feminism. See in particular the monographs and anthologies by Ruby Rohrlich and Elaine Hoffman Baruch (1984), Sarah Lefanu (1988), Nan Bowman Albinski (1988), Frances Bartkowski (1989), Libby Falk Jones and Sarah Webster Goodwin (1990), Angelika Bammer (1991), Jane L. Donawerth and Carol Kolmerten (1994), and the prolific work as critic/editor of Marleen S. Barr (1987; 1992; 1993; 2000). These works have established women writers as important contributors to, and innovators of, the genre, noting specifically the intersections between feminism(s), postmodernism, utopia, dystopia, and sf. Despite the abundance of feminist utopias and a large body of criticism dealing with them, some critics continue to fail to notice women writers' contributions to utopian literature. For example, Hoda M. Zaki writes in her in many respects insufficient study that "[o]nly four noteworthy utopias have been published in this century" (21n37) and lists apart from Wells's A Modern Utopia, B.F. Skinner's controversial Walden Two (1948), and Huxley's Island only one feminist utopia: Gilman's Herland. Unsurprisingly, Zaki similarly neglects feminist dystopian novels (cf. 22n44). For German publications on Anglo-American female utopia, see Dagmar Barnouw (1985), Annette Keinhorst (1985), Barbara Holland-Cunz (1986; 1988), and Mario Klarer (1993).

[18]In fact, a whole subgenre of eco-feminist utopian writing emerged. For an introductory discussion of eco-feminist utopias, see Maureen Devine's discussion of eco-feminist utopias (1992).

Bersianik sends her hopeful but naive extraterrestrial messenger in *The Eugélionne* (1976) to find. These feminist utopias vary from projected primitive, quasi-tribal, non-urban societies in non-industrial, rural settings—shown as in Charnas's second book, *Motherlines* (1978) of the Holdfast series or Gearhart's *The Wanderground*—to highly advanced technological societies, for instance, in Russ's *The Female Man*, to societies with advanced biological knowledge, as in Joan Slonczewski's *A Door Into Ocean* (1986) and its sequels. Some women authors extrapolate separatism (e.g. James Tiptree, Jr.'s, alias Alice Sheldon, famous story "Houston, Houston, Do You Read?" 1976) and suggest all-female, often parthenogenetic (*Motherlines*) or lesbian societies (*The Female Man*). Others opt for gender equality as in Thea Plym Alexander's *2150 A.D.* (1971) and Dorothy Bryant's *The Kin of Ata Are Waiting for You* (1976) or for matriarchal role reversal as in Marion Zimmer Bradley's *The Ruins of Isis* (1978). In the 1970s, the utopian novels "presented a range of explanations for male violence, grouped roughly around an 'essentialist' pole (men are *by nature* violent) ... and a more materialist one, according to which male violence is socially produced" (Fitting 1992, 33). To gain admission to all-female utopia, male characters need to be re-educated, since their destructive way of life and violent disposition would otherwise threaten the survival of the species. Importantly, in most cases the problem of male violence is not considered insoluble, as "the manless societies usually reveal ... the intention (or wish) to allow men in" (Russ 1981, 78). Bryant, for instance, suggests individual change, whereas Sheri S. Tepper's *Gate to Women's Country* (1988) resorts to eugenics, a draconian measure Tepper revokes in her dystopia *Gibbon's Decline and Fall* (1996) which ends on a note of coexistence.

In the 1980s, along with the charges of an all-white feminism, feminist utopias were reproved for neglecting issues of racism, ethnicity, and postcoloniality. Allusions to racial superiority pervade, for instance, Gilman's *Herland* and many feminist utopias of the 1970s and 1980s tackle gender but not necessarily racist issues. Non-white female protagonists such as Connie Ramos in Piercy's *Woman on the Edge of Time* or the multi-racial Riding Women in Charnas's *Motherlines* were still the exception. Women of color called for an aesthetic representation of human diversity, a call the African-American writer Octavia Butler anticipated and answered by introducing strong black, female characters to the genre, although mostly in sf narratives such as the *Xenogenesis* and the *Patternist* series.[19]

Increasingly, women writers juxtapose utopia and dystopia within the same text, for example, in Piercy's *Woman on the Edge of Time* or

---

[19]*On the growing ethnic diversity in utopian and sf writing, especially Butler's contribution,*

Russ's *The Female Man*. The most elaborate early example for this narrative alternation between utopian and dystopian strands is the *The Dispossessed* (1974), originally subtitled "An Ambiguous Utopia," by Ursula K. Le Guin. I agree with Kumar, who uses *The Dispossessed* as an example, that contemporary utopia is "fragmented, both in its form and in its audience" (1987, 420), since utopia can no longer address or even wants to provide a blueprint for everyone or for society at large. Notably, during the last forty years utopia, dystopia, and sf are no longer easily distinguishable, thus the alternative term "speculative fiction"—originally proposed by Robert A. Heinlein in the 1940s to denote sf that extrapolates from known rather than unknown science and adapted by Judith Merril in 1966 to describe sf not predominantly dealing with science—has appealed to a growing number of critics, while others reject the term for its inclusion of fantasy (cf. Wolfe).

1.2. The Twentieth-Century Sibling: Classical and Feminist Dystopia

Dystopia, utopia's devilish generic sibling and antonym, is predominantly a modern literary phenomenon of the twentieth century. Although utopia and dystopia share a discontentment with the present, their approaches are diametrically different. Creating what Brian Attebery has so aptly described as a literary "intaglio effect ... an inverted form of low-relief sculpture, in which instead of carving away background to leave the figure ... the most prominent features are sculpted most deeply" (5), dystopia reverses, mistrusts, and parodies the ideal of a perfectly regulated utopian state, often unintentionally inclined towards totalitarianism. Where utopia uplifts the reader, dystopia holds up a hellish mirror and describes the worst of all possible futures. Although both utopian and dystopian imaginings of the future refer readers to the present and seek to implant a desire for societal transformation, they evoke different effects: the utopian defamiliarization takes the avenue of arousing readers' desire for utopia, whilst the defamiliarized dystopian society appals readers. Where utopia compares social vision and reality by creating difference, dystopia presupposes and thrives on the correlation and similarity of the present social order and the near-future scenario. Using opposed strategies, both utopia and dystopia, however, share the same

[continued] *see Salvaggio (1984) and Green (1994). See also the recently published anthology of black writer's speculative fiction (including sf and fantasy)—featuring established African-American writers of speculative fiction such as Butler, W.E.B. DuBois, Walter Mosley, and Delaney, and newer black writers such as Nalo Hopkinson and Evie Shockley—edited by Sheree R. Thomas (2000). This anthology contains also an essay section with insightful contributions by Delaney, Butler, Mosley, and Charles Saunders, who discuss racism in sf from various angles.*

objective: sociopolitical change by means of the aesthetic representation of a paradigm change.

Dystopia represents gloomy prognostications, as seen by the author, the negative extrapolation of and the logical conclusion or the outcome of current trends, of the flaws ailing contemporary society. The term itself, *dys*topia, meaning "a non-existing bad place," was allegedly coined by John Stuart Mill who first used this term in a parliamentary speech in 1868.[20] Dystopia matches utopia's formulation of humankind's highest hopes by voicing humankind's deepest fears. The grim literary projections of non-existing bad places have been given various names that critics notoriously debate over: "reverse utopias, negative utopias, inverted utopias, regressive utopias, cacoutopias [sic], dystopias, non-utopias, satiric utopias" (Lewis 27), yet the most commonly used terminologies are dystopia, anti-utopia, and utopian satire. The older and more narrow labels anti-utopia and utopian satire apply only to certain literary works. Satire shares a strong link with dystopia in that both share a critical view of the author's actual society, and satire is frequently a narrative element of dystopian literature. Dystopia differs from utopian satire as it warns of future social developments and calls its readers to action, whereas the utopian satire/parody mocks utopia by presenting "the same kind of social goal [of an ideal world-state] in terms of slavery, tyranny, or anarchy" (Frye 1966, 28).[21] Anti-utopia misleadingly implies that its primary aim is solely to attack the concept of utopia; it connotes a mere negation of utopia. Anti-utopia thus exclusively thrives in relation to utopia. Kumar notes an "antithetical yet interdependent" relationship between these contrasting concepts in which anti-utopia merely "feeds parasitically" on utopia: "[u]topia is the original, anti-utopia the copy" or the "negative response" (1987, 100). In contrast, the widely accepted term dystopia denotes a broader concept, allowing criticism of

---

[20]*Kumar quotes the* Hansard Commons *(1868): "As MP for Westminster, Mill in a speech in the House of Commons in 1868 mocked his opponents: 'they ought rather to be called dys-topian, or caco-topians. What is commonly called Utopian is something too good to be practicable; but what they appear to favor is too bad to be practicable'" (1987, 447n2). Today's use of dystopia, however, originates less in Mill's speech than in its popularization in the anthology* Quest for Utopia *(1952), jointly edited by Glenn Negley and J. Max Patrick, in which the latter called a seventeenth-century utopia a "dystopia" (cf. 298).*

[21]*According to Frye, satire combines two components. On the one hand, it darkly relies on "wit or humor founded on fantasy or a sense of the grotesque or absurd" (Frye 1957, 224) and, on the other hand, it ironically attacks an actual object or situation. Subsuming anti-utopia and dystopia under the term "Menippean Satire," which deals "less with people as such than with mental attitudes" (ibid. 309), Frye denies dystopia an earnest desire for narrativization and literary characterization and, to a certain extent, annuls its social criticism. His use of the paradigmatic dystopian classics—Zamyatin's* We, *Huxley's* Brave New World, *and Orwell's* 1984—*as examples of the utopian satire comes hence as somewhat of a surprise. On the relation between utopia and satire, see also Robert C. Elliott (1970, esp. 21–22) and for the intersection of utopian satire and dystopia, see Alexandra Alridge (esp. 5–8).*

1. The Classical Vision

utopia, but also directly deals with contemporary social evils and posits thus an independent term far less linked with utopia/eutopia. It is precisely not *only*, as Alexandra Alridge remarks, "utopia in reverse" (ix). Therefore, I accede with Sisk who favors dystopia as the generic category:

> *Dystopia* is preferable to anti-utopia for two main reasons. Rhetorically, it exactly reverses the common misreading of More's *eutopia* ... as "bad place." Dystopias concern themselves with the moral structure of a fictive society, not its physical location. Furthermore, although dystopian societies may appear to exist "out there," they criticize the reader's world—"displacing" the reader.... Second, dystopia as a genre encompasses a spectrum of works ranging from a few anti-utopias ... through novels that create miserable societies without attacking directly utopian ideals... [5–6].

Unsurprisingly, the proliferation of dystopian images coincides with the utopian heyday of the nineteenth century, the rise of technology, evolutionary theories, and Social Darwinism. Where utopia prophecies industrialism as panacea, and utopias such as Edward Bulwer-Lytton's influential *The Coming Race* (1871) praise evolution and anticipate a superior human race, others satirize industrial utopias such as Bellamy's *Looking Backward* and attack the industrial revolution for technology's increasing influences on social conditions, impersonal machinery, exploitation, and alienation. Dystopia thus projects an "admonitory image of the future, [and] fuses two fears: the fear of utopia and the fear of technology" (Beauchamp 1986, 53). With the exception of Swift's early utopian satire *Gulliver's Travels* (1726)—especially the satirical depiction of the filthy and despicable Yahoos in the land of the Houyhnhnms in Book Four—Butler's *Erewhon*, the many satiric responses to *Looking Backward*, and especially Wells's prophetic *When the Sleeper Wakes* (1899)[22] and his other dystopian sf novels mark,[23] as Alridge argues, the transition of "anti-scientific utopian satire to the [anti-scientific and anti-technological] anti-utopias and dystopias of the late nineteenth and early twentieth centuries" (7). Just as the utopian vision then began to diminish at the fin de siècle, dystopia thrived.[24]

---

[22]*When the Sleeper Wakes anticipates many of the dystopian themes that prevail in classical dystopias: when the sleeper Graham awakes in London in the year 2100, he finds a technologically advanced yet sociopolitically oppressive system based on class antagonism, where the few idle rich exploit the dehumanized and degenerated worker-slaves (a re-exploration of the central theme of his sf classics* The Time Machine *and the allegorical* The Island of Dr. Moreau*); where media technology has replaced literacy, and consumerism and a mindless pursuit of pleasure prevail; and Graham's own intervention triggers the threat of dictatorship.*

[23]*Mark Hillegas declares Wells the originator of dystopian images: "the most important influences ... were the scientific romances, utopias, and future histories of H.G. Wells" (4).*

[24]*The utopian impulses that shortly prospered in the fine arts at the turn of the century—especially in the avant-garde movement futurism outlined in the* Futurist Manifesto *(1909) with its mandate to break with the past and to celebrate instead power and technology—quickly vanished with the incorporation of Marinetti, its most prominent advocate, into the Italian Fascist move-*

After Nietzsche had proclaimed God's death, science stepped into the vacuum as the new god, and it is precisely this prevailing unquestioning belief in the "scientific worldview" that dystopia criticizes, since technological progress went not only hand-in-hand with lifestyle improvements and inexpensive goods for the masses but also with long working hours, increased child labor in the factories, and an im-pov-erished mass proletariat. Witnessing how modern science develops ever more sophisticated techniques for social control, modern dystopia describes "an advanced totalitarian state dependent upon a massive technological apparatus—in short a technotopia" (Beauchamp 1986, 54).

While the emerging sf genre lauds technology and optimistically celebrates its liberating power, dystopian visions consider technology as dehumanizing and destructive, answering in the negative the question whether technology is an instrument in the hands of totalitarian rulers or an autonomous force. Beauchamp differentiates between technophile dystopias that "contend that technology is value-neutral, merely a tool that can be used for good or ill depending on the nature and purposes of the user. Man remains in control," and technophobe dystopias, viewing "technology as a creation that can transcend the original purposes of its creator and take on an independent existence and will of its own" (1986, 54), what Isaac Asimov has called the "Frankenstein complex."

Technological determinism haunts dystopia that chiefly portrays technology not as misused neutral tool but as the totalitarian logic of the future.

In fact, old anxieties about the hybridization of human/machine, the merging of biological and mechanical systems—which can be traced back to the Jewish Golem myth, homunculi stories, E.T.A. Hoffmann's automata, and Mary Shelley's *Frankenstein* and have been revived in contemporary images of robots, androids, and cyborgs—re-emerge and culminate in what Beauchamp calls "mechanomorphism": "man [sic] will so completely introject the ethos of technology that his highest aspiration will be to become a machine himself. Then the machine, like Hell for Milton's Satan, will be inside him" (1986, 61–62). Whilst some technocratic dystopias, for instance, Anthony Burgess's *A Clockwork Orange* (1962) and Kurt Vonnegut's *Player Piano* (1952) equate the state organism with a mechanism; others such as Bernard Wolfe in *Limbo* (1952) envision a total and literal conversion in that mechanical prosthetics

---

[continued] *ment in the 1930s. On the rise of classical dystopian fiction, see the notable studies of Chad Walsh (1962), Mark R. Hillegas (1967), and Alridge (1984; esp. chap. 1), who also supplies a detailed critique of Walsh and Hillegas.*

replace human body parts. Inspired by the *angst* that humans can be transformed into machines, E.M. Forster's "The Machine Stops" (1909) and D.F. Jones's *Colossus* (1966)—*Colossus* depicts how the supercomputer Colossus gains consciousness and usurps the world: the servant becomes the master—elaborate this theme, and prophesy the domination of machines and the mechanization of human life. Anticipating today's reverence for information technology, postmodern dependence on communication technology, and the total prevalence of technology in every aspect of life in the twenty-first century—themes contemporary cyber(punk) novels celebrate or critique—Forster describes a mechanistic society, literally controlled and regulated by a machine, in which technology replaces individual contact. The totality of human dependence on technology is elucidated when the machine malfunctions and the society collapses.

Obversely, not only technological progress but the historical polarization into capitalism and communism, and the thereby changed attitudes towards the state, were the major stimulus of dystopia. Previously, the state, embedded in a religious world order, had been considered a historically grown and necessary construction to protect its citizens. Now, it had turned into a Leviathan devouring the helpless individual. These fears were embodied in anti-capitalist dystopias such as Jack London's *The Iron Heel* (1907) and anti-socialist dystopias such as the lesser known *The Unknown Tomorrow* (1910) by William Le Queux or *Crucible Island* (1919) by Condé B. Pallen.

The violation of all ethical norms and the unspeakable atrocities committed in the First and Second World Wars and by totalitarian systems, such as Stalinism in Russia and fascism under Mussolini in Italy and, above all, in Hitler's Nazi Germany, had an enormous, shattering impact on the individual's view of the world and on writers' imaginations. Visibly, these demonstrations of the horrible potentialities of centralized governments combined with advanced technology changed utopian literature and resulted in dystopia that extrapolates from the current trends and thus intimates visions of totalitarian, barbaric societies to come.

Commonly, the logical extrapolation of the abuse of mass technology for mass extermination in the Second World War led to literary depictions of ideology as the mental control mechanism using technology as the physical tool for manipulating and repressing citizens. In 1947, George Orwell ascertained this future function of utopian literature: "making people *conscious* of what is happening outside their own small circle is one of the major problems of our time, and a new literary technique will have to be evolved to meet it" (312). This "new technique" that Orwell postulated—and expertly put into aesthetic practice only two years after this statement in his famous classical dystopia *1984* (1949)—became dystopia with its applied literary shock therapy. In contradistinction to the dislocation of space and the far future projection many utopias and much of sf employ, most dystopias are time-oriented rather than located in a different space. Deliberately, dystopia designs a claustrophobic, though quite realistic near-future scenario by exaggerating contemporary tendencies to heighten the moral pressure on readers: "Just as distance in space was once essential to the positive utopia, so the date of a dystopia had to press hard and close on readers urged to avoid its seeming inevitability" (Mezciems 92–93). The pressure is increased by the recurrent use of eschatological archetypes, i.e., the end of the world and the post-apocalypse motif.

Where utopia expands space, tucking the individual securely into the tight grasp of the perfect state, and the utopian traveller returns to his or her society to relate happily the desirous wonders, the dystopian protagonist seeks nothing more than to escape the strangling grip of the state's total control: "Dystopias present 'shrinking' worlds where nothing escapes the 'hallucinatorily' intense force of attraction of the center" (Mihailescu 217). Revolted by the disastrous outcome of the compulsive collectivism of fascism, Stalinism, and communism as implementations of an ideology of perfection that ruthlessly repress pluralism, dystopia describes collectivism *in extremis*, curtailing any inclination towards individualism: "Whatever encourages individualism, 'I-ness,' is the enemy, for it separates the one from the many, man [sic] from the God-like State" (Beauchamp 1973, 288). All the canonized dystopian classics, Burgess's *A Clockwork Orange*, Aldous Huxley's *Brave New World* (1932), and Orwell's *1984*, attack collectivism and behavioral engineering. In dystopia, the individual is placed in opposition to and then usurped by the state:

> Dystopias are stories that contrast the failure of the main character with the unstoppable advance of society towards totalitarianism. The loss of the self is the character's final acknowledgement of, and ultimate contribution to, society's being definitely victorious. This story of hope, deception, and decay strongly opposes dystopia to its eutopian predecessors [Mihailescu 215].

With his famous Russian dystopia *We* (English translation 1924), by many considered to be the first full-fledged modern dystopia upon which other authors drew,[25] Yevgeny Zamyatin was among the first to attack ruth-

---

[25] Cf. Hillegas: "the anti-utopian tradition after Wells pivots on We" (99). Critics disagree on what novel or story describes the first dystopia. Mihailescu perceives the story "The Great Inquisitor," told by Ivan in Dostoevsky's *The Brothers Karamazov (1880)*, as the first dystopian story. Kumar names Machiavelli's *The Prince (1532)* as one of the earliest precursors of dystopia (cf. 1987, 101).

lessly the violations of freedom, the total thought control and brainwashing, the surveillance, terror, brutality, and rationalization of totalitarianism that turns the individual into an anonymized, alienated automaton. Poking at the ugly underside of human civilization and scaring up its truths, dystopian novels feature the stock topics of nationalism, militarism, slavery, exploitation, class antagonism, racism, barbarism, enforced and controlled gender relations, rape, overpopulation, drug dependence, sexual perversion, pogroms, degeneration, nuclear devastation, and increasingly also catastrophes such as (terminal) ecological pollution, and authoritarian/totalitarian regimes that oppress the masses. Monotonous conformity, surveillance, denunciation, and the degradation of humans to object status are the standard features of dystopia. Such a future scenario might also extend to the artificial mass production of humans according to selective genetic criteria—with the breeding of five different human models for society's needs *Brave New World* indeed predicted today's possibility of cloning—and to use medication to manipulate and tranquillize the citizens' emotions (for instance, with *soma* in *Brave New World*) for maximum control. Media technology is employed as a propaganda tool, for manipulating and rewriting history, and brainwashing and stupefying the willing populace of a leisure-oriented consumerist society into intellectual numbness (e.g., in *1984* and in Ray Bradbury's *Fahrenheit 451* 1951). Access to information, knowledge, and literacy is hierarchized and restricted, just as language in general as an instrument of power is manipulated (e.g., the euphemistic Newspeak in *1984*), themes that Atwood in particular picks up in *The Handmaid's Tale* with the added twist of gender-specific restriction on literacy and that Elgin reworks in the *Native Tongue* series in terms of class-specific access.

The change in content, the introduction of the oppositional drive, has narrative repercussions that render dystopia, narratively speaking, more exciting than utopia. Dystopian narrative thus benefits from the dramatic struggle against its parody of utopia. Since the protagonist/narrator is an inhabitant of the future society, and although the dystopian dissident remains in the role of social outsider, the role of the visitor thus shifts, up to a certain extent, to the reader who is required to compare and contrast the fictional society with her or his own. To avoid the reader's complete identification with the protagonist (who may fail in his or her rebellion), it is a narrative necessity to undercut the narrative voice.[26] As

---

[26] *This double strategy of a "contradictory discursive impulse" that Gleen Deer has identified in Atwood's* The Handmaid's Tale, *holds true for the majority of dystopian novels that "cannot avoid complicity in using the mechanisms or rhetoric of that very intolerable world. Hence, a trope that might characterize the rhetorical gestalt of the novel is* paralepsis, *the figure of verbal dissimulation and duplicity that asserts its lack of rhetoric while using rhetoric" (216).*

the utopian traveler mutates into the dystopian rebel, the utopian guide metamorphoses into a representative of the oppressive system. Customarily, the (predominantly male) protagonist of classical dystopia is a member of the nameless, faceless, numbered, and normed mass, and initially accepts the coercion by the dictator or the omnipotent regime. The crucial dystopian dramatic conflict revolves around the protagonist's political awakening and ensuing rebellion against the totalitarian system and the state's subsequent hunt of the rebel.[27] Sometimes his new awareness is triggered by his love for a female rebel (Clarisse in *Fahrenheit 451*, Julia in *1984*, Nick in *The Handmaid's Tale*), or in the case that she is a fervent supporter of the system (Lenina in *Brave New World*) he seeks to convince her of the system's injustice. Female characters are thus cast in the stereotypical feminine role of accessories; Linda and Lenina remain flat cardboard characters, entirely taken in by the system or, at the most, initiate the hero's rebellion, before receding to the background. In any case, the state attempts to prevent and obliterate any emotional experiences involving privacy and any act of reinstating the ego. Therefore, individual bonding is abolished, as "[c]oupling represents a 'political act,' a 'rebellion' against the state, because it points to that genuine union of opposites" (Grossmann 140) and consequently individualism, and sanctions sexual intercourse solely in the form of coupling without emotional attachment: "One way to deal with the disruptive consequences of sex is to make it so frequent and so mechanical that it will not generate any love" (Rabkin 1983, 5). In the end the protagonist is left with three options: escaping to a colony outside of the system's reach, disappearing into an underground movement, or openly confronting the regime. The latter results in the protagonist's inevitable death, either by suicide or by execution.

The first female writers enter the male literary (sub)genre of dystopia in the 1930s. The earliest female dystopias are Katharine Burdekin's *Swastika Night* (1937), dealing with a future where Nazi Germany rules Europe and Hitler is apotheosized from political ruler to deity, and Ayn Rand's *Anthem* (1938), featuring a primitive future society of literally self-less humans where the very concept of identity and any sense of an ego has been erased. Both Burdekin and Rand introduce issues female writers of dystopia in the 1960s explored more extensively from a feminist perspective. Rand's dystopia disconcertingly remains within the masculine paradigm; its otherwise unspectacular plot culminates in the male protagonist's dissociation from the collective "we" and his progressive cognition of the ego, "[t]his god, this one word: 'I'" (97). In Burdekin's text, the purposely narrative absence of female characters,

---

[27]*For a detailed discussion of the hunt theme in dystopia, see R.E. Foust (1982; esp. 83–84).*

apart from the three marginal female characters who do not get beyond speaking a few lines, reflects fascism's contempt for and obliteration of women, who are considered hardly conscious beings, closer to animals than to humans, and only worth keeping for breeding purposes. Both themes, the discovery of the forbidden narrative (female) subjectivity and the animality of femininity refigure in feminist dystopia, notably in Charnas's *Holdfast* series and to a lesser degree in Atwood's *The Handmaid's Tale*.

Along with the beginnings of the Women's Liberation Movement and the revival of literary utopia in the late 1960s, renewed interest in the genre's dystopian sibling was aroused. With the shift to (dystopian) sf settings, the somewhat dwindling classical literary dystopia was revitalized by women writers, who challenged the traditional definitions of masculinity and femininity and explored sexual politics. Early examples are Doris Lessing's *The Four Gated City* (1968) and Angela Carter's *Heroes and Villains*. In the 1970s, the strong women's movement, especially by questioning heterosexual relationships as the perpetuator of women's subjugation, really sparked off a surge of feminist dystopias, for example Piercy's *Dance the Eagle to Sleep* (1970), Lessing's *The Memoirs of a Survivor* (1974), Charnas's *Walk to the End of the World* (1974)—the first book of the *Holdfast* series—Carter's *The Passion of New Eve* (1977) and Zoë Fairbairn's *Benefits* (1979).

Even more female writers were drawn to dystopia by the backlash of the 1980s—so aptly traced and disclosed in popular culture (media, fashion, movies, television), in science, academia, economy, reproductive body politics, and politics by the former *Wall Street Journal* reporter Susan Faludi in her identically named, scintillating book *Backlash* (1991)—that experienced under the conservative governments of Reagan in the USA, Thatcher in Great Britain, and Mulroney in Canada the rise of the Moral Majority and the revocation of many achievements of the women's movement of the 1970s. Social benefits were curtailed, and reproductive and abortion rights were restricted in an attempt to push women back into the kitchen. Equal opportunity politics came to a standstill, women's organizations received cutbacks, dubious and often inaccurate scientific research spread by the media insinuated that successful career women suffered from severe health problems and underwent identity crises. All this was, as Faludi writes, conveniently blamed on feminism and feminists were pathologized: "Identifying feminism as women's enemy only furthers the ends of a backlash against women's equality, simultaneously deflecting attention from the backlash's central role and recruiting women to attack their own cause" (1991, xviii). While politics paid lip-service to equality, factual discrepancies between men and women persisted in all major areas (cf. also Faludi 1991, xiii–xv), or were even increased by budget cuts that especially affected programs aimed at serving women.

Extrapolating from these contemporary politics women authors

> posit dystopian futures in which women's rights had been extinguished altogether, in which women were valued only as breeders, in which the moral majority had ascended to establish tyrannical theocracies, in which technology had become the sophisticated means by which women could be successfully oppressed once again [Nixon 230].

Women writers do use the stock conventions of dystopia, but—carrying patriarchy, technological advances, and the oppression of women to a logical extreme—they refocus these to expose their interrelation with questions of gender hierarchy, biological reproduction, and women's rights; in short, with sexual politics. Charnas and Carter, for example, use the nuclear catastrophe device to emphasize that the ultimate outcome of patriarchy is destruction. And women writers of dystopia take the stock dystopian features of slavery, exploitation, extreme collectivism, and oppressed individualism and present them from a feminist angle. Moreover, feminist dystopia inserts feminist images and critiques, addressing new issues such as sexual polarization, restrictive gender roles, female textual/actual absence, the cult of (superior) masculinity and the essential inferiority of femininity, lesbianism/homosexuality, misogyny, patriarchy, patriarchal views of femininity, the male gaze, patrilinearity, male violence against women, female complicity, and sexism inherent in phallogocentric language. The latter and language in relation to power structures are frequent topics: language fails altogether to depict adequately reality in Carter's *Heroes and Villains*; in *The Handmaid's Tale* women are excluded from literacy; and in the *Native Tongue* trilogy women linguists construct a secret female language called Laádan to express a female reality.

Female sexuality, the female body, and its abuse are also key issues in feminist dystopia, whereas racism, ethnicity, and women as conquered sex/species feature in some and more so in recent contemporary feminist dystopias. Where feminist utopias emphasize the sexual autonomy of women, feminist dystopias describe the opposite, "the denial of women's sexual autonomy…. They show women trapped by their sex, by their femaleness, and reduced from subjecthood to function" (Lefanu 71). Reproduction is another central theme, for instance, in Fairbairn's *Benefits*, where the British state controls the birth rate by adding contraceptive drugs to the water supply. Only those women, whom the state considers to be ideologically fit, are allowed antidotes. Lesbians, single mothers, and feminists are subjected to re-education programs. To keep women in traditional roles, the "Family Party" pays mothers with children "benefits" under the condition that mothers withdraw from the labor force and "voluntarily" participate in a fertility control program. Other important topics are rape, enforced sexual intercourse in marriage, the disrupted relationship between the sexes, and misogynist religion, especially Christianity. In feminist dystopia, women in particular lose all civil rights. Elgin's *The Native Tongue* (1984), for instance, is based on a fictional amendment to the American Constitution that declares women legal minors.

While most feminist dystopias use direct temporal extrapolation, for instance, Atwood's *The Handmaid's Tale* and Elgin's *Native Tongue* trilogy, other retrogressive dystopias such as Lessing's *The Memoirs of a Survivor* and Carter's *Heroes and Villains* are modeled on prehistoric barbaric times, whereas Charnas presents a curious mixture of both with the *Holdfast* series. However, a preference for temporal extrapolation and an increased interest in technological and scientific developments go hand-in-hand with a turning to sf, a generic development that becomes evident in the 1980s and intensifies with the emergence of the originally male-dominated cyber(punk) novel in the mid-eighties and women's appropriation of this sf subgenre in the 1990s. Sf's own turning from the exploration of outer to inner space has been conducive to the convergence of utopian, dystopian, and science fiction and has thereby facilitated in particular the fusion of feminist probings of social constructs as natural laws with the investigation of scientific laws. Sf has thus become a concomitant element of much of today's feminist dystopian and utopian writing.

1.3.1. Science and Fiction

With the end of the agrarian worldview, the closing American frontier, the fast progress of industrialization, the exploding advances in technology, and the rise of the city in Western societies, a new literary genre emerged that celebrated technology and science: that of *science* fiction. While America in the nineteenth century in particular had been organized by the "two adjacent worlds" of civilization and wilderness, separated as Brian McHale observes, "by an ambiguous and liminal space, the 'frontier'" (1987, 49), this concept of space quickly changed with the advent of the twentieth century. The end of the historical exploration and colonization of geographical space announced the successful subjugation of the natural frontier—signified by the rapid rise of the metropolis, symbol of conglomerated technology and the locus of social upheaval as an infernal, crime-ridden, dirty melting pot—and North American society and specifically U.S.-American writers turned to the new frontier of the mind: science and the advance of technology.

Contradictory in itself, the oxymoron *science* fiction—in 1926 Hugo Gernsback coined the word "scientification" that John W. Campbell, Jr., soon changed into the generally accepted term "science fiction"[28]— emphasizes what these narrations strive to combine: two opposed languages. While the language of literature does not necessarily represent the truth, although it may contain fictionalized or even historical truth, the language of science aims precisely at an accurate description of what we agree upon as reality. Sf, however, extrapolates either from real (natural) science or from what could be possible in accordance with the laws of contemporary sciences, but it investigates the future consequences with literary devices. The language of fiction provides the story; the language of science contributes the hypothesis. Sf at its best aims to impart an understanding of science with the means of aesthetic representation.

Generally speaking, due to the heterogeneous nature of this particular literature sf is probably one of the least and most defined terms in genre history: "Science Fiction is an undefined term in the sense that there is no generally agreed upon definition of it. To be sure, there are probably hundreds of individual definitions, but that is as bad as none at all" (Asimov 158).[29] Similar to the multifarious definitions of utopia and dystopia, there are in use various terminologies for as well as multicomponential definitions of sf. Arguments have raged over what exactly sf is and what it is not; generic demarcations are disagreed upon at large and become increasingly confusing and perhaps irrelevant as contemporary utopian, dystopian, and science fiction converge, intersect, and ultimately implode these very generic distinctions, just as sf originally emerged from a cross-fertilization of, among others, Gothic and scientific romances, fantastic literature, travelogues, the tall tale, and adventure/voyage stories. Many literary works are therefore listed under various labels, depending on the critic's approach and use of definitions, but also because a definite and unambiguous classification is impossible. Speculative fiction, fabulation, science fantasy, and social sciences are all terms that are used to denote sf; Gothic romance and voyage literature are considered antecedents of sf; and contemporary use of sf as an inclusive genre name can subsume fantasy, fairy-tale, folk-tale, myth, alternate history, and utopia/dystopia. Although it is almost impossible to agree upon

---

[28]*On the professional relationship of Gernsback and Campbell and a comparison of their genre theories of sf, see Gary Westfahl's informative essay (1992).*

[29]*Gary K. Wolfe lists a vast number of sf definitions in the encyclopedic* Critical Terms for Science Fiction and Fantasy *(1986).*

1. The Classical Vision

and probably not even desirable to construct rigid definitional categories in postmodern times of increasingly murky generic boundaries and crossovers, there are, however, a number of important distinguishing features common to utopia/dystopia and sf, and to sf and fantasy.

Despite the numerous differences, a shared concern with the future, nourished by a discontent with social realities and technological progress, and joint narrative strategies, such as defamiliarization, extrapolation, and alternate societies, forge a generic interrelationship between sf, utopia, and dystopia. Yet while the division between fact and fiction is blurred in all three genres, "classical" sf thematically foregrounds *scientific* fact. Key elements of the sf narrative are therefore science, technology, and a futuristic (not always plausible) setting often involving Aliens (actants) and space opera. In general, the sociopolitical content, the representation and critique of historical empirical reality, distinguishes classical utopia/dystopia from classical sf, which as an escapist literature of entertainment has been more often than not preoccupied with adventure or horror for its own sake. However, contemporary sf, dystopia, and utopia overlap and borrow settings, stock conventions, and staple themes from each other.

As sf and fantasy collide and overlap in many areas, other critics, for instance, Tzvetan Todorov, Eric S. Rabkin, and Rosemary Jackson favor the label "fantastic literature" for all non-realistic literature. From a structuralist approach, Todorov has termed fantasy a literature of uncertainty with an "event which cannot be explained by the laws of this same familiar world" (25) at its narrative core, a literature that even requires the narrative violation of the laws of reality. For Todorov, the fantastic occurs between the two poles of the uncanny, when the laws of reality remain intact and the narrated event is a mere illusion, and the marvelous, when the (supernatural) event is real but laws apply that we do not know. In Todorov's definition, sf features as the "scientific" marvelous along with the hyperbolic, the exotic, and the instrumental marvelous. Rabkin annexes fairy-tale, sf, detective fiction, and religious allegory to fantastic literature, stating moreover that "a work belongs in the genre of science fiction if its narrative world is at least somewhat different from our own" (1976, 119). Similarly, fantasy is for Rosemary Jackson a "literary mode from which a number of related genres emerge" (7), and a mode that assimilates romance literature, the marvelous (containing fairy tales and sf), and fantastic literature.[30]

Such very broad and vague definitions overlook that there are notice-

---

[30]*Such a definition leads Jackson to lump together in the same category of "fairy romance" the fantastic work of J.R.R. Tolkien and sf novels by, for example, Le Guin. Jackson elaborates on the subversive function of fantasy literature that brings to light what a given culture attempts to silence; an approach that Sarah Lefanu adopts for feminist sf, whose primary objective is also subversion and giving voice to what has been previously silenced.*

able differences between sf and the literature of the fantastic. For one, fantasy does not distinguish between animate/inanimate objects and allows supernatural beings. Although sf makes use of alien actants instead of human characters, it endows these non-human actants with scientifically explainable rather than inexplicable supernatural abilities. Both introduce factors of discontinuity or strange elements, but once these are established, the logic of the sf world does not violate the natural or scientific laws, whereas this violation is an important element of the (il)logic of fantasy fiction. Fantastic literature functions by rules created for the fictional world that are not required to correspond with those of our real world, though the fantastic needs the real as referent to be recognized as fantastic. The fantastic describes the phenomenon of the supernatural or what we take as beyond the normal, and, obversely, sf deals with the natural of consensus reality. Without claiming "scientific accuracy in the extrapolated realia," sf nonetheless aims at producing plausible consistent science, a "futurological foresight in technology, ecology, sociology" (Suvin 1979, 28) that adheres to scientific logic. Therefore, despite acknowledging that sf "shares with myth, fantasy, fairy tale, and pastoral an opposition to naturalistic or empiricist literary genres" (ibid. 3–4), Suvin hastens to emphasize that folk-tales, fairy-tales, and fantasy evade the empirical laws of science and create parallel worlds that are "inimical to the empirical world" (ibid. 8).

In turn, Robert Scholes has worked up yet another all-inclusive term, that of "fabulation" (1967)—Marleen S. Barr has reclaimed this term as "feminist fabulation" for feminist fictions—to denote all non-realistic literature that simultaneously encompasses and questions worlds discontinuous of our own empirical reality. Fabulation thus provides a blanket description covering not only magic realism or absurdist literature but also much of postmodern fiction. In addition, ten years later, Scholes introduces the term "structural fabulation" (1975; 1977) for sf and any literature that is acutely aware though not restricted to the application of scientific findings and explores the impact of science on humans.

Again, as in the case of utopia, the most commonly agreed upon definition of sf—Tom Moylan acknowledges that Suvin's definition of sf "holds to this day" (2000, 42)—has been charted by Suvin who, concentrating on the formal definition of sf as the *"literature of cognitive estrangement"* (1979, 4), defines sf as

> a fictional tale determined by the hegemonic literary device of a *locus* and/or *dramatis personae* that (1) are *radically or at least significantly different from the empirical times, places, and characters* of "mimetic" or "naturalist" fiction, but (2) are nonetheless ... simultaneously perceived as *not impossible* within the cognitive (cosmological and anthropological) norms of the author's epoch [ibid. viii].

This jarring disjunction and discrepancy of the norms of the presented text and the norms of the experienced world of the reader ultimately and intentionally create what the prolific sf writer Philip K. Dick has called the "convulsive shock in the reader's mind, the *shock of dysrecognition*" (xv). It should be noted, however, that many sf novels strive to create the obverse effect by trying to familiarize the reader with the implausible. Sf is, Suvin argues, a literature that explores "a realistic irreality, with humanized nonhumans, this-wordly Other Worlds ... the space of a potent *estrangement*" (1979, viii) with what he calls an "interest in a strange newness, a *novum*" (ibid. 4) that, in contradistinction to fantastic literature, demands a scientific explanation. Suvin then distinguishes between the extrapolative model, based on direct temporal extrapolation, dictatorship, social oppression, global catastrophe, and cybernetics,[31] and the analogic model of "extrapolation backwards ... to the past of the Earth, from geological through biological to ethnological and historical" (ibid. 29).[32] As I have previously pointed out, others such as the sf writers Robert A. Heinlein, Judith Merril, and Samuel R. Delaney stress the speculative nature of sf, its mode of teaching and learning, and have thus opted for the term "speculative fiction" to deemphasize the pre-occupation with technological *science* in sf and to denote sociologically oriented literary explorations. Contemporary usage, however, applies the term speculative fiction to sf, fantasy, and utopia/dystopia.

As befits a heterogeneous and "impure" literature defying a clearcut definition, the historiographers of sf claim various literary origins for sf apart from the more general distinction between U.S.–based genre sf and a more mainstream-oriented sf in Great Britain. As a genre proper, as a sufficient body of fiction constituting a distinct genre, the generic history of sf begins in the twentieth century, when sf indubitably first prospered as pulp fiction in the U.S., where the magazine *Amazing Stories*, founded by Hugo Gernsback in 1926, supplied sf not only with a literary home, but also ghettoized sf as a propaganda literature of technological progress. In the late 1930s, John W. Campell, Jr., joined Gernsback's efforts with the magazine *Astounding Stories*, later renamed *Astounding Science-Fiction*. Some studies, however, take a retrospective approach and locate the roots of sf in the nineteenth century, and name Jules Verne and Wells as the "two founding fathers" of sf,[33] since they were

---

[31] Suvin names Wells's Men Like Gods, Zamyatin's We, and Stapledon's Last and First Men *as examples for the extrapolative model.*
[32] *Probably the purest example of the analogic model is Edwin A. Abbott's satirical* Flatland *(1884), which uses a mathematical model.*
[33] *E.g.:* The Time Machine, The War of the Worlds *(1898)* The First Men in the Moon *(1901) by Wells and Verne's proto-science-fiction* Voyage au center de la terre *(1863),* Vingt mille lieues sous les mers *(1870) and* De la terre à la lune *(1865).*

the first writers of immensely popular novels that combined adventure tale, fantastic voyage, and scientific/technological imagination. Another such approach acknowledges the Gothic mode as an important precursor of sf and argues that by combining social criticism and scientific ideas Mary Shelley wrote with *Frankenstein, or The Modern Prometheus* (1818)[34] the first sf novel (cf. Aldiss and Wingrove),[35] whereas others appropriate utopian literature and utopian satire as the literary precursor to sf.

With the upsurge of sf in the pulp magazines of the 1930s and 1940s, the "Golden Age" of juvenile sf began, examples of which are the early stories and novels of the eminent Arthur C. Clarke (e.g., *The Sands of Mars* 1951), the early work of John Wyndham, A.E. van Vogt, Heinlein's *Beyond This Horizon* (1942) and Asimov's *The Caves of Steel* (1953). As an optimistic genre embracing if not heralding industrial technology and scientific progress, it privileged populistic, positivistic narrations of technological futurism and produced teleological narratives of scientific progress. During this time the stock conventions of classical conservative sf proliferated, including time-travel, post-apocalypse, future interstellar war, alien encounters, space opera, gadgets, and the modern myth of the invasion from outer space. These early stories stage the scientist/inventor as the artist and cultural hero of the new technological age—a hubris Wells already had deconstructed in *The Island of Dr. Moreau* and *The Invisible Man* (1897). Classical sf populates its space ships and outer worlds with monastic fraternities of such scientists, engineers, and space explorers all set upon the invasion of space, the conquest and colonization of new planets, and the subjugation of aliens. Conversely, xenophobic fears led to visions of alien invasion. Positing a dichotomy of human/alien, such masculinist sf conflates the metaphor of the Alien with misogynist depictions of the female/cultural *other*.[36] Since the main objectives of these juvenile adventure stories were action and a fast-paced plot, characterizations remained weak, and linguistic innovation was the exception.

In the 1950s, sf began to shift away from the physical sciences of hard sf, manifested in the gadget stories and space operas of the 1930s and 1940s (which has been resuscitated to a certain extent in the cyper-

---

[34]*Because of the theme of childbirth/artificial creation and the critique of the male hubris of god-creator in* Frankenstein *to which Ellen Moers (1976) has so articulately drawn attention, feminist sf criticism has claimed Mary Shelley as progenitor of feminist sf, despite the novel's lack of significant female characters. For her treatment of gender metamorphosis in* Orlando, *Nathalie M. Rosinsky goes as far as naming Virginia Woolf a "spiritual forebear" (4) of feminist sf.*

[35]*The Gothic romances of Edgar Allan Poe, the use of sf images by writers such as Nathaniel Hawthorne—notably, his stories revolving around scientists, "The Birthmark" (1843), "The Artist of the Beautiful" (1844), and "Rappaccini's Daughter" (1844)—Herman Melville (e.g. the mechanical man in "The Bell-Tower" published in 1855), and Villiers de l'Isle-Adam with* L'Ève future *(1886) also contributed to percolate science into literature.*

[36]*I return to a closer analysis of classical sf as a colonial discourse in Chapter 3.1.*

1. The Classical Vision 43

punk stories of the 1980s and 1990s) that foregrounded technology and (un)critically reflected the attitude of Western society towards science and nature, and turned to the speculative soft sf. Writers such as Frederik Pohl, Philip K. Dick, and C.M. Kornbluth turned to the social sciences (e.g., psychology and anthropology); sf developed an interest in telepathy, psi powers, and the like, the cardboard character of the scientist faded, and with the introduction of ordinary protagonists sf eventually began to emphasize problems of identity and consciousness.

From the 1960s onward, two movements invigorated sf and effected the most radical changes: the New Wave and feminism, which initiated a shift from *science* fiction to science *fiction*, from the foregrounding of outer space to inner space, from object to subject, from the male subject to the female subject. Along with the cultural shifts of the 1960s came a growing ecological awareness and cultural pessimism and New Wave authors such as Brian Aldiss (*Report on Probability A* 1968) and J.G. Ballard (*The Drowned World* 1962; *The Terminal Beach* 1964) changed the content and the style of the genre. New subject matters dealing with inner space, psychology, drug experiences, sexual encounters, religion, and a shift towards the dystopian visions predicting overpopulation (e.g. John Brunner's *Stand on Zanzibar* 1968) or the downfall of industrial society were explored in narrative strategies adopted from outside sf, engaging in imagist and metaphorical styles and entering an ongoing flirtation with experimental writing. Science was no longer an end in itself, but was used as a metaphor. However, despite the gain in literary quality from crossing into mainstream literature, its narrative experimentation and shift in content, New Wave writing did not turn away from the androcentric and ethnocentric worldview of male sf.

Indeed, up to the late 1960s, sf has been an ultra-conservative genre, written by men from a male if not masculinist point of view, with male protagonists at the narrative center for a male audience. Women writers of sf remained the exception, and those who did venture into the male dominated genre almost always used male protagonists (as Leigh Brackett did). In the 1930s and 1940s, authors such as C.L. Moore and Leigh Brackett wrote under androgynous abbreviated versions of their names, while others assumed masculine pseudonyms, as Andrew North (alias of Andre Norton) and much later James Tiptree, Jr. (alias of Alice Sheldon), widely celebrated as writer of distinctly masculine sf, did. The pioneering Canadian writers Judith Merril and Phyllis Gotlieb extended the subject matter of sf to children and nurturing, although Merril has been charged with orthodoxy and retaining an element of the sentimental.[37]

---

[37] See *Roz Kaveney (1989, 84). On the role of anglophone and francophone Canadian sf/fantasy writers and Canadian themes, see David Ketterer (1992).*

In the mainstream of malestream sf, female characters are virtually absent; the few female characters are cast as quintessential *other*, as toys, robots, alien threats, enigmas, or love interest, blatantly tacked on to the story only to validate the masculinity of the male hero.[38] For this cliché attitude, it may suffice to quote the narrator of Heinlein's *The Moon Is a Harsh Mistress* (1966) who smugly observes, "[w]omen are amazing creatures—sweet, soft, gentle, and far more savage than we are" (14). Inevitably, women as represented in sf fall into the stereotypical categories of attractive, young, single sexbomb, housewife, and asexual middle-aged mother with grown-up children—John Clute and Peter Nicholls also list the "Timorous Virgin," the "Amazon Queen," and the "Frustrated Spinster Scientist" (1343) as the standard portrayals of women in sf—or are described as mere breeders. In this role, women are either instrumentalized objects of conquering Aliens, for instance, mothers of implanted alien offspring as in *The Brain-Stealers* (1954) by Murray Leinster or *The Body-Snatchers* (1955) by Jack Finney, or the convenient means for messianic heroes set on conquering and populating earth or other planets, as in Philip José Farmer's *Flesh* (1969) or in D.F. Jones's *Implosion* (1967). Caught within a patriarchal heterosexist paradigm, radical visions of gender equality had simply not occurred to a majority of male sf writers, who excelled in reproducing within an sf setting a Eurocentric/North American, white, middle-class status quo of heterosexual gender relations, where masculinity is synonymous with power and femininity equals passivity and powerlessness. As Russ writes, "women were perceived as inferior and men were encouraged in machismo" (1981, 72). If women ruled in anti-feminist male sf, for example in Edmund Cooper's *Five to Twelve* (1968) and *Gender Genocide* (1972), Richard Wilson's *The Girls from Planet 5* (1955), and Parley J. Cooper's *The Feminists* (1971), the dreadful gynocratic matriarchies of cruel but positively lecherous women were eventually overthrown by the return of the Father, who firmly reestablished male supremacy.[39]

"The people, in SF, are not people" (1975, 209) but pawns in a literary exercise of power hierarchy, as Ursula Le Guin diagnosed, and she criticized that male sf circles around the male self, excluding or objectifying the female, racial, and social *other*. Sf, Le Guin concluded elsewhere, needs to move away from archetypes to literary characterizations, from

---

[38]*In an early study on the changing image of women in gadget, adventure and social sf, Beverly Friend notes that women appear as gadgets, robot-androids, and the object of rescue in the former two subgenres of sf (cf. 141–148) and lauds the latter for more mature representations. Examples of the latter are novels by Philip Wylie, Russ, Le Guin, and Sturgeon.*

[39]*On the topic of the Amazon and masculinist depictions thereof and portrayals of female rule in general in sf from the 1870s to the late 1960s, see Sam Moskowitz (1976; esp. chap. 4). See also Russ (1980b) on the war of the sexes as portrayed in anti-feminist sf.*

1. The Classical Vision 45

a literature of ideas, objects, and icons to an experimental literature of human nature and of the human subject. She argues that sf needs to take snapshots of Virginia Woolf's Mrs. Brown aboard the space ship or in utopia and to observe "what goes on *inside* Mrs. Brown" (1979a, 109; my emphasis). In regard to the image of women, sf literature differed not from mainstream literature, as Russ drily observed: "Women in twentieth-century American literature seem pretty much limited to either Devourer/Bitches or Maiden/Victims" (1973b 8). (The only good woman in literature in general is basically a dead woman, as Elisabeth Bronfen (1992) would point out in a later study, though in a different generic context.) With the acknowledged exception of Sturgeon, Delaney, and Damon Knight, who cast female characters as scientists and explorers, sf not only lacked strong female characters but had essentially ignored women. A growing number of feminist critics and feminist writers, who entered the genre in a constant trickle in the late 1960s and in droves in the 1970s, and applied the new science "feminism" to the field of sf began to point out: "There are no female heroes, where are the women in sf?" Women writers busily created strong female heroes and populated their future visions with a variety of female characters, since they found that, again in Russ's words, "[t]here are plenty of images of women in science fiction. There are hardly any women" (1973a, 91).[40] To highlight this discrepancy, women writers, for instance, Judith Moffett in "Surviving" (1986) or Russ in "When It Changed" (1972), played with stereotypical reader expectations with regard to a character's sex and gender role.

With its particular amenability to experimentation and its explorative affinity to feminism, sf became a genre popular with women writers, who recognized the radical potential of sf, because, as Robin Roberts observes, "realism by definition is grounded in the actual, patriarchal world, *only* Science Fiction, with its embrace of fantasizing and the impossible, can fully sustain a feminist vision of the future" (1990, 137).[41] Sarah Lefanu characterizes the liberating potentiality of sf for feminist writers thus:

> Unlike other forms of genre writing, such as detective stories and romances, which demand the reinstatement of order and thus can be described as "closed" texts, science fiction is by its nature interrogative, open. Feminism questions a given order in political terms,

---

[40]*See Russ (1973a; 1973b; 1980b; 1981), Le Guin (1975; 1979a; 1979b), and Scott Sanders (1981). On the image of women in sf, see also Jacqueline Pearson (1990; esp. 9–15). For a history of the female character in sf up to the early 1980s, see Betty King (1984). Among the first writers who have recast women's role in their revisionary narratives are Russ, Le Guin, Piercy, Tepper, Charnas, and Carter. See also my discussion of women as Aliens in Chapter 3.1.*

[41]*See also Robert's extremely useful overview of feminist sf (1993).*

while science fiction questions it in imaginative forms.... If science fiction demands our acceptance of a relativistic universe, then feminism demands, no less, our acceptance of a relativistic social order [100].

With the questioning of a given reality—whether scientific or social—as the joint core of sf and feminism, sf in conjunction with feminist theory therefore provides female writers with a unique tool to speculate about feminist issues, focusing in detail not on technological progress but on *social* evolution, on femininity as a social construct, and on societal reconstructions, notably on the abolishment of sexual power. Inevitably this shift first to gender issues and sociopolitics, and somewhat later to a growing awareness of ethnic issues, led to a merging with utopian/ dystopian elements and themes, as I have outlined above. Established tropes of sf, such as time travel, the search for a unified field theory, Aliens, colonization, and entropy, were pushed into the background or parodied and recycled into a background sf setting primarily used to estrange readers from previously accepted stereotypes and assumptions and to re-examine "the social and sexual hierarchies of the contemporary world ... through the process of 'estrangement,' thus challenging normative ideas of gender roles" [Lefanu 21–22].

Apart from those women writers privileging utopian and dystopian fiction, sometimes using a sf setting, women writers such as Vonda N. McIntyre, C.J. Cherryh, Joan D. Vinge, Gwyneth Jones, and Melissa Scott have entered sf to tackle sf tropes. They center their novels around alien cultures and races, distant planets, spaceships, and biotechnology. With the blurring of (sub)generic boundaries, however, such a classification is, of course, problematic; particularly since female mainstream writers such as Atwood, Lessing, Piercy, and Fay Weldon have occasionally ventured into utopian, dystopian, and science fiction, albeit adamantly and ardently rejecting the labeling of their books as such. Similar to feminist utopia/dystopia, the battle of the sexes loomed darkly over feminist sf in the 1970s, and separatism, sometimes gynocentrism, was one of the dominant themes. In fact, as Barr notes, "[m]ost male SF writers imagine men controlling a universe once dominated by nature; most female SF writers [of that era] imagine women controlling a world once dominated by men" (1992, 4). Although titles from that period, such as Slonczewski's *A Door Into Ocean*, Tepper's *The Gate to Women's Country*, and Pamela Sargent's *The Shore of Women* (1986), insinuate a transitory societal position, they often suggest separatism or matriarchy, and cast men and women as two different species; or they reverse masculine metaphors of otherness and perceive men as alien. The two female characters in Tiptree's "The Women Men Don't See"

1. The Classical Vision

(1973), for instance, elect to board a starship with Aliens rather than staying with the male *other*. Men are marginalized characters confronted with the choice of elimination because they are too violent (e.g., Tiptree's famous rewriting of a male invasion story of an all-female society in "Houston, Houston, Do You Read?"); or being taught or bred for different behavior (Tepper). Innovative in many respects, many of the feminist sf novels remain, however, caught in the binarism they attack, positing men and women as distinct species in two disjointed hemispheres.

In reaction to the New Wave's turn to inner space and women writers' introduction of sexual relations to sf, the distinct literary movement of "slick, colloquial, and science-based" (Nixon 220) cyberpunk novels—reminiscent of William S. Burroughs's nightmarish, drug-induced, biomorphic surrealistic fictional world, and narratively modeled on the hard-boiled private-eye stories of Raymond Chandler, Dashiell Hammett, and Ross Macdonald—developed in the 1980s, embracing technology, capitalism, and consumerism with new fervor in the belief that technology can be used to oppose the establishment. Although Bruce Bethke coined the name of the subgenre with his story "Cyberpunk" (1983), the most prominent author associated with this era is probably William Gibson with his famous trilogy *Neuromancer* (1983), *Count Zero* (1986), and *Mona Lisa Overdrive* (1988) that were followed by his more literary hightech novels *Virtual Light* (1993) and *Idoru* (1996). Other cyberpunk novels include Walter Jon William's *Hardwired* (1986) and Bruce Sterling's *Islands in the Net* (1988). Cyberpunk projects bleak, computer-driven, hightech, near-future worlds of neon-lit, sky-scraping mega-cities ruled by multinational corporations, featuring streetwise and anarchic data-cowboys and information pirates jacked into cyberspace decks, hooked on technological drugs, implants, and the next digital image injection. These cyberpunks attack the globalized multi-corporations that rule in place of nations from (in the terminology of Gibson) the squalid urban *sprawl*. Turning from outer space to cyberspace and its hyper or virtual reality and focusing on a new human/machine hybridization effectively captured in the metaphor of the cyborg, cyberpunk prophesied from a transhumanist perspective and often with a postmodernist stance the replacement of *homo sapiens* by *homo digitalis*.[42]

---

[42]*Referring to Frederic Jameson's praise of cyberpunk as "the supreme literary expression if not of postmodernism, then of late capitalism itself" (Jameson 1991, 417), Brian McHale analyzes the coalescence of the poetics of postmodernism and cyberpunk in that cyberpunk "translates or transcodes postmodernist motifs from the level of form (the verbal continuum, narrative strategies) to the level of the projected world" (McHale 1992, 150) and hence "literalizes" postmodernist ideas and themes. Moreover, McHale identifies "worldlessness," the "centrifugal self," (ibid. 150) and individual as well as collective "death imagery" as three motifs shared by postmodernist fiction and cyberpunk.*

Cyberpunk, however, parades weak, depoliticized, sexualized and hence marginalized female characters in a world of alpha-males, desiring the ultimate penetration of the matrix. Furthermore, feminist critics have heatedly charged cyberpunk as a literary "aggressive anti-feminist backlash ... [that] figured feminists as emasculating harridans and ballbusters" (Nixon 228).[43] Among the few women writers associated with cyberpunk are Pat Cadigan, Rebecca Ore, Laura J. Mixon, Candas Jane Dorsey, and the French-Canadian writer Élizabeth Vonarburg with regard to her novel *Le Silence de la Cité* (1981) that represents an early employment of the idea of simulacra, an image central to cyberpunk. Perhaps one of the best known feminist re-appropriations of cyberpunk is Piercy's *He, She and It* (1991), published in Britain as *Body of Glass* (1992). Like Mixon and others, Piercy turns to a thorough questioning of dualism in that she employs the hybrid figure of the cyborg—that Donna Haraway has designated as the deconstructive and potentially liberatory figure of the future in her seminal study "A Manifesto for Cyborgs"—not as an image of hyped artificiality/technology, but as a metaphor transgressive of binary oppositions such as human/machine, organic/inorganic, male/female, creator/creation, and subject/object.[44] In this respect, Piercy's cybernovel represents a good, albeit sf-oriented, example of what the next chapter explores: the turn from the feminist critical utopia and dystopia to the transgressive utopia and dystopia, the rupture of boundaries.

---

[43]*There is a multitude of literature on cyberpunk, cyborgs, media adaptations, film studies, genre and gender issues, and feminist criticism about these topics. For short discussions of genre/gender in relation to masculinist and feminist sf, see Nicola Nixon (1992), Karen Cadora (1995), Mary Harper (1995), and Lauraine Leblanc (1997); also Wolmark's insightful study on woman as the Alien/other (1994; esp. chap. 5 on the intersection of cyborgs, cyberpunk, and feminism), and the essays in the recent anthologies edited by Wolmark (1999) and by Barr (2000; esp. those in section 2 and 3). For a discussion that includes television, software, comic books, and recent films, see Claudia Springer (1996).*

[44]*The cyborg, Haraway argues, is a distinctly utopian figure that resists and challenges artificial Cartesian dualisms; it is "about transgressed boundaries, potent fusions, and dangerous possibilities" (154). Essentially, Haraway argues, the cyborg is a creature of a post-gender world where not only gender differences, but also the corporeal mother-child unity or dyad respectively dissolve. The cyborg "skips the step of original unity" (Haraway 151) without undergoing the painful Lacanian process of separation and individuation of the self mirrored by the other. Such a self opens up a whole new venue for the imagination of differences. Without a concept of unity, a notion of difference can emerge that is not defined by the Cartesian paradigm of two opposites but perceived as a parity of pluralities. See also Mohr (2001), for a further discussion of Piercy's novel following this argumentative trajectory.*

2
Demanding the Possible?
The Artificiality of Boundaries

> *But then are we in order when we are most out of order.*
> —William Shakespeare [2H6 IV.ii.203–204]

    What is order? Is it the opposite or perhaps the very absence of disorder? Are order and disorder intrinsically connected in yet another less exclusionary sense, as William Shakespeare has suggested? Habitually, to define one pole we refer to the other, although our postmodern age has questioned, if not ruptured, the already fissured boundaries of traditional thought, and science has disproven the exclusively dual nature of matter. In the field of neurology, researchers have recently begun to discard the fundamental Cartesian error of dichotomizing body and mind, as the U.S.-American neurologist Antonio Damasio attests in his latest book (1999). Modern physics has also revolutionized our thinking for some time now. The spacetime continuum of relativity theory has replaced the Newtonian separation of space and time. Moving beyond the distinction between particle and wave of classical mechanics, quantum mechanics describes sub-atomic objects that are simultaneously particle *and* wave— depending on the observer, as Schrödinger's famous cat has illustrated— or are perhaps neither, but something that we cannot grasp yet. Last but not least, chaos theory has displaced the Newtonian world of stability and linear progress by proving that structuring elements are part of disorder, and thus dissolve the opposition between disorder and order. Perhaps we are indeed most in order when we are in disorder. Above all, our way of thinking and our perception of reality construct binary poles that are not necessarily manifested in reality, as (to quote Shakespeare once more) Hamlet remarks: "for there is nothing either good or bad, but thinking makes it so" (*Ham*. II.ii.259–261).

    To move beyond binary thinking, we need to imagine something else. Literary representation, experimentation, and imagination of other realities that are less riven by opposites provide cognitive maps for such a paradigm shift. Within the literary realm, utopian, dystopian, and sf literature are predisposed to defamiliarize us from these false dichotomous categories of thought and familiarize us with new, transgressive notions of existence. Yet, although expressing discontent with the status quo, classical utopia and dystopia have acted within and have in fact reinforced binary opposites, whereas contemporary feminist literature that addresses the construction of the future disrupts and transgresses dualisms on the generic, narrative, and content level.

The first part of this chapter first examines the recent new generic developments towards what Tom Moylan has called "critical utopia" (1986)—a term Lyman Tower Sargent has extended to include the "critical dystopia" (1994)—and then explicates Lucy Sargisson's perceptive and useful notion of the contemporary transgressive utopia, a concept that I extend to denote what I describe as "transgressive utopian dystopias": dystopias that contain a utopian subtext transgressive of binaries. The ensuing section introduces Sargisson's concept of transgression and discusses the transgressive aspects she locates in the often intersecting theories of postmodernism, poststructuralism, and feminism(s). Additionally, transgression is linked with postcolonial notions such as hybridity, because—surprisingly—Sargisson's study does not extend to an examination of postcolonial theories. Finally, I briefly mention which binaries are criticized and transgressed in the exemplary transgressive utopian dystopias by Elgin, Charnas, and Atwood.

2.1. From Critical Utopia and Dystopia to Transgressive Utopia and to Transgressive Utopian Dystopia

As delineated in the previous chapter, since the 1970s a general dissolution and cross-fertilization of generic and narrative boundaries can be discerned in contemporary utopian, dystopian, and science fiction. Especially during the past 25 years feminist utopias and dystopias—represented, for example, by Piercy, Russ, Le Guin, Carter, Butler, Atwood, Elgin, and Charnas—have created a generic fluidity and a thematic dialogue, so that classifications such as utopia *or* dystopia are indeed in many cases obsolete.

By merging and hybridizing utopia and dystopia traditionally defined as antinomies—sometimes situated in a sf frame—and presenting utopia and dystopia as interactive hemispheres rather than distinct poles, feminist literary utopias and dystopias in particular contest the standard reading of utopia and dystopia as two discrete literary subgenres and expose the artificiality of rigid classifications. These utopian/dystopian texts not only negotiate the continuum between utopia and anti-utopia, to paraphrase Tom Moylan (cf. 2000, xiii), but constitute—as I suggest in the case of dystopias—a dystopian utopian continuum or, in other words, an interweaving of utopian and dystopian narrative strands that form "utopian dystopias."[1]

More important, however, a number of these feminist utopias and utopian dystopias successfully suggest ways of *transgressing* binary thought, forming in the process the new subgenre of "transgressive utopias" and "transgressive utopian dystopias." These texts refuse a logic of sameness, dissolve hierarchized binary oppositions, and embrace difference, multiplicity, and diversity. Transgressive utopian dystopian texts discard the polarization of static dystopia and static utopia, of thesis and antithesis, and thus never arrive at a definite synthesis that comprises the blueprint for perfection. In the logic of transgression, thesis and antithesis do not exist; they are neither, and in a movement of fluidity these texts, describing the interplay, incorporate both.

In the mid–1980s, Moylan first notes in his seminal work *Demand the Impossible: Science Fiction and the Utopian Imagination* (1986) this formal and narrative content shift in the predominantly feminist utopian literature of the 1970s. Following Russ's observation about the interconnectedness of oppositional movements and the oppositional stance of these critical utopian texts (cf. Russ 1981), Moylan identifies recent feminist utopias as the literary products of the diverse liberatory and countercultural movements of the time, offering the "contradictory and diverse multiplicity of a broad utopian dialogue" (1986, 210) between text and social reality.[2] Investigating recent literary utopias by Russ, Piercy, Le Guin, and Delaney, Moylan asserts that these utopian visions, which he terms "critical utopias," refrain from the classical utopian notion of perfection and stasis, and "reject utopia as a blueprint while preserv-

---

[1]*In his introduction to* Scraps of the Untainted Sky *(2000), Moylan also once uses the term "utopian dystopia," yet not to emphasize a successful and continuous utopian subtext, but merely to denote the insertion of oppositional strategies within these new dystopias.*

[2]*In her study* The Concept of Utopias *(1990), Ruth Levitas contests Moylan's view that the feminist writers' engagement in oppositional movements translates into the texts, and that these literary texts thus effect a strong reader reaction resulting in political action, because "the education of desire ... will not automatically be read off into political action. Desire must be transformed into hope, the wish for change into the will for change and the belief that there is an agency available to execute it" (174). For Levitas, critical utopias display a disillusioned lack of confidence in social transformation and, therefore, do not address the problem of agency: "The function of utopia thus reverts from that of goal and catalyst of change to one of criticism, and the education of desire, without any necessary move forward into action" (196).*

ing it as a dream" (1986, 10), a dream of a better but not of an ideal and fixed society. In contrast to classical utopias, feminist critical utopias thus remain ambiguous and, consequently, defy charges of totalitarianism. This view is shared by Angelika Bammer, who also notes that the introduction of change differentiates contemporary utopias from classical static utopias that envision "a state in which change seems neither desirable nor possible, and even more significantly in their reconstruction of precisely the kind of dichotomous categories ... that they claim to refute, they tend to reinforce established ways of thinking even as they set out to challenge them" (2). By presenting what Bammer calls "partial visions" of utopia, contemporary feminist utopian texts preserve the utopian impulse, a utopian desire that refrains from prescriptions of perfection, and advocates "a politics of change cast in the subjunctive instead of the imperative mode" (51). Significantly, these "partial visions" or "critical utopias" no longer implement the state as the superior principle of order, but stress taking individual *action*, since these texts value the personal engagement of the individual, driven by discontent to participate in the negotiation of a larger social transformation. As outlined in Chapter 1, this change in content is also reflected by the changed narrative form that—compared to classical utopias—accentuates character development, non-linear narratives, and multiperspectivism. According to Moylan, these texts, focusing on self-criticism, the element of process, and the very construction of a utopia that is never attained, "dwell on the conflict between the originary world and the utopian society opposed to it so that the process of social change is more directly articulated" (1986, 11), whereas classical utopia obscures its very origin and revels in the very absence of historical progress and process. With a less fixed, non-normative content, the contemporary utopian texts do not present a finished "product" but the exploration of the very construction of an alternative and improved societal vision. Such a notion of "imperfection within utopian society itself" (ibid. 11) creates a dynamic interaction between fictional present and future and, therefore, allows a mode of diversity, difference, and a multiplicity of perspectives.

Similar to static classical utopias, classical dystopias are equally resistant to the idea of change. With the defeat of the rebel—whose rebellion, as Chris Ferns argues, "expresses itself through a series of binary oppositions" (1999, 120)—classical dystopias depict the reinstatement of a totalitarian order and preclude any notion of progress. In this gap between described dystopian present and the anticipation of a potential utopian future that classical dystopia evades, the new contemporary feminist dystopia with its utopian subtext is located—which early on Sarah Lefanu has recognized as "hidden utopian streak" (75) and recently Raffaella Baccolini has identified as the "utopian core ... a locus of hope"

(13). These "utopian dystopias" initially present a dystopian world, and then narrate the point of transition to show glimpses of the historical processes that lead from dystopia to utopia and resist narrative closure. Without ever narrating or exactly defining utopia, these new feminist dystopian texts map not a single path but rather several motions and changes that may lead to a potentially better future. For Baccolini, this utopian element emerges, on the one hand, from the generic crossover, the "use, revison, and appropriation of generic fiction that constitutes ... an opening for utopian elements" (13), and, on the other hand, it is primarily contained in the ambiguous ending, "rejecting the traditional subjugation of the individual" (18).

In contrast to Baccolini, I argue that the utopian subtext is interwoven as a *continuous* narrative strand within the dystopian text, as the close textual analyses in the second part of this study show. This collapsing of generic boundaries—which Baccolini correctly aligns with a general poststructuralist "deconstruction of genre purity" (18)—essentially produces what I call hybridized "utopian dystopias." Despite this generic impurity, Lyman Tower Sargent, however, names these texts "critical dystopias" (1994, 7) in analogy to Moylan's earlier term of critical utopias. While Baccolini affirms critical dystopias as a new genre, neither Moylan (2000)—who in turn takes up Sargent's term and, apart from providing a critical survey of the literary history of and recapping the academic criticism of utopia/dystopia/sf, discusses at length Kim Stanley Robinson's *Gold Coast* (1988), Butler's *Parable of the Sower* (1993), and Piercy's *He, She and It* as examples of critical dystopias— nor Sargent consider critical dystopias (nor critical utopias for that matter) as a distinct new genre. Instead, Moylan identifies the critical dystopia as the new literary motor of utopian agency, providing "a space for a new form of political opposition, one fundamentally based in difference and multiplicity" (2000, 190).

While Sargent, Baccolini, and Moylan acknowledge the generic hybridization, the shift in form and content, the British political scientist Lucy Sargisson notes in her groundbreaking study *Contemporary Feminist Utopianism* (1996) the important innovation of transgression. Sargisson's book investigates feminist utopianism from a broad perspective, including feminist political thought and theorizing, feminist literary utopia/dystopia, and literary theory. Favoring the less restrictive term "utopianism" over utopia that, she notes, verges on cultural imperialism because it exclusively reduces utopian moments to the form of the literary genre, Sargisson follows a trajectory that delineates utopian moments not as a definite oppositional movement but rather as an opening of utopian spaces in a variety of theories—here she finds feminist, postmodern, and poststructuralist theories particularly useful—and as a literary practice.[3] These utopian spaces can no longer be described with a conventional understanding of utopianism as the perfected ideal, since they emphasize constant change, renegotiation, imperfection, and process.

In accord with Moylan, Sargent, and Baccolini, Sargisson discerns in contemporary feminist utopia a generic blurring, a resistance to closure, and a movement towards the dynamic process of a pragmatic utopia rather than the static perfectionism of the dogmatic utopia as blueprint. Sargisson finds in particular Moylan's reconceptualization of literary utopia as a critical vision emphasizing process, imperfection, and multiplicity, and his analysis of the critical utopia as "part of the political practice and vision shared by a variety of autonomous oppositional movements ... [a] new historic bloc of opposition" (Moylan 1986, 11) a useful approach that steps out of the classical binary tradition: "Opposition thus understood is a bigger concept than the either/or position; it is comprised of multiple critiques" (Sargisson 55). In contrast, other non-literary conceptualizations of utopia—for instance, Mannheim's socialist oppositional theory—represent opposition as fixed dualism. Yet Sargisson strongly repudiates Moylan's attempt to unify oppositional movements as an element of "normative prescription" (56), for he neglects the diversity and multiplicity of oppositional movements.

Sargisson notes moreover that specifically feminist oppositional approaches deviate from a dualistic positioning and postponing of change into the future, and thus produce a paradigm shift because they "anticipate the possibility of radically different 'nows'.... This new utopian function operates in the political present, not in the desired future ... [moving] utopia from a speculative (or concrete) future to a no place/good place that is an alternative reading of the present" (52). Sargisson identifies transgression—the critique and displacement of meaning "constructed by a complex and hierarchical system of binary opposition" (4) and the suggestion of an alternative approach that values difference and multiplicity (the concept of transgression is examined in more detail in the next section)—as an important element of all these oppositional practices, and she extends Moylan's and Sargent's notion of critical oppositions to the transgression of binary oppositional thought. Sargisson introduces the new term "transgressive utopianism," and she also asserts this hitherto unrecognized tendency of contemporary feminist utopias to challenge and to *transgress* binary logic. Thus, in Sargis-

---

[3] *Cf.*: "'Utopianism,' then, the umbrella term, concerns the propensity or phenomenon, and under this umbrella I place utopian thought, utopian theory and utopias ... eutopias, dystopias and utopian satire" (Sargisson 2). Sargisson sets out to explore and assess existing content-, form-, and function-based approaches to utopia(nism) and—favoring function and recalling Bloch's, Sargent's, and Levitas's definitions—she arrives at a broad understanding of utopia(nism) as 'social dreaming' and desire.

son's view, transgressive literary feminist utopias are *one* expression of transgressive utopianism.

This essentially postmodern view of utopia—envisioning a pluralistic society that values heterogeneity, diversity, and difference—also intersects with what both Michel Foucault and Gianni Vattimo have called "heterotopia." While Sargisson omits any reference to the potentially transgressive concept of heterotopia, Moylan asserts—with reference to Foucault's analysis of heterotopian spaces as destabilizing the present—that "heterotopia ... preserves the utopian impulse, releasing it from the traditional utopian genre, and stakes out the terrain of a radically new development in that particular discourse where our dreams and fictions intersect" (1986, 161). In contrast to the imaginary realm of utopia, Foucault, however, situates heterotopia in reality as "counter-sites, a kind of effectively enacted utopia in which the real sites ... are simultaneously represented, contested, and inverted. Places of this kind are outside of all places.... I shall call them, by way of contrast to utopias, heterotopias" (1986, 24).[4] Unlike utopias that reside in the spatial and temporal no-place or fictional elsewhere, heterotopias exist in the real realm of society, a position that reflects Foucault's critical view of utopia and his insistence to replace utopian dreaming with real experiences and experiments lived in the here and now.

Reappropriated by postmodern narrative strategies, heterotopia as an aesthetic principle celebrates, in Vattimo's terminology, the liberatory function of differences, multiplicity, and heterogeneity and embodies a carnival of utopian visions that refrain from metanarratives. By focusing on the shift from stasis to dynamic, from the universal blueprint to plurality and diversity, the terminologies of heterotopia, critical utopia, and critical dystopia, however, only partially address the innovative potential of postmodern feminist utopia/dystopia. In contrast, Sargisson's concept of transgressive utopianism captures the most important and the potentially most utopian shift in contemporary feminist utopian and dystopian narratives: that of a destabilization, a subversion, and ultimately a transgression of binary categories.

2.2. The Concept of Transgression

Noting the crisis of standard notions of utopianism and the standard notion's inadequacy to describe contemporary feminist utopianism,

---

[4]*On the intersections of heterotopia and utopia, see also the articles anthologized in Tobin Siebers (1994), especially Judith N. Shklar's essay "What Is the Use of Utopia?" (40–56) that explores the emergence of the postmodern heterotopia of disorder and of individual subjectivity from the classical utopia of order and collectivism and links heterotopia to the philosophy of the Frankfurt School, reformulating utopian desire on the grounds of diversity and multiplicity.*

I. Literary History and Theoretical Background

Sargisson advances a "critique of utopianism as perfection-seeking ... [that] hinges on a critique of the equation of perfection with closure and is related to ... debates on the construction of meaning" and hence advocates that "utopia need[s] to be reconceived" (3). Consequently, Sargisson explores those open-ended, multidirectional, and multisourced utopian tendencies and spaces in feminist utopian literature, feminist theorizing, political and postmodern literary theory, and particularly in poststructuralism; her work specifically investigates changed concepts of the body, sexuality, identity, power, and feminist politics that are not grounded in binary oppositions.[5] For Sargisson, "[d]ebates concerning equality and difference, the construction of meaning through language, and the construction of subjectivity" (3) prove useful for the articulation of a new approach to utopianism. Such a radically new transgressive utopianism, subverting meanings derived from binarism—in the language of binary logic, meaning is referential and to define the dominant term requires a subordinate *other*—and refusing universalism, emerges from the interstices of feminist, postmodern, and poststructuralist discourses, particularly from the theories of Derrida and Cixous.[6] Sargisson deduces from her investigation of theories and utopianisms that a transgressive utopianism is especially manifested in feminist utopianism.[7]

Because contemporary feminist discourse is no longer singular and monolithic, but has evolved to speak in the plural and from many positions, it "sets the tone for a new utopianism" (Sargisson 64). Through a long process of introspection and internal discussions, feminism has come to reject universalist and essentialist notions, therefore concurring that "no one solution can be proposed" (ibid. 64), and, informed by

---

[5] *Sargisson also discerns a dynamic and transgressive utopianism in Carol Pearson's political theory, which is grounded in the paradoxical principles of the relativity of time and locates the act of change in the present and demands a paradigm shift (of abandoning all notions of control) before social transformation. Such a political theory, Sargisson concludes, "lets go of the quest for truths, certainties and fixed categories" (58).*

[6] *The mechanics of binary thinking, Donna J. Haraway writes, "have been persistent in Western traditions; they have all been systemic to the logics and practices of domination of women, people of color, nature, workers, animals—in short, domination of all constituted as others, whose task is to mirror the self. Chief among these troubling dualisms are self/other, mind/body, culture/nature, male/female, civilized/primitive, reality/appearance, whole/part, agent/resource, maker/made, active/passive, right/wrong, truth/illusion, total/partial, God/man. The self is the One who is not dominated, who knows that by the service of the other; the other is the one who holds the future, who knows that by the experience of domination, which gives the lie to the autonomy of the self. To be One is to be autonomous, to be powerful, to be God; but to be One is to be an illusion and so to be involved in a dialectic of apocalypse with the other. Yet, to be other is to be multiple, without clear boundaries, frayed, insubstantial. One is too few, but two are too many" (177).*

[7] *Sargisson associates "transcendence" with a privileging of the mind over the body, and thus finds "transgression" the more appropriate and her preferred term.*

poststructuralism, has come to reject closure as a political act that "privileges sameness and oneness and favors self over other" (ibid. 65). Sargisson starts with the axiom of feminisms' well-known conundrum of being torn between the strife for "integrationist thought in order that women might be able to articulate and act as *women*" (66) and the necessity to acknowledge the diversity of and differences among women (an inherent paradox with strong transgressive potential). From this axiom, the "equality versus difference" debate within feminisms, she believes it is most important to move towards a refusal of an understanding of equality as sameness, so that difference can be approached as a relational concept and not in opposition to equality. Sargisson thus posits the contemporary equality versus difference debate as the pivotal issue from whence the prevailing binary logic can be deconstructed and transgressed.

Where liberal feminism foregrounds equality on the basis of the irrelevancy of gender distinctions and the claim that women and men share the same capabilities,[8] radical feminism rejects equality within the existing system.[9] As cultural feminism—also referred to as gynocentrism or gynandry—radical feminism moves on towards a rejection of equality as a masquerade of sameness and a celebration of women's difference, embracing an inverted dualism by revalorizing feminine qualities as superior.[10] Yet all three positions have been charged with essentializing and

---

[8]*Historically emerging in the 1960s—a key text is Betty Friedan's pioneering* The Feminine Mystique *(1963)—liberal feminism of the first wave has tried to eliminate difference and has argued along a basis of "androgyny" (complementary differences) of the sexes and an emphasis on socialization for the sameness of the sexes, and hence for the same capabilities and the same treatment (e.g. the Equal Opportunities programs in Britain). The key tenet of liberal feminism is the demand for the equal power of women, a desire for equality with men, within the hierarchical system and thus, its opponents criticize, liberal feminists essentially try to become female men and remain complicit to the existing power structure of patriarchy. Reacting to these reproaches, second wave liberal feminists—among these being Betty Friedan this time with her book* The Second Stage *(1981)—rejected not equality but an equality within the existing system.*

[9]*Informed by the New Left movement as well as the black Civil Rights movement of the 1960s, the early, more radical advocates of egalitarianism have sought the abolishment of patriarchy and capitalism in the belief that the overthrow of the system will change the distribution of power and thus liberate everyone who is oppressed. Sexuality is considered to be the major cause for oppression. For instance, Shulamith Firestone in* Dialectic of Sex *(1970) views the sexes as two classes, and to abolish inequity she suggests that in addition to the abolishment of the nuclear family there needs to be changes in the reproductive biology/technology, urging women to own their bodies and to seize reproductive technologies.*

[10]*For cultural feminists, women differ from men, and thus cultural feminism takes a separatist stance. An equality that requires women to acquire masculine characteristics to become the same, to turn in fact into female men, is not desirable; nor are feminine traits seen, as in liberal feminism, as complementary to masculine traits. Revaluing the "feminine mystique," gynocentrism elevates women to a superior position, favors female qualities, and considers women to be closer to the concepts of body, nature, and nurture, a stance that the ecofeminist positions extend to equalize the elements with woman. Mary Daly argues along these lines and in her endeavor to expose*

universalizing "woman." While lesbian feminism attacked the heterosexual straightjacket of early feminism and added "identity politics" to feminisms' agenda,[11] black feminism has drawn attention to the very differences *between* women by adding the categories of race and ethnicity to feminist discourse.[12] Black feminism charges Western (white) mainstream feminism, on the one hand, with the cultural imperialism of a feminist Eurocentrism that speaks from a newly established and homogenized center of subjectivity that either excludes women of color or constructs women of color as yet another *other*, and, on the other hand, for homogenizing and objectifying "Third World Woman" into a monolith devoid of differences (cf. Mohanty).

Sara Suleri investigates these interstices of feminism and postcolonialism to question how to negotiate the categories of race and gender, and provocatively demands to know "which comes first, gender or race?" (273). Angelas de la Concha wisely answers this question by emphasizing that only a dialogue (or perhaps a polylogue?) of the diverse feminist approaches will bring about empowering insights and solidarity, precisely because of the specific historically varied *and* the shared common differences according to the following categories:

> the matrix of domination is structured along axes that are not limited to gender but include race and class, to which other axes might be added such as age, physical appearance, sexual orientation, individual personal biography, group or community life, and larger social and political institutions, gender is nevertheless a discernible substratum underlying all the others. All this social and relational plurality notwithstanding, there is a clear, specifically female voice narrating a plurality of stories... [63].

Feminist discourses—whether informed by postcolonialism, poststructuralism, liberalism, or Marxism—need to embrace this plurality and diversity of female voices and must abandon notions of a monolithic coherent feminism.

[continued] *oppression she also analyzes (masculinist) language as a major tool of (psychological) oppression, calling for a reclamation and reappropriation of terms used to denigrate women in Gyn/Ecology (1979). Obversely, Adrienne Rich in* Of Woman Born *(1976) addresses the physical oppression of women, and specifically discusses motherhood.*

[11]*For a good overview of lesbian feminist criticism of generalized representations of (women's) sexuality as heterosexuality, see Bonnie Zimmermann (1981). In a later essay, Rich (1980) questions the necessity for women to identify with men, and proposes that women want to identify with other women—which renders them potentially lesbian—and thus they would inhabit a "lesbian continuum."*

[12]*African-American feminists such as Alice Walker and bell hooks have repeatedly challenged white feminism for universalizing women's experiences. From a black and lesbian point of view, Audre Lorde has critiqued the nexus of heterosexual/white/Eurocentric writing, explicitly lambasting Daly for representing women of color as predominantly victims (1983; see also her essay collection* Sister/Outsider *1984). Otherwise more engaged in postcolonial studies, Gayatri Spivak has also blamed Western feminism for its color-blindness.*

2. Demanding the Possible? 59

Echoing Teresa de Lauretis's earlier warning that feminism needs to turn away from essentialist notions of emphasizing sameness over difference—"a homogeneous, monolithic Feminism ... is something that must be resisted" (de Lauretis 15)—Sargisson postulates that feminist theories must reject patriarchal conceptualizations of difference in terms of universalized reference, such as "Woman is not-a-man—'she' is different" (Sargisson 68). In Elizabeth Grosz's words, patriarchal difference signifies "inequality, distinction, or opposition, a sexual difference modelled on negative, binary or oppositional structures within ... the other is defined only by the negation of the first. Only sameness or identity can ensure equality" (339). Taking a critical stance towards a feminism of "an equality-versus-difference polemic" (71) that moves towards exclusion and is "representative of a suppression of otherness (difference)" (72), Sargisson argues for a feminist politics that simultaneously aims at equality *and* difference as linked and not counterpoised concepts. Only the rejection of the impossible choice between the either/or binarism will lead to the recognition of the interrelationship between equality and difference, and will result in a truly postmodern feminism that affirms differences but transgresses patriarchal differences.

Joan Scott argues, informed by poststructuralist approaches, along a similar trajectory for the displacement of dichotomous terms and pleads for a more relational rather than an antithetical view:

> A binary choice has been created to offer a choice to feminists.... When equality and difference are paired dichotomously, they structure an impossible choice. If one opts for equality, one is forced to accept the notion that difference is antithetical to it. If one opts for difference, one admits that equality is unattainable.... In fact the antithesis itself hides the interdependence of the two terms, for equality is not the elimination of difference, and difference does not preclude equality [137–138].

For Scott, equality and difference are also not mutually exclusive concepts, and equality must not be restricted to the applicability of sameness. As Sargisson argues, from such a standpoint "[e]quality no longer negates difference, but rather is reliant upon this concept for its own meaning" (74). Instead of challenging differences, the call for equality should embrace the notion of difference, just as "power is constructed on and so must be challenged *from the ground of difference*" (Scott 145; emphasis added). Similarly, Irigaray does not place difference in opposition to sameness, for in her understanding, difference is not based on a dualistic principle. For Irigaray, "[a] solution will only come through sexual difference.... Equality between men and women cannot be achieved without a *theory of gender as sexed* and a rewriting of the rights and obligations of each sex *qua different*" (1993, 12–13). Such a feminist understanding of difference would not perceive difference "as different *from* a pre-given norm, but as *pure difference*, difference in itself, difference with no identity.... Difference viewed as distinction implies the pre-evalutation of one of these terms ... pure difference refuses to privilege either term" (Grosz 340). Difference would then not imply inferiority, lack, and deviance from a norm of sameness, but could be valued as difference in terms of desirable diversity. Sargisson concludes that a "feminist politics of difference ... denormalizes sameness, to which difference is no longer opposed. Difference ... is [then] representative of dissimilarity and non-identity ... of the impossibility of similarity of identity" (75). This understanding of difference describes, Sargisson argues, critical utopian thinking in Moylan's sense and at the same time transgressive utopian thinking, aimed at transforming the dualisms of the present from an oppositional stance "whilst transcending the limitations of patriarchal binary oppositionality" (77).

To conceptualize new utopian spaces, however, feminist theorizing must allow a diversity of approaches appropriate for the diversity of relational differences that women (and men) represent and experience. In Elisabeth Spelman's words, "though all women are women, no woman is only a woman" (187), and consequently feminism needs to "recognise the existence of many kinds of women, many genders" (176).[13] Moving thus from the universal to the particular and from the particular to the universal—not as an opposition but rather as a flux of appreciation and connection—would expand the notion of choice from either/or to a plurality of choice, to multiple choices. Such a move would, as Sargisson states, "transgress the binary position of either/or and say both, neither and more" (95). From this utopian space, "[w]e can ... simultaneously accept and reject, thus creating a new space beyond binary opposition in which something else (the unforeseeable) can be foreseen. Thus we neither (fully) accept nor (fully) reject, and either/or is no longer a meaningful position" (Sargisson 95).

In her search for transgressive utopian spaces, Sargisson turns also to the dynamic interaction between feminisms and poststructuralism/ postmodernism(s). Feminism profits from the postmodern desire to undermine and disrupt boundaries, to reject universal truths, and to

---

[13] *The notion of more than two genders has been interjected by Monique Wittig, arguing for a third, a lesbian, gender or sex (cf. Sargisson 95–96 and 171–172), a concept that Charnas specifically contests. See also my discussion of lesbian sexuality in Chapter 4.4.2 (also n68). With regard to lesbian identity, Judith Butler has also called into question the notion of a binary theory of gender and gender identity and draws attention to the performative nature of gender, the very "imitative structure of gender itself" (137), that simultaneously constitutes and expresses the miming subject.*

destabilize the confounding of traditional markers of "difference": "Postmodern feminism asserts difference, and it also destroys the concept of difference as we know it. It transgresses the conceptualization of patriarchal difference and renders it redundant" (Sargisson 83). In particular the poststructuralist and postmodernist theories of Jean-François Lyotard, Jacques Derrida, and Emmanuel Levinas are ideas that Sargisson recognizes as potentially liberating approaches to difference that are less fixed on opposition implying the hierarchical ordering of sameness and difference into superiority and inferiority, and instead focus on dissimilarity as a welcome incommensurability.[14]

In this context, Sargisson reads in particular Derrida's deconstructivism and Hélène Cixous's theory of libidinal femininity as profoundly transgressive discourses whereby transgressive, open-ended utopianism can be best approached. Derridean poststructuralist deconstruction is not finite—it does not offer a final reading—but rather represents an ever-changing activity of reading, of working from inside a (cultural) text. Just as deconstruction tries to "expose and transform the text" (Sargisson 101), utopia(nism) aims at disclosing and transforming the present via extrapolation and defamiliarization. Where deconstruction defers meaning, transgressive utopianism embodies "the endless displacement of possibility, of the possible"; as neither approach offers "the final interpretative word" (ibid. 103), both thus resist logocentrism, the handing out of the (monolithic) truth. Furthermore, deconstruction *is* inherently a utopian project insofar as it "venture[s] into regions as yet uncharted and to dismantle the edifice of tradition is to practise utopian thinking" (ibid. 103).

Both deconstruction and transgressive utopianism describe an open-ended process and are thus profoundly resistant to closure, because they invite continuous change. Sargisson declares deconstruction utopian, using extensive references to Christopher Norris's reading of Derrida in *Deconstruction: Theory and Practice* (1982), and particularly addresses Derrida's deconstructive reading of Saussure—whereby speech is no longer prior to and constitutive of writing but rather dependent on writing as understood in the broader sense of inscription. As Norris explains, Derrida thus situates speech in the cultural text of logocentrism, and thereby debunks as illusory the very notion of truth reached via reason (cf. Norris 18; qtd. in Sargisson 104). As Sargisson states, "[d]econstruction, then, like utopianism, does not just reverse an existing hierar-

---

[14]*Briefly put, the "silencing of a 'player' in a language game.... The inability to articulate one's cause in the same idiom or language creates a* différend*" (Sargisson 69). Lyotard's* différend*, connotes the unarticulated difference between two speakers, whereas Derrida's* différance *addresses the very construction of language itself; and Levinas suggests with* alterity *the acceptance and celebration of the existence of the other not as referent but as independent from the self.*

chy; rather it subverts and undermines the system which constructs hierarchical relations ... [and] represents an alternative in itself" (104–105). As in utopianism, deconstruction opens up new conceptual spaces.

Sargisson takes as an example Derrida's deconstructive reading of Claude Lévi-Strauss (who deduces from the universal occurrence of incest that it is natural), which unmasks the incest taboo as both a natural phenomenon *and* a cultural construct and reveals its discursive nature, and she asserts that deconstruction not only destabilizes but also does not partake in binary logic and can also be seen as a transgressive method. Similarly, Sargisson argues, Derrida's concept of *différance*, of deferred meaning that "subverts and operates in the gaps of binary oppositional thought" (108), exists outside of a hierarchical understanding of language and, remaining "unconceptualizable," denotes a "transgressive utopian moment" (108) in Derrida's philosophy. Significantly, Derrida turns from the Saussurian notion of difference as "spacing by contrast," whereby meaning is constructed by contrast and the negation of one term, to difference as "temporalization," whereby the sign in language always "represents the present in its absence.... The sign, in this sense, is deferred presence" (qtd. in Sargisson 109) and, in Sargisson's own words, the sign "then both signifies absence and compensates for absence by implying presence" (ibid. 109). Because of their spatial and temporal interplay, differences and the thus deferred meaning, which is enmeshed in this interplay—what Derrida captures in the polysemic neologism *différance*—cannot be construed in terms of opposites but instead remain relational and fluid, Sargisson reads *différance* as an elusive concept transgressive of an either/or logic: "Rather it is both and perhaps neither, in their 'pure,' discrete senses" (110). Moreover, as with transgressive utopias, *différance* is rooted in the present or in the cultural text it deconstructs: "both deconstruction and utopianism destroy and create simultaneously, and ... the one act cannot occur without the other" (Sargisson 111).

The second profoundly utopian concept that Sargisson identifies is Cixous's theory of a libidinal economy that addresses femininity, which turns away from a masculine concept of a phallocentric world structured in oppositions.[15] For Sargisson, libidinal femininity is therefore a utopian concept, because "it provokes a *paradigm* shift in consciousness" (113). Deconstructive in its approach, libidinal femininity also borders on the

---

[15]For an accessible introduction to what Toril Moi designates as Cixous's "imaginary utopia," see Moi's invaluable guide to feminist literary theory Sexual/Textual Politics *(1985; chap. 6)*. *In* What Is a Woman *(1999), in which Moi turns from a poststructuralist stance to a Beauvoirean feminism, she continues her investigation of as well as revisits her understanding of feminist theorists, such as Cixous and Irigaray, and connects contemporary feminism with a rereading of Simone de Beauvoir's* The Second Sex *(cf. chap. 1, 2, and 8).*

2. Demanding the Possible? 63

twofold transgressive utopian aim in that "[t]he future must no longer be determined by the past" and a new approach must attempt "to break up, to destroy; and to foresee the unforeseeable" (Cixous 1976, 875). Consequently, Cixous dismisses the past and present discourses of masculinity as unacceptable, invalid, and non-constitutive for the future. According to Cixous, femininity, which Cixous suggests has been defined as lack, absence, negativity, passivity, the body and ultimately has been linked with death,[16] needs to be revalued—from *within* this system of masculinity that is stabilized by such a concept of femininity—as lifegiving. Additionally, she advocates speaking in a feminine language that destabilizes, subverts, inverts, and "explodes" phallogocentrism, the collusion of logocentrism and phallocentrism. By using body metaphors, by conceptualizing a different framework, the body enters the text "in a move which privileges the corporeal whilst ... transgressing the body/mind divide" (Sargisson 115).[17] Likewise, Sargisson views desire as a transgressive force in Cixous's work. In contrast to the masculine gift of appropriation situated in the Realm of the Proper within an all-pervading "economy of exchange," Cixous proposes a feminine libidinal economy located in the Realm of the Gift that allows an opening up and letting go, and is driven by the desire to give generously with no expectation of a return: "Who could ever think of the gift as a gift-that-takes? Who else but man, precisely the one who would like to take everything? If there is a 'propriety of woman,' it is paradoxically her capacity to depropriate unselfishly" (Cixous 1976, 888–889).[18] Such a concept of a gift that gives without taking and, therefore, neither operates within hierarchical binary logic nor expounds the truth, and hence arrives at a lan-

---

[16]Cf.: "Men say that there are two unrepresentable things: death and the feminine sex. That's because they need femininity to be associated with death" (Cixous 1976, 885).

[17]In response to charges of essentialism or biologism for a certain conflation of the terms "feminine," "female," and "woman" Sargisson interprets Cixous's work as "a manipulation of this attitude," because the "female body is [not only] privileged in her work in a move of inversion, but the concept is also transformed" (118), in that Cixous reformulates the equation of woman-body-silence such that woman resides within her body from which she speaks.

[18]Cixous links the desire to give with birth as a transgressive moment that neither subtracts nor adds, but occurs. She states, "giving birth is neither losing nor increasing. It's adding to life an other" (1976, 891). Feminine desire is structured by love and not by jealousy: "But I do desire the other for the other, whole and entire, male or female; because living means wanting everything that is, everything that lives, and wanting it alive.... What's a desire originating from a lack? A pretty meagre desire" (ibid. 891). Cixous concludes her essay by stating that woman's exchange stems from and results in desired difference: "she is the desire-that-gives. (Not enclosed in the paradox of the gift that takes nor under the illusion of unitary fusion. We're past that).... She gives more.... She gives that there may be life, thought, transformation.... Wherever she loves ... she finds not her sum but her differences" (ibid. 893). Although the feminine libidinal economy seems to be intrinsically linked to women, Cixous specifies elsewhere that it is, in Sargisson's words, "the cultural experience of the body, rather than the body itself, that brings women closer to femininity than are men" (Sargisson 122) and, therefore, men can inhabit this position as well (e.g., homosexuals).

guage open to multiple meanings, is also characteristic of feminist utopian texts, which "are marked by the absence of the 'gift' of the blueprint.... The feminine [utopian] text ... presents to the reader the strange, the stranger, the other, the self, without fetishization or the creation of a new cult of the same" (Sargisson 126).

For some reason Sargisson omits postcolonial studies, an important discursive field that proves fruitful for the concept of transgression and is a repeatedly employed feature in transgressive utopian literature. Postcolonial issues are, for instance, relevant to the discussion of Charnas's and Elgin's texts.[19] As with feminisms and postmodernism, postcolonialism shares a concern "with the state of what we could call ex-centricity" (Hutcheon 1991, 172). Dealing with the binary politics of colonization, postcolonialism is engaged in the deconstruction of binarisms, such as the borders of colonialist white self and colonized colored other; center and margin; past, present, and future; and in the destabilization of the status quo.[20] Perhaps the most useful potentially transgressive concepts of postcolonial theory are cultural and linguistic hybridity[21] and the connected processes of the decolonization of the mind

---

[19]*An excellent and detailed introduction to the diverse field of postcolonial studies and postcolonial literature is Ania Loomba's* Colonialism/Postcolonialism *(1998). See also* The Post-Colonial Studies Reader *(1995) edited by the Australian scholars Bill Ashcroft, Gareth Griffiths, and Helen Tiffin.*

[20]*In this context, it is, however, important to note that the term postcolonialism has also undergone change and remains controversial. While originally addressing specific historical circumstance and specific localities—that is, the process of imperial colonization exporting the value system of white European men into "Third World" countries—the term now implies at least some flexibility, if not total severance from national histories. Where postcolonialism "once referred exclusively to the discursive practices produced by the historical fact of prior colonization in certain geographically specific segments of the world, it is now more of an abstraction available for figurative deployment in any strategic redefinition of marginality" (Suleri 274), and postcolonial feminist theory has linked feminist and postcolonial discourses precisely from this new perspective of shared marginalities. In my reading of Elgin's* Native Tongue *trilogy as a postcolonial counter-narrative and of Charnas's* The Furies *(the third volume of the* Holdfast *series) as the formation of a neocolonial system, postcolonialism is not restricted to the period after colonialism, but is used exactly in the above-mentioned broader sense "as the contestation of colonial domination and the legacies of colonialism" (Loomba 12), "indicating a general process with some shared features across the globe" (ibid. 19). Postcoloniality, thus understood as "oppositionality to imperializing/colonizing ... discourses and practices" conveyed as a "multiplicity of ... parallel narratives" (Alva 245), shares feminist desires for opposition to patriarchal discourses and practices: where feminism dismantles the Law of the Father, postcolonialism opposes the Law of the Empire. Both discourses recover the histories, voices, and concerns of peripheralized subjects that the dominant colonial/patriarchal center denied subjectivity.*

[21]*Hybridization was originally a problematic term and referred to the cross-breeding of two distinct species/races within the colonial context (cf. Young 10f.). Postcolonial notions of hybridity, particularly Bhabha's usage of the term, suggest that hybridity is not only an irrefutable fact of colonialism but is also an enabling strategy. Bhabha counters Frantz Fanon's polarizing view in* Black Skin, White Masks *(1967) of the colonized subject fixed in a position of subordination and psychic trauma, resulting from the attempt to slip on a white mask (the master's white skin) while being "trapped" in the black skin. Bhabha posits an unstable colonial identity in flux,*

and the body—what Homi K. Bhabha describes with the "aesthetics of liberation"—as well as of transculturation that, according to Marie Luise Pratt, occurs after the culture clash in the "contact zone." There is, however, an important distinction between hybridity and transculturation on the one hand and transgression on the other. The transgression Sargisson proposes is meant to be voluntarily chosen, while transculturation and hybridity can be culturally produced forms of existence and exchange that one is subjected to without choice or they can be consciously desired modes of existence and cultural learning (or a mixture of both).

Instead of reading colonialism solely as a one-sided act of superimposing the dominant culture, Pratt insists on a more nuanced perspective and exposes the social interactive process that takes place in the "contact zones," those "social spaces where disparate cultures meet, clash and grapple with each other, often in highly asymmetrical relations of domination and subordination" (4). What Pratt terms "transculturation" is not a superficially one-sided infiltration of the dominant group's culture into the culture of the subordinate group, but a less obvious back flow or seepage of indigenous cultural norms, values, and behavior that also reshapes the dominant culture. These cultural crossovers, the mutual transportation of values, emphasize the artificiality of neat divisions, and allow a transgressive perspective that does not focus on either colonialist subject or colonized object, but speculates about the interchange or interplay and the creation of an oscillating something else, something more that escapes bipolar categorizations.

Taking a similar trajectory, Bhabha also notes that the colonial process encompasses more than just a simple application of polarization that neatly separates into colonialist subject and colonized object and can be instead perceived as a dynamic and complex process of ambivalent dependency that involves both parties.[22] This experience of an exis-

[continued] *not divided but doubled: "being in at least two places at once" (1994a, 117). Although the colonialist views the colonized other as different, select members of the colonized other are invited to join the dominant group on the basis of yet another implied difference (e.g. education). This "ambivalent use of 'different'—to be different from those that are different makes you the same" (ibid. 117)—produces an incoherent discourse of sameness and difference, and thus the colonialist self reveals the cracks of colonial bipolarity. Oppositional movements can arise from these ambivalent interstices, where "the disturbing distance in between [the colonialist self and the colonized other] that constitutes the figure of colonial otherness" (ibid. 117).*

[22]*Postcolonial feminists, such as Gayatri Spivak and the Subaltern Studies group, criticize Edward Said's notion of a homogenous colonial discourse and Bhabha for diagnosing primarily the cosmopolitan diaspora of a transnational migrant elite. These feminists/postcolonialists are concerned with retrieving and reinserting the alternative indigenous voices within (post)colonial discourse, the obscured subaltern voice of the colonized majority; that is the non-elite rural populace (cf. Guha and Spivak 1988). Moreover, in her notable and famous essay "Can the Subaltern Speak?" Spivak (1993) expounds on the double colonization and effective silencing of indigenous women by the combined oppression of patriarchy and colonialism.*

tence between cultures, of a cultural hybridity, and of an indeterminate hybrid identity creates a borderline position from which subversion can infiltrate the seemingly fixed oppositions of colonialist self and colonized *other*.[23] Instead of being a borderline, as Bhabha writes, "the boundary becomes the place from which *something begins its presencing*" (1994b, 5). Bhabha thereby describes a process of hybridization that refrains from a simple inversion or dissolution of oppositions. Rather, his "aesthetics of liberation" creates a double vision, a vision that does not choose between either/or but is situated in the in-between, opening up a potentially transgressive utopian "third space" in which identity and alterity are no longer subjected to hierarchization but participate in an open-ended fluidity of exchange and an overlap of the incommensurable. Similarly, code-switching between discourses—the abrogation of the imperial discourse and the (re)appropriation of the indigenous discourse—creates a dynamic linguistic hybridity and a "nomadic" consciousness, a locus of communicative creativity and of jarring perceptual blanks from whence the master-discourse can be dethroned, subverted, and transgressed.[24] As Ania Loomba explains, "there is no neat binary opposition between the coloniser and the colonised, both are caught up in a complex reciprocity and colonial subjects can negotiate the cracks of dominant discourses" (232).

Sargisson is predominantly concerned with formulating a new political theory of transgressive utopianism focused on process instead of results, and thus seeks transgressive notions in various theories which she then exemplifies with brief glances at select contemporary feminist utopian literature. Sargisson, however, never succinctly defines transgression; this silence is perhaps the most serious flaw of her otherwise stimulating argument for new avenues of utopianism. On the other hand, this absence of a definition is consistent with the elusive nature of a concept that strives to abolish the fixed and the static. Sargisson gets closest to defining transgression in the following description of transgressive utopianism as an alternative approach to what we perceive as reality:

> it transgresses, negates and creates new conceptual spaces from which to reapproach the world in a non-dualistic way that is not driven by the desire to possess. Considered within an alternative ["feminine"] economy, though, the profit does not consist in the possession

---

[23]*Bhabha's universalizing view of "the" colonial subject is somewhat problematic, since different locations and dislocations, national histories, and other involved categories such as class and gender, result in diverse experiences of colonialization, marginality, and hybridity, as several critics have pointed out. See Stuart Hall (1994).*

[24]*Similarly, migrant and indigenous writers employ a hybridized literary discourse, mixing the formerly hierarchized discourse of dominant (English) literature and vernacular, of literacy and the orature of orality.*

of truth, but rather in the opening of further alternatives and possibilities ... [in] diverse conceptual shifts ... [that] transgress dominant and restrictive ways of construing the world. This, then is, utopianism of process [168].

Transgression, then, is a phenomenon that can be discovered in a variety of theories, whether postcolonial, feminist, postmodern or poststructuralist. It details fluid moments of suspended binary logic, when distinctions between either/or are nullified. Transgression, however, must not be misunderstood as the dissolution of binary order to produce a permanent unity; rather, transgression contests the notions of unambiguity and authenticity. Transgression is a utopian move towards a dynamic process of "neither and more," signifying multiple and previously unconceptualized possibilities beyond our persistent binary structuring. Transgression is a phenomenon of overlaps, of slippage, of the interdependence of relational concepts taken out of and diluting the hierarchizing binary order and the limiting principle of dualistic choice. In summary, transgression occurs as hybridity, as transculturation, as the gift that does not take, deconstructivism, and *différance*, and allows a particularly feminist oppositional position that is grounded in equality *and* difference.

This utopian activity and ability of transgression—perhaps best captured in the image of borderwalking, of the borderwalker who recognizes but learns to disrespect boundaries and, thus changed, acquires a nomadic consciousness of polylogous perspectives—can be approximated in the imaginary realm of fiction, of utopian fiction in particular. How, then, does transgression occur in what I have termed transgressive utopian dystopias? The very fact that the novels by Charnas, Elgin, and Atwood cannot be neatly categorized as either dystopia or utopia indicates the most obvious transgression, that of generic conventions; hence my terminology of transgressive utopian dystopia. As Part Two of this study shows, other genres these novels hybridize include sf, myth, quest, adventure tale, fantasy, fairy-tale, and satire. These postmodern novels mix discourses, fact and fiction. They use multigenerational cluster characters and single characters; societal and individualized narrative voices; and create a polyphony of alternating voices and multiple perspectives. As the textual analyses will demonstrate, the thematic concerns of feminist, transgressive utopian dystopian literature, and especially the texts of Elgin, Charnas, and Atwood, involve transgressions of subject/object, male/female, human/animal, human/alien, human/non-human, master/slave, nature/nurture, nature/culture, mind/body, spirit/matter, sanity/madness, self/other, literacy/orality, codes/stereotypes, the relation between myth/history with regard to the (im)possibility of a representation of reality and truth(s).

68   I. Literary History and Theoretical Background

The texts likewise probe language for its phallogocentrism and exclusory representation of one worldview.

All eight novels under discussion share the denial of what Sargisson identifies as the characteristic feature of feminist transgressive utopian literature: the rejection of "a determinist, teleological link between past, present and future" (225). Feminist transgressive utopias and transgressive utopian dystopias offer multiple or heterogeneous alternative views, expressing wonder at rather than the possession of *one* reality and *a* future. Their mark on the utopian/dystopian genre is one of multiplicity: "The future cannot be programmed in terms of the present, as constructed by the past. It must be dreamt and imagined according to desire. This utopian break is perhaps the most transgressive and is illustrative of the scope of such a feminist project" (ibid. 225). As the ensuing textual analysis in Part Two will show, describing the artificiality of boundaries and the potentiality of persistently transgressing these boundaries is then not a matter of demanding the impossible but of imagining the possible.

Part II
Textual Analyses

3

Rewriting the Colonization of Physical and Mental Space
Suzette Haden Elgin's Native Tongue *Trilogy*

> *There's no inherent reason whatsoever why things couldn't be divided into threes (or more) instead of twos, or understood as continua instead of as dichotomies. The either/or and on/off constructs don't impress me as having been discoveries of something real but as a phantom "order" imposed by human beings....*
> —Suzette Haden Elgin [Mohr 2000c, 26]

Suzette Haden Elgin, American author and former professor of linguistics with a long-term interest in tribal languages, transformational grammar, psycholinguistics, feminism(s), and postmodernism/poststructuralism, satirically rewrites the stock conventions of a large conservative bulk of mostly masculinist sf novels.[1] Her postmodern counter-narrative re-positions the colonial object (Aliens) as subject and the Earth/center as peripheral to the universe. Moreover, Elgin's trans-

---

[1]*In an interview Elgin stresses: "[Feminism] plays a major role....The situation of women keeps getting worse, and so I feel more urgently the need to explain where that is sure to lead" (DuPont 62). Although she has read Cixous, Irigaray, Lacan, Rich, and Daly (Elgin 1987b, 177), Elgin labels herself "a feminist in the nontechnical sense of the term" (DuPont 62) and gives the following definition of the term "feminist": "A feminist is someone-devoted-to-replacing-patriarchy-with-Reality-O," "Reality-O" being her "cover term for a society and culture that can be sustained without violence; patriarchy requires violence in the same way that human beings require oxygen" (Elgin 1995, 46). In a recent interview that I conducted with Elgin, she hypothesizes that "if patriarchy were eliminated it would yield nonviolence" and a new society could emerge where anyone "interested in and fascinated by violence is considered as pathological" (Mohr 2000c, 18).*

gressive utopian dystopian trilogy, *Native Tongue* (1984), *The Judas Rose* (1987), and *Earthsong* (1994), connects a postcolonial criticism of masculine space imperialism/colonialism with a feminist criticism of the patriarchal exploitation of women and the colonization of women's minds; and she postulates a decolonization of physical and mental space. The incorporated utopian subtext emerges as the driving force of the narrative, suggesting ways of transgressing the various dystopian chasms that draw on historical sociopolitical realities of the 1980s, more generally on a Western colonialist history, and on a biologistic nineteenth century context. The utopian dystopian narrative thus slips between reality-orientation, defamiliarized reality, and the desire for hope. Moreover, Elgin satirizes and rewrites generic, Biblical, literary, scholarly, scientific, legal, media, and other discourses, exposing hypocritical pathos and concealed sexism/racism.

In the first two books of the series, Elgin proposes a slow linguistic subversion of the dystopian Terran dichotomy that posits men at the center and marginalizes women. According to Elgin, a mental decolonization process, a transgression of psychological borders, can be achieved through a new female language grounded in inclusion rather than phallogocentric exclusion. Drawing on poststructuralist and deconstructionist linguistic theories, the weak form of the Sapir-Whorf hypothesis, and Gödel's Theorem, Elgin depicts how this female language called Láadan threatens sociocultural norms and codes expressed in phallogocentric language, and how Láadan, consequently, undermines a society based on patriarchal values and exclusive concepts of difference.[2] In the third book, Elgin moves within a holistic Native American reference framework from the previously privileged notion of mental liberation, of language as the primary source of power, to the acknowledgement of the body and of physical subversion. Elgin proposes a non-violent musical nourishing process called Audiosynthesis to eliminate hunger and thus violence that she now considers as the deeper source of oppression and the masculine colonizing drive.

Clearly, the themes of the books run parallel to theoretical discussions, following the drift of literary theories from mind to body, from the feminisms of the 1980s to a joint-venture of feminist and transcultural perspectives of the 1990s. With the third book Elgin covers three deficits of the previous two books: from privileging language and the mind, she turns her attention to the body. By including male Native Americans as participants in the utopian Audiosynthesis project, she no

---

[2]*Elgin came first across the hypothesis "that existing human languages are not adequate to express the perceptions of women" (1987b, 177), when she reviewed Cheris Kramarae's book* Women and Men Speaking *(1981).*

longer stereotypically aligns only the female sex with the progress toward utopia, although, in defense of Elgin, not *all* female characters are involved in the utopian movements. And with this inclusion of another ethnic group, she moves away from a primarily white focus, what Gert Fehlner has criticized as "simplifying along a black and white frame" ("simplifizierendem Schwarz-Weiß-Raster" 119).

Instead of aligning differences with the categories of sex, gender, and culture, Elgin pinpoints the hierarchical and elitist distribution of power as the structural element that causes exclusory difference.[3] Elgin aims at the abolishment of masculine power hierarchies between all creatures and replaces these with an ethics of feminine sharing and communal cooperation. In the trilogy, despite her critical depiction of men as the dominant sex, she carefully draws attention to the fact that characters of both sexes and members of various ethnic backgrounds are capable of (ab)using their (language) power to master those marked as *others* either by class, culture/race or sex/gender. However, she does locate the motor of human evolution among women who develop as tools for a utopian evolutionary process a new language and the free access to non-violent nourishment for all people. Elgin equates masculine language acquisition with power, exclusivity, and an expansionist drive and, in short, with dystopia, as opposed to feminine language acquisition as a means of liberating resistance, disempowerment, and inclusion. Language is thus the primary locus of colonialist and patriarchal domination *and* of transgressive resistance.

This chapter reads the texts as blatant critiques of racism and colonization, sexism and patriarchy. First, Elgin's postcolonial counter-narrative is placed into the context of sf as a colonial discourse. Next, I examine the generic hybridity of the trilogy, the merging of the subgenres of sf, dystopia, and utopia, and I briefly look at the postmodern narrative structure in terms of transgressive aspects. In the next section, the analysis focuses on the dystopian/colonial aspects of the trilogy: the masculine abuse of physical and mental space in terms of power and possession as organizing principles; and the patriarchal concepts of difference as ways of excluding the *other* along lines of class, culture/race/

---

[3] *When questioned whether women and men speak different languages, Elgin takes an oppositional stance to Deborah Tannen's position in* You Just Don't Understand *(1990), where Tannen claims that gender-based language constitutes the root of gender difference. For Elgin, power-linked language is expressed in "two kinds of English," "dominant English" and "subordinate English" and "both sexes know both of those styles of language" (cf. Elgin 1996; cf. also Mohr 2000c, 25). Nor does she support gender-specific writing in terms of a feminine or masculine style; for her, writing as a way of communication is power-linked (cf. DuPont, 64). Elgin diagnoses a "metaphor split" (usage of same words but connoted with different meanings), "shifting scripts" and "difference in voice" (both behavioral expectations) as relevant factors for a communication breakdown between the sexes (cf. Elgin 1996, see also Elgin 1993).*

species, and sex/gender categories. I then turn to the transgressive utopian aspects: the decolonization of physical and mental space; how Aliens and women use space and language in terms of sharing, empowerment, and inclusion; and how they acknowledge differences *and* equality.

3.1. Science Fiction as Colonial Discourse

The earliest examples of masculinist sf have been very much part of a colonial, often Eurocentric discourse that extrapolates issues of racism/sexism into (fictional) space by bringing the "gift of civilization"— i.e., imperialist cultural patterns of thought—to naturally less intelligent mostly evil alien species, or fearing the reverse, the invasion of malign imperialistic Aliens.[4] In other words, according to Frederic Jameson, "all SF of the more 'classical' type is 'about' containment, closure, the dialectic of inside and outside" (1987, 58).

Fictional geographical space has been treated as a tabula rasa. As the literal conquest of land ended with the closed Western frontier in the New World, a new fictional space opened up that demanded a mental shift to the open frontiers of outer space.[5] Some of the most memorable examples of such space operas were written in the 1920s and 1930s, for example, Edmond Hamilton's stories about the battles between Terran heroes and evil Aliens or Edgar Rice Burroughs's *Barsoom* novels that depict the conquest of Mars and battles with various "non-whites." These narratives foreground an invasion of space, the usurpation of planets— conquest being the Darwinian birthright of the naturally superior human (male) species.[6] In analogy to the past conquest and colonization of Earth, fictional planets are conquered and settled, and these Imperial Galactic Empires and Earth-clone worlds are almost always ruled by humans warring with Aliens. Critical views of the conquest of space gained influence from the late 1950s on, for instance, in Poul Anderson's story "The Helping Hand" (1950) and in Robert Silverberg's *Invaders from Earth* (1958), while Thomas M. Disch criticizes human prejudices against other beings in general in *The Genocides* (1965).

[4]*This very short survey of the treatment of space and aliens in sf is naturally limited and superficial, covering by no means all aspects. The inclusion of certain themes and novels as examples presupposes the exclusion of others.*
[5]*The transcription of colonial exploitation into space led to see-through sf Western, e.g. Robert A. Heinlein's* Time Enough for Love *(1973). Analogous to the Wild West, starship "cowboys" roam the space frontier, called the "rim." Recently, female characters have assumed this role, notably in C.J. Cherryh's novels.*
[6]*In* Return to Tomorrow *(1954), the notorious L. Ron Hubbard even promotes the total genocide of all alien races to guarantee the hegemony of humans. John W. Campbell, Jr., not only supported slavery, but further argued that because, in his opinion, progress depends on (Darwinian) competition, we need enemies. The survivalist fiction of the 1980s has reverted to this theme.*

3. Rewriting the Colonization of Space 75

The transfer of imperialistic, territorial desires to the unknowable Alien led to sf stories that posit Aliens as genocidal colonizers of Earth. Taking the colonial history of the British Empire as a model for the Martian invasion, H.G. Wells's *The War of the Worlds* (1898) provides one of the earliest and best-known examples of human xenophobia of technologically superior Aliens. More recent examples of Alien invasion stories and the subjugation of humankind are *The Puppet Masters* (1951) by Robert A. Heinlein and *Footfall* (1985) by Larry Niven and Jerry Pournelle. Less common are notions of a possibly benign alien invasion, as in Arthur C. Clarke's *Childhood's End* (1953). Additionally, the "monster movies" of the 1950s and 1960s perpetuated the image of Aliens as predators. Furthermore, the paranoia about the unrecognizable *other* is captured in sf novels about conquering Aliens disguised as humans. Jack Finney's *The Body-Snatchers* (1956) provides one of the most popular examples, as indicated by the current tally of three film versions.

Later depictions of the colonization of other worlds satirize terrestrial human behaviour, or enact sociological experiments on alien worlds, as in Poul Anderson's *Virgin Planet* (1959), Gene Wolfe's *The Fifth Head of Cerberus* (1972), and Joanna Russ's *And Chaos Died* (1970). John Clute and Peter Nicholls differentiate between romantic and realist colonization stories (244–246) and argue that in the romantic version exploitation becomes a non-issue, because humans and humanoid Aliens coexist in an exotic but quasi Earth-like pastoral environment. The native (alien) population may rebel against the colonizers, but more commonly human adaptation to alien environments works well.[7] Realist colonization stories, though, appeared only after World War II. Arthur C. Clarke, for instance, deals realistically with colonization methods in *The Sands of Mars* (1951).

In analogy to the various indigenous populations of the conquered and colonized countries on Earth that the conquerors define as cultural or subhuman *other*, the sf topos of the Alien is used as a foil for the cultural/ethnic or even biologically *other*. Of course, in the case of sf, this imagined *other* is in fact *alien*. Additionally, the propensity of masculinist sf to negatively conflate the generic metaphor of the Alien with the construction and depictions of female/cultural others—this *othering* of the "sexual Alien, and the social Alien, and the cultural Alien, and finally the racial Alien" (Le Guin 1975, 209)—has been noted by several feminist scholars.[8] The Alien represents predominantly the natural com-

[7]*Women writers, for instance, Marion Zimmer Bradley in her* Darkover *novels and Anne McCaffrey in her* Pern *novels, most commonly use this trope. Pamela Sargent's* Venus of Dreams *(1986) and* Venus of Shadows *(1988) describe the reverse process of "terraforming," the adaptation of worlds to the colonists.*

[8]*See especially Roberts (1987); Wolmark (1994), who analyzes alien/woman as central metaphor;*

petitor and enemy, a mostly inferior bug-eyed monster (BEM), which must be eliminated or subjugated. Unsurprisingly, benevolent Aliens strongly resemble humans, whereas the BEM reflects racist beliefs in biological differences, notably in John W. Campbell Jr.'s short story "Who Goes There?" (1938), or A.E. van Vogt's short stories "Black Destroyer" (1939) and "The Monster" (1948). However, a growing body of texts deals seriously with cultural and biological differences, particularly novels by Jack Vance, Michael Bishop, and, among women sf writers, by C.J. Cherryh.

Those sf novels that value the encounter with other life forms as enriching juxtapose Aliens with humans to criticize human racism. More rarely, Aliens are also redeployed in transcendental roles, for instance, as spiritual tutors in Robert Silverberg's *Downward to the Earth* (1970). Furthermore, the late Star Trek series, notably its sequel *The Next Generation,* or Ian M. Banks's *Culture* novels incorporate diverse views of Aliens as incredibly advanced, benign *and* as less-advanced, possibly malign beings. Representations of innocent and altruistic Aliens as philanthropic observers of human endeavours are less common. One early example is Eden Phillpotts's *Saurus* (1938). Lately, the desire to meet Aliens—for example, through SETI as in Carl Sagan's novel *Contact* (1985), recently turned into a major movie—has been accompanied by the anxiety that we might be considered too coarse for alien contact.

Against this large bulk of predominantly masculine and conservative sf, women sf writers raise their voices. For example, Le Guin (*The Word for World Is Forest* 1972), Slonczewski (*A Door Into Ocean* and its sequels), Gwyneth Jones (*White Queen* 1992), and Butler (especially her reworking of slave narratives in the *Patternist* series 1976–1984) have criticized racism, imperialism/colonialism, and sexism in sf, sometimes by depicting gender relations as contact with alien species (e.g. Le Guin's *The Left Hand of Darkness*). Far from technological escapism, feminist sf merges with utopia/dystopia and is thus grounded in the sociopolitical concerns of the present. As Penny Florence points out, feminist sf is less concerned with outer space than with inner space:

> Feminist SF does not often foreground or evidence the conservative game of projecting the idea of threat onto outsiders and then playing out its destruction.... In other words, the threat is not that aliens might invade the established order; nor is it simply the opposite. It is that the established order might overcome or re-possess the new, which, far from appearing from outer space, developed out of inner space [77–78].

[continued] *and Jane Donawerth (1997; esp. chap. 3) for concise discussions and overviews of women sf authors who rewrite these stereotypes.*

This connection between outer/inner space and the process of *othering* groups of people as inferior according to class, race, and gender is a key issue in the *Native Tongue* trilogy. Throughout the novels the re-positioning of Aliens and women inverts and subverts this "Manichean allegory" (60ff.)—to use Abdul JanMohamed's term referring to the binary opposition between races—that creates outsiders *and* insiders. As the ensuing analysis shows, both Aliens and women linguists deconstruct the patriarchal/colonial colonization of outer and inner space.

3.2. Transgressions of Genre and Narrative Form

3.2.1. Plot

Elgin's satiric dystopia replicates the all too familiar pattern of hierarchized gender, class, and ethnic relations. Primarily set in the U.S. between the twenty-second and the twenty-fourth centuries, society is polarized into humans/aliens, men/women, linguists/non-linguists, male linguists/female linguists, and U.S./USSR. Drawing on a nineteenth century context, particularly on biologism and on the Victorian "angel of the house" mentality, the genetic inferiority of women has been proven; two Amendments to the U.S. Constitution of 1991 have repealed the 19th Amendment (granting women the right to vote) and have declared women legal minors.[9] In this future scenario, equal rights are, in fact, history. This future Earth claims its place in an alien-ruled universe through interplanetary trade and the colonization of other planets. Alien language acquisition, achieved by interfacing linguist babies with AIRYs (humanoid Aliens-in-Residence), is the monopoly of thirteen dynastic linguist families, the "Lines." Society is basically divided into two classes (linguists and non-linguists) with the government and the church taking the top position within the non-linguist power pyramid. The government furthers this social split with propaganda about idle linguists who exploit the masses, and who are, perhaps, altogether genetically different *others* of debatable human status.

The primary plot of *Native Tongue* focuses on the women linguists, who secretly create Láadan—a women's language which represents female perceptions of reality—while they officially create the baroque language travesty "Langlish" to deflect any suspicion. Nazareth Chornyak, a highly gifted inventor of new Láadan words, persuades the hesitant women lin-

---

[9] *The actual 24th and 25th Amendments to the U.S. Constitution were ratified in 1967 and 1971. The former abolished the Poll Tax requirements for voting rights and the latter outlines the procedure of succession and replacement in the Vice-Presidency.*

guist to disseminate Láadan. Finally, they surreptitiously teach Láadan to their daughters, for whom it will eventually be a *native tongue*. Meanwhile, the government, desperate to crack the linguist trade monopoly, interfaces non-humanoid Aliens with human and test-tube babies, but the incompatibility of non-humanoid alien and humanoid perceptions of the world leads to mutual self-destruction. To bridge the perceptual and communicative gap, Terran whales are (unsuccessfully) interfaced with human babies and with non-humanoid Aliens. Another sub-plot centers around the nurse Michaela Landry who takes revenge on her husband for having volunteered their son for this government project in which the infant dies. Michaela begins to work for the much-hated linguists with the intent to kill them off one by one. Gradually, the women linguists befriend her, and when Thomas Chornyak detects Láadan and threatens to destroy it, she kills the linguist "topdog" (*NT* 61).[10]

In *The Judas Rose*, Elgin moves towards a flagrant criticism of the Judaeo-Christian paradigm, especially of the Catholic Church. The female linguists disseminate Láadan beyond their own closed community via translated bible readings in "Thursday Night Devotionals" that are open for all women. Sister Miriam Rose—illegal daughter of a woman linguist, raised by nuns to infiltrate the omnipotent Catholic Church—sabotages the clerical attempt to revise the "feminized" Láadan bible. As the supervisor of the nuns, Sister Miriam makes sure these revisions are turned into ugly travesties; meanwhile, she secretly makes and distributes handmade copies of the feminist Láadan Bible. Upon detection of her double agency, the Catholic Church condemns Sister Miriam Rose as a female Judas and labels her the "Judas Rose." In another narrative strand, Heykus Clete, Chief of the Department of Analysis & Translation (D.A.T.), monomaniacally carries out his "All Souls Mission" to colonize and christianize the whole universe. Meanwhile, the Terran whales have been successfully interfaced with non-humanoid Aliens, yet they refuse to cooperate with humans. Macabee Dow, an ambitious Professor of Mathematics, challenges the Lines' language monopoly and has his son Gabriel interfaced with an Alien. The differences between linguists and non-linguists shift from genetics towards the field of social conditioning, when it turns out that multilingual Gabriel—for lack of further social contact with linguists beyond the interfacing—has no desire to be a professional interpreter. In a third subplot, the nurse Jo-Bethany, like Michaela, grows fond of the female linguists *and* of the AIRYs. The novel closes with the Alien Consortium, dedicated to non-violent ethics, putting Earth under quarantine for being too violent. Because of the

---

[10]*References to the trilogy are given in the text in parentheses with the following abbreviations:* Native Tongue (NT), The Judas Rose (JR), *and* Earthsong (ES).

female linguists and their language project, the Alien Consortium harbors, however, hope for barbarous Earth, for the women linguists "understand the mechanisms of change" (*JR* 362).

Published ten years after the first book, *Earthsong* relinquishes the linguistic project and turns towards the liberation of the body. In the chaotic aftermath of being abandoned by the Aliens, the men helplessly watch the cataclysmic deterioration of life on Earth: the Alien technology is increasingly dysfunctional; the economic system dependent on interplanetary trade crashes; the space colonies question the hegemony of Earth; and a predicted Icehouse Effect threatens to extinguish all life on Earth. With the destabilization of the class system, translation becomes superfluous, but their amassed wealth keeps the linguists in power. To re-establish contact with the Aliens, computers are modified to resemble whale brains. Helped by the Chief of the Pan-Indian Council of the Americas (PICOTA), Delina seeks the advice of her dead great-grandmother, Nazareth, in a vision quest. Following the first directive of Nazareth to end hunger and thus (male) violence, Delina develops "Audiosynthesis," a form of active chanting that nourishes humans with soundwaves similar to the photosynthesis process for plants. "Mouthfood" and the resulting need to kill are consequently rendered obsolete. Upon Nazareth's second directive, women of the Lines take Native American husbands.[11] Moreover, they secretly teach Audiosynthesis in religious music schools. Once Audiosynthesis is sufficiently wide spread, they make it public. In a hastily organized United Nations of the Earth (UNE) meeting, the (male) delegates are torn between an ethically expected positive response and their desire to stamp out Audiosynthesis, and with it the implied threat to the very basis of (patriarchal) society. The chairman of the UNE summarizes their dilemma: "*The end of hunger for all mankind* [sic] *has arrived; I should rejoice.... The end of my life has arrived; my heart is broken; I can only mourn*" (*ES* 229). Grudgingly, Audiosynthesis is officially made available to everyone. The novel closes on a note of hope: the whales send out a message to the Aliens that the elimination of violence has begun on Earth.[12]

---

[11]*Similar to Elgin's proposal, Octavia Butler suggests a "genetic marriage" in her* Xenogenesis *trilogy, written in the late 1980s, where almost extinct humans survive by trading genes with aliens. In return, they must abolish violence, and the colonizer's "hunger" for new territories ceases. Elgin, too, pleads for the "marriage of races," indicated in the alliance of PICOTA and linguists.*

[12]*The framing prefaces of Book One and Two indicate that women's position in this anticipated future society has significantly improved, although it is not discernible whether this is a two-sex or single-sex future society. The end of* Earthsong, *however, suggests a future world where women and men live and evolve together.*

3.2.2. The New Hybrid: Generic Merging

On the generic level, the trilogy merges a sf frame (Aliens, Earth colonies, Interfaces, FTL-travel) with aspects that are dystopian (oppression of women, class differences, surveillance, control of communication technology) and utopian (Láadan, Audiosynthesis) and alternate history (Amendments to U.S. Constitution).[13] Generally speaking, the Aliens, women linguists, Native Americans, and whales represent a transgressive utopian principle, and men and women of all classes and nations represent dystopia.

Elgin has classified the series as "[n]ear future Science Fiction" (1987b, 175) and not as dystopia, although she opines that Atwood's dystopian *The Handmaid's Tale* depicts "precisely the scenario in *Native Tongue*" (ibid. 176). David Sisk claims the series as "science fiction with strong dystopian overtones," but he also notes that the "science fiction trappings of alien contact, advanced technology, and space travel merely set the stage" (109). Lucie Armitt misleadingly classifies *Native Tongue* and *The Judas Rose* as "akin to the 'harder' techno-fiction novel" (130), a classification that is based on the Interface device (in which human babies acquire alien languages) as a "central feature." This view disregards that Elgin is not interested in lengthy descriptions of technology (e.g. of Interfaces), but rather in language acquisition (as made possible by Interfaces) and its implications for the perception of reality and for society at large. In fact, Elgin plunders generic sf conventions, such as highly advanced communication computer technology (Interfaces, Intercom, wrist computers, comset, comunit)[14] and "first contact" with Aliens and outer space, only to subvert them. The most characteristic topos of hard sf, technology, thus plays a marginal role, and the narrative centers instead around human/human or human/Alien interaction and communication. Precisely the lack of elaborate descriptions of alien or human technology reveals Elgin's scorn on technophile hard sf and stresses her interest in the dystopian sociopolitical structure, the creation of myths excluding *others,* and the power humans exert via language. Rather, the sf elements satirize sf tropes. Especially in *Earthsong*, the author comments on our increasing inability to understand technology and on our dependency on it. Like the Terrans—"pushing buttons that read PUSH and pulling levers that read PULL" (*ES* 48) without knowing how the

---

[13] *Thelma Shinn has located a similar merging of genres in Elgin's "hybrid science fiction/fantasy tale" (218),* The Ozark Trilogy *(1981).*

[14] *For an analysis of media, social and personal communication, and communication devices in* Native Tongue, *see Dagmar Priebe (1998). Applying Niklas Luhmann's systems theory, she discusses influences of contemporary media discussions, but does not include* The Judas Rose *and* Earthsong.

alien technology works—we depend on technology without understanding all of it. In the novel, the Aliens and their sophisticated technology acquire the elevated status of almighty gods to which men in their hubris aspire. The lack of recognizable hardware renders the alien technology incomprehensible to the Terrans. For them, the genuine technology represents therefore a sophisticated hoax with "nothing inside ... *connected to nothing at all*" (*ES* 49).

As the narrative foregrounds sociopolitical issues and concentrates on gender and class relations on Earth, the Aliens do not function as mere science fictional backdrop setting, but represent the cultural/racial other on a larger scale.[15] Elgin depicts a feminist dystopia where the male and the colonial gaze as well as the ethnic and gender stereotyping have led to a dystopian world in which oppression along class and gender lines is legitimated by Judaeo-Christian religion and science. Unlike classical dystopia where rebellion fails, women successfully create a new, expanding utopian space within the dystopian world, a space which provides possibilities of approaching one another in a non-dualistic, non-possessive way. The trilogy continues the central utopian themes of Elgin's earlier novels, as Thelma J. Shinn notes: "community, communication and faith in the sisterhood of woman.... Elgin believes we can even pull men through into a better, more egalitarian future" (220). The novels describe the progress from dystopia towards utopia, but utopia is never shown. Utopia is *desired* without knowing how it will look. This interaction of utopia/dystopia and of female/male/Alien perspectives inspires a dynamic, open text that deconstructs dystopia as we know it. This fluid dialogue between the genres creates a contesting and satirical polyphony of male, female, and alien voices that continually demands of the reader to change his or her perspective. Thus the texts cannot be labelled as either dystopian or utopian. Rather, they describe a utopian dystopia within a rewritten sf context.

3.2.3. "Begin at the Beginning": Spirit-Narrator, Cluster Characters, and Other Postmodern Narrative Adventures

Transgression pervades and shapes the postmodern trilogy, its dialogic metafictional metatext, and the polyphony of narrating voices. The

---

[15] Sisk blatantly fails to recognize Elgin's play with the Alien as foil for the cultural/racial other. For Sisk, this misogynist, racist future Earth "seems like paradise" where "the problems of racism...have been effectively solved" (112).

subplots weave together three levels of action—four if we count the Aliens—mirroring the class perspectives of linguists, government/church, and non-linguist citizens. These levels subdivide into the male and female perspectives of different characters. To deconstruct monolithic truths, the representation of the world according to one's own view, Elgin uses a postmodern narrative technique that transgresses order and linearity. Though conventional in other respects, the narrative conjures multiple universes and a plurality of voices, and thus challenges the singularity of the dominant patriarchal perspective of the Terran center. This plethora of narrative voices, complementary characters, levels of action, metatext, and discourses constitutes what, in a different context, Bonnie Zimmermann has called "an egalitarian, democratic novel" (1990, 135). The satirical double-staging of constantly recasted perspectives represents the problem of incomplete mimetic representation, the question of "who speaks for whom on what assumptions." To this end, the narrative form emphasizes what the content analyzes.

Chronological chapters create an illusion of narrative order, while the narrative is, in fact, full of gaps. The borders of narrative time and form are transgressed and disrupted by a metatext and chaotic episodic jumps in the narrative, which flash forwards and backwards between plot and subplots, between male and female (and alien) perspectives, and between linguist, non-linguist and governmental points of view. The trilogy covers the dates from the winter of 2179 to the year 2289 and corresponds with the lifespan and afterlife of Nazareth Chornyak. If we include the metatext, the narrative time reaches back to the 1970s and ends with the twenty-third century. If we further include the ideological/religious subtext with the Judaeo-Christian religion pointing towards much earlier roots in human history, there is no exact beginning. Neither can the end of the future narrative time be ascertained. The fictional editors of the prefaces comment from an even farther, presumably more egalitarian future of an unspecified date. Juxtaposed real past and present and fictive futures lead thus to textual deconstruction. Furthermore, the inclusion of fictional forewords, prefaces, appendices, and chapter epigraphs taken from various discourses—they incorporate songs, poems, academic lectures, magazine articles, letters, interview transcriptions, and the like—transgresses the narrative form of the novel. Layer upon layer of new ironic facets peel off the narrative, making a unitary interpretation or reading problematic. Moreover, the postmodern metatext calls attention to the text as text, "it is a NOVEL" and a "found ... manuscript" (*NT* 5), and points towards the unreliability of these fictional texts and the possibility of editing. On the intertextual level, the framing device connects, on the one hand, with the tradition of the genre; and, on the other hand, it links the series with the beginnings of the colonial discourse within the English novel, especially Daniel Defoe's *Robinson Crusoe* (1719).

Since the prefaces claim the novels as factual reports, the borderline between (fictive) reality and (real) fiction is transgressed from the start, stressing the central topic of the trilogy that language mediates and shapes, or fictionalizes, reality.[16] What is real and what is fiction? The government eliminates or fictionalizes any memories of attempts at or achievements of equality in the past. In the novels, professional women doctors and the vote for women (the reality of our time) are removed into the realm of fantasy along with legendary dragons and unicorns. Similarly, the fictional reality of the Books One and Two, of women linguists working six days a week, quickly turns into myth in *Earthsong* (cf. *ES* 106). And in like manner, the past "reality" of Aliens on Earth in the first two books transmogrifies into sf in the interspersed soaps of *Earthsong*: "You *know* those are science fiction threedies. You *know* there were never really Aliens living on Earth" (*ES* 190). Anything that proves that equality *was* (partly) achieved in the past becomes very important to the women linguists. Forbidden surgical instruments, contraceptives, "books from the time of the Women's liberation movement," videotapes, and their version of female historiography—the women linguists' secret, collective "archives of a time when women dared to speak openly of equal rights"—are distributed via the "underground railroad of sympathetic women" (*NT* 124).

The chapter epigraphs quote from different discourses of various periods, ranging from the 1970s to the twenty-fourth century. They enter a multiple textual self-commentating dialogue, and their ironic comments from male/female perspectives deconstruct the topics addressed in the chapters. The epigraph to Chapter 11 in *Native Tongue*, for instance, provides a "lecture" on "women and religious mania" by a "feminologist," while Chapter 11 deals with the linguist Belle-Anne pretending religious mania to save Láadan. The epigraphs do not qualify as sources of truth, and the boundaries between discourses, between science and fiction, between high and low art are crossed and re-crossed, until ultimately we arrive at a form of narrative hybridization. The epigraphs reflect the sexually connotated discourses and opposition of the *patrius sermo* of the

---

[16] Elgin also includes distinct references to our reality of the 1980s: Earth continues our past in the form of a "reaganic tradition" (NT 51) with "Reagan Medals for Statesmanship" (JR 9) and national holidays celebrating "Reagan's Birthday" (NT 77). Additionally, Elgin transgresses the fiction/reality polarity by constructing and distributing Láadan for real: she teaches Láadan at the "Ozark Center for Language Studies" in Huntsville, Arkansas; she has written a Láadan dictionary and Láadan grammar books, and Láadan is available on tapes; short stories are published in English and Láadan on the Internet. The short stories can be accessed on the Internet at: <http:/www.interlog.com/~kms/Laadan/> [Accessed: 20.10.1998].

official public male discourse (e.g. jurisdiction, talk shows, academic lectures, interviews, articles; governmental briefings, scientific reports, bible quotes), and of the *materna lingua* of the private female discourse (e.g. manuals from the women linguists' archives, feminist poems, Nazareth's diaries).[17] Yet both oral and written sources share the notion of unreliability and questionable authenticity. The male epigraphs cement male traditions; they incorporate ideologies and prejudices into scientific discourses, and thus objectify the representational construction of cultural and gendered difference. In short, they describe and legitimate patriarchal reality *ad infinitum* in the past, present, and future.

In contrast, the female epigraphs focus on the process of how women perceive and change reality. As a result, the female epigraphs puncture the very monolithic truth that the male epigraphs claim. Through this narrative strategy of a double perspective, of the private discourse resisting the exclusive view of the official discourse, the reader is galvanized into a deconstructive reading process of noting differences in the feminine and the masculine narratives, and thus recognizes the bias of the official discourse of "truth" and "objectivity." This juxtaposition of literary and non-literary texts also emphasizes that neither discourse is necessarily "objective"; on the contrary, both represent and mediate subjective realities.

In *Native Tongue*, the first chapter and the last six chapters are set in the (future) "present," and thus frame a long inserted retrospective narration. Formal coherence is demonstrated by chapter epigraphs in Book One and Two; in *Earthsong*, only four chapters carry epigraphs. In *Native Tongue*, these chapter epigraphs are additionally dated with specific years and, therefore, facilitate a reconstruction of chronology. Conversely, the lack of such time specifics adds to the disjointed narrative structure of *Earthsong*. While Book One and Two keep to a somewhat chronological narrative time despite retrospectives and narrative gaps, *Earthsong* dislodges time. As the *post mortem* spirit-narrator speaking from the beyond, Nazareth warns us in her Foreword to *Earthsong*, "[T]his story is going to be disorganized ... it will have to come in chunks and pieces tumbling out of time" (*ES* 10). Nazareth's story is filtered by so-called "trancers"—"[This story] will come ... through many different voices all trying to give utterance to the single instrument that is *my* 'voice'" (*ES* 10)—and thus we are reminded that storytelling mediates other voices.[18] *Earthsong* is told by three trancers in three parts, and Parts Two and

---

[17] On the sexual bias of discourse see Sandra Gilbert and Susan Gubar (516ff.).

[18] *An accurate translation is an illusion: "[It] is not a matter of substituting words in one language for words in another language. Translation is a matter of saying in one language, for a particular situation, what a native speaker of the other language would say in the* same *situation ... [the trancers] have to fall back on metaphors" (ES 9).*

3. Rewriting the Colonization of Space

Three are interrupted by interspersed fragmented chunks of "soaps," various snippets of stories/lives on Earth and the colony planets. *Earthsong* presents thus the most jarring narrative of the three books. This truncated narrative form parallels, on the one hand, the content level of a chaotic Earth after being quarantined. On the other hand, these constant interruptions of the narrative flow—the "empty spaces left by this method of taletelling" (*ES* 11)—reflect the succession of interruptions in women's lives. The life of Marilisa, for instance, epitomizes this discontinuity. Marilisa gives up the so-called multiversity and a professional life precisely because "[she was] interrupted every few minutes ... [and] considered herself fortunate when there were five minutes free of interruption" (*ES* 145).

While the feminine narrative in *Earthsong* can only be told in disordered chunks with gaps, the masculine narrative still maintains chronological order, a linearity of beginning and of closure. When Delina is unsure how to formulate her request for a Native American husband, PICOTA Chief Will Bluecrane encourages her: "Try the simplest method.... The ancient one. Where you begin at the beginning, go on till you're through ... and then stop" (*ES* 92). And in another episode, when one of the security officials fumbles for the "*perfect* word[s]" for his report on the women's Audiosynthesis conspiracy, the President chides him: "Begin at the beginning ... go on to the end. Nothing could be simpler" (*ES* 210). Both these answers echo the impatient answer of the King to the seemingly illogical and silly question of the White Rabbit about just *where* to start reading a poem in Lewis Carroll's *Alice's Adventures in Wonderland* (1865).[19] However, Elgin reformulates Carroll's stance that radical violations of habitual logic lead to nonsense and to the questioning of the logical linear approach as not necessarily being congruent with reality, and argues instead that a radical violation of habitual logic potentially leads to an equally arbitrary reorganization of events. Like the child character Alice, who represents the logic of the adult world and experiences the absurdity of a manipulated reality/dream in Wonderland, male and female characters of Elgin's trilogy equally experience the dissolving of the logical categories of order, time and space, rationality, identity, and hierarchy in their universe.

Like other women sf writers, Elgin breaks with the genre convention of the single male narrator. In her analysis of women sf writers' use of cross-dressing male narrators, Jane Donawerth includes Elgin's series as an example for the *naive* male narrator (cf. 113ff.).[20] The male narra-

---

[19]"*'Begin at the beginning,' the King said, very gravely, 'and go on till you come to the end: then stop'" (Carroll 93).*
[20]*As briefly indicated in Chapter 1, cross-dressing narrators are used, for instance, by Gilman*

tor's *limited* point of view, excluding all realities other than the parochial masculine perspective, leads to comic parodies of stereotyped masculinity with blatantly obvious misogynist, colonialist attitudes, and to stereotyped feminine behaviour in feminist dystopias, and particularly in the *Native Tongue* series. Readers of either sex thus refrain from identification and critically witness "[from] a position of superiority" (Donawerth 122) the insensitivity of male characters to and ignorance of the agonies of female characters and, on the other hand, the automatized unquestioning feminine responses. This narrative strategy leads to a "blurring of boundaries of gender that define science fiction as a genre" (ibid. 115), in other words, it leads to (male) readers' transgression of gender roles. Donawerth differentiates between three forms of multiple narration (cf. 131ff.), all of which are used in the *Native Tongue* trilogy. The "heterosexual romance" with alternating male/female points of view calls attention to "the *power* of point of view" (Donawerth 132; emphasis added), and orchestrates in the novels a blatant satire of double-staged female/male perspectives that deconstruct predominantly the male characters—caricatures of stock characters in sf—and expose gender roles as stereotypes. Nazareth, for instance, describes her husband Aaron—characterized by other men as entertaining, attractive, sensible, and tolerant—as an abusive, unsympathetic, egocentric, and cruel misogynist.

The "human and alien narration" (ibid. 132) with male, female, and alien narrators further destabilizes the categories of gender and race. This is doubly true in *The Judas Rose*, where the alien point of view breaks up the either/or binarism of gender perspectives. In accordance with what Donawerth calls the "communal voice" (ibid. 132) that speaks for several characters, a series of female narrators frequently speaks with the authority of such a communal voice (e.g. the Archive Entries of the Women of Chornyak Household are written by various women linguists) in *Native Tongue*. The boundaries of "I" and "we" narration are thus transgressed. In *Earthsong*, the narrative successively enters various female points of view, which are mostly undistinguishable, and only Delina speaks as a distinct narrative "I." Again, this "sequential communal narration" (Lanser 256) is born out of the women linguists' speaking as individuals *and* as members of a female community.

As I have outlined in Chapter 1, male authors often assign female characters marginal roles in utopian, dystopian, and science fiction. In Elgin's books, female characters occupy a central but not a singular position. The main female characters complement one another in the functions of the artist, the rebel, and the convert; and all share the stigma of

[continued] *in* Herland *and by Tiptree in her famous short story "The Women Men Don't See." Moffett in "Surviving" and Russ in "When It Changed" also mislead reader expectations with female narrators who cross-dress as male narrators.*

3. Rewriting the Colonization of Space

bodily or mental deviance such as deformity, disfigurement, mutation, and madness. Consequently, there is no central character or individual heroine; the women linguists' community forms instead a multigenerational cluster character composed of changing feminine voices that carries through the polyphony.[21] The narrative form thus reflects once more the content, because precisely this sense of community and networking provides the seed for the women linguists' actions.[22] Often (most characteristic of *Earthsong*) the identity of the narrative "I" is only disclosed at the end of a chapter, leaving us with a textual uncertainty. Moreover, the fictive editor of *Native Tongue* confirms the whole narrative as a joint-venture: "It was signed simply 'the women of Chornyak Barren House.'" (*NT* 6). Significantly, most female characters carry the first names of aunts, grandmothers, great-aunts, and great-grandmothers in different combinations at different times, hence it gets increasingly difficult to distinguish between female characters. For instance, the inventor of the Audiosynthesis, Delina Meloren Bluecrane Chornyak, reappears as a Delina Bluecrane Jefferson at the end of *Earthsong*—possibly this Delina is her daughter or granddaughter. Similarly, the Aquina of *The Judas Rose*—the *unmarried* mother of Sister Miriam Rose—is the great-granddaughter of the rebellious Aquina of Book One. And Belle-Anne Jefferson Chornyak of *The Judas Rose* is "named after the famous poisoner and lunatic" (*JR* 63), Belle-Anne of Book One.

Elgin's texts, however, retain remnants of the single protagonist's narrative. The distinct narrative voices of Nazareth and her great-granddaughter Delina serve as narrative anchors and unifying narrative links. Nazareth is the only character present in all three novels, and the narratives of *Native Tongue* and *The Judas Rose* guide us through key incidents of her life, whereas *Earthsong* foregrounds Delina's life. Together they form a kind of "continuous character," as both Nazareth and Delina strongly resemble one another physically and mentally. Neither of them fulfills the stereotypical, masculine ideal of woman as "tall, slim and beautiful." Delina, for instance, is described as "small and stocky and not particularly pretty" (*ES* 17); and Nazareth is referred to as "a plain, ordinary gawk of a girl" (*NT* 118) and as a "repulsive," worn-out, and ill woman with a "gaunt body" (*NT* 18). Both carry a stigma of deformity in that Delina suffers from a twisted spine, and Nazareth is forced to undergo a radical mastectomy due to cancer.

---

[21]*What I term cluster character corresponds with Nina Auerbach's notion of the "collective protagonist," who replaces "individual heroes or sealed couples with groups" (179). Several feminist sf novels call the construction of character into question; the fluid narrative "I" of Russ's* The Female Man *that enters multiple identities provides the most prominent example within feminist sf.*
[22]*This "vision of communal strength" (Shinn 209) is a recurring motif in Elgin's work. Shinn also notes about Elgin's earlier work that "[t]he individual hero, or heroine, is not for Elgin" (209).*

Both Nazareth and Delina are stubborn, resourceful, and gifted with extraordinary talents and "unruly mind[s]" (*NT* 20), and symbolize the sf equivalent of the artist/inventor who propels the community with her visions into action. Delina, in fact, inherits this role of the artist from the then deceased Nazareth. Both symbolize the female history of resistance: Nazareth turns into a "talisman" (*JR* 70), and Delina becomes an obliterated "ancient manuscript ... to be painfully deciphered" (*ES* 60). Moreover, Nazareth and Delina are the initiating guides for the women linguists towards utopia, while another set of "twin" or "continuous characters," the two nurses Michaela (*NT*) and Jo-Bethany (*JR*), are 'travellers to utopia' in new clothes. As members of the non-linguist public that despises the linguists, the two nurses are initially citizens of dystopia; yet they come to revise their prejudices at least against the female linguists through contact and interaction. Eventually, Michaela and Jo-Bethany share the utopian projects and the utopian dream of the women linguists.

Another set of "twin characters" are the female linguists Aquina and Belle-Anne. They share the function of the rebel, yet their forms of rebellion are diametrically opposed. As a defiant radical and troublemaker and a "feminist activist ... [who is] planning direct resistance" (Sisk 125), Aquina situates herself outside of the women linguists' community and their project of non-violent, clandestine resistance. Ready to sacrifice individual needs for the supposed common good—Aquina plans to poison Nazareth so that the girl will be infertile and can move to the Barren House to invent more Láadan Encodings—Aquina, in fact, applies the egoistic principles of the male dystopian community. In this respect, Thomas Chornyak is Aquina's male alter ego. Unscrupulously he manipulates others and does not hesitate to sacrifice fellow linguists if they threaten his top position of the linguists and of Chornyak Household.

Belle-Anne, on the other hand, personifies the feminine way of rebellion. Belle-Anne voluntarily sacrifices her own individual needs for the communally agreed upon common good of the women's community: she takes the blame for Aquina's poisoning of Nazareth to prevent an investigation that would inevitably lead to the discovery of Láadan. Similarly, the female linguist Cleo St. Andrews falsely admits to the poisoning of the President's secretary to disclose (rather than conceal) the Audiosynthesis project in *Earthsong*. These forms of sacrificial resistance, however, lead to death. Belle-Anne is incarcerated as the proverbial "madwoman in the attic," and Cleo is locked away in a prison.

3.3. The Brittle Dystopian Map: The Colonization of Space and Mind

Postcolonial and feminist scholars have noted the importance of geographical, bodily and mental space in the exertion of power and resistance. In different historical, geographical, and social contexts, public and private spaces and their mimetic representations have been inscribed with gender, class, and race differences. The need to disrupt these static mappings of space necessarily creates the need to re-map, or perhaps not to map at all, dynamic spaces for the future. As Alison Blunt and Gillian Rose write:

> Through such critique, more fragmented, complex, and often contradictory notions of both space and subjectivity can emerge. Rather than map apparently unproblematic and transparent space, its construction and contestation are then revealed. In this way, transparent space is disrupted by subject positionality, the politics of location, and the situatedness of knowledge that reflect partial and multiple mapping strategies [19].

Elgin presents us with such a brittle dystopian map of spatial and mental differences, full of cracks through which we glimpse fluid utopian spaces. Primarily concerned with geographical conquest, this future Earth, in fact, resembles very much European colonial history. In the trilogy, language and religion are the vehicles to expand (on Earth and into the universe) or to narrow geographical space (confinement of women, segregation of the Lines), and to possess the "space" of the female body (the marital act, procreation). Moreover, the underlying patriarchal concepts of difference that define everyone not identical with the dominant self as *other* colonize mental space. From the Terran perspective, such binary thinking divides the two sexes, the classes (linguists, government/Church, ordinary citizens), cultures (humanoid Aliens), and species (whales, non-humanoid Aliens). A combination of legal repressions (women as legal minors) and internalized consent (manipulation and indoctrination via Church, science, and media) ensures the hegemony of men over women and of elite classes (linguists, government) over the masses. Ideological conditioning creates willing subjects of both sexes and all classes and races, who are ready to collaborate in their own oppression.

3.3.1. No Limits but Limits: The Expansion and Narrowing of Geographical Space

Imperialist and colonialist attitudes characterize this future patriarchal Earth. Colonialism, defined as the "conquest and control of other people's lands and goods" (Loomba 2), is taken into space with language as the fulcrum of male power. Language and spatial colonization are intrinsically linked, because only the acquisition of alien languages and negotiations with Aliens allow a colonization of outer space. Therefore, Earth is caught in an "endless cycle of negotiations for conquest" (*NT* 265). Whoever controls the language acquisition controls the interplanetary trade and the expansion into space. Church, government, and linguists, all desire and constantly battle for the possession of languages, and thus for economic and political power on Earth as well as in space. Science, religion, and ideology/patriotism are all semantic frameworks for this conquest.

On Earth, Panglish, the future version of English, dominates all other languages. Similarly, the almost exclusive U.S.-American point of view symbolizes the supremacy of the West, especially the global political and economic hegemony of the U.S. Furthermore, the location of ten Lines in the U.S.—two are located in Europe and only one in Africa—stresses the spatial and political domination and the "linguistic imperialism" (*NT* 270) of the U.S. However, patriarchal and colonialist attitudes prevail globally, as the UNE meeting at the end of *Earthsong* demonstrates, when men from Asia and New Ireland alike react with disgust to the women linguists' Audiosynthesis project.

Following a capitalist creed, Earth settles as many planets as possible, taking "more room, more opportunity, more new frontiers" (*NT* 91), because "every new Alien people contacted meant new Alien treasures ... a new market for the products of Earth" (*NT* 269). Clearly, economics is not driven by dire need but greed, as a Pentagon official ponders, "[W]e always 'need' ... we *want* what they've got" (*NT* 50). Whatever the colonized planets have to offer in terms of raw materials or live samples is shipped back to Earth for manufacturing. The Earth government only refrains from violently seizing the Aliens' technology and conquering other planets, because "there's no way of getting it *without negotiating*" (*NT* 50; emphasis added).

Ideology and religion further legitimize this economic desire for colonization. The interstellar competition for planets between the U.S. and the Soviet Union satirizes Reagan's Strategic Defence Initiative (SDI) program of the 1980s—Elgin's satire gains a new topicality in the light of George W. Bush's recent plans for a National Missile Defense System—and the maxim of Western capitalism to make or do anything "bigger and faster and better than the Russians" (*JR* 154). Both systems, however, attempt to rule Earth as well as the colony planets.

In *The Judas Rose*, Elgin poignantly criticizes both the early colonial abuse of "religious conversion ... as a justification for economic plunder" (Loomba 114) and the Catholic Church in particular for its politics of missions and crusades. Heykus Joshua Clete, Chief of the D.A.T., carries out his private Christian war to colonize and christianize the whole universe in a neverending competition over planets, colonies, and souls with the geopolitical enemy, the atheistic and communist USSR. His firm belief in the Judaeo-Christian religion fuels his desire to colonize space and every other being's thinking, he "carr[ies] the Good News out to all *other* worlds ... still condemned to outer darkness" (*JR* 22). Clete's invocation of inspired missionaries who set "Earth's colonies afire with that same love" (*JR* 20) for his God jars with his subsequent combined use of religious and militaristic vocabulary that reveals his true aim of subjugation. Clete's "battalions of missionaries" must besiege rival religions: "[e]ven the religions of Aliens ... would fall before the soldiers of Christ" (*JR* 22).

Economic, political, and religious motifs intricately converge, as Clete literally maps the militaristic takeover of space. Graham Huggan has described the role that cartography and maps play in colonial discourse as symbolic epitomes of patriarchal and colonial acquisition of land:

> The exemplary role of cartography in the demonstration of colonial discursive practices can be identified in a series of key rhetorical strategies implemented in the production of the map, such as the reinscription, enclosure and hierarchization of space, which provide an analogue for the acquisition, management and reinforcement of colonial power [126].

In like manner, Heykus Clete claims every inch of the universe for his Judaeo-Christian God: "one God, *his* God, had created everything there was, no matter where it might be located" (*JR* 132) and maps the progress of occupation with colored "tiny light[s]" (*JR* 11). These lights are visual signifiers of his control over places and of the enlightenment he (his God) brings; Clete thus inscribes his authoritative power as God's representative. Spatial and mental colonization converge in the image of the color-coded ideological, atheistic *other*: "A world lost to the Soviet *hordes* glowed red" (*JR* 11; emphasis added). The expression "hordes" homogenizes the *other* and constructs a discriminatory classification of the stereotypically less civilized, culturally, and ideologically different *other* in that he equates "civilization" with Christianity and the U.S., and "primitivism" with heathenism and the Soviet Union. Additionally, his choice of colors—"clear bright yellow" for the U.S. and "bloody red" (*JR* 11) for the USSR—aligns the former with light/reason and God, and the latter with danger/blood and the devil.

Clete's map becomes an emblem of location, of national territory, and of ideology/Christianization, but it also signifies his attempt to represent the unknown as knowable, to normalize and neutralize the alien difference. For Clete, the universe is either a tabula rasa, a virgin space, onto which he can inscribe his religious beliefs—"a discovered but as yet unclaimed world—still available for exploration and colonization ... and still neutral" (*JR* 11)—or it is a space settled by inferior human or alien beings who must be erased. Clete's map metaphorically visualizes the perceptual transformation of yet unspecified geographical space into something which can now be named, known, claimed, and possessed. It turns into (American) territory, and becomes "an image of land claimed and conquered" (Blunt and Rose 15).

The relationship between Earth/center and satellite planets/periphery mirrors historical "First World" colonial attitudes toward the "Third World." In this hierarchization of outer space, dependency, dominance, and contempt characterize the colonial relationship between space colonies and Earth, and the names of the space colonies connote this cultural, religious, and colonial subjugation.[23] Analogous to the historical transfer of European place names to the landscape of the "New World" and their associations with the landscapes of the "Old World," Terrans attach their sociocultural memories of Earth's landscape and society to the new planets.[24] Recalling British-Australian history, the center in fact settles space colonies to "outsource" unsolved social problems such as violence and poverty: "[each] planet dedicated to your particular favorite variety of trouble" (*ES* 178). Spatial displacement thus mirrors social aberration from the standard, and the Earth colonies replicate the distorted Terran microcosms; they are islands of inclusion and exclusion in outer space. Ironically, the governments of Earth use those individuals, potentially rebellious and thus dangerous to the Terran hierarchy, as representatives of Terran hierarchy in space:

> People ... who thrived on violence and danger; they had tremendous value to society ... on the frontiers. The government had no intention of providing them with facilities that would make them less frustrated.... [T]he attitudes which made them misfits here made them potential leaders in the spaceboonies... [*JR* 128].

All space settlers carry a stigma of difference and otherness; they are "Criminals. Foreigners ... Refugees" (*JR* 143). Again evoking the "Old"

---

[23]*Mentioned are "Fruited Plain," a "tourist asteroid ... specialized in rowdy parties and big drunken brawls; it had been established to preserve the peace in communities once plagued by such activities" (ES 115), heavily populated "Savannah," "[a] world of limited resources, settled by one hundred African-American families of Earth origin" (ES 117), Polytrix, Gehenna, and Eden.*

[24]*These new localities are strangely devoid of native inhabitants. There are no descriptions of indigenous alien species living in these colonies, or of their interaction with the human colonists.*

World's historical settlement of the "New" World, those who settle on the space colonies quickly turn notions of displacement and dislocation into constructions of belonging and superiority. The colonial settlers claim and name their place in space and consider themselves as "Founding Famil[ies]" (*JR* 142) and a new "settler aristocracy." The settler Daryl, for instance, invites his wife Benia to share this myth: "You'll be *Old* Polytrician ... you'll be like people in Philadelphia that had family come over on the Mayflower" (*JR* 142). However, Benia never desired space, she "never once thought of herself being a colonial wife" (*JR* 142), because she never wanted to leave her home in Philadelphia. Benia cannot share Daryl's myth of social mobility, since the position of women in space does not change. As colonial wife and mother, as a member of the female sex, she can never attain the superior class position her husband claims for them as a family.

When the Aliens abandon Earth and expose the Terran hegemony as farcical and the Terran center as peripheral to the universe, the hierarchical spatial Terran system is imbalanced. With the breakdown of the economic system, the space colonies immediately challenge the hegemony of Earth, and the relationship between the colonies and the former colonial Terran center is reversed. Now the inhabitants of space colonies are "prejudiced against Earth and all things Terran"; they criminalize Terrans as "Terroes" (*ES* 151) and deny Terrans a human status: "[t]hey're nothing but animals" (*ES* 152). However, a certain fixation on despised Earth ensures a balance among the space colonies, "[w]ithout Earth to hate, they'd fight each other" (*ES* 170). Earth therefore continues to serve as the locus for channelled aggression as long as the colonies still revolve around a system of patriarchal/colonial domination.

However, the dwindling power of the American President and his Oval Office—now merely "symbols of such antiquity, symbols of the very heart of what it meant to be Terran, to be of *Earth*" (*ES* 161)—symbolize the onset of a new age and a new concept of space. The Oval Office, once the symbol of the ultimate Terran power, acquires a museum status with its real books, wood, and flags in a world where reality and illusion converge. In the end, the American President—once a symbol of supreme political and economic power, of independence and stability, "around whom a carousel of civilizations, mired deep in the consequences of blunders, revolved" (*ES* 169)—is demasked as a puppet and simulacrum.

Just as expansion into space serves to consolidate the colonialist rule, the narrowing of geographical space on Earth—the isolation and segregation according to class and/or gender—consolidate the patriarchy on Earth. The less physical contact the differing social classes and cultures have, the better myths and propaganda can flourish. Spatial segregation leads to a lack of interaction and furthers prejudices, as the PICOTA Chief observes: "separate buildings made gulfs easier to carve out and maintain" (*ES* 43). Particularly the separate living space of the linguists as a group symbolizes the social divide between linguists and the public. Seeking "security in numbers" (*NT* 81), the linguists live communally in inconspicuous Households that are literally shelters dug into the Earth. Each enclosed, self-sufficient unit resembles a "fortress" (*NT* 81) to be reached only via the narrow space of a tunnel. Hence, the architecture demarcates the social boundaries between linguists and non-linguists, and it minimizes the interaction between the classes.

In contrast to the seemingly abundant universal space, the linguist class lives puritanically in an archaic self-inflicted confinement—"91 of us in the Household proper ... 42 more at Barren House" (*NT* 122)[25]— to counteract government propaganda about the luxurious lifestyle of linguist "exploiters." Conveniently, the lack of privacy also allows the monitoring of every movement of each member of the Household. Originally designed to keep non-linguists out, the Households' architecture emblematizes the linguists' seclusion and their walled-off existence. The Household becomes a prison that keeps the linguists in solitariness *cum* group confinement: "no light filtered in here ... no sound" (*NT* 255).

Geographical space is limited for women. On Earth, women of all classes cannot move about freely "beyond the city limits without a male escort and a man's written permission" (*NT* 268), and women can only settle on space colonies as wives and potential breeders. Whether on Earth or in outer space, women are isolated either as a group or as individuals. Non-linguist women are isolated in their private homes to keep them from unsupervised gatherings of solidarity and rebellion. Ironically, the narrowed geographical space—the separate female communities of nuns in convents, of menopausal or sterile female linguists in Barren Houses, and at the end of Book One of all linguist women in Women Houses—furthers the building of a female parallel society and allows the women to develop utopian projects.

3.3.2. Of Usable Bodies, Servo-Mechanisms, and Wife Robots: The Invasion of Body Space

In the patriarchal mental topography, the human body is an exploitable commodity, a machine, and the female body in particular provides another tabula rasa for inscription. Heykus Clete's map symp-

---

[25] *This quotation exemplifies the gender marking of words in that it marks the feminine (Barren and Women House) as a deviation from the male norm (Household proper).*

3. Rewriting the Colonization of Space 95

tomizes this attitude. Customarily, Clete depersonalizes all people into objects and has "every known *usable body* in space indicated on his map" (*JR* 11; my emphasis).

Particularly the female body represents another unknown space to be mastered. Just as the colonial male gaze (ab)uses geographical space as an object of penetration and possession, as "virgin" (feminine) land, the physical space of the female body is constantly conquered, possessed, discovered, violated, and curtailed. Women, especially women linguists, and their living spaces are classified according to their reproductive capacities (e.g. the "Barren Houses"). The female body is described, legislated, and dismissed. The trilogy describes how men use civilization (scientifically legitimated biologism, advanced medicine) and Judaeo-Christian religion to exploit the (female) body for power politics; the novels thus reflect what Kadiatu Kanneh has stated about the historical colonial attitude toward the (female) body: "Civilization and Christianity ... lie on the road to covering up, concealing, neutralising, and taming the body" (347). Both the metaphorical invasion (images, Biblical representation) and the physical invasion of the female body (scrutinizing analysis in medical science) inscribe the body, and turn it into a testimony of oppression. In the trilogy, all instances of bodily contact and emotional involvement, such as marriage, love and sexuality, birth and medical treatment, turn women into objects. For men, women represent only an economic value as reproductive and/or translation machines.

Worn out from giving birth to nine children, Nazareth's gaunt body bears the mark of this exploitation of her reproductive and linguistic capabilities: "[She] looked like nothing so much as a battered servomechanism.... Ready to be traded in. Ready for scrap" (*NT* 17). The constant verbal, psychological, and physical abuse leaves her with "bruises of spirit and mind as well as body" (*NT* 239). Nazareth can only truly work on her Encodings for Láadan once she is past the reproduction stage. Delina suffers from scoliosis, but she has been sterilized at birth; and, therefore, she is not caught in the reproductive cycle. On the one hand, Delina's twisted spine symbolizes the collective forced deformation of women who are robbed of their subject status and of the control over their own bodies. Delina, however, refuses the medical treatment aimed at fulfilling prescribed standards of beauty—a medical treatment that Nazareth desires and that is denied to Nazareth—because Delina is convinced "that she did not and could not ever measure up to the standards coming at her" (*ES* 95). Thus, Delina's body symbolizes, on the other hand, female resistance to the male rule over the female body.

In this profit-oriented masculine economy, highly advanced medicine describes a measure of power and of authority. Once an admired female profession, medicine is only practiced by men; computers have replaced the human factor of providing comfort, and demeaning labor is left for nurses. In this context, the stethoscope is not a symbol for healing but an "antique symbol" of "the power of tradition" (*NT* 56). In this medical economy, women deserve only second-rate medical treatment, despite the emphasis men put on the reproductive function of the female body. The deteriorating architecture epitomizes this attitude: "the maternity ward, since it only served women, would be the last place anybody would spend money on renovating" (*NT* 57).

Consequently, her failing body devalues Nazareth, who was once valued for her "superb genetics" (*NT* 147). The male linguists dismiss her request for a medical treatment that would preserve her breasts and order her to undergo a mastectomy, because her now cancerous breasts are no longer useful in a masculine economy geared towards male pleasure and breeding: "Nazareth is barren now.... She's nearly forty.... What earthly need has she got for *breasts*? It's absurd. It's a non-issue" (*NT* 12). Yet the painful loss of her secondary sexual organs—"Nazareth's hands moved, one to each of her breasts, and she covered them tenderly, as a lover might have covered them against a chill wind" (*NT* 19)—also affords Nazareth "a kind of freedom" (*NT* 243), because a woman without breasts becomes a woman liberated from the desirous male gaze: Nazareth moves to the Barren House.

The female body is on constant display for the male gaze. The female body is exposed and exhibited, covered or discovered by clothes, and promises (sexual) excitement. Women are thus subjected to a constant social/sexual body competition, "never set[ting] a foot outside their homes, or invit[ing] guests into their homes, without the obligation of ... being the best-dressed person present" (*JR* 262).[26] While the male dress code emphasizes profession, authority, and social status—the doctors, for instance, signal their professional competence with "white labcoats" at work and with "black labcoats and ... miniature stethoscopes [pinned] to their neckties" (*JR* 262) in the evening—female clothing marks sexual availability and object status.

In a parody of (Western) women's factual history of marriage as the only career option, women—for example, the nurse Michaela—are sent to marital academies to become perfect wife-servants.[27] Within this masculine economy, marriage becomes an economic contract in which

---

[26] *Women linguists are exempted from this dress code and beauty contest; they are instead required to wear plain tunics that render them uniform. However, true to their profession, women linguists compensate for this lack of diversification with "excessively ornamental...naming"* (*JR* 29).

[27] *Michaela is cast in the double role of the "perfect wife-servant" and as rebel, whereas Melissa Klander acts like a "wife-robot"* (*JR* 56), *a barely human domestic appliance designed by her husband Ham Klander.*

women are commodities of a genetic transaction from father to husband. However, a similar bio-logic of reproductive and genetics applies to lower-ranking men. For Thomas Chornyak, Aaron, too, is merely a genetic object, serving as a "prize stallion" (*NT* 151) first for Nazareth and then as a "stud for Perpetua" (*NT* 233). Perpetua's name ironically signifies the interchangeability of women and their perpetual fate of maximized child-bearing: "marriage at sixteen, allows the husband to space his children three years apart and still see that the woman bears eight infants before the age of forty" (*NT* 146). Professor Macabee Dow aptly describes the function of woman in marriage: "to run my bed and board and bear my children and look decorative" (*JR* 103). With perfidious deviousness, Nazareth's husband Aaron thus desires a speedy divorce from her after her mastectomy, because she no longer fulfills these requirements. The fake suicide note the Vice President writes for the murdered secretary of the President gives in a nutshell the decisive factors—youth, beauty, and marriage—that define woman in relation to man: "I am growing old, and I can see that I will never marry" (*ES* 163).

While in classical dystopia (heterosexual) love often represents a subversive force that destabilizes the system, love fails from the start in Elgin's trilogy. The relationship between the sexes is one of master and slave where love is impossible: "loving any adult male ... would be a perversion, loving your masters while their boots were on your neck" (*NT* 258). Men's attitudes, behavior, and mentality, render them virtually alien to women, as Jo-Beth notes of her abusive brother in law:

> [S]he would far rather have taken her chances in bed with one of the AIRYs ... than with Ham Klander. Who was supposed to be her species.... A human man, as she was a human woman.... It was Ham Klander that [she] found alien. Four arms, she could understand ... [he] was an absolute mystery [*JR* 233].[28]

In this context, love becomes an empty concept signifying nothing. Ned, for instance, tells his wife, Michaela, that he loves her, because "[w]omen liked to hear that" (*NT* 43). Unlike Michaela, Nazareth falls for the myth of romantic heterosexual love, when the linguist Jordan Shannontry treats her kindly, pays her compliments, and gives her a yellow rose. Traditionally a symbol of love, the rose symbolizes instead miscommunication. Jordan and Nazareth differently interpret the sign and what it

---

[28]*Elgin explicitly denies that she deals with female characters as* other. *For her, "it is the male characters who are 'other' and 'alien'.... Most of the things men do and say mystify me; they might as well be sentient gas clouds ... males as alien and other—I do deal with consciously and deliberately" (DuPont 64). Recently, she has revoked this comment as "it no longer represents me accurately.... I just don't believe in the dichotomy any more" (Mohr 2000c, 30).*

signifies. While she regards the rose as a symbol of tender affection if not love, it is quite literally a simple flower to Jordan.[29] When Nazareth declares her love for Jordan, he not only rejects her, but further violates her feelings by reporting her emotional outburst to her father and husband. The men's rational tongue-lashing and cruel laughter at her naiveté and romantic inclination stun Nazareth into immobility. The verbal abuse and the emotional pain transform Nazareth's body into "nothing but a bruise twisted round a core of shame" (NT 200), and she experiences the impossibility to express her feelings in the masculine standard discourse: "there were no words, not in any language, that she could use to *explain* to them what it was that had been done to her" (NT 201-202).[30] She can only regain control over her body when she is spatially removed from the men. Nazareth seeks solace and a mental refuge from the male world in Láadan, "saying the litany of the Encodings aloud ... like a charm against evil" (NT 201).

Elgin's fictional universe is restricted to (abusive) heterosexuality. It is perhaps one of the most serious flaws of the novel that Elgin painstakingly neglects any transgressions of sexual borders. Despite the cloistered space that women linguists and nuns inhabit, despite all the myriad possibilities alien actants offer, Elgin does not include lesbian, or homosexual, and cross-species relationships.[31] (Hetero)sexuality becomes a controlled exchange of genes within marriage, a masculine domain of power and sexual abuse. In the *Native Tongue* series, connubial rape signifies, in de la Concha's words, the "triumphant wordless assertion of male power over woman's body as the last and conclusive statement" (65). Men's sexuality is aligned with violence, whereas female sexuality is denied. Thomas, for instance, denies his mistress Michaela an autonomous sexuality when he sanctions his own lust while expressing abhorrence at the very idea of lustfulness in a woman. Smugly, he believes himself to be "a master of the erotic arts" and is convinced of Michaela's "reciprocal pleasure," since this is "precisely what *he* would have asked for" (NT 223; emphasis added).

---

[29]*The context, of course, changes the meaning. Sister Miriam Rose becomes a symbol of the successful dissemination of the feminist Láadan bible; and the women linguists plant rosebushes as secret signs of their defiance against the patriarchal law that forbids such extravagances.*

[30]*Examples of such curious lexical gaps for existent but previously unnamed situations or experiences that are, therefore, hard to pinpoint are sexism, racism, sexual harassment, and mobbing. See also Dale Spender (1980, esp. chap. 6).*

[31]*It is arguable whether, as Val Gough claims, the mere existence of a strong female community that steps out of heteropatriarchal boundaries creates a "pro-lesbian (or anti-heterosexuality) subtext" (35). Elgin has commented that she never decided "to leave out lesbianism ... it just never ... occurred to me" (Mohr 2000c, 29). However, she retrospectively and somewhat haltingly classifies the relationship between Nazareth and Michaela as an asexual relationship "of deep love.... When lesbianism is defined as love between women, without the stipulation that there be sex involved ... Nazareth and Michaela were a lesbian 'couple'" (ibid. 29).*

The linguist Belle-Sharon has perfected the art of faking passion for the pleasure of her husband Jared without getting emotionally involved. For Belle-Sharon, sexual intercourse becomes an act of performance in that she "carefully arrange[s] [herself] for Jared's pleasure as an earthwise plant arranged for sunlight or for rain" (*JR* 292). Belle-Sharon withdraws mentally from her body and recites scientific "ugly word[s]" such as "vagina," "penis," and "menstruation" (*JR* 293) to dissociate from the physical act of abuse and to stamp out "every last *scrap* of desire" (*JR* 296). However, to violate one's own (com)passion, desire, and feeling will not help women nor men, as Nazareth exhorts Belle-Sharon: "If true passion is driven out of our women ... then what hope is there? How are the men ever to *learn*, if we do that?" (*JR* 297). The end of desire would be tantamount to the end of hope for change, and it is the women's desire to change that builds utopia.

Sexual bodily contact is geared towards "female growth." A woman's reproductive capacity is exploited to the maximum, stopping just short of fertility drugs for multiple births and of polygamy. The men nonetheless practice a form of serial monogamy, replacing a "used up" barren wife with a new woman. True to the context of nineteenth century biologism, women only incubate what man creates: "The *man* goes to the trouble of impregnating the woman.... To attribute any credit to the woman who plays the role of a receptacle is primitive romanticism ... and entirely unscientific" (*NT* 11).

The female reproductive capacity is also used to settle and populate space colonies. Inherently, the penetration of space is thus linked to the penetration of the female body. For instance, the forest ranger Daryl marries Benia simply because only couples or families are sent into space: "[w]ithout her to make him eligible, without her to produce Bran [their child], Daryl couldn't have carried out the Plan" (*JR* 144). Benia, however, refuses the myth of the doting mother, although she superficially complies to the expectations of society, "making the soothing noises that the microfiche said she was supposed to make" (*JR* 140), even though she hates her son.

Children also become commodities within this economy. Quite literally, linguist children are the investment for the future; they represent the most valuable constant in the interstellar economic equation that "acquired alien languages equal power." Hypocritically, the government accuses the linguists of breeding children "like flyers come off assembly lines, they're just products to you ... like they were stocks and bonds" (*NT* 91), while profiting from the thus maximized alien language acquisition. Alluding to the hypocritical attitude of the "First" World comfortably living off the cheap child labor in the "Third" World—a past barbarism of the twentieth century that translates into the more sophisticated variant of child linguist labor in this future world—Thomas Chornyak demasks the governmental display of shocked innocence: "*your* children ... could not be provided with perfect food and perfect housing and perfect education and perfect medical care and the leisure to thrive and live the good life.... You love your children ... on the weary backs of ours" (*NT* 94–95). In return, the government legitimizes its kidnapping of a linguist baby (for interfacing) by claiming to save the child from the exploitative maltreatment the linguists inflict on their children. The government, however, equally maltreats infants in the governmental secret project of decoding non-humanoid alien worldviews for even greater profit. This government project totally objectifies the human body. The scientist create test tube babies and interface them with non-humanoid Aliens. When the "tubies" self-destruct, they are drugged with hallucinogens to alter their brains to more readily accept non-humanoid alien worldviews.

3.3.3. *The World According to His Word: Mental Traps*

For the linguist Elgin, the colonization of the mind obviously plays a primary role in the construction of the *other*. She scathingly critiques the androcentric discourses inherent in the (Western) history of religion, literature, and culture. Colonization always implies domination and suppression, often in a context of physical violence and always in a context of mental violence; it homogenizes and objectifies the *other*, as Heykus Clete's aforementioned "All Souls Mission" demonstrates. The "objective" discourses of science and law in particular participate in the oppression of the *other*. Clearly, Elgin's critique of language and discursive practices intersects with historical and contemporary discourses in different parts of our world; and this criticism casts light on how preconceptions of the *other* filter encounters between sexes, classes, cultures/races, and species. A language of differences and sameness shapes to a large extent not only the dystopia of the twenty-third century but also our contemporary world(s), as Trinh T. Minh-ha ascertains about factual colonial/patriarchal relations: "Words manipulate at will ... 'difference' is essentially 'division' in the understanding of many. It is no more than a tool of self-defense and conquest ... [a] semantic trap which sets us up against each other as expected by a certain ideology of separatism" (266).

In Elgin's novels, the dystopian use of language provides therefore not a concept of mutual/dialogic verbal/body communication, where words/signs are exchanged on a level of equality. Instead, language becomes a tool of dominance, of talking *at*, not to or with, someone from a superior/inferior position. Patriarchal conceptualizations of difference are manifested in language, and lead to a process of *othering* that science, legal texts, religion, and government propaganda legitimize. Language thus promotes the mastery of others, and communication is not aimed at understanding. In the novels, men use militaristic language, disallowing any doubts about who is in command, deliberately instilling hatred as the masculine "index of your power" (*JR* 40), while desire for harmony is considered a feminine weakness, because "[o]nly women wanted to be 'liked'" (*JR* 40).[32] Patriarchal and colonial discourses represent the *other* as unalterably *alien*, and define difference as lack and incompleteness, as unequal to the (male) self. Scientific and religious language, education, traditions, ideology, myths, and propaganda express exclusively the masculine worldview and suppress the female perception of reality.

Religious discourse is particularly foregrounded and deconstructed in *The Judas Rose*. Elgin exposes Judaeo-Christian religion as a patriarchal and misogynist construction and attacks the patriarchal structure of the hurch. Furthermore, she underlines that the Bible with its "kings and masters and battles and rods and staffs and foreskins" (*JR* 174) has been written, after all, by male scriveners. Well aware of language as a "powerful instrument for change" (*JR* 352), the Catholic Church employs religious language to stabilize the status quo. The Catholic Church uses this ancient and "most reliable of all conversion mechanisms" to channel worship of a feminist goddess into Mariolatry and ultimately into a "wholesome worship of the Lord and of His Son" (*JR* 184).

Unsurprisingly, the Catholic Church execrates the feminist Láadan version of the Bible as "theological pornography" (*JR* 337), because this version threatens the maintenance and contentment of women in their inferior role. Against this patriarchal church, Elgin posits Aquina, the mother of Sister Miriam Rose, and Sister Miriam Rose as the two founding mothers of a feminine Christian religion. Her name ironically aligns Aquina with Thomas Aquinas, one of the founding fathers of the misogynist Church. Moreover, her immaculate conception of her daughter (Sister) Miriam aligns her with the Virgin Mary, and, consequently, places her daughter (Sister) Miriam in the saviour function of Jesus. Symbolically, Elgin thus reclaims both the Virgin Mary and Jesus for women.

---

[32] *Power and the desire to dominate are explicitly linked to sexuality: "Powerful men had always been hated, they fed on it the way infants fed on mothers' milk ... hatred was like the satisfaction of sex" (JR 39).*

However, the Virgin Mary (representing the divine feminine principle) and Joseph (representative of the human but patriarchal principle) also appear as corrupt human incarnations. The Virgin Mary turns into the frightened subordinate Sister Maria, who confesses to Father Joseph upon her deathbed the double agency of Sister Miriam, herself, and the other nuns. In this context, Sister Miriam, who works on the liberation of women, becomes the prophet Miriam of the OT, who intones a new hymn of renewal and liberation after the Exodus.[33] In her *function* as a woman of the Church, Sister Maria *cum* Mary of the NT betrays Sister Miriam *cum* Miriam, the feminist revolutionary of the OT and the female incarnation of Jesus.[34] The true inheritor of the Biblical Mary is therefore Sister Miriam, who is additionally characterized with the oval face of "the traditional Madonna" (*JR* 178), the looks of an "El Greco Saint," and the stately behavior of a "medieval queen" (*JR* 302). Looming tall over the priests, Sister Miriam with her "magnificent voice" (*JR* 304) incarnates a feminine divinity so ingeniously that even Heykus Clete reluctantly feels blessed by her presence.

In Elgin's rewriting of the NT, Joseph betrays Mary. Like Moses, who, in a patriarchal act, expels his insurgent sister (Miriam) from the community, *because* she has turned into a sovereign and liberated woman, Father Joseph breaks the seal of the confessional for the same reasons.[35] By not excommunicating him but absolving his violation of the sacred vow of sanctity, "Holy *Mother* Church" betrays God in the aspect of the *feminine* divine principle. Hypocritically, the superiors justify this absolution in that they compare *his* betrayal with Jesus driving the moneychangers out of the Temple, "there are times ... when it is right to break even a good and holy rule" (*JR* 339). Jesus, however, violated certain commandments to drive institutionalized materialism out of the House of God. His intent was to reestablish a personal relation to God without religious regulations and to advocate a return to pure spirituality. The argumentation of the Church, however, distorts and abuses the temple scene to sanction the infringement of a Church law and to maintain the institution and its hierarchy. Posthumously, Sister Miriam Rose—and thus the textual female incarnation of Jesus—is anathematized as "Judas Rose": "Judas for the treachery; Rose for her false perfection. Rose with

---

[33]*Miriam is derived from the Hebrew name Mara which translates into "the unruly."*
[34]*I use incarnation here not in the sense of an avatar, a bodily reincarnation, but figuratively as the incarnation of the principles Jesus stands for and the betrayal he was subjected to.*
[35]*Miriam and Aaron doubt the political and religious leader Moses in his dominant position and mediatory role between god and humans (cf. Exod. 12; also Num. 26, 59), yet only Miriam, not Aaron, is punished. In view of the highly probable fact that Jewish male scribes have aetiologically reinterpreted the patriarchal acts of Jewish history as divine acts, it seems highly probable that the punishment of Miriam that is attributed to God in the bible has really been carried out by Moses.*

3. Rewriting the Colonization of Space 103

a worm at its heart, a venomous worm, rose with poison tipping its thorns" (*JR* 334).[36] Although the patriarchal Church in fact betrays the preachings of Jesus and his maxim to liberate *all* humans, the clergy reverses this to women's of betrayal of Jesus. In effect, spirituality and divinity are reduced to irrelevance and, moreover, are abused to oppress and to disavow the feminine divine principle as represented by women.

Language acquisition and communication are, of course, the key issues of the *Native Tongue* series. The whole Terran system is based on the successful communication with the alien *other*, yet all human-to-human communication, such as government negotiations, public and private communication, the communication between social groups and the sexes, is based on miscommunication, (self-)deception, and misperception. Indicating patriarchal/colonial supremacy and demarcating one group from the other, manipulative, deceitful usage of language as a tool of power marks intra- and interpersonal communication. The surface communication between women and men remains a facade; the deceptive use of language allows men to gain or keep power (myths, lies), whereas women deceive to cover that they destroy power (Langlish, the falsification of food data).

Both body and verbal language underline and express the hierarchical stratification and impervious binary structure of human society. The linguists' reference to their extended families as "Households" and "Lines" establishes, on the one hand, a patrilinear genealogy. On the other hand, this form of reference linguistically separates them as a superior social/racial group from the public in that these phrases recall the interchangeable use of "race," "lineage," and "household" practiced in the sixteenth to eighteenth centuries (cf. Loomba 118). In like manner, language marks woman's reproductive and social status, as in "Barren House" and the title "Mrs."[37] Phallogocentric discourse defines woman as an appendage and not as an individual; for instance, all married women of Chornyak Household are either addressed as "Mrs. Chornyak" (*NT* 177)—a form of address that obscures their identity and erases their individuality—or are referred to by the number of their children. This linguistic practice, in fact, dates back to the nineteenth century; it stresses that a woman is defined by her husband and her children. In addition, Lucie Armitt—attributing the original idea to Mair Evans (cf. n18)—has

---

[36] *The worm symbolizes the devil and sexuality, and the rose, read here in connection with Judas and the NT, stands for the ultimate female betrayal of patriarchal Judaeo-Christian religion. These lines also recall William Blake's poem "The Sick Rose" ("O Rose, thou art sick! / The invisible worm, / That flies in the night" 1–3).*

[37] *On the linguistic abuse of women, the historical background of generics and pronouns, and the double standard applied to names and (social) titles with regard to women, see Casey Miller's and Kate Swift's dated but excellent study (1980).*

suggested that the last name of Aaron Adiness describes "a pun on the phrase 'add an s,' the letter 's' at the end of the name referring originally to 'son of'" (137), and thus designates masculine lineage. Perhaps "Adiness" can also be read as an allusion to the originally French feminine-gender suffix "ess": woman is an "addition," a substandard variation to male standard words.

The social hierarchy is linked with the subject position in language and with the participation in the communicative process of society, and women are excluded from both. For example, men regard women linguists as translation machines, and a nun may only respond with the ritualized formulaic phrase "[i]t is my privilege to obey" after a priest has issued the permission "you may speak" (*JR* 179). Woman takes on the "role as listener" (*NT* 36); listening becomes thus the image of the exclusion and the silencing of female speech, but this silence is often mistaken as consent as, for example, in Michaela's case.[38] Her husband Ned Landry appreciates her ability to focus attentively on his droning monologues that he thinks of as brilliant conversation. Thomas too finds in his mistress Michaela the projection space he needs. The less verbal space that Michaela takes while listening "with her whole heart and her whole mind" (*NT* 278), the more Thomas can usurp space. Her silence allows him to feel enlarged to "*taller*" (*NT* 222) physical proportions. Ned likewise needs to be the center of her "total" mute attention to nurture his narcissistic ego. Once Michaela's attention is diverted to their newborn baby, Ned volunteers the baby for the Government Project and thus eliminates the "competitor." With the destruction of all memorabilia, "like there'd never *been* any baby" (*NT* 41), he falsely hopes to erase her memory. Michaela, however, never *talks* back, but effectively retaliates for her loss: she locks Ned into a room full of wasps.

Women of all classes are disempowered, but at the same time they are the necessary referents for the masculine self. Their exclusion from power, decision-making, and public professional life in general is disguised by the pretense that "women are cherished. Treated tenderly. Indulged in every way. Looked after, deferred to, sheltered" (*JR* 19). In fact, they are reduced to adornments of masculine life; they are declared irrational and their actions are trivialized: "as if it had been a major contribution to civilization" (*JR* 91). In this context, a female conspiracy of the size of Láadan or Audiosynthesis must seem impossible. As Donawerth comments, paternalistic language and thought occludes or at least "deafens men to others' realities—they stop hearing language other than their own" (123). This deafness leads Heykus Clete, for instance, to the

---

[38]*Similarly, female speech is referred to as "gossip" while the "solid useful talk of men" signifies "real conversation"* (NT 273).

assumption that he is an "*expert* on women" (*JR* 92), knowing their minds and needs much better than they do.

Scientific discourse reverts to biological determinism, and social Darwinism justifies a hierarchy of genes in which male genes keep the human race from degenerating into an inferior species of females with smaller brains, i.e., lower intelligence. Like religion, sociobiology is based on a patriarchal ideology and effectively primitivizes and objectifies women. The *female* linguist baby Selena Opal Hame, who transgresses the perceptual barrier between humanoid and non-humanoid worldviews, later disproves the pretense of scientifically proven female inferiority.

In Elgin's dystopia, linguistic/discursive practice therefore classifies the female sex into four categories: machine, legal minor, colonial subject, and animal. All four categories imply binary oppositions with man as active, rational, speaking adult human subject and woman as passive, irrational, mute subhuman/non-human object. For Thomas, his mistress Michaela is a "lovely piece" (*NT* 71). In like manner, linguist and non-linguist men treat women linguists as mindless machines that transmit words and process information without understanding. The priests sanction the professional work of female linguists, because "[t]hey do not act *alone* ... they simply function, much as a servomechanism would function ... [the linguists] *provide* them with their instructions" (*JR* 213). Of course, Nazareth is acutely aware during government negotiations with Aliens that "history was being *made*" (*JR* 80), but without her having any share in the actual shaping of power. Additionally, every woman is treated like a "sophisticated child" (*NT* 110) and she is addressed as "girl." Analogous to the treatment of colonial subjects, women are subjected to the same "prejudice that had once been attached to racial differences" (*NT* 229). Moreover, comparisons with "chimps" (*NT* 17) and the attribution of "sly animal cleverness" (*NT* 102) allocate women to a subhuman/non-human status.

The same linguistic practices, however, apply to any member of the male sex who displays "feminine" characteristics, attitudes, or behavior that is denounced as "effeminate." The patriarchal paradigm equates desirable "masculine" attributes, such as courage and boldness, with *human* qualities. When the subsidiary character Kenneth Chornyak displays *human* qualities such as compassion and empathy—these are equated with deplorable femininity—he is derogatorily insulted as "girlish"(*NT* 12). Heykus Clete chastises himself for his "womanish" (*JR* 129) fear of space travel, and another character is shamed by "womanish crying"(*NT* 81). When a colleague associates the desk of Professor Macabee Dow with "the inside of a giant egg" or a "womb" (*JR* 247), the mathematician indignantly rejects any associations with sex, birth, and blood and instead favors "masculine" rationality—for him the desk visualizes the number nine.

Although women at large, according to Elgin, are the *victims* of colonized thinking—"deformed of spirit through no fault of their own" (*NT* 227)—they neither constitute a homogenous gender group nor are they exempted from patriarchal dualistic thinking. Female characters also participate in the masculine hierarchy and apply patriarchal concepts of difference, when they use "tongue-lashing" and "body-parl" for literally putting other women into their place. Several scenes illustrate how women appropriate the masculine gaze, and how they use phallogocentric language to describe other women. The nurse Jo-Beth perceives her own sister Melissa as the epitome of masculine sexual expectations—"large breasts and a pretty face and long red hair" with "no discernible intelligence or common sense"—and pejoratively dismisses her sister's utterances as "drivel" (*JR* 55) instead of recognizing in Melissa a woman utterly intimidated by an abusive husband. When Rachel, wife of Thomas Chornyak, accuses Aaron of being "stupid, and vindictive, and petty— he's worse than any woman" (*NT* 151), she too succumbs to masculine characterizations of "woman" as inferior and base. In the hospital, non-linguist women denigrate Nazareth as a human *Alien* and devil because of her *social* status as a linguist: "as if her skin had been pale green, or as if linguists had horns to identify them" (*NT* 226).

Sent to deliver the men's decision against a mastectomy, the linguist Clara first perceives Nazareth as "repulsive" and "battered servomechanism," before this "unsavory image" (*NT* 18) strikes her for what it is: the internalized male gaze that reduces Nazareth to the status of an object and machine. Consciously, Clara decides to break free: "I will *not* see her that way! This is a living woman" (*NT* 18). Her act of mental "decolonization" leads to the silent recognition of enforced compliance under the male rule, as (verbal) messenger and as (body) victim: "The two women looked at each other, silently. And in the same way that Clara ached for the woman who must accept the wholly avoidable mutilation, Nazareth ached for the woman who had been ordered to carry that message" (*NT* 19).

Nazareth achieves a similar act of decolonization, when she understands that her abusive husband Aaron—"that disgusting parody of a man and his ego" (*NT* 156)—truly lives "in constant terror of ... [his] own ego" that is consumed by self-hatred. Only then she can turn from hate and fear to empathy and compassion: "*Poor* Aaron. That was a new thought" (*NT* 183; my emphasis). When she discerns Aaron's true motives for abuse—namely his need to externalize his terror of his *own* self which fears and hates the *other* he then terrorizes—Nazareth is liberated from being an object that reflects him. Once Nazareth has deci-

3. Rewriting the Colonization of Space 107

phered this mechanism, she no longer reacts but acts to trigger the desired response, despite never precisely comprehending "*why* men did things, but predicting *what* they would do in response to a particular stimulus" (*JR* 349). Essentially, stimulation and response constitute the principle of resonance that the utopian projects are based on.[39]

The dichotomization of society is similarly based on social, religious, and scientific myths and on propaganda aimed at consolidating insurmountable differences between the known and the unknown, the self and the other. Verbal barriers, not different languages, insinuate a fixed dualism and silence the repressed. Anxious to counteract the linguistic monopoly on Alien languages and, therefore, on power, the government (ab)uses the media for polemic propaganda about the "linguist dynasties" (*NT* 11) and "Aristocrats" (*NT* 70) of the future, acquiring wealth with Mafia methods. In the words of the government propaganda, Thomas Chornyak is the "Lingoe godfather" (*NT* 61), and the Lines live "off the backs and the blood of decent people" (*NT* 54). Analogous to the historical linguistic abuse of colored people as "Negroes," the derogatory term "Lingoe" denotes linguistically the envious exclusion of the socially and educationally superior class of linguists as inferior human *others* within the social stratification of mainstream Terran society. Their lifelong interaction with Aliens renders them virtually *alien*, "a little *other* than human" (*NT* 14; emphasis added),[40] while their earth-sheltered communal households evoke animal associations, "packed into a hole in the ground like animals" (*NT* 112).

Because linguists are experts at controlled verbal/body language use, non-linguists feel helplessly inferior and manipulated. With controlled gestures, modulation of tone and voice, and conscious use of "bodyparl," the linguists use body and voice as "mechanism[s] of power" (*NT* 287), and rigidify the lines of social schism between linguists and non-linguists. In contrast, women's body language—of the women of the Lines and of the public alike—signals inferiority. Their body language is geared towards a socially accepted and expected display of erotics, sexual availability, and bodily/intellectual inferiority. To this effect, the PICOTA plants Marthajean Brown as secretary in the presidential Oval Office: to seduce and influence the President. Conscious of their bodies as "erotic weapons" (*NT* 152) and the manipulative potential of bodyparl, women linguists in particular play their bodies and voices "like exquisitely tuned instruments" (*JR* 35).

---

[39]*Jo-Beth also notes this way of manipulation: "how easily a man could be made to believe you when you were saying exactly what he wanted you to say, no matter how improbable it was"* (JR 231).

[40]*A number of text passages refer to linguists as human* others *or Aliens (cf.* NT 94; JR 42, JR 314, *and* JR 319*)*.

The two attempts at breaking the Lines' linguistic monopoly are not aimed at the dispersion but the usurpation of power. The myth of *genetic difference*—analogous to historical biologisms about color and gender (cf. *NT* 67)—is refuted, when the ambitious Professor Macabee Dow challenges the Lines' language monopoly and interfaces his son Gabriel with humanoid Aliens.[41] However, Macabee does not pursue the noble objective to reconcile the classes. Academia too desires power within the hierarchical class system. Unlike the linguist infants who enter the Symbolic Order, the social order of patriarchy, as members of the dominant social group that controls it, the non-linguist Gabriel has to enter a Symbolic Order that is not his. Gabriel and all the other non-linguist children of high-ranking citizens subsequently sent into Interfacing reject the career as translator, because they lack the *social* conditioning, the interaction, and the group pressure necessary to work as devoted linguists and translators. Only the indoctrination and total immersion into a social environment solely concerned with linguistics—analogous to the long tradition of circus families[42]—mold humans into the cyclical reality of linguists, who pray the mantra: "A linguist is a human being is a linguist is a human being" (*JR* 253). Closer involvement between linguists and selected members of the non-linguist upper class leads to the recognition of the linguists' *real*, little to be envied, life of "priesthood ... celibacy, poverty, [and] obedience" (*JR* 317). As prejudices ease, the *social* split between non-linguists and linguists begins to heal (cf. *JR* 355). To his father's disappointment, Gabriel, however, desires unlimited fun and the immediate power of a despot; he wants to "run the place, a whole asteroid of my own, just exactly any way I please" (*JR* 255). Driven by megalomania and almost apotheosizing himself, Macabee conversely desires the unlimited power of an emperor-god of the universe: "to control the fate of entire planets, and of whole alliances of planets" (*JR* 255). Unlike his son, Macabee recognizes the "difference between real power and the illusion of power" (*JR* 256), between unlimited, divine power and the limits of an acting representative.

The government unsuccessfully attempts to crack the linguists' alien

---

[41]*Macabee Dow's compound name personifies the synthesis of economics and religion. The religious hero Maccabeus of the Apocrypha led a revolt in Judea against the advance of pagan Hellenism brought by the Seleucid king, and the American economist C.H. Dow compiled, together with his colleague E.D. Jones, the first average of U.S. stock prizes in 1884 (Dow-Jones index). At first, Macabee appears as an innovator, yet he drops this mask when he reveals the true nature of his desire; as a historical traditionalist, he wants the power of the ancient tradition. The naming of his sons after the heavenly agents of revelation (the archangels Gabriel, Raphael, and Michael) indicates Macabee's desire for divine power; only, these modern, mundane archangels are content with asteroids.*

[42]*Elgin confirms this interrelation: "The Linguist Lines I got ... from the circus families that I'd observed in Sarasota, Florida ... in the [19]50s" (Mohr 2000c, 24).*

language monopoly by interfacing non-humanoid Aliens with human infants and with test tubies desensitized with hallucinogenic drugs. The name of the project's location, *El Centro,* signifies its aim: to be at the center of "power through language." With the drug experiments—an extreme version of the linguistic nativism that Noam Chomsky has propagated—the government hopes to heighten the mind's awareness and to strengthen the language acquisition device; yet with this belief in language as innate ability, the government disproves its own myth of genetic difference. Oblique language enables the involved workers to deny their own agency and responsibility in the child abuse. Once more, the government workers legitimate their otherwise unjustifiable share in the barbaric treatment of infants and other species with religion: "For the greater good of all mankind [sic] ... Christ would understand ... God allowed *His* beloved Son to be sacrificed, for a greater good.... You see the parallel" (*NT* 49). Only the computer technician Lanky Pugh draws a parallel between humans and (non-humanoid) Aliens: "How do we know it [the Alien] hasn't got a wife and kids it'd like to go flicker at instead of us" (*NT* 138). The workers deny the unbearable reality of their participation in and their responsibility for willful acts of murder because this reality collides with their self-image of civilized, virtuous heroes. They erase their knowledge of guilt by pretending to act "for honor and glory" (*NT* 47), and not for money like mercenaries. The government euphemistically circumscribes the kidnapping of Selena Opal Hame as "temporary custody" (*NT* 62), which Thomas spells out for what it is: "barbarism" (*NT* 87). To mask their own monstrosity, the workers label the drugged test tubies, who do not self-destruct but remain mute after Interfacing, "little monsters" (*NT* 169). Assigned to erase all incriminating data—all "acts that are past illegal and criminal, and so far into unspeakable and unthinkable, that we can't even keep records on them" (*NT* 51)—from the computer memory, Lanky Pugh turns into the human memory of all names of sacrificed children. Ironically, the repeated action of deleting names inscribes them indelibly in his memory.

While the linguists work with humanoid Aliens that roughly fit into some familiar categories—"It was possible to look at one of theirs and at least assign labels roughly to its parts"—the form or concept of these non-humanoid Aliens cannot be classified: "it flickered (??) [sic], and never any pattern to the flickering (??), it drove the Terran eye to a constant search for order ... you profoundly wished that you *couldn't* see it" (*NT* 47). This immediate reality of the *other*—in contrast to a reality removed by simulation or media—unsettles the government workers. The simulacrum of an Alien, a sophisticated hologram, cannot represent the "presence" of the *other*: "An Alien in a holo was exotic; an Alien in the flesh was *alien*" (*JR* 227).

The interfaced and drugged tubies develop no language whatsoever; they suffer from an "absence of lexicalization," because they cannot grasp the different *psychic* "nonverbal experiences and perceptions for which no [humanoid] language offers a surface shape" (*NT* 167). They slip into psychosis and remain in the Imaginary Realm. The successful interfacing of the linguist infant Selena Opal Hame with a non-humanoid Alien, however, disproves the assumption that something completely alien *and* non-human cannot be included into one's worldview. Moreover, Elgin indicates how important interaction is for the development of communication. After years of speechlessness, Selena acquires the basic concepts of lexicalization, of sign and signifier, under the care of the women linguists: "there is first the real chair, inside their head" (*JR* 202); but, lacking the interactive communicative element of "[s]haring what is in your head" (*JR* 203), she cannot articulate her perceptions.[43]

Speciesism allocates the whales—successfully interfaced with non-humanoid Aliens on the presumption that both are cetaceans—to the inferior position in relation to *man*. Yet the whales deliberately refuse to be *forced* into communication with human infants; they do "a Ghandi" (*JR* 199). With their immobile bodies they plainly signal "*We won't play your silly game*" (*JR* 200), and defy man's claim of dominance. Yet the government workers merely conclude that they have "drawn the lines in the wrong places" (*JR* 284), and begin to redefine the borderlines between humanoid/non-humanoid. Unwilling to accept this refusal to cooperate, they begin to modify a computer to resemble a whale's brain.

The Aliens' superiority, only known to the governmental and linguist elite, poses a fundamental threat to this hierarchical organization of human society. Only if the public keeps believing in a firmly established hierarchy of humans/Aliens, Earth/colonies, men/women, elite/public, the government and the linguists can keep their elite positions. The public must be kept under the illusion of (male) human superiority; and tradition and unquestioned hierarchy must be preserved to resist destabilization through contact with the alien *other*. Thomas Chornyak, for instance, dismisses divorce on the grounds that only the preservation of the "cultural fabric" keeps the nation that suffers from "shocks of contact with the Alien civilizations" (*NT* 232) from disintegration. Furthermore, ancient uniforms are kept as symbols of the past: "Tradition. Respect of historical values. Antidote to Future Shock Syndrome" (*NT* 51). For the same reasons, Heykus Clete wears glasses despite his perfect vision, because the glasses provide him with a protective barrier, a "slight edge of privacy" (*JR* 10) in that they keep everything *alien* at a

---

[43]Oddly, there are no stylistic and narrative indicators of Selena's language difficulties (truncated sentences etc.), she is (mis)represented as a coherent narrative "I."

distance. The glasses also align him with the ancestral male gaze, the powerful "tradition to which male heads ... in *his* family subscribed" (*JR* 10).

Human racial differences are not explicitly the subject of the novels, yet Elgin addresses these when she attacks the seeming futility of education and the tragedy of history repeating itself. Education perpetuates an androcentric and colonial history of "Great Events Through the Ages" that consists of "wars and kings and extrapolations and conquests" (*JR* 238). Despite superficial public outrage at "history tapes where the little black kids walked into schools between rows of policemen with dogs, and white people spitting ... a time so barbaric that people based their estimate and treatment of others on skin color.... It was like hearing that your ancestors were cannibals" (*JR* 189), the very same prejudices are transferred to Aliens because they are *different*. In contradistinction to most sf novels, Elgin refrains from elaborate and detailed descriptions of Aliens. Some Aliens appear physically bizarre, some such as the Jeelods are "nearly Terran in physical appearance" (*NT* 23). No matter how minimal the physical differences are, those officials involved in negotiations with the Aliens suffer from culture shock, as one government representative reports: "you get close to an Alien.... Everything goes on red alert, and everything you've got to feel with is screaming ALIEN! Alien!" (*NT* 45). Incapable of including the very concept of *superior* Aliens—a superiority *not acted out*—and the alien perceptions of the universe into their own worldview, the officials *need* to demonize Aliens for the sake of sanity. Some have an inkling that possibly the differences between Aliens and humans are not irreconcilable, but "we don't know and we can't afford to care" (*NT* 138). In contrast to the men's own reaction, the Aliens do not react with resentment, but with mild interest: "the Aliens didn't hate them.... The Aliens thought they were *cute* ... a word you used for females, and children ... small animals ... you, an adult male were considered 'cute'" (*JR* 40). Caught in the binary classification system, the officials must suddenly perceive and categorize *themselves* as the stereotypical uncivilized inferior: "[l]ittle naked heathen ignorant savages, strutting our stuff, rattling our beads" (*JR* 41). Within this reversed relationship, the government officials struggle to keep the *illusion* of superiority. For interplanetary negotiations, they pump up their injured egos "to such monstrous inflated proportions that it would carry you through the session" (*JR* 38). The hilarious mental litany goes like this: "I AM ONE OF THE MOST POWERFUL MEN ... I OWN A PRIVATE ASTEROID WHERE I AM KING AND POPE AND SULTAN AND MAGUS AND THERE IS NO OTHER POWER BEFORE ME" (*JR* 38).

In like manner, men deny reality and "wall off everything" (*NT* 96) that interferes with their delusive self-perception. Colonialist and sexist attitudes are euphemistically superseded by the exact opposite; reality is perceived through "mental filters that kept from the masters even the realization that they were slavers" (*NT* 96). Utterly terrorized by the sight of an Alien in an Interface, Ham Klanders, for instance, self-deceptively represses all memory of his repulsion and "make[s] up a story about his total indifference to the AIRYs ... he would also manage to *believe* the tale he concocted" (*JR* 227) to keep his self-image of a brave and intrepid man. The President likewise successfully convinces himself that his sexual encounter with the secretary never actually happened. When the linguists, formerly essential to the economic universe, become superfluous after the abandonment of Earth, they remain in a state of limbo, because "trained to *remember* having it [the power]" (*ES* 237) they cling to the *memory* of power. Reality, the novels suggest, is what we are either pre-conditioned to perceive as reality, or what we fabricate as such. Reality depends on the subject/object relation and the capacity to express it:

> [T]here's no such thing as reality. We make it up by perceiving stimuli from the environment—external or internal—and making statements about it ... people get used to a certain kind of reality and come to expect it, and if what they perceive doesn't fit the set of statements everybody's agreed to, either the culture has to go through a kind of fit until it adjusts ... or they just blink out... [*NT* 142].

Increasingly, reality and imitation merge; even objects such as the three factitious moons that orbit around the settler planet Savannah have lost "all the marks of manufacture" (*ES* 131) and are no longer recognizable as simulacra. A dialogue between the President and the investigator Zlerigau expresses this increasing difficulty to differentiate between what is real and what is not. Incredulously, they discuss the Audiosynthesis conspiracy that undermines the reality they both know:

> "Nothing that ... extravagantly absurd," declared the President, finally, "could possibly be true."
> "I'm sorry to have to disagree, sir.... In spite of every rational consideration, it's as true as it is true that I sit her before you now."
> "Perhaps you are a simulacrum, Zlerigau."
> "And perhaps you are, Mr. President. It's equally likely."
> *I* could be a *simulacrum*, he thought. Certainly he was not the same man who had sat here and talked to the President with such serene self-confidence.... He was a man in some kind of shock.... The world he knew had been a rug under his feet.... And then that rug had been pulled out from under him [*ES* 212].

This inability to adjust to changed stimuli is captured in the violent image of patriarchal culture verging on self-destruction and still keeping a dead "system ... running, the way the male praying mantis keeps right on thrusting at the female even though she has already bitten off his head" (*ES* 90). According to Elgin, patriarchal culture and any system based on exclusive opposites resist by definition change and evolution. The BASIC computer command of the last epigraph of *Native Tongue*—"1Ø REM HERE WE GO AGAIN / 2Ø GOTO 10" (*NT* 301)—captures this infinite self-perpetuation of coming round full circle without having changed. The final static image of the computer whiz Lanky Pugh, who watches captive whales swimming "[r]ound and round and round, in a lovely endless loop" (*NT* 301), epitomizes this infinite self-perpetuation. A (female) bird who sings "'*A-F-Of-L!*'" (*ES* 171)—recognizably an abbreviation for "A Female of the Lines"—announces the human advocates for change that I will focus on next. Simultaneously, the bird's song also signals in an ironic prolepsis the inevitable downfall of patriarchy. The Vice President, however, fails to decipher the meaning of the song, although he nonetheless recognizes the song as that of a male bird and associates the song with the sound of "water going down a drain" (*ES* 171).

3.4. Utopian Glimpses: Decolonizing Space and Mind

3.4.1. XJH$_i$ Reports: The Alien Bird's Eye Perspective

Moving between the alien "bird's eye perspective" from outer space and the women's perspective from within the system, we get a dual critical view of dystopia. Both *others*, Aliens and women linguists as their Terran counterparts, move with their utopian projects from the deconstruction, i.e., the reversion, of binary oppositions to a transgression of binarisms. Both movements employ the "double gesture" that Derrida considers fundamental for deconstruction:

> Deconstruction cannot be restricted or immediately pass to neutralization: it must, through a double gesture ... put into practice a *reversal* of the classical opposition *and* a general *displacement* of the system. It is on that condition alone that deconstruction will provide the means of *intervening* in the field of oppositions it criticizes.... Deconstruction does not consist in moving from one concept to another, but in reversing and displacing a conceptual order... [1977, 195].

By inverting the stereotypical colonial relations between male human as subject and Alien as object in sf and by reversing the Earth/center and universe/periphery relation, Elgin deconstructs and displaces the colonial and hierarchical human order. From the perspective of the alien *other*, Earth is by no means central to the universe. Unlike in most sf stories, *humans* must therefore learn alien languages. Contrary to xenophobic invasion scenarios of classical sf, these Aliens have neither an interest in colonizing Earth and its inhabitants, nor do they fit the stereotypical sf concept of the Alien as the enemy. Human concepts of usurpation, subjugation, and exploitation—all based on dichotomization and power relations—do not apply to the Alien Consortium that implicitly relies on non-violent interaction between different but equal humanoid and non-humanoid cultures and species. For Elgin, technological and psychological progress are interrelated: "any ET [extra-terrestrial] culture sufficiently ahead of humankind technologically ... would also be sufficiently ahead ... spiritually to be nonviolent" (Mohr 2000c, 25). Respecting the difference of Earth, the Alien Consortium allows Terrans space; it gives or shares planets and alien technology with both Terran power blocks in the hope that Terrans will thus unlearn the repetitive irrelevance of possession and expansion and will learn instead the principles of non-violence, non-possessive sharing, integrative communality, and non-hierarchical empowerment.

Conflating the generic with the content level and reality with fiction, Elgin ridicules and deconstructs the colonial discourse of sf as imperialistic fictionalizations about space grounded in mostly male behavior that is projected onto the alien *other*. Sf stories' true nature as constructs is exposed, when the quarantined Terrans cannot even fall back on fiction, since sf writers have not even *imagined* the possibility of being abandoned by Aliens: "Plenty of ancient stories about the *arrivals* of alien beings, but none where they settle in for generations and then leave without a word" (*ES* 38). The "past" referred to in the quoted passage below may refer to the fictional past of the narrative, but it may also refer to the literary discourse of sf that inscribe colonial attitudes into fictional space:

> All the years in the past spent dreading the marauders from outer space, the monsters that would subjugate Terra and make her peoples their slaves! It *was* funny. Because the Aliens, no matter which part of the Interstellar Consortium they had been sent from in their mysterious rotation of duty, had no more interest in taking over Earth and its colonies than the United States government would have had in subjugating an Appalachian pig farm and persimmon grove. Earth was a reservation planet, a place where dear little primitives lived in quaint but deplorable squalor. Earth was not to subjugate; Earth was to *help*. To the very limited extent that Terrans could be trusted not to hurt themselves or others with the Alien knowledge and the Alien gadgets [*JR* 41].

Reflecting the self-centered male position on the narrative level, the interrelation between Terrans and Aliens is mostly described from the male human point of view, although Book Two gives twice the alien perspective. These episodes are unspectacular and conventional rather than linguistically or narratively innovative. We are only given a classification of alien languages, and we gain little insight into alien life or social customs, although the Alien *Consortium* may be intended as a reminder of peaceful cooperation and of cultural multiplicity. Gender equality *is* an option for the females of "a large number of extraterrestrial cultures," who have an "equal or roughly equal status" (*NT* 180).

The problems cultural interaction creates if one culture disrespects the laws and norms of another culture is the topic of intergalactic negotiations between humans and Jeelods in *Native Tongue*. For Jeelods, the color blue is taboo, a cultural specific that Terrans have been unaware of, when they shipped goods in blue containers. The Jeelods penalize the government representatives with absence rituals and, well aware of Terran customs, retaliate by sending a *female* negotiating team. In its ethnocentric hubris, the Terran government obstinately extends the Terran law that denies females legal rights automatically to *all* female species, and hence nearly triggers a diplomatic planetary crisis.

The only direct encounter between an Alien and a human, narrated by an Alien in Chapter 21, describes notably a brief encounter of females, who transgress the human/Alien divide. Observation and the gathering of data are the tasks of the anonymous, non-humanoid female agent to whom it is "categorically forbidden ... to cause distress to any Terran" (*JR* 277), or to intervene in any way. Yet the now grown-up Selena, who was subjected to neurological brain alterations and who was exposed to non-humanoid Aliens in the government project, perceives the agent. The governmental experiment disabled Selena's language acquisition, but also enhanced an additional, unspecified sensory system normally degenerated in humans. Thus transgressing the borderline between human/non-human, Selena has turned into a human with the initial "mind" or "perception set" of a non-humanoid Alien.

The epilogue of *The Judas Rose* contains the second alien narration, in which a not discernibly specified humanoid or non-humanoid Alien of possibly plural identity with the cryptic name "XJH$_i$," (*JR* 363)[44] reports to the Alien Consortium. We are told that the Consortium, dedicated to non-violent ethics, has only intervened, because formerly irrelevant and peripheral Earth verges on the brink "of moving [violence] into space" (*JR* 357). Devoid of paternalism, and instead of monopo-

---

[44]*I read this letter-glyph as "ex jay age (subscript) eye/I," which in turn translates into "I see this from the bird's eye perspective," or even "from another time (age)."*

lizing their technologies, the Aliens have *shared* "FTL travel ... miraculous medicines ... [and] anti-gravity techniques" (*JR* 44). With the "carefully orchestrated introduction of technological advances in the *guise* of 'interplanetary trade'" (*JR* 359; emphasis added) the Aliens mask their superiority, and thus allow Terrans the illusion of being equal trade partners. Far from domination, the Aliens wish to integrate humans in their difference and on equal terms into the Consortium. In fact, the intergalactical trade becomes a farcical game of indulgence: "You asked; they [the Aliens] asked you why; you told them; they thought a minute or two; much of the time they said 'Yes, of course....' [If they refused it] was something that children could not be allowed to play with, so sorry" (*JR* 44). Moreover, the Aliens carefully avoid anything that might disrupt the fragile balance of powers on Earth and on the respective space colonies. To this end, the Aliens prevent a monopoly of resources and know-how; the eternal geopolitical U.S.-American "race against the Soviet Union for the staking out of this galaxy and ... all galaxies beyond" (*JR* 23) always ends in a draw. The Alien Consortium maintains "absolute neutrality toward Earth politics," so that "neither East nor West ever gained any scrap of knowledge that was not immediately transmitted to the other side" (*JR* 43).[45]

From the Alien perspective, Earth and its space colonies are "*plague* worlds ... filthied by a disease" (*ES* 51) called "intransigent *violence*" (*ES* 50) with which mainly male Terrans are infected, whereas the majority of women have passed this violence-driven stage of evolution, because Láadan immunizes them like a charm against "the state of violence" and provides them "with the patience necessary to bring the men *out* of those endless loops of violence" (*JR* 355). Presumably, Láadan resonates also among men: "a small but significant percentage of males ... had become aware that it [violence] was undesirable and were going beyond it" (*JR* 357). Gender difference consists then of an "evolutionary lead of females" and a "lack of developmental synchrony" (*JR* 358). However, XJH_i reports to the Consortium that the limited trade has merely exacerbated violence and has retarded (male) evolution; the trade has made the "endless expansion of that violence not only possible but *easy*" (*JR* 360)—culminating in a "threat to the indigenous species of the colony world" (*JR* 360)—and has "*widened* the gulf between the genders" (*JR* 361). The agent pinpoints the ethical dilemma the Consortium faces if

---

[45] *The Aliens' behavior reads almost like a homage to Le Guin's* The Dispossessed, *where the theoretical physicist Shevek undermines all plans of competing nations and planets to buy the monopoly on his "Theory of Simultaneity" by sharing it as a gift with everyone: "I want to give this ... to you all! So that one of you cannot use it ... to get power over the others, to get richer or to win more wars. So that you cannot use the truth for your private profit, but only for the common good" (277).*

it wants to stop Earth from spreading violence. Separatism would be "an open totalitarian act" (*JR* 361), and it would allow violence to continue on Earth; the annihilation of Earth or the genocide of its population would infringe the Alien Consortium's policy of non-violence, yet such an act would effectively stop the violence on Earth.

Hope for Earth might be found among female linguists who, according to XJH$_1$, "understand the mechanisms of change" (*JR* 362). Elgin's central argument is that change cannot be instigated from outside or above (Aliens), but must develop from those within (women linguists), from the oppressed who are willing "to step outside what you're doing and look at it *from* outside, even while you are most deeply occupied with it" (*ES* 47), as Delina explains the excruciatingly necessary step of transgressing the inside/outside borderline. Change cannot be forced upon others, but has to be learned from the earliest phase of childhood on. To judge the other by alien standards, that is to apply a concept of sameness, is considered absurd, because in the inversion *Terran* "psychology is so alien to us that we have no foundation on which to *build* understanding" (*JR* 362). The closer the physical and mental resemblance to the dominant human model, however, the more likely "the same idiot taboos turned up in so many humanoids from all over the universe" (*NT* 23). To turn the argument on its head, humans must then become more alien to transgress these taboos. Only by isolating Terrans can humans be pushed toward "find[ing] their *own* way to harmony or to annihilation" (*JR* 361; my emphasis). As the title *Earthsong* indicates, Earth does find harmony virtually by singing (Audiosynthesis).

3.4.2. The Nazareth Principle: Female Transgressions

The Terran constellation of a misogynist colonial center (men) that patronizes and exploits the colonized periphery (women) and that women begin to undermine mirrors the inverted Alien/male relationship. Relegated to the margins, the very separate all-female communities further the development of utopian projects. Out of their hybrid existence, living in their own female system within a male system and being in contact with the cultural/racial alien other, the women linguists develop their two transgressive utopian projects to free the mind (Láadan) and the body (Audiosynthesis). Moreover, they challenge the patriarchal power base of language *and* of society by restructuring linguistic and social frameworks through Láadan and Audiosynthesis. Unlike the male colonizing drive, their expansion into geographical space deterritorializes space to bridge the chasms of isolation between women of all classes; additionally, they reclaim the female body and develop Audiosynthesis to eliminate violence. Verbal decolonization as a process of personal and cultural transformation presupposes first the identification with and then the dissociation from a violent colonial discourse and its replacement by a counter-discourse. From their privileged and exposed position of being at the center of language production and formation, the women linguists perceive the inconsistencies of languages that represent chunks of reality. With Láadan they articulate those rhetorical spaces yet unmapped and the unspoken gaps of dominant discourse. With the creation and occupation of a liberating mental space beyond dualisms—hence opening up a third space between the present they live in and the future they anticipate—the view of the dominant male group is challenged and slowly altered. Far from a mere role reversal such as positioning themselves at the center, they aim at the dispersal of the masculine monopoly on power in that they eradicate mental and bodily power structures and wish to empower first women and eventually men *in their differences*. Hoping for resonance, the women of the Lines intend at long last to effect society's transformation.[46]

3.4.2.1. Let the Body S(w)ing: Audiosynthesis

The linear law of causality that Thelma Shinn notes in the series— "Communication is the key to community" (213)—grasps only part of Elgin's utopian notion, which is one of an intricate interconnection and mutual dependence between space and community, between communality and communication. Rather, Elgin's concept of Láadan corresponds with what Sargisson notes about feminist utopias in general: "new and inventive languages can best be imagined and employed in a new space" (41). The separate geographical spaces of Barren and Women Houses, Convents, and the quarters of the Meandering Water Tribe, allow women linguists, nuns, and tribal members to form temporary communities and communication of their own. Men forcefully establish the female community of the Barren Houses because they presuppose that inferior "barren" women are jealous of superior reproductive women. With cruel sarcasm Thomas Chornyak acrimoniously downplays the significance of labeling a lack: "women who *are* barren no longer make any connection between their condition and the name. It's just a name" (*NT* 121). How successfully women altered by Láadan instigate

---

[46]Obviously referring to Earthsong, *Elgin's statement indicates her interest in changing first one's self, and then wait for a resonating echo: "My primary concern [at the time of the interview] is with the concept of resonance, as it applies in physics, in music, in psychology, in linguistics, in theology, in medicine. The next novel I do will be overtly about resonance" (DuPont 67)*.

change is demonstrated at the end of *Native Tongue*, when the men willingly build Women Houses, a separate space the women desired and thus indirectly designed. Similarly, the convents of the Catholic Church also offer temporary separate female communities initially created by men. Deviant women, however, seek *by choice* refuge in convents as "a compromise of sorts," as an alternative to "a life of unrelenting silliness" (*JR* 245) and catering to males.

At times removed from male control, but without being isolated in spatially and thus communicatively disconnected households like the individual non-linguist woman, this communal bond enables the women linguists to develop Láadan and Audiosynthesis. Banned to dystopian islands of isolation as a gender and class group, the women linguists reorganize these into utopian islands of integration and enclaves of decolonization. The insulting name "Barren House," associating lack and a vacuum, now becomes a privilege synonymous with "Paradise on Earth House" (*JR* 119). Shared knitting and embroidery symbolize the secret networking, the invisible web of Barren and Women Houses in *Native Tongue*, infiltrating the convents in *The Judas Rose* and including Native Americans in *Earthsong*. The harmless and socially accepted circle of women doing women's work is the deceptive camouflage for their subversive scheming. Using the domestic as camouflage, Láadan is passed from Household to Household in recipe collections. Similarly, the double-voiced discourse of Langlish that affirms patriarchal linguistic structures deflects attention from Láadan.

While men live in seclusion and erect architectural borders between outside and inside, between linguists and non-linguists, between women and men, space is not used to isolate but to integrate in the Barren and Women Houses: "twenty-three women in twenty-three narrow beds, all in one big room with twelve beds down each side in rows that *faced* each other" (*NT* 204; emphasis added).[47] In contrast to the windowless claustrophobic rooms in the Households that rob the inhabitants of any vision and any sense of connection with the world beyond the walls, these rooms have "high windows along both sides, so that ... every woman [has] a view of the Virginia woodlands outside.... If the room had been cut up into cubicles, only a few of them could have watched ... the trees" (*NT*

---

[47]*Similarly, the women literally prefer to* face *a difficult situation, while men avoid actual interpersonal confrontations and prefer computer communication technology to put* space *between themselves and the adversary. Clara and Michaela stop Thomas from sending Nazareth the message that she is to be divorced from her husband Aaron by wrist computer "without even a human face attached" (NT 237). Instead, they break the news to Nazareth, just as Clara takes it on to inform Nazareth about the breast laser surgery. The male linguists use* face-to-face *communication when they want to make the best use of deceptive body-parl, which is less effective if transmitted via comset.*

204). Everyone is literally given an equal share of the view without privileging anyone, and symbolically all women thus share and participate in the same utopian vision.

Appalled by the crowding and apparent lack of privacy, Michaela learns that "[i]t was our own choice.... The men, now they had every intention of putting 'private rooms' on this floor.... We wanted none of that" (*NT* 205). Although they live in a close-knit community, communality is not enforced. Anyone tired of company can retreat to the privacy of a separate bedroom. Elgin suggests that to transgress the individual/community dualism it is necessary to reconcile the self with the community without suppressing individual needs. In place of the reader, Michaela gradually realizes that she judges from her own conditioning to value privacy. However, a potentially physically and mentally liberating private room of one's own can deprive the inhabitant of (female) community. Enforced privacy turns the room of one's own into a physical/mental prison of solitary confinement.

The women have designed rooms that embrace on the physical level the light and openness of the outside; metaphorically speaking, they have torn down the walls that men have put up between women, between inside and outside. Consequently, the women fear as much the loss of their "own space" and their community as they fear the discovery of Láadan, if the investigation upon the poisoning of Nazareth is carried out. A dispute between Aquina and the women of Chornyak Barren House further illustrates the architectural and spatial transgression of the individual/community opposition. By violating Nazareth's privacy (clandestinely Aquina reads her diary in search of precious Encodings) and poisoning the adolescent Nazareth to make her quickly barren, Aquina strikes against the only thing the women linguists *own*: their trust in privacy.[48] Moreover, Aquina hierarchizes the mental liberation of the community of women above the personal interest of Nazareth. Priebe (cf. 198) interprets this as a totalitarian move similar to the Ministry of Truth's silencing of Winston in *1984*, but she neglects that Aquina acts purposefully *against* the communal decision of the Barren House to respect the privacy and the individual rights of Nazareth.

For the women linguists, colonization simply transfers unsolved physical/mental problems into space: "it was as ridiculous to be expanding forever out into space as it had been to be all crowded together and stuck on Earth" (*JR* 146). Especially, since gender and class relations are

---

[48] *The woman linguist Susannah rebukes Aquina: "we have so little privacy! It's so precious. You can't violate Nazareth's privacy by sneaking her notebook" (*NT* 30). The other pillar of their lives is truth, women of the Lines do "not lie to one another" (*ES* 62); this is also reflected in the many speech act and evidence morphemes of Láadan.*

left unchanged in the space colonies. Confined into cubicles and tied to household chores and child care founding mothers cannot share the men's illusion of usurping new worlds: "Benia couldn't see that bright future, herself. She had this day to get through.... That was as far as her imagination could stretch" (*JR* 142). The women linguists and the nuns travel geographical space, concurrently expanding mind and body, without mapping and claiming territory. They deterritorialize and liberate space from patriarchal and colonial claims. They break up the perpetuated dualism of inside(r)/outside(r) from exactly these closed, feminine private spaces that they turn into loci of mental and bodily decolonization. Furthermore, they reach over the chasm of class isolation by teaching Láadan to non-linguist women in the Thursday Devotionals. In *Earthsong*, the women linguists even found their *own* order called "Our Blessed Lady Of The Star Tangle" (*ES* 102). In special music schools and in mobile space habitats, the field chapels, they popularize Audiosynthesis via songs; and they practice resonance medicine on Earth and on space colonies, moving from the enclosed feminine Terran cloister into the now "open territory" (*JR* 235) of masculine outer space.

The women linguists reject a retreat to a separate all-female society—"a colony of our own" (*NT* 268) as Aquina suggests—as counterproductive for a reconciliation between genders. Both separatism and matriarchy are *implausible* feminist utopias for Elgin, who defines "a *possible* feminist utopia" as "a society in which women no longer had to fear *human violence*" (1992, 43). She has stated elsewhere:

> Even if it were possible for women to upset the political, economic, religious, and bureaucratic foundations of this country and to take over the present position held by men, what would have been accomplished if the result were only an exchange of roles, with women as the abusing group? The point of liberating women ... must be to produce a better state of affairs, not a mirror image of the one now being objected to [1980, 286].

Aquina assumes that only an austere place devoid of any potential capitalist profit will escape the profiteering male gaze. This isolationist colony would have to be "far away and so lacking in anything worth money, that men would never be interested in taking it away from us" (*NT* 268).[49] In *The Judas Rose*, a satellite scanner detects such an all-female colony on a barren planet in the wilderness sector, where women killed men, choosing a rough but free life rather than slavery in luxury. Not com-

---

[49]*Le Guin describes such a place in* The Dispossessed. *Anarchists from the patriarchal planet Urras, modeled on Earth, can retreat only to the bleak moon Anarres, because there is nothing Urras could possibly want to possess on Anarres.*

prehending the immense despair that led to this choice, Heykus Clete condemns—"Satan was eleven souls richer" (*JR* 88)—and dismisses them as childish and illogical madwomen: "Free to starve. Free to die of exposure. Free to choke on foul air. Free to die of diseases no doctor has seen in a century. Free to suffer unspeakably. They want to be *free*, to do all those things" (*JR* 90).

Picking up the academic discussion of the 1990s, Elgin focuses on the body in *Earthsong*, because Láadan does not sufficiently advocate the necessity of non-violence. If Cartesian dualism is to be transgressed, reason alone can no longer subdue the potential violence of the body, yet Audiosynthesis dispels the very *need* for bodily violence. Unlike the fundamentalist conceptualization of a mind that controls the body, Audiosynthesis transgresses the spirit/matter dualism and calls for a holistic approach to nature, the world, and every living being. This notion of the mind as part of the body, of humans as part of nature, of both working not in opposition but together, of neither functioning without the other, describes a philosophy that corresponds with Susan Griffin's view that "[t]he mind is made up of tissue and blood, of cells and atoms, and possesses all the knowledge of the cell, all the balance of the atom" (qtd. in Sargisson 138). Charlene Spretnak likewise includes the spiritual as part of material life and arrives at the formula "the spirit works in the mind works in the body": "spirituality is an intrinsic dimension of human consciousness and is not separate from the body" (ibid. 138). Elgin achieves such a utopian linking of body, mind, and spirit by connecting Láadan to Audiosynthesis and by the distribution of both via religion.

The women start several projects to decolonize the body and to transgress the body/mind dualism. Among these, Audiosynthesis is the most prominent project, but medicine, reproduction, and childbirth are also issues where women regain control over their bodies and strive to remove violence. The impersonal technology and mechanization of medicine, irrespective of the human and dissociating body from mind, is replaced by "the nonverbal communication of live hands" (*JR* 118). Reassuring physical and psychological bonds, women constantly touch one another and use terms of endearment such as "dearloves," whereas men keep an emotional and bodily distance and insist on titles of respect such as "Sir" instead of the informal "Dad" that stresses family bonds. Additionally, nuns and women linguists administer resonance medicine. Although Elgin[50] claims that no fusing of body and mind takes place I disagree; the healer focuses her mind on her own healthy body and fuses both into holistic energy, which then resonates in the body and mind of the sick. For example, Sister Cecily's inability to cure a man from can-

---

[50]*Personal communication.*

cer of the stomach illustrates this fusion and exemplifies the inherent danger of neglecting the difference of the other. When she treats his abdomen according to the anatomy of the female body the imposed sameness cannot trigger resonance.

Various instances illustrate how women strive to repossess their deeply marked and violated bodies and minds. Women of the Lines celebrate the first menstruation of a girl instead of hiding it away as "mark of shame" (*JR* 33) as patriarchy and the Church stigmatize it. Elgin also deconstructs the threefold curse women have to suffer because of "woman's original sin": accursed if barren, upon conception, and by the agony of childbirth in fulfillment of God's curse. The biologically unproductive women of the Barren Houses metaphorically give birth to Láadan, and they are the midwives of Audiosynthesis. Robbing men of their control of progeny, the linguist Belle-Anne takes back her body "by the force of her own will kill[ing] the lustiest little wiggler of a sperm," or induces a "spontaneous abortion" (*NT* 127). This sabotage of enforced motherhood and her refusal of the "naturally nurturing and doting mother" myth brands her an unnatural woman within the dystopian paradigm. Demystifying the third Judaeo-Christian dogma, Aquina, the great-granddaughter of Aquina-the-rebel, ascertains that there is "nothing to scream about.... Such silly ignorant superstition" (*JR* 35). Horrified that Aquina does not agonize in her labor and remains silent, the devout nuns literally translate the phallogocentric word of the Bible— "a woman must bring forth her children in sorrow, that she might be cleansed of the guilt of tempting Adam and causing the Fall of all humankind" (*JR* 31)—into physical violence and clamp her legs tightly until Aquina screams. Contentedly misinterpreting this cry of pain as acknowledgement of original sin, the nuns then allow her to give birth. The far more interesting but neglected issue of sexuality and the question just how a sexuality free of violence and domination could be lived in a transgressive utopia remain a matter of speculation. Presumably, the new perception of women's reality expressed in Láadan will change sexuality and the perception of female sexuality, and both will radically improve in a non-violent society no longer set on the eradication of (female) bodies and on desire driven by violence.

In the first two books, numerous scenes describe the various shades of bodily and verbal violence. Yet the paradoxical and fallacious belief that violence can be eliminated by violence or legitimized and legalized with euphemisms such as defense or punishment—obviously a comment on the legal system of and the death penalty in the U.S. as a repressive system breeding violence—is drastically elucidated in the "Judge Story," one of the soaps contained in *Earthsong*. A Judge induces fierce pain to convicts, after he has paralyzed the vocal tract to ensure that the bodily pain cannot be verbalized and must be contained within. But this philosophy of pain—"when you truly know how it feels to suffer the kind of pain you inflict on others, you *will not do* it. Not ever again." (*ES* 192)—does not turn a violent man into "a *different* man" (*ES* 193).[51] The futility of forcing a change of paradigm from outside is aptly captured in the final image of the disillusioned judge, who turns away in disgust and despair from a second offender once again strapped to the torture table, and commits suicide in the vaporizer.

After Earth has been quarantined by the Aliens and struck by the Icehouse Effect, food is scarce and the hunger of the body becomes the most pressing problem, especially for those at the end of the food chain: women, children, and the lower classes.[52] Instructed by the spirit of Nazareth to find a way to end hunger, Delina researches the mechanisms of food and hunger, looking for a "universal food that every culture would turn to willingly ... available everywhere at little cost" (*ES* 55), but finds that often new low-cost food has been rejected by a starving population, "because in the context of their culture it was repulsive" (*ES* 53). The mind, religion, and ideology, seem to govern the body. Realizing that the capitalist system of accumulation will not solve starvation, Delina remembers 'Chomphosy's Law': "Don't learn ways to get more of what you want; learn not to *want* it" (*ES* 56). The inversion, how to decrease the need for food and still sustain the body, leads her to the history of religious groups who thrive on chants to supplement their meager diets. She dismisses the ideological or religious content and develops Audiosynthesis—a "nourishment from waves of *sound*" (*ES* 58) similar to the photosynthesis of plants—that is based on the resonance principle. Radical change and the onset of evolution towards an ethics of nonviolence are the consequences: "But human beings who have never eaten mouthfood ... who have *never* had to say.... 'This substance in my mouth was once a living creature like me, until it was caught and killed and cooked for me to eat' ... won't just be the *same* creatures eating a different diet" (*ES* 88–89). Audiosynthesis undercuts the necessity for violence at the basic root, the very "*definition* of being human" (*ES* 88), and makes change unpredictable: "People who've never known mouthfood ... what will they be *like*?" (*ES* 85). Presumably, with Audiosynthesis making

---

[51]*The factual gender specifics of violence, i.e., women's lower propensity to violence, is reflected in the succinct parentheses that the Judge never "found a prisoner there [on the torture table] who was a woman"* (ES 194).

[52]*However, Elgin also posits women as the natural survivors, capable to adapt more easily to this changed environment because of the otherwise denounced larger amount of fat cells in the female body. Again, Elgin includes a negation of a single-sex society: women take on great sacrifices to save the men from extinction and the surviving men understand the environmental catastrophe as a global "warning to be kinder to the women"* (ES 180).

physical violence obsolete, humans will evolve towards alien ethics of non-violence. In the utopian future, humans will be less recognizably human; the incorporation of this alien element into the human definition might very well transgress or even dissolve the opposition human/Alien. To prevent early discovery, Audiosynthesis is taught secretly and computer statistics on planetary food supplies are falsified to cover the decreasing need for food. Once Audiosynthesis is sufficiently spread, men cannot "stop evolution by force" (*ES* 219).[53]

The repercussions of Audiosynthesis on human society are far-reaching. It "destabilize[s] the inhabited universe" (*ES* 175) and eradicates the profit-oriented economy based on an ever-increasing spiral of supply and demand. Audiosynthesis is not subject to profit or to economic laws and thus affects (in)directly every segment of economy. Anthropologically speaking, Audiosynthesis ends the ceaseless fight for food and its distribution, because it is available to everybody for free and on demand. Audiosynthesis describes the "end of *this* world.... All of human life from the beginning of time, all of culture, all of economics, everything, has revolved around the need for food. Take that away ... you don't have human life any longer" (*ES* 216). If the fight for food ceases, the social strata of a class system based on exclusivity and power of possession is also abolished, as the advantages of the rich and powerful class are "to a substantial degree *cancelled*" (*ES* 223). In fact, the women practice what Cixous has called the libidinal economy, to give without the desire to appropriate a return gift. The men cannot grasp this concept of altruism: "a conspiracy that size, to do good" (*ES* 213). Their androcentric and patriarchal paradigms are based on hierarchy, possession, and exclusivity, and do not include a concept of benevolent sharing and selflessness:

> all of human society, all of human culture, rests on the knowledge ... that human beings are only capable of really buckling down and working together in groups when their goals are *evil*. They'll do it for money or power or conquest ... they'll do it to be famous.... But a conspiracy to *feed everybody* [*ES* 214]?

The members of the UNE can only recognize the "*ultimate power*" (*ES* 215) Audiosynthesis would offer if owned, and conclude that it must have originated from a "*man* ... driven only by an all-consuming lust for *power*—running that pack of females" (*ES* 228). The reaction of agent Jay Zlerigau mirrors the resistance to change paradigms and the totality

---

[53] *The saved food money is invested in social projects such as "meals for people in famine areas," in "supplies of vaccines and medicines" (ES 217), and in the acquisition and closing down of armaments factories.*

of displacement: "I would have sworn that I was *not* somebody who wanted to see babies starving.... I thought I was a decent man ... if fixing it so babies don't starve means my life has to be changed into something I don't recognize, I'm willing to let them starve. I'm *eager*" (*ES* 218-219). The holding on to the status quo animalizes men as in the image of the head of the United Asian Alliance whose hands curl "like claws" (*ES* 227). To deflect pangs of guilt and to demonstrate power, the UNE hypocritically condemns the women as "Unspeakably filthy Judases. Betrayers of all humankind" (*ES* 232-233) and debates retroactive punishment for the "willful withholding of information critical to the survival of the human race" (*ES* 236). As polarized absolutes are displaced and binarisms can no longer construct meaning, as fundamental dualisms dissolve and converge, men find it impossible to differentiate between "*good* and ... *evil*, because it all ran together" (*ES* 219).

3.4.2.2. Láadan: A Language of Our Own

With the first utopian project, the counter-discursive Láadan that prominently features in Books One and Two, Elgin *dis*covers the cultural structures and inscriptions that constitute racist, sexist, ethnocentric, and androcentric values in the seemingly natural structures of language. The problematic nexus of language, thought, and action has been at the center of speculation within the sf genre—after all, language immerses us into an unfamiliar fictive world—and it has a long tradition within feminist theories and critical linguistics.[54] Beginning with the neologism "utopia," speculation in linguistics has been a key concept of utopia to express new liberatory concepts, phenomena, gadgets, realities, and places,[55] whereas dystopia, concerned with thought control and the total-

---

[54] *See, for example, Gunther Kress and Robert Hodge (1979), and for a discussion of the intersection of language and thought in terms of the categories race, sex, and class, see Bolinger (1980); Eschholz, Rosa and Clark (1982); and Boltz and Seyler (1982).*

[55] *Among those works that speculate about the construction of alien languages, about the power of language in politics and psycholinguistics, about artificial languages, and about future English, Orwell's "Newspeak" and Le Guin's "Pravic" are probably the most well-known examples. Increasingly, women writers have explored gender-specific elements of language, for instance, Wittig in her experimental* Les Guérillères, *or Slonczewski in* A Door into Ocean *and the sequels. Scrutinizing the bias of language Piercy changes in* Woman on the Edge of Time *the gender specific pronouns "he/she" to "per," derived from "person." Le Guin tries something similar in* The Left Hand of Darkness *by introducing gender-free neologisms such as "ammar," but she falls back into phallogocentrisms. Le Guin has defended the consistent use of the generic pronoun "he": "I call Gethenians [the fictional alien people] 'he,' because I utterly refuse to mangle English by inventing a pronoun for 'he/she.' 'He' is the generic pronoun, damn it, in English" (1979b, 168), a position she has been lambasted for and which she has revoked years later in an annotation to the same essay contained in the reprinted 1989 edition. For detailed analyses of language and sf, see*

itarian restriction of language, has used, as Sisk argues, "language as the primary weapon with which to resist oppression" (2). With regard to Elgin's work, Mary Kay Bray notes that it is a novelty "to combine a representation of female experiences in a male-dominated culture with linguistics as a central speculative concept" (49).

Yet the problem of questioning linguistics within a fictional linguistic construct is how to demonstrate this in the narrative structure. Originally thinking about improving English for the usage of women, Elgin moved toward the construction of an entirely new language, with the result that "Láadan is not English, but it features repair of what Elgin sees as defective in present-day English" (Bailey 234).[56] To reach a large audience otherwise excluded had she written the series in Láadan (cf. DuPont 60; Elgin 1987b, 178), and to popularize basic linguistic concepts (cf. Mohr 2000c, 19–20) such as language acquisition, translation, and the Sapir-Whorf hypothesis, Elgin has succumbed to known codes of reading and a mixed conventional *cum* postmodern form to get the content intelligibly across.

Both Armitt and Penny Florence have criticized this lack of experimental style and syntax, and Kristine J. Anderson has reproached Elgin for the lack of avant-garde style: "[a]lthough Elgin has invented a language, her novels are not written in it" (1992, 7).[57] Open to criticism are also, as Armitt has noted, the "political implications of syntactic structures ... [that] are not concreticised within the narrative form," while Elgin's "polarising of language as dialogue and language as literary medium oversimplifies ... the impact of feminist theories of the impor-

[continued] *Myra Edwards Barnes (1975), Walter E. Meyers (1980), Delaney (1977;1984), and Sisk (1997, esp. chap. 6, 107–136). M. Lynne Murphy (1992) provides a selective bibliography on Elgin and on woman-made language within the genre. Richard W. Bailey (1991) examines the cultural history of English, its colonial aspirations towards a world language, and gives a brief survey of the idealized view of imaginary English in utopian literature (chap. 8, 215–236), which has often envisioned that the different languages originated at the Biblical Tower of Babel—that Michaela aptly recalls as "Tower of Babble" (NT 215)—coalesce into one evolved language of linguistic excellence that everyone can understand. Furthermore, Bailey summarizes how words coined by utopian/sf authors—for example, astronaut, robot, and spaceship—have entered the real world (cf. 221).*

[56]*In her newsletter* The Lonesome Node *(1981), Elgin has proposed examples of additions to English: "acantophile A woman who repeatedly chooses to form relationships with persons who abuse or neglect her, despite apparent unhappiness each time (From Gr. 'acanthos,' 'thorn.')." "To granny To apply the wisdom and the experience of the elderly woman to any situation." "L-harmonics The theory whose basic hypothesis is that the purposeful language of women has, as organizing principle, a set of strategies for reducing communicative dissonance (failure of communication) to its minimum level." (n. pag.) Presumably Láadan is also based on L-harmonics.*

[57]*Florence, however, acknowledges the radical potential of Láadan and the difficulty of writing in it: "Elgin has only to bring her language-fiction together. Only!" (83). The characters, however, communicate in an unremarkable English (Panglish) of the 1980s with a few exceptions such as "perceive," which the women linguists prefer to verbs such as "see" and "look," because those verbs privilege sight.*

tance of language as a means to change" (135). Anderson in turn criticizes Elgin for separating "invented language from fiction [which] renders her basic premise somewhat suspect" (1992, 8).

In defense of Elgin, to actually sell the novels need to be readable. Upon the publishers' demand, only a few examples of Láadan (morphems, Encodings, passages of the King James Bible) had to suffice (cf. Mohr 2000c, 31) and, according to Cheris Kramarae, the publishers also declined to include the grammar or dictionary of Láadan (1987, 185). The lack of actual Láadan words, however, is somewhat consistent with the content; after all, Láadan is a *secret* and, therefore, less visible language within a patriarchal world. My aim, however, is to look from a feminist/postcolonial perspective at the transgressive utopian potential of Láadan rather than to discuss the (in)consistencies of the linguistics, which has been done elsewhere.[58]

Elgin's approach to the bias of language corresponds with what Julia Penelope has so aptly defined as a "patriarchal universe of discourse" and a "cultural model of reality" (36) or a "consensus reality" imposed by men that is accepted as an "accurate description" of reality, even if "its assumptions and predictions override contradictory evidence" (37). Language then does not describe all of reality; it distorts, limits, and predetermines our thoughts and, therefore, restricts our range of conceptual exploration. Unless we unlearn this static pre-cognition, we modify people and situations to meet our thought/reality model. Elgin is predominantly concerned with this "inadequacy of words, seeking communication that comes from inside, that is not fooled by sensual perceptions, communication that goes beyond the lies" (Shinn 221), a theme she explored in her earlier novels in terms of direct mental communication. Upon reading Douglas Hofstadter's *Gödel, Escher, Bach* the linguist realized that the closed system of human languages is essentially paradoxical:

> [P]erhaps for any *language* there are certain perceptions that it cannot express because they would result in its self-destruction ... you might hypothesize that the reason contemporary English does not express the perceptions of women is that ... it would cease to be English. It would become some other language; that is, it would self-destruct ... for any culture there are certain languages that it cannot use because they would result in its self-destruction ... the main-

---

[58]*The few scholarly articles on the first two books focus primarily on the application of the Sapir-Whorf hypothesis. See Booker's brief abstract (1994), Klarer (1993, esp. 98–104), Anderson especially for a thorough historical approach to the hypothesis (1992, 1991), Armitt (1991), Fitting (1989), Bray (1986), and Shinn (1985). Julia Penelope discusses Láadan from a lesbian perspective (1990, esp. 223–227); Priebe (1998) concentrates on communication and mass media in* Native Tongue.

stream culture of the United States could not use Láadan, or any other women's language, any language that did express the perceptions of women accurately, because that would result in the culture's self-destruction [Elgin 1987b, 177].[59]

Drawing on Gödel's theorem that is explicitly referred to in one chapter epigraph in *Native Tongue*, Priebe has argued that the women linguists develop Láadan to destroy the male cultural and thus the male communicative system,[60] while Booker—persistently missing the numerous references to spreading Láadan beyond class and gender boundaries to *all* humans—fears the reverse, namely that Láadan "by existing entirely outside the bounds of male language and of ... male power structures ... threatens to marginalize women even further" (144). Fitting levies a similar criticism against Books One and Two for what he reads as a retreat into a closed, separate all-female system instead of a rebellion against the status quo:

> [R]ather than providing a way of transforming the world, this new language will condition the women to their inferior and exploited state. Allowed [sic!] to live separately, even with their own language, they will still be little more than slaves. Reality will not be changed by this new language; it will become an instrument of self-deception, the bleeding off of the rebellious energies of a group of exploited women [1989, 159].

In the reading of Priebe, Booker, Fitting, and Aldiss (cf. Aldiss and Wingrove 550–551), Elgin simply aims at a reversal of reality or at separate societies. Elgin, however, has refuted these readings: "The social change I was focusing on ... was improvement in the status of women, with ... a corresponding improvement in the lot of humankind as a whole" (Mohr 2000c, 20). In the trilogy, she aligns women's use of language with dynamic growth, change, and life, whereas the phallogocentric discourse is equated with stasis, destruction, and death. She advocates less a totalitarian elimination of a masculine cultural system than a slow displacement of totalitarian masculine values by feminine values and an incorporation of feminine perception into masculine reality. The existing language is not altered; and, therefore, it will not self-destruct, as

---

[59]*This view coincides with the "muted group theory" that, as Cheris Kramerae argues, applies when "[t]he language of a particular culture does not serve all its speakers equally.... Women (and members of other subordinate groups) are not as free ... as men are to say what they wish ... because the words and the norms ... have been formulated by the dominant group, men" (1). After Láadan has not been embraced by women at large in reality, Elgin has drawn the conclusion that "the muted group theory does not hold for English-speaking women" (1994, 18).*

[60]*Cf.: "Láadan soll eine solche Sprache sein, die in die Zerstörung der von den Männern errichteten Kultur mündet" (Priebe 157).*

Gödel's theorem hypothesizes. Láadan does not replace and dominate all other languages and perceptions, but disrupts the status quo and *adds* to existing languages, eventually transforming the cultural values, and it will then "produce a radically different world" (Kramarae 1987, 185). Only shared multiple concepts and perceptions of reality make an equality that respects difference possible.

Furthermore, Booker criticizes that women remain without "political power" (144), but he overlooks the fact that the women linguists have no desire to share a masculine concept of power. Instead, they develop and share both utopian projects to destroy power relations in all segments of human life. Moreover, Elgin links the desire for change not with gender but with the powerless who know from experience that power at either end of the stick leads to violence and war. Elgin locates verbal and bodily violence as the shared cultural metaphor that affects men and women, but women more so. While we look back on a "long history of attempts to bring about change by force" (Elgin 1992, 45), non-violent and passive attempts by people such as Ghandi and Martin Luther King, or by legislation (e.g. civil rights laws and the Equal Rights Amendment), have been the exceptions. Yet both these approaches hypothesize that "social change comes first, and then the language changes to reflect the social change" (ibid. 45), whereas Elgin postulates the very opposite— "language is the most powerful mechanism available to human beings for bringing about social change" (Mohr 2000c, 20)—and suggests the boycott of all communication (videos, shows etc.) that perpetuates violence and the objectification of women (e.g., romance novels), and urges to be more attentive to language and language violence. What we really need, according to Elgin, is a new cultural metaphor and, she claims, "[t]he only tool available for metaphor insertion is LANGUAGE" (1992, 46).

Elgin supports the weak form of the Sapir-Whorf hypothesis—the linguistic relativity principle, formulated in the 1930s by the U.S.-American anthropological linguist Edward Sapir and his student Benjamin Lee Whorf[61]—"which means that language does become a mechanism

---

[61]*Sapir and Whorf never actually defined an exact formulation of the hypothesis. According to Sapir, language and thought influence one another—"language is ... a prepared road" (Sapir 15; cf. also 12–17)—while Whorf's more narrow approach claims that words determine the concepts conceived: "We dissect nature along lines laid down by our native language" (Whorf 213). Other linguists hold against the hypothesis that ideas are independent of language and rather shape language; Hudson reformulates Whorf: "We dissect the universe along lines laid down by nature and by our communicative and cognitive needs, rather than by our language" (105). And Hockett argues that human history proves a constant struggle against limitations of language: "Speech habits were revised to accommodate those [cultural] changes.... The causality is in all probability from 'philosophy of life' to language, rather than vice versa" (132–133). For further discussion of the hypothesis, see Brown (1958, 229–263), Carroll (1964, chap. 7), Slobin (1971); and for a historical grounding, see Penn (1972).*

3. Rewriting the Colonization of Space 131

for social change" (Elgin 1987b, 178).[62] In George W. Grace's words, the correlation between language, thought, and culture determines "reality construction ... [as] the primary function of human language" (139). The Sapir-Whorf hypothesis has been much debated, and its strong forms of linguistic determinism (language constitutes reality) and linguistic relativism (each language encodes concepts differently and constructs its own worldview) have been rejected in favor of the notion that language takes a considerable *role* in the construction of reality and the predisposition of a person's worldview.[63] Far from neutrality, the discourse of any language describes the *one* encoded vision of a particular social reality. The way patriarchal discourse categorizes cognition and its semantic mediation and vice versa, passing its subjective bias off as objective/scientific monolithic truth, intersects with Lyotard's concept of the *différend* and Derrida's *différance*. As I have outlined in Chapter 2, Lyotard argues that a speaker can be silenced, because the language both speakers use restricts what s/he perceives as *différend*, whereas Derrida locates *différance* contained in the very construction of language. By imposing their perceptions on language, the dominant speakers hence restrict any discourse. Láadan tackles this problem by adding the *différend* in terms of a new language discourse that addresses the previously lacking concepts and idioms, and by reconstructing language formation.

Elgin focuses on language as a linguistic filter of what we perceive of reality. As language organizes thought and speech, all verbal communication depends on our linguistic concepts and is limited by the available vocabulary and its contained cultural codes. In a sideswipe on the sf stock device of universal translating machines, the difficulties of mediation and translation between language systems is addressed by the intergalactic negotiations, where cultural codes and symbols easily clash, and by the failed communication with non-humanoid Aliens that presumably rely on different communicatory organs (e.g., sensory organs). Communication includes sign language, cultural signs, and body language, which are, Elgin insists, "at least as important as the dialogue" (DuPont 66), and if communication is the basic element in the formation of social

---

[62]*Priebe reproves Elgin for an inconsequent use of the Sapir-Whorf hypothesis because the women linguists develop their own language within a masculine system, while Oldspeak and Newspeak, for example, coexist in Orwell's* 1984, *thus allowing Winston "a rebellion of thoughts" (cf. 171n164). This argument is oversimplified as both systems coexist here too, and the multilingual women linguists partake simultaneously in the masculine and in the evolving feminine system.*

[63]*The Sapir-Whorf hypothesis without feminist implications is also applied in Jack Vance's* Languages of Pao *(1958) and in Delaney's* Babel-17 *(1966). In* 1984, *the control of language leads to thought control, an example of a combination of linguistic determinism and relativism. In* The Futurological Congress *(1974), Stanislaw Lem satirically extrapolates how linguistic inventions shape the future.*

systems as Niklas Luhmann claims (cf. also Priebe 11ff.), they all influence society and thus part of reality.

From a postcolonial perspective, the women linguists apply their own "aesthetics of liberation," to borrow Homi Bhabha's term (1994b), and they are the "primary advocates" (*JR* 160) of the Sapir-Whorf hypothesis that the male linguists criticize. The women linguists revert to the postcolonial practice of code-switching, and with Láadan (analogous to lower-case English) they challenge the privileged masculine standard discourse "Panglish" (analogous to upper-case English). In fact, the Sapir-Whorf hypothesis intersects with Bhabha's postcolonial understanding of language theories in that he claims that the process of communication involves a gap between what is said and what is heard. Panglish reflects the colonial discourse, but its use for translating alien perceptions leads to a replication process that renders the colonial authority "hybrid," and hence it "open[s] up spaces for the colonised to subvert the master-discourse" (Loomba 89). Bhabha claims that subversion and rebellion are the products of the colonists' failure to perpetuate their authority in its entirety, and suggests that only this gap allows subversion; a view that Benita Parry has criticized, because Bhabha's concept of the dominant language as a transformative tool of colonial encounters presents "The World according to The Word" (9).

Elgin, however, seeks not only the gaps within the master-discourse or simply turns the dominant language around, but grounds the women linguists' oppositional discourse in a *new* language supposedly free of the bias of dominant languages.[64] According to Elgin, precisely an inversion, the construction of a new language, will avoid the cultural codes embedded in standard discourse. Eventually, women too will experience the world according to words, *but in words created by women.*

Elgin takes the subversion one step further by showing a literal "voyage inside," respectively a voyage "out into the void" (*NT* 254). To bridge gender segregation boys and girls alike are taught Láadan (cf. *JR* 355), and hence for both sexes the perception of reality and of one another will change. This, of course, is the prerequisite for a rejection of violence, colonization, and imperial and sexually-biased attitudes. Here, as Mario Klarer notes (cf. 1993, 101–102), the primacy of language acquisition during subject formation converges with Lacanian psychoanalysis and its adaptation for feminism by Julia Kristeva. Lacan places language acquisition within the patriarchal realm of the Symbolic Order, the law

---

[64]*Feminists and linguists have extensively discussed the gender bias of the English language and the question whether women need to reform the existing language or ought to create a new one or a new context. For a good introduction to feminism and linguistics, see Spender (1980), Deborah Cameron (1985), Susan Ehrlich (1995); and from a lesbian angle, see Mary Daly and Jane Caputi (1987), and Penelope (1990).*

of the father, and categorizes the Imaginary Order as pre–Oedipal and ruled by the mother. In the Imaginary order, the infant experiences a dyadic unity with the mother; upon the entry into the Symbolic Order this changes into the Oedipal shock of difference and disparity. Replacing Lacan's Imaginary Order with "semiotic chora" (Greek for enclosed space or womb), Kristeva argues for a coexistence of the semiotic and the symbolic without abolishing the initial dualism of the mother/father realm and Klarer concludes that Láadan replaces the Symbolic Order of a patriarchal language and world. Yet, clearly, Elgin does take this a step further with the suggestion that these children will enter full subjectivity into a world speaking Láadan *and* multiple other languages, since words and concepts (Encodings) derived from the semiotic chora, which make up the content difference of Láadan, *add* to the Symbolic Order. This double-voiced language acquisition transgresses the polarities of Orders without abolishing them. Instead of losing the realm of the chora and entering the world as fragmented speaking subjects, the new language constructs new subjects supposedly moving fluidly between realms. Given the revision of the aforementioned theoretical standpoints of Lacan and Kristeva by the American feminists Sandra Gilbert and Susan Gubar, who have argued that "verbal signification arises ... from a confrontation with the lure and lore of the mother" (537) *before* the father breaks up the dyadic unity, Láadan might even be seen as an expression of the retrieved *materna lingua* existing alongside the *patrius sermon*.

Yet the pivotal question remains, where do oppositional ideas emanate from in this misogynist, patriarchal society? Elgin suggests three major components. First, linguistic socialization has trained the women of the Lines to probe (alien) languages for the very concepts they hold, and it has taught them to be sensitive to ideological traps codified by languages. Second, on a daily life-long basis they are confronted with *other*, alien cultural worldviews. After all, interpreting is a twofold process; on the one hand, it "necessitates a significant understanding of one culture's set of structural principles in order to reconstruct another's through language" (Armitt 131). On the other hand, it involves a fluctuation between one's own and the Alien's culture as well as a confrontation and questioning of cultural structures and modes in general. Thirdly, the women linguists live in large all-female communities. This separate physical and mental space allows female linguists to start a process of disengaging from internalized masculine thinking. As a result, they possess hybrid, dual consciousnesses and live hybridized lives, outwardly complying with the dominant language, but also speaking the language of resistance. They access what Cixous has called the "Realm of the Gift," the otherwise oppressed creative vision of alternatives (cf. Cixous and Clement 1986). Temporarily outside of phallogocentrism, they perceive the gaps and "lack" of the appropriating language of the masculine "Realm of the Proper" with its barked commands and a grammar based on patriarchal ideology. Because "the only mechanism available to women for explaining this situation [that language lacks women's expressions] ... was the very language that was inadequate" (Elgin 1987b, 177), the women linguists construct Láadan to escape this paradox and fill these very gaps.

Láadan is an artificial language, constructed to be easily pronounced and universally accessible for everyone,[65] in contrast to constructed languages that are defined as mostly restricted to private use or limited to a certain era (cf. L. Murphy 3).[66] On the other hand, Láadan shares the developmental characteristics of contact languages that eventually transmogrify from pidgin and creole into a native tongue (cf. *NT* 216–217, *NT* 266–267). Yet while pidgin takes phrases from and simplifies other languages, Láadan evolves with every new major or minor Encoding into a more differentiated language. Unlike real contact languages that have developed out of trading necessities, Láadan emerges from emotional and psychic necessity. In correlation to minoritized people of color, women perceive a discrepancy between language and reality, yet unlike colonial subjects, women never had a language of their own. As Nazareth notes, "women are not precisely a conquered people with an existing language ... but the analogy is close enough" (*NT* 217).

Láadan does not join the competition of languages, but as an auxiliary language it constructs new linguistic and psychological modes of expression; it stresses perceptual information and equalizes the relation between speaker and listener. Láadan refrains from pouring new wine into old bottles, i.e., merely changing the vocabulary by offering new meanings for old words or by coining new words. Elgin deconstructs language on the content as well as on the formal and the structural level. For Penelope, the most notable innovation of Láadan is that *"inner sensory information becomes as important as outwardly obvious material phenomena if we have the words to describe it"* (224). With a variety of required speech acts, repetition, evidence and state of consciousness morphemes, degree markers and suffixes that indicate the emotional quality and attitude towards what is said as well as the source of the information, Láadan as a consequential linguistic translation of feminist standpoint theory dethrones the privileged speaking subject. The sentence structure forces

---

[65]*To avoid dominance by pronunciation, Láadan is composed of eighteen sounds equally accessible to all speakers (cf. NT 160).*

[66]*A constructed language is purposefully created by one or more persons to either link speakers of different languages (e.g. the international Esperanto created by L.L. Zamenhof in 1897), or to express concepts previously unexpressed in that particular language (Gottfried Leibniz in the seventeenth century), or for fictional purposes (e.g., J.R.R. Tolkien's Middle Earth languages in* The Lord of the Rings*).*

the speaker to mark the reliability of all utterances and her/his subjective standpoint, purpose, and emotive state; hence it involves the listener on a more equal basis and draws feelings into the speech act. The very structure of Láadan transgresses the "subjective-objective divide between speaker and language, potentially a radical linguistic shift" (Florence 83).

Nevertheless, the given choice of morphemes might serve to disguise a standpoint. And although parts of the Láadan vocabulary mirror a more differentiated perception of femininity—Penelope lists, for example, eleven variations on the word love—it leaves conceptual patriarchal structures intact: "[t]here are words for Jesus of Nazareth [sic], penis, and testicle, but none for clitoris or Lesbian [sic]" (Penelope 227). This reproach has been met by Elgin, who claims that the "degree to which a language expresses the perceptions of women ... cannot be determined by looking at its vocabulary" (1998, 1). Although Elgin invites everyone to coin new Láadan words—since Elgin designed the actual Láadan by no means as a closed off and definite language—and Láadan thus remains open to further inventions (just as any language is subjected to a process of change by its speakers), it is puzzling that, for example, only the words for *female* sexual body parts and *all-female* sexual relations need invention. Last but not least, might not less benevolent native speakers of Láadan, who are also deeply immersed in the patriarchal universal discourse, potentially misuse and manipulate Láadan into yet another language of power?

The dominant stratum of reality expressed in language are lexicalized masculine concepts that blot out all other realities however diffusely sensed. Far from providing a blueprint of the world, language, in fact, "foregrounds those aspects of experience deemed significant by a culture and, simultaneously, backgrounds concepts for which it provides no labels" (Penelope 203). In effect, Láadan answers Luce Irigaray's question "How can women analyze their exploitation, inscribe their claims, within an order prescribed by the masculine?" (qtd. in Wiemer, 163). Láadan adds experiences and realities otherwise excluded and inexpressible *without* denying those realities already conceptualized in other languages. If there are no words to express specific conditions, situations, emotions, and perceptions, they will remain "in the realm of the invisible, the unreal" (Penelope 236).

The Encodings, previously unlexicalized concepts that materialize "out of nowhere" (*NT* 22), originate exactly in this non-verbal pre-conscious realm, and correspond with what Irigaray calls *le parler femme*, defined as spontaneous utterances resisting existing forms, figures, and concepts. By definition, Encodings give "a name for a chunk of the world that ... has never been chosen for naming before in any human language ... .[that] has never before impressed anyone as sufficiently important to *deserve* its own name" (*NT* 22). Major Encodings are "truly newborn to the universe of discourse," whereas minor Encodings add "related concepts" (*NT* 158). We get two examples of Encodings; one describes a certain behavior: "[t]o refrain from asking, with evil intentions; especially when it's clear that someone badly wants you to ask" (*NT* 29). Another (re)constructs a new body space:

> Now, there is a continuous surface of the body, a space that begins with the inside flesh of the fingers and continues over the palm of the hand and upon the inner side of the arm to the bend of the elbow ... I will name that the "athad" of the person.... Where there was no athad before, there will always be one now.... And I have made the athad appear ... now it *exists* [*NT* 242].

The Encodings are not only linguistically valuable but also in terms of female historiography. The memoriziation of the names of those "women of valor" who coined Encodings creates a consciousness of female history: "And Emily Jefferson Chornyak in her lifetime gave to us three Major Encodings and two Minor; and Marian Chornyak Shawnessey, that was sister to Fiona Chornyak Shawnessey, in her lifetime gave us one Major Encoding and nine Minor" (*NT* 159). In contradistinction to the written genealogy of the begats of the Biblical OT that inscribes tradition, this oral secular genealogy of mothers and sisters celebrates innovation.

As touched upon repeatedly, men use religion to cement traditions, whereas women use it as another locus of potential subversion. The hybridized Láadan version of the "monumentally male King James Bible" (*JR* 174) does draw on patriarchal Christian sources, but transforms these into feminized versions. Other "books of blasphemy," giving voice to formerly excluded female disciples, prophets, and visionaries, are "The Theology of Lovingkindness. The Discourse of the Three Marys. The Gospel of the Magdalene, that began: 'I am the Magdalene, hear me, I speak to you from out of time. This is the Gospel of women.'" (*NT* 124). A feminine revelation of the original content preached by Jesus of *Nazareth*, who mutates here into the female Jesus figure Nazareth Chornyak, deconstructs the masculinist exegesis and androcentric discourse of the Bible, especially of the OT. Like Jesus, Nazareth preaches non-violence—the peaceful distribution of the women linguists' knowledge—she patiently suffers humiliation, and in a way she is also resurrected when she speaks from the beyond as spirit-narrator, who even appears in her disciple's (Delina's) visions. Thus the women linguists' method of sharing and teaching knowledge follows what we aptly might call the "Nazareth Principle" of compassionately setting an example of a non-violent life, allowing others to perceive by themselves and by their own free will rather than compelling anyone. In Elgin's strong feminist rewriting of the NT's notion of empathy, non-violence, sharing, and love for the other, the women linguists act out these intrinsic teachings of Jesus to uncreate the world of a male god (cf. *NT* 198). Against a long history of male antagonism to female visionaries, women such as Nazareth and Delina have visions no matter what religious background they come from.[67] The fish as Christian iconogram of resistance, community, and renewal is replaced with the feminist sign of the circle, symbolized by the wild vine wreaths in the chapter headings of Book Two, and similarly, alluding to the Native American context, a corn wreath stands for Audiosynthesis in Book Three.[68] Two epigraphs (*JR* 331, *NT* 242) turn the masculine divine trinity of Father, Son, and Holy Ghost into the feminine trinity of the "Discourse of the Three Marys," author(s) unknown. This Discourse of the Three Marys allows three interpretations: it may have been written communally by three generations of women linguists all named Mary, yet it also implicates an ancient pagan worship of a triple goddess and earlier matriarchal social structures, and it alludes to all three of the Marys present at Jesus' crucifixion, the disregarded females of the patriarchal Bible. The stately and authoritative Biblical "I" of God and the "I" of Jesus, already distorted in the NT, are met with a colloquially talkative "I" in *Native Tongue* that is then replaced by the communal 'we' of the three Marys in *The Judas Rose*.

The only direct Biblical quote and its Láadan equivalent describes the fifth verse from the Twenty-Third Psalm: "Thou anointest my head with oil" As a symbol of special honor, a sign of zest for life and affluence, priests and prophets anointed with olive oil the king of Israel, other prophets and priests, and objects dedicated to God, for example, the holy stone of Bethel (cf. also 1. Sam. 10:1, 16:1, and 16:13).[69] Originally, the holy cultic deed elevated the anointed to the inviolable sacral representative of God—Messiah is Hebrew for "the Holy" or "the anointed"—and was later turned into a useful patriarchal gesture of profane secular power. Even in the patriarchal Bible, the Psalm of David—a royal prayer and song of trust—evokes a very different kind of image of God: not as

---

[67] *The deceased Nazareth's experience of being given the triple choice to "go on, go back or stay and help" (ES 7) disproves a primacy of either one of the manifold human religious speculations about afterlife.*

[68] *Disclaiming my interpretation, Elgin states that both wreaths symbolize resonance. Personal communication.*

[69] *In fact, Biblical parallels refer to women performing anointings. Maria, the sister of Lazarus, anoints the feet of Jesus (John 12:1); and a prostitute does the same out of gratitude because Jesus has forgiven her failings (Luke 7:37). By rehabilitating her in front of society, Jesus acknowledges the rightfulness of her deferential deed. Incidentally, the Psalm acquires also a very literal interpretation in Chapter 23, when Belle-Sharon anoints her head and body with lilac oil before she meets her husband Jared in the rendezvous room.*

a patriarchal, avenging God but as the Good Shepherd and kind host, who treats us like guests in his house, preservs our lives, and nourishs our souls. This is not a patriarchal but a benign god of loving kindness, who offers protection against enemies through the act of anointing.

In the Láadan translation, the fifth verse of the Twenty-Third Psalm reads "Thou braidest my hair with Thine own hands" (*JR* 210), and thus breaks down the fixation of gender roles and the colonial perspective.[70] Here, Elgin pictorially reinscribes a transgendered and transcultural divinity, where the patriarchal bible written by men disclaims feminine divinity.[71] Because the priests *have* made the divine into the image of a male god, the translation contains for them a blasphemous maternal and luscious image, a heretical "reference ... *perforce* to a goddess" because "the braiding of hair is not something that men *do* in our world" (*JR* 212). Sister Miriam beats the priests at their own game of exegesis, when she rebukes them that it is idolatry "to anthropomorphize God" and heresy to suggest that there is any "human act of which God is ignorant" (*JR* 212).

3.4.2.3. Collapsing the Boundaries of the Other

The principal representatives of the utopian process are not presented as a *perfect* utopian foil for "woman." Female characters such as Aquina, who supports "masculine" ways of aggressive action, contradict such a reading. In fact, as Michaela notes, the women linguists are "not perfect ... no saints—if they had been, it would have been easier, because they would have been so *other*" (*NT* 212). Michaela judges the linguists according to her internalized binary thinking, and rejects the linguist females at first on the grounds of class antagonism, but in the end she comes to transgress this class divide. There is no instant "sisterhood" on the basis of gender, as an essentialist and universalist position might represent it. Not biological essentials or sociological and anthropological universals are the basis of Michaela's transgression, but the recognition that despite some differences there is a likeness of shared experience of sociological and biological oppression.[72] Close interaction between lin-

---

[70]*In a different cultural or historical context, the braiding of hair is something men do and have done. Additionally, all references to God as male are rewritten in the Láadan bible; for example, the phrase "son of God" is replaced with the Láadan phrase for the "child of the Holy One"* (JR 240).

[71]*As a "radical pacifist Christian" (Mohr 2000c, 33) Elgin firmly rejects the idea of a patriarchal god or the implication of a male deity, "God has no gender," although the language the Bible is written in "forces the constant choice of sexual gender" (ibid. 33).*

[72]*Cf.:* "the [linguist] women were as controlled as any other women" (JR 28), "and except in their work they probably had less *freedom than other women"* (JR 29).

guist and non-linguist women makes the gradual collapse of prejudices possible. Like Jo-Beth, Michaela learns that the women linguists do not "fit the profile" of "repulsive characteristics she'd been brought up believing marked the woman linguist" (*NT* 212). Confronted with *experienced* reality, Michaela dismisses these stereotypes as invalid.

Life-long contact with Aliens teaches women linguists respect for physical, sociological/cultural, and psychological differences. For Elgin, interactionism (language is learned by communication) transports not only language acquisition (syntax, grammar, and vocabulary) but also the cultural values and worldviews contained in language. The Interface device is such a version of intense communicative interaction. Interfaced at the mirror stage, the infant perceives through the transparent barrier the Alien and merges or identifies with it *before* language acquisition even begins. One reason why interfaced male babies do not significantly alter their perceptions may be that this sense of "the self within the other" of the Imaginary is broken up, when they enter as members of the dominant group the patriarchal Symbolic Order and the patriarchal universe of discourse. Perhaps, because they view interpreting as a mechanical rather than a creative process, men repress at an early stage the otherwise involved sub- and unconscious. Because female infants can only take the place of subordinates in the patriarchal Symbolic Order, the repressed dyadic unity with the alien *other* of the Imaginary is more likely to resurface. With Láadan as the conscious expression of concepts derived from the Imaginary, women linguists do not need to eradicate or assimilate external and internal differences. For example, the two highly gifted linguists Nazareth and Delina are perceived as "*truly* interesting Alien[s]" (*NT* 26), but their *difference* is seen as enriching and valuable. Moreover, women as terrestrial *other* recognize the Aliens as extra-terrestrial *other*. Nazareth, for instance, eagerly appreciates the very difference of an AIRY: "The Alien was interesting.... She looked forward to knowing more about its culture and its language.... Three legs rather than two, and a face was more 'face?'" (*NT* 20). The very concept of Aliens as such becomes even a necessity, a beacon of hope: Delina feels frightened by the prospect of a "life alone in a universe of Terrans" (*ES* 62), because without Aliens there are only male Terrans.

In the first two books, only women propel the utopian movement; ethnicity as such remains a minor topic. This failure to make ethnicity explicit is a flaw that Elgin repairs in *Earthsong*. The marriage of the two peripheries of linguist women and of the men of the PICOTA suggests a transgression of ethnic and gender boundaries. Moreover, the PICOTA societies are less riven by extremes: women and men of the Native American societies live together, and their Tribal Councils are democratically organized. Anne Bluecrane, for instance, talks irreverently to her husband Chief Will Bluecrane; and they are on equal and good terms as her use of endearments such as "love" and "dear man" (*ES* 29) indicates.

In a central passage, Delina and Will establish differences and common ground without assimilating or attempting to possess the difference of the other. Both are cautious of a "false sense of equality and unity within and among the correlative subjects such as Native ... Woman, Man" (Emberley xiii). As "a master of resistance" (*ES* 18), Will recognizes the same quality in Delina, who lives "in resistance as fish live in water" (*ES* 15). She earns his respect with her patient sit-in outside the PICOTA domes, waiting for help with her vision quest. Both learn to demask cultural myths and constructs they have been conditioned to believe. Will is no medicine man mumbling "monosyllables and wise grunts and noble platitudes" (*ES* 28), nor is Delina a super-human linguist chameleon or witch who "can look any way" (*ES* 26) she desires. They come to acknowledge a familial human relationship beyond racial and biological boundaries, and eventually call each other daughter and grandfather *without* denying the cultural and ethnic differences of their "Anglo" and "Indian" (*ES* 21) heritage. On the grounds of shared biology, Delina invalidates Will's objection that Native American ceremonies are useless for a member of a different cultural background: "Anglos are human beings. They are just like you, and just like all your relatives" (*ES* 21). Along a similar line of argumentation, she also rejects his theological quibbles that "[Anglo] *souls* are very different from ours" (*ES* 22).

With the new community of women linguists and PICOTA men, a "marriage of the highest of technologies" (*ES* 43) takes place. Chief Bluecrane gives the hybrid Native American female linguists the honorary title "Meandering Water Tribe" for their method of non-linearity, fluidity, and soft obstinacy: "You go this way a while, and that way a while, and this way again, instead. And you go gently and quietly.... You meander, as water meanders, headed for the oceans ... and then you arrive" (*ES* 98). The meandering water, a feminine symbol of the psyche or the subconscious, represents the indestructibility, tenacity, and variety of life.

Furthermore, Delina's recurring dream of supposedly inferior "blue corn and red corn, black corn and purple corn, fields of short stubby corn growing implausibly in hills of plain dry sand" (*ES* 36) indicates a similarity between women and the PICOTA, inasmuch as the diverse ethnicities challenge the (mono)cultural domination of the white, male colonialists. In her dream, the colonialists are symbolized by "tall lush green and yellow Anglo corn" that grows only linear "in dark rich ground in long logical rows" (*ES* 36). In comparison, the native corn, symbol for the archaic and indomitable, grows randomly against all odds, whereas the corn of rational capitalism based on the sterility of sameness can only flourish under the best of conditions.

For the UNE meeting the women of the Lines "put together a delegation of five, one for each of the traditional colors of humankind" (*ES* 229).[73] In an ironic carnival of stereotypes, the delegation represents whites as "tall and imposing and gifted with presence" (*ES* 230), implying that other colors represent absence. A yellow woman personifies strategic overpopulation with a baby as "superb prop"; a black woman with a "compelling voice" demonstrates exceptional musicality; browns are defined by the body ("grace of bearing and her beauty") and a red female dresses up with beads, feathers, and bells like a "bird of plumage" (*ES* 230). The one reminder of the provisionality of all cultures is left out: the alien human of the space colonies, naturally turned green from adopting alien ways of life. This representation of the "races" in terms of "traditionalism" (*ES* 231) is meant to appease the UNE. At the same time, the women acknowledge ethnic difference and suggest that human evolution may eventually render racism obsolete, once that colonial stigmas no longer apply.

The relationship between animals and humans, formerly characterized by domination and abusive arbitrariness, also changes. Delina's quilt composed of "blocks of black and white sea-waves in the dolphin curve" (*ES* 30) foreshadows a transgression. The whales that rejected communication with humans in the Cetacean Project (a reminder of the factual interspecies communication experiment "Project Dolphin" of National Aeronautics and the Space Administration in 1962) communicate with the envoy of the PICOTA. Here, animal-human communication is not a matter of dominance; the whales are *asked* to contact the Alien Consortium. Gentle giants, Native Americans, women linguists, and Aliens—species, races, sexes and the *other*—are linked as a peaceful, holistic counter-force to the destructiveness of Western colonial men. According to Elgin, the interaction of cultures, species, and sexes and the renunciation of bodily and verbal violence indicates the level of human evolution.

Booker and Fitting assert that nothing much has changed at the end of Book Two, and Florence accedes that "it is difficult to gain a sense of what her 'third reality' might be" (82). All three critics neglect the small instances of change depicted. Transformations are introduced on an "eternal time" (*JR* 292) scale, so that even the vigilant and omnipotent Thomas Chornyak is blind towards them, although he searches for a

---

[73]Like an afterthought, this ethnic mix reminds us that all along the women linguists have been from different ethnic backgrounds, although the narration centers on the American/Eurocentric/Western view.

"small difference ... something that deviated from the familiar. The women had a tendency to accomplish change by altering things one infinitesimal fraction at a time, spread over months and months, so that you never saw it happening until suddenly it was just *there*" (*NT* 102). Láadan frees women from "tongue-binding," as Elgin puts it in an allusion to foot-binding, it releases them "from the constant tension and frustration that comes of not having words for things you want to say" (Wells n. pag.).[74] The women linguists are not simply "*the same women with a different language added on ... we were different*" (*ES* 88). True enough, there are no explicit descriptions of what exactly this difference is composed of, yet women increasingly live in a parallel reality, which eventually *meets* men's reality. Women, as men knew them and defined them in patriarchy, are extinct, as male linguists note: "you *know*, that their minds are a thousand miles away. They're not really looking at you—and not really listening" (*NT* 289). In this temporary perceptual reversal, women are like mirrors gone blank that no longer reflect the male ego, because "foreground and background in the male perceptual framework have shifted. Where women were once invisible to men, now men are invisible to women" (Bray 55). Several instances show how Láadan provides women with an alternative; it fills the lack of patriarchal discourse in times of mental and emotional distress. For example, Nazareth recites Encodings to ease her mind and body; Láadan soothes Jo-Beth and makes "the tension inside her melt away" (*JR* 123–124); and without the women's language to turn to Delina would be diagnosed neurotic: "*Borderline personality disorder. Hysteria*" (*ES* 68). In *Earthsong*, Elgin, however, revises her earlier universalist assumption that Láadan is a language for *all* women. The women linguists admit that the "Láadan project failed" (*ES* 74) because their own interest in Láadan, in languages as such, was not necessarily shared by *all* women to the *same* extent. Contrary to Elgin's earlier statements that "[l]anguage is the only source of real power" (1989, 5) and "the only real high technology" with linguistics being the "property of the elite" (1992, 45), the body turns out to be a more common denominator: "Hunger is a powerful motivator" (*ES* 75).[75]

Both utopian projects are taught and dispersed not as superior knowledge but are randomly learned, and thus follow the same resonance principle that the Aliens use. Men are to keep the illusion of appropriating Láadan and Audiosynthesis on their own: "*let them 'discover' it.... So they feel that it is their knowledge, gained by their efforts, and won by their*

---

[74]*Láadan means literally "the language of those who perceive" (Elgin 1994, 17).*
[75]*Book Two already connects mental and real food: "As if we had food ... and other women were starving all around us"* (JR 75).

skill at overcoming your puny attempts to prevent them" (*ES* 223–224). Even Thomas Chornyak is forced to acknowledge that everything is subjected to the flux of time because change is a necessity of life and part of reality. Infuriated, he orders "NO CHANGES not specifically initiated by males" (*NT* 102), only to recognize the absurdity when the women literally stop all gardening activities until the Chornyak property resembles a jungle. Ironically, this character, Thomas Chornyak, comes round full circle in the much milder version of his own great-grandson Thomas Chornyak at the end of *Earthsong*. This process of the "domestication" of patriarchs already takes place in the second book, when the surprising revelation dawns on Jonathan Asher Chornyak, the new head of all Lines and himself in comparison "a very mild alpha male indeed" (*JR* 350), that the linguists "had too many *Emperor types* in a row and it was time for a *correction* in the curve" (*JR* 110; emphasis added). As another example of how men change, the secret agent and half-cyborg Benedicte Mondorro is another representative of a changing or changed male attitude. Contrary to the logic of the patriarchal gaze, he feels drawn to the eyes and *face* of his wife, wanting "to hide in there *with* her" (*ES* 180), and prefers her eyes and hair—symbols of her psyche, the female gaze, and her sexuality—unchanged.

The trilogy avoids closure and does not depict utopia, but ends with the hopeful message that "the end of the plague of human violence had begun" (*ES* 243). There is no victory and no arrival at the ultimate truth but a desire for reconciliation. Elgin refrains from presenting us with a programmatic blueprint of how precisely this new world with new humans may look. Many feminist utopias and dystopias have centered on the distribution of power either as patriarchy (men in power), matriarchy (women in power), or androgyny (power independent of gender), whereas, according to Elgin, "Reality-O" "in which power is irrelevant" (1995, 46) has not been considered. Reality-O according to Láadan and Audiosynthesis, however, cannot possibly be predicted. The future, the very object of sf, cannot be known, because one can no longer extrapolate from past experiences as Nazareth rejoices:

> all our plans were based on the *old* reality. The one *before* the change.... We have pseudo-sciences, in which we extrapolate for a reality that would be nothing more than a minor variation on the one we have ... but the science of actual reality change has not yet been even proposed, much less formalized [*NT* 296].

What Sisk (cf. 116) sees as a narrative conflict—he asserts that the epilogue of Book Two (the possibility of Earth's self-destruction) contradicts the very existence of the prefaces—appears to me as the inevitably evasive answer of an open narrative that resists the very closure Sisk apparently desires. To some extent the prefaces, however, provide what the end refuses to tell. From the prefaces we can conclude that in the distant future gender inequality is solved and Láadan is widely available. A fictive *female* editor, the "Láadan Group," and "WOMANTALK Earth section" sign the prefaces, indicating that the cultural isolation of Earth has been removed. Presumably, Terrans have overcome violence and have been accepted into the galactic community.

Elgin walks the knife edge between describing the binarisms that structure our past and present and providing us with glimpses of a future vision where dualistic thinking is abolished. Her trilogy can be summarized as a plea for the allowance of transgression and progression. By rejecting the imperial masculine discourse and by inventing their own discourse as well as eliminating the very basis for competitive exclusion and violence, women, and eventually men, can move towards a global progressivity that, in turn, will allow an exchange with the alien/*other* on terms of equality and *difference*.

Elgin's proffered vision creates an important paradigm shift in readers by first analyzing and criticizing the present (dystopia) and then suggesting ways of transformation, and then making us wonder what a non-sexist and non-racist society not riven by language bias would look like. What sort of language would we and could we speak? How would humans act and live, if killing for food were unnecessary? Precisely by depicting the very throes of change, so often glossed over by utopias and dystopias, by making social achievement or change palpable without the blueprint we desire to cling to in terms of an ideology or manifesto, Elgin draws readers into the trilogy and asks *us* to imagine a future in a hybridized world. As readers we become part of the narrated hybridized voices, we are part of the destabilized center in the process of dissolution, and ask ourselves "What does a world without a center and with no margins look like?" It will not be a world free of contradictions because there is no abolition of polarities, but it could be a world of fluctuation, of merging and of continuous exchange, a world where humans would live as equals, who respect and value each other's multifarious differences.

4

Beyond Separate Worlds and War
Suzy McKee Charnas's Holdfast *Series*

> *We have to get beyond simplistic dualism and learn how to deal with polarity. We need to manage the idea of parity among a number of different things rather than between two opposites. We must break down and destroy the definition that creates polarity and get to a plain of parity. Parity meaning that two terms hold the same value, they are both valuable, one is not dominant over the other, or by definition better or worse.*
>
> —Suzy McKee Charnas[1]

In the epic *Holdfast* tetralogy, American sf and fantasy writer Suzy McKee Charnas looks at the interrelating categories of gender, race, class, and the often neglected factor of age/generations, and presents us with a harsh (eco)feminist comment on extreme dualism, hierarchical patriarchy/matriarchy, and colonialism.[2] The dystopian society Charnas devises is riven along well-known binarisms that she simultaneously undermines from the start by re-mixing some stereotypical bipolar equivalencies, such as homosexuality and white men. Within feminist sf, the *Holdfast* series is unique in that it not only reflects twenty-five years of feminist theorizing,[3] but, unusual for the 1970s, also voices in *Walk to*

---

[1]For the full quotes of this shorter part of the interview that I conducted with Suzy McKee Charnas, see the appendix. The longer part of this interview has been published in The New York Review of Science Fiction (*cf.* Mohr 1999c, 1999d).

[2]Walk to the End of the World *and* Motherlines *won the Retrospective James Tiptree Jr. Award in 1996,* The Furies *was short-listed in 1994 for the annual literary James Tiptree Jr. Memorial Award, awarded to the best sf novel exploring gender-bending and expanding gender roles in new ways, which* The Conqueror's Child, *the final volume of the series, then received in 1999.*

[3]Charnas has defined feminism as the challenge "to treat women as full-fledged human beings" (1988, 157), and recently claimed favoring "an economic model" of feminism as money is the

the End of the World (1974) postcolonial concerns, a topic revisited especially by the last book, *The Conqueror's Child* (1999).[4] Remarkably, *Motherlines* (1978) envisions hybridity long before Bhabha analyzed these issues, and, with the Amazonian culture of the Riding Women, *Motherlines* anticipates Haraway's transgressive concept of the cyborg, if not in the technical sense of the human/machine fusion, then as a merging of human/animal. Instead of venturing into outer space and drawing on the sf trope of aliens for a utopian model, as Suzette Haden Elgin does, Charnas also mines here the terran space of mythical/historical Amazon culture, though these "Amazons of the future" (Charnas 1981, 104) with their "alien ideas and values" (Mohr 1999c, 8) could be Aliens.

Most explicitly in *The Furies* (1994), Charnas investigates the raging war of the sexes, the anger and the violence involved; and she describes in unusual and painful detail the slow and grim process of change leading from dystopia towards an emerging potential utopia transgressive of bipolarities, as well as the painful purging of psychological and physical violence involved. This description of a literal war between the sexes is quite unusual and remains as yet extraordinary for the genre, although Wittig's *Les Guérillères* and Gearhart's *The Wanderground: Stories of the Hill Women* also include to some extent the war of the sexes. According to Charnas, however, this very foregrounding of the actual struggle involved in bringing on change, the necessity of a factual working through anger and pain, the experience of oppression and victimization as well as mastery, allow the release of rejuvenating energy and a final catharsis. The foregrounding of the struggle also addresses the fact, often neglected by privileged white middle-class women, that in Charnas's words "for most women in the real world, the fight for recognition as full-fledged humans with human rights has barely started" (Mohr 1999c, 10).

Exploring the pathology of our society's sexism and racism taken to extremes, and alternatively inflicted by both sexes, Charnas even-handedly criticizes masculine and feminine domination, and the colonial attitudes of the Western world. The series oscillates between the possibilities

---

[continued] *"primary standard of value [in Western culture]," therefore "a feminist is someone who insists on equitable income policies and their enforcement" (Mohr 1999c, 10). She claims, however, to have "specifically stayed away from feminist theory" in order not to be influenced by feminism and "avoided reading much about postmodern theory" (ibid. 10). However, the fact that the social structure, the cultural and sexual practices of the Grassland fictionally implement feminist political theorizings induced Jones to sarcasticly comment that the series reads like a "transliteration of feminist theory" (185).*

[4]*In the early sixties, Charnas traveled in Africa, worked as a Peace Corps volunteer and taught in Nigeria, an experience that changed her "understanding of race and the frictions that develop around it" (Mohr 1999c, 10), leading to an early recognition of the intersection of gender and race issues.*

of a (re-)formation of dystopia and a negotiation of a transgressive utopia that we, however, never witness. The *Holdfast* series moves from the feminist dystopia of *Walk to the End of the World*, to the almost pastoral separatism of *Motherlines*, to a masculinist dystopia and establishment of a neocolonial system in *The Furies*, and finally arrives at a potentially utopian reconciliation of the two sexes and the races in *The Conqueror's Child*. Unlike many feminist dystopias and utopias, Charnas does not stop at describing the outcome of patriarchy, or at focusing on women's struggle towards full humanity, but returns to consider men from a different angle. With *The Conqueror's Child*, in many ways a revisiting and rewriting of the previous books and their issues of the 1970s and late 1980s, Charnas comes full circle and formulates perhaps the most important remaining questions, if not of the next century, then at least of the next decade: How can men undo their past deeds? How can men recreate masculinity to acquire full human subject status? In this sense, the last book of the saga envisions the destroyers of the world of *Walk* as co-builders of the future.

Unlike Elgin, Charnas does not suggest specific utopian projects; instead, all societal and personal aspects take part in the transformation of society. The far too often monopolized and monolithic past, in its various manifestations of history, religion, and myth, must be counterbalanced and replaced by multiple perspectives, allowing previously muted groups and the subaltern voices to be heard.[5] External oppression will be eternally inflicted if internal programming does not change. The Western concept of relationships, based on master/slave binaries, needs to be restructured according to principles of non-violence and non-possessiveness. Charnas also stresses the necessity to shift from biological to psychological ties, to move from the destruction of the nuclear family to families of affinity, and to separate possession and progeny, i.e., to let go of genetic parent-child relations and to turn to generational progeny. The absence of fathering and stereotypical masculinity that contributed in particular to destructive patterns of bonding is met by new roles of masculinity and shareparenting, modelled on the Riding Women's sharemothering. Only the experience of both roles, of being victim and oppressor, slave and master, breaks up the dualism that previously permeated all aspects of Holdfast life. This individual experience that transcends the double bind of being master *or* slave, man *or* woman and the recognition of the coexistence of two, or more, modes of being leads to the societal disruption of cluster oppositions.

---

[5]*Originally used for military officers below the captain status, the term "subaltern," as used by Spivak and other postcolonial critics, is "shorthand for any oppressed person" (Loomba 51), but denotes specifically the double oppression of native women under colonialism and patriarchy.*

The potentially utopian society of the Riding Women serves as an inspiring alternate model and contrasting experience, yet it is not an alternative to be unquestioningly transferred to human society. Their society represents less a model for copying than a stimulus for transculturation. Charnas advocates the experience of borderwalking, of slipping in and out of different societies and cultures, of transgressing binaries of self/other, male/female, master/slave, human/animal, sanity/madness: "The books attempt to show that if you can reach across some of those lines then you can reclaim that energy [needed to retain boundaries] as social and personal resource."[6] This energy, otherwise used to maintain stasis, can then be used for the dynamic process of borderwalking. The acquired double vision and the marginalization that turns into hybridity furthers the cultural, sexual, and ethnic transmissions essential for the making of a postpatriarchal, multicultural, and multi-ethnic society, imagining the fulfillment of human potential and new ways of coexistence.

To reinforce preceding ideas, this chapter contrasts the dystopian Old Holdfast and the forging of an increasingly improving New Holdfast with the society of the Riding Women and their sometimes problematic role as alternative. It elucidates the construction and deconstruction of the past, the distortion of collective and personal memory contained in religion, myth, written and oral history. The analysis then turns to the contrasting cultural, social, familial, generational, personal, and sexual relationships. The last section pursues the question of how a future of parity can be obtained. An investigation of Charnas's deconstruction of the traditional concept of heroism analyzes how various characters transgress binaries and turns briefly to the very *making* of the new society.

As pointed out earlier, critics have not focused on *The Furies* and *The Conqueror's Child* so far, perhaps for the very reasons Lefanu stated, that critics had been waiting in vain for a sequel for more than ten years. Lefanu had maintained then that *Walk* and *Motherlines* investigate "dissolution rather than resolution,"[7] arguing that this emphasis "precludes a third book ... that will 'round off' or 'complete' the trilogy," allowing "a different reading" (149). This chapter provides therefore another reading of the now complete, but open-ended tetralogy that offers less a resolution, as Lefanu correctly anticipated, than a vision of dissolution resulting in the formation of new alliances that dismiss dualistic principles.

---

[6]*Interview with Charnas. See the appendix.*
[7]*Lefanu reads* Walk *quite similarly as "a novel of disintegration rather than renewal" (157).*

4.1. Plot

Walk to the End of the World introduces a dystopian society driven by the exploitation of women and the land, and set in a bleak post-holocaust environment known as the "Wasting." White men's cruel exploitation of nature, irresponsible (ab)use of science, and biochemical and nuclear pollution has caused an ecological disaster; the crisis, however, is conveniently blamed on women, people of color, and rebellious youth, all subsumed under the umbrella term "unmen." The surviving white males (re)build a misogynist patriarchy divided along age and gender lines, reducing the surviving females to an animal status and younger men to an uneasy submission. Referred to as "fems" (a cruel pun on females and feminists), women are used as breeders and slaves: biology is literally their destiny. Contaminating sexual contact with fems is limited to the necessities of reproduction, and consensual heterosexuality is outlawed; the intergenerational relationship between senior and junior men is characterized by homosexuality. Institutionalized violence, food scarcity, superstition, fear, and (Dark) Dreaming induced by drugs and violence ensure a fragile ritualized life that terminates in the nirvana of a poisonous drink, administered by the Endtendant, at Endpath.

The larger part of *Walk* revolves around two deviant juniors, the outlawed DarkDreamer, Servan d Layo, and the Endtendant, Eykar Bek, as they search for the latter's father, Raff Maggomas. On their journey to the city of 'Troi, where Maggomas has re-established industrial science and experiments with cannibalizing fems, they are accompanied by the slaverunner and messenger Alldera. After the ultimate objectification of becoming a commodity when she is raped by Servan and Eykar, the formerly silenced Alldera acquires the status of a narrative "I," claiming subjectivity and humanity. At the journey's end, Eykar declines his patrimony and commits patricide. In the turmoil of the juniors' uprising against the seniors and the destruction of 'Troi, Alldera literally walks to the end of her world and escapes into the surrounding wilderness.

With *Motherlines*, the narrative shifts to a female focus and an alternative all-female potential utopia. The pregnant Alldera is taken in by Riding Women, warriors and nomads living in the Grasslands. Free from male restraints and heterosexist pressures, they have created a non-hierarchical culture of their own structured by non-possessiveness, communality, cooperation, and tribal kinship. The Riding Women do not understand such concepts as war—though they fight feuds—the conquest of land, the telling of untruths, and possessiveness. Having escaped from laboratories where scientists designed them to be parthenogenetic, the Riding Women mate with horses to trigger reproduction, and they practice a non-possessive naming of the resultant offspring, whom they sharemother. *Motherlines* also depicts the society of escaped Free Fems at the Tea Camp, whose matriarchal society reinvents patriarchy and rebuilds and perpetuates slavery. Nurtured by the Riding Women who hope that way to start a new motherline, Alldera gives birth to a girl. Slowly Alldera adapts to the Grassland society and its customs, even taking a Riding Woman as lover. Not all Riding Women, however, welcome Alldera. Most explicitly, Sheel resents a fem living among them. Leaving her daughter to grow up among the Riding Women, Alldera sets out to live with her own kind at the Tea Camp. After getting caught up in the rivalries of the Free Fems and in particular in the schemes of the pet fem and storyteller Daya, Alldera, eventually followed by Daya, departs to live with a lone Free Fem, the dye-maker Fedeka. From a solitary and healing sojourn in the desert, Alldera returns with captured wild horses. Accompanied by Daya, now her lover, Alldera attends the naming ceremony of her daughter, whom she names Sorrel. The Free Fems leave the Tea Camp and join Alldera in the Grasslands, claiming kinship. The novel ends with the Free Fems' considering their choices: either to return to Holdfast to free the fem slaves and use captured men as studs, or to witness their own extinction and recede into the past.

The Furies abandons the utopian Grasslands and returns to dystopia. It is an angry story of revenge that explores the corrupting influence of power. Sixteen years after the events depicted in *Motherlines*, Alldera the Conqueror leads the furious Free Fems in their victorious return to the Holdfast, followed by Sheel and a small group of Riding Women. They succeed in subjugating the men and take revenge on collaborating fem overseers. Some Newly Freed, however, resent the liberation, and rivalries erupt among the fems. Imitating the only form of power they know, the Free Fems reverse roles and turn back towards the very tyranny they sought to supplant. Afraid of an uprising, they too rule by fear and brutalize the enslaved men, who in their victimization begin to learn the horrors of their own previous rule. One major concern among the Fems is progeny: how can the sexual act be imagined without violence? In the hope of starting a new motherline, Sheel sends one pregnant Newly Freed as kin to the Grasslands. Sheel, however, overlooks that Holdfasters are dual-sexed: the baby Veree turns out to be male.

In *The Furies* Alldera re-encounters Eykar, handicapped by a failing and mutilated body, and now guardian of the library, and both undergo a painful process of recognizing their shared humanity despite all the disparities dividing them. Eykar becomes spokesman for the dying men who have been herded like cattle into prison pits. He is assisted by the mad cut-boy Setteo—he has been castrated by men—who is obsessed with distorted Christian symbols and with visions of mystical bear spirits. Accused of tyranny and betrayal for negotiating with Eykar, Alldera finds herself walking a tightrope. Two Newly Freed, along with her old lover and now jealous and treacherous foe Daya, try to assassinate Alldera, but fail. Both Alldera and Eykar are introspective at the conclusion. Alldera withdraws from both societies to Endpath and eventually re-emerges as a politician in the council of Fems, their attempt at democracy. Eykar comes to realize that the war has been about women and not about men, as men in their hubris would have it: women must now learn to govern themselves autonomously without surrendering to division and discord.

The Conqueror's Child opens with Sorrel's venturing into the New Holdfast in a double movement: her search for her mother and her father—both Eykar and Servan raped Alldera and both might hence be Sorrel's father—recalls Eykar's quest in *Walk*, and like Alldera journeying pregnant to the Grasslands, Sorrel arrives with a child. Yet the girl she can initially pass off as female "bloodchild," i.e., her own child, is publicly denounced as the boy Veree by her confidante Daya, now priestess of Moonwoman, the Free Fems' cult; and Veree is taken away to a children's house. The New Holdfasters struggle to establish a postwar daily routine, addressing the questions of how to deal with their newfound liberty and how to resist the corruption of power. Sorrel's focusing on the male child Veree formulates the most pressing question—essential to a healing process—of how to bridge the chasm between the sexes, and between generations, despite the atrocities committed on both sides. While *Motherlines* and *The Furies* are predominantly concerned with the liberation of women, *The Conqueror's Child* considers the men of *Walk* from a different angle: how can men rehumanize themselves?

An external threat mirrors these internal problems. Fulfilling the liberation prophecies of the Sunbear cult that has developed among captive men, Servan d Layo returns with a small renegade crew of marauders from his ventures into the Northern lands and with some people of color he took prisoners in the Pooltowns; he seeks to reconstitute the Old Holdfast. A combination of opportunism and necessity induces Sallali, the wife of the slain leader of the Pooltowns, to become d Layo's mistress. Holding her children captive, Servan blackmails Sallali into worming her way into the New Holdfast to kidnap Sorrel, and thereby hopes to gain access to the Holdfast. Together with her male lover Galligan, the ever-scheming Daya, planning to regain the Fems' admiration by killing Servan (or so she later claims on her deathbed), joins Servan and is quickly reduced to her old pet fem status. Impelled by his mystical bear spirits, Setteo flees with Veree as a sacrifice to the Sunbear, but Sheel intercepts and kills him. Convinced by Servan that Sorrel killed his beloved Setteo, Eykar also joins Servan. When Servan threatens Sorrel with rape, Eykar is forced to choose between his old lover Servan and the girl who may be his daughter. He kills Servan. Accompanied by the half-blind Eykar and other New Holdfasters, Sorrel ventures into the Grasslands to search once more for her mother, who has returned to the Grasslands. Alldera, however, has vanished, along with the Riding Women, leaving the plains and their history as a gift to the New Holdfasters. The imagining and building of the future now becomes the responsibility of both sexes in league with the other races represented by the Pooltown people and by the additional hybrid cultures evolving around the New Holdfast.

4.2. Generic Multiplicity and Dissolving Narrative Conventions

Generic multiplicity and hybrid merging of echoing subtexts avail the Holdfast tetralogy a fluidity of contrasting and weaving together fiction and reality. It combines and interlocks a variety of genres: adventure tale, epic, fantasy, sf, dystopia and utopia, and it re-appropriates classical texts and myths. Among these, the nexus of myth/quest and of dystopia and utopia are the most striking, whereas sf overtones are few.

Walk depicts a feminist dystopian society, yet can be read as a postmodern rewriting of the Oedipal quest narrative, as Bartkowski notes (cf. 85–86). As in Homer's *Iliad*, the Oedipal twist of *Walk* leads to the fall of 'Troi, easily deciphered as the ancient Greek city Troy, and Homer's Achilles, the swift-footed runner, is reworked into a new female version: Alldera the runner (cf. Vasey). Despite borrowing from the classical content, however, Charnas "refuses the simplistic reductionism of ... the situation-complication-resolution structure [that] becomes an affirmation of the unified coherent hero" (Cranny-Francis 184) and underwrites the deconstruction of classical concepts of heroism with the emerging female protagonist Alldera, who is anything but a unified hero. Alldera's own quest, and later Sorrel's quest, displace and decenter the patrilinear quest theme, the traditional tale of "a young hero adventuring with two male companions in search of his father" (Charnas 1981, 103). Alldera develops from a "boring, cowardly, ordinary person" (*F* 368)[8] to, in Charnas's words, "a reluctant hero" (Mohr 1999d, 20), from passive slave runner and messenger of men's words to messenger of fems' freedom, from escapee and outsider to conqueror and politician, to a mythic godfigure. With the all-female society of the Riding Women in *Motherlines*, Charnas seemingly creates a separatist feminist utopia, but by modeling

---

[8]*References to the tetralogy are given in the text in parentheses with the following abbreviations:* Walk to the End of the World *(W),* Motherlines *(M),* The Furies *(F) and* The Conqueror's Child *(CC).*

them on the mythical Amazons, she also weaves a "feminist mythopoeia" (Vasey). Likewise, the return of the furious Free Fems to the Holdfast in *The Furies* establishes, on the one hand, a masculinist dystopia. On the other hand, as the title of Book Three so aptly suggests, they are modern personifications of the ancient Greek spirits of punishment, revenge, and justice.

Classifications of the *Holdfast* series as "powerful science fiction" (Jones 184), or "science fantasy" (Fitting 1985, 157), are arguable, since elements of sf are few. Certainly, if the series is placed in an sf context, the narrative structure and content as well as the introduction of Alldera as strong female hero underscore the chiefly masculinist focus of sf in the 1970s, which often lacked female characters altogether.[9] Principally rejecting escapist masculinist space operas which are not grounded in (f)actual social realities, Charnas focuses very little on gadgets and other sf tropes, but foregrounds sociopolitical inequities of contemporary society seen through the defamiliarizing lens and magnifying glass of dystopia/utopia, taking "new questions ... [o]ut of the culture I live in" and formulating answers less "from a plan ... or a blueprint" (Charnas 1988, 149), than via theoretical/fictional speculation. Apart from its destructive potential, leading to the Wasting and to Maggomas's reimplementation of industry and technology in 'Troi, evoking "Detroit, the epitome of the rational thought" (Clemente 2004, 83), technology features only insofar that scientists designed parthenogenetic women, who then escaped and founded the culture of the Riding Women. It is less their different social structure than the alien reproductive process that turns the Grasslanders into a disguised alien species, however, with strong mythical roots. They detail less an sf than a mythical element and function mostly as a utopian alternative to the "masculinist dystopia" (Bartkowski 81) of the Holdfast, and to the matriarchal rule of the Tea Camp in *Motherlines*. While the first two books thus juxtapose dystopia and utopia, the third and forth sequels emerge as utopian dystopian hybrids, as the New Holdfasters struggle with dystopian relapses and the reluctant realization that the building of a better society involves the inclusion of both sexes. In this respect, the single-sexed Grassland society cannot function at all as a desirable utopia for the Holdfasters.

[9]Walk *rewrites to some extent Heinlein's masculinist utopia* Space Cadet *(1948), as Brian Attebery has pointed out (cf. 7–9), which describes a society where homosexual undercurrents and external control prevail, the nuclear family is removed, the chanting of male names occurs, and female characters are negligible. Signed by both Charnas and Russ, the preceding blurb of* Walk *clearly puts Charnas's novel outside of mainstream masculinist sf, defining the following text as part of a new feminist tradition within the genre. The dedication of* Motherlines *to "J.R.," easily deciphered as Joanna Russ—who dedicates* The Two of Them *(1978) to Elgin—stresses further this notion of genealogy and growing intertextuality among feminist writers of utopian, dystopian, and science fiction.*

In fact, whether *Motherlines* depicts either a utopia or a separatist feminist utopia is debatable. Although the society of the Riding Women has some distinctly utopian features, I disagree with Lefanu and other critics who consider the Grassland society as "unmitigatedly utopian" (147). The Grassland is a parallel world, a contrasting but imperfect society, as Alldera finds out when she discovers that there is brutality, albeit of a different kind, in the Grassland. Contrary to her expectations, Grassland life is not clean and sanitized: "She had wanted the women to be perfect, and they were not" (*M* 84). There is no perfection, not even in the Grassland utopia. Not at all a real alternative to be unquestioningly adopted, the Grassland serves predominantly as a foil, an inspiration for Holdfasters. The Riding Women's return to nowhere, to textual and physical absence at the end of *The Conqueror's Child*, indicates the negation of any ideal. Figuratively and literally, there *is* no utopia, no-place to turn to and no ideal to be achieved, *but* to go indeed by one's own imagination. As much as Alldera's healing sleep does resemble a utopian traveller's initial dream taking him or her to utopia, this narrative is rather, in Charnas's words, a "culture-clash story" (Mohr 1999c, 8). In contradiction to Anne Cranny-Francis's reading of *Motherlines* as a purely separatist "essentialist argument which condemns men virtually unequivocally and offers no hope for female autonomy beyond a total rejection of any society containing men" (184), *Motherlines* instead transgresses the subgenre of separatist utopias, specifically in its function as part of a series dealing primarily with the Holdfast's two sexes. Many separatist all-female utopias—such as Gilman's feminist classic *Herland*, Russ's *Female Man*, Tepper's *Gate to Women's Country*—propagate an essentialism that *Motherlines* renounces. Some link men almost exclusively with violence,[10] while others consider the sexes effectively as different species or races, as Gearhart does in *The Wanderground*.[11] In Charnas's novel, there is no need to reintroduce the male sex to Grassland society, as, for instance, in Gilman's *Herland*, where the Herlanders gladly embrace the three male explorers, because the alternative Grassland society is not the utopian allegory of human society.[12] Exactly this absence Marleen Barr has criticized. Barr alleges that in comparison to other all-female societies where invading men are killed (e.g., Tiptree's story "Houston, Houston Do You Read?" and Russ's *The Female Man*), *Motherlines* "presents the least radical solution to the 'male problem'" (1987, 7), since Grasslanders "have no desire to harm the men" (ibid. 8). Yet

---

[10]*E.g., in Tepper's* Gate to Women's Country *the sexes clandestinely reconcile, since the ruling women secretly select only non-violent men for procreation.*

[11]*For a discussion of* Wanderground *and* Motherlines, *see Wolmark (1994, chap. 4). On separatist feminist sf, see Fitting (1992).*

[12]*For a comparative study of* Motherlines *and* Herland, *see Margaret Miller (1983).*

the Grasslanders have no desire for invasion, since men are simply *irrelevant* to their society's structure, unless a man accidentally enters the Grassland; men pose hence a passive threat.[13] Thus, the Riding Women do not *need* to tackle the "male problem." It is essential to the forging of the New Holdfast that the Riding Women's model of the transgressive single-sex interaction can be transferred to, and adjusted for, the needs of a dual-sex human society.[14] Quite appropriately, the Riding Women then disappear into what they verged on from the beginning: the realm of myth.

With Lefanu, who sees *Walk* and *Motherlines* as "interrogative ... of order, of unity" (149), I argue that an establishment of order, i.e., stasis and perfection, is not desired and runs counter to the author's intention of advocating constant diversification and the necessity to "change things all the time" (Mohr 1999d, 19). This element of fluidity, the concept of transgression, is most obviously embodied by the Riding Women's merging of human and animal. Other Holdfast characters also transgress sexual, gender, cultural, and body/mind boundaries, exemplifying that neither one nor two but the participation and interaction of various, if not all, supposed binaries leads from dystopia to utopia. This generic interlocking is symbolized by Holdfast characters of both sexes, "working towards this transgressive utopia."[15]

Narrative transgressions are less obvious. In fact, at first glance the narrative technique, especially of Books One to Three, seems quite conventional, as the novels are neither experimental in style nor self-referential as, for instance, Russ's *The Female Man*; a flaw that closer scrutiny somewhat mollifies. Generally speaking, with each sequel the fractured, multiperspective but otherwise conventional narrative structure of *Walk* dissolves into an increasingly diversified and polyphonic narrative. If we look at the *Holdfast* series as a whole, pillars of postmodern narratology, such as narrative diversification, complexity, slippage, deconstruction, and pluralism, can be identified in the novels. The texts neglect or conventionally deal with other postmodern issues such as fragmentation, a metatext in the sense of interwoven various discourses, or the rejection of chronology. This puzzling contradiction does make sense, if we take into account to what extent the narrative form and character development reflect the narrative content.

On the structural level, the content's shift from singularity to diver-

---

[13] *Only a man who crosses the border and might discover them is hunted down and killed—the "'macha' warrior" (Charnas 1988,154) Sheel prides herself for having killed seven men—a reversal of the stereotypical literary motif of men as hunters and women as prey.*

[14] *The women in Sargent's* Shore of Women *arrive at the same realization as the fems in* The Conqueror's Child: *only the inclusion of men will bring on utopia.*

[15] *Interview with Charnas. See the appendix.*

sity is reflected by the progress from four successive limited male/female viewpoints in *Walk* to the multiperspectivism and polyphony of alternating male, female, and subaltern points-of-view in *The Conqueror's Child*. The conventional linear narrative turns as a series into a cyclical structure: *Walk* is about men versus fems, *Motherlines* about women versus fems, *Furies* about fems versus fems and fems versus men, and *The Conqueror's Child* deals with fems, men, women, people of color, and children. In their linearity, the five episodes of *Walk* mirror the male rule of rationality. Just as men occupy the center of the Holdfast and assign women a liminal status, the narrative centers around men. Three out of five sections, for example, are told by consecutive male narrators (Captain Kelmz, Servan d Layo, and Eykar Bek), and only the fourth and the last section from the female point of view (Alldera). This textual absence of female characters represents the physical absence, the linguistic negation of and the virtual silencing of fems, whom men have literally muted by cutting their tongues out. In this respect, *Walk* has been wrongly criticized for its "nonfeminist narrative structure" (Barr 1983, 50). Focusing as a critic or reader on the male narrative and neglecting the female subtext relegates women once more to the narrative margins.

Following Alldera as focal point, shifting between the Tea Camp and the Riding Women, *Motherlines* describes a more "contrapunctual than episodic" (Bartkowski 95) narrative. Reflecting the momentary separatism of the sexes, the narrative absence of male characters replaces the prevalent absence of females in *Walk*, and the female point of view now expands to include the societal voices of the Riding Women and the Free Fems of the Tea Camp. Lefanu has argued that Charnas successfully creates "multiple protagonists" and "group protagonists" (150), while Barr criticizes that individual voices merge with the respective female community and regrets "the loss of particular female character's individuality" (1987, 15). Yet, although each motherline presents a collective character—similar to the cluster characters of the women linguists in the *Native Tongue* trilogy—individual characters have distinct voices, most notably the counterbalancing voices of Alldera's lover Nenisi and of her antagonist Sheel. Similarly, among the Free Fems of the Tea Camp, the voices of Daya the storyteller, of Kobba, literally the voice of muted Elnoa, and of Fedeka the Dyer gain substance. Just as *Walk* overemphasizes male voices, *Motherlines* tends to overemphasize female societal voices; *The Furies* and *The Conqueror's Child*, on the other hand, gradually progress towards narrative individualization, which is in accordance with these novels' particular contents. With the frictions among Free Fems and Newly Freed, the female voices individuate further in *The Furies*, while Sheel essentially fuses the voices of "those harsh judges, the Riding Women" (*F* 303) and functions like Setteo as external com-

4. Beyond Separate Worlds and War 157

mentator of human actions in Books Three and Four. *The Furies* also (re)introduces the two juxtaposed male voices of Eykar and Arjvall, the former emerging as spokesman for the negotiation of new male roles and the latter holding on to male superiority. "[T]he absence of any convincing male voice" (189), as Jones remonstrates, seems to me less a matter of unconvincing narration than an absence of convincing new male roles that only begin to develop in Book Four. Notably, *The Conqueror's Child* features Sorrel in a first person narrative, introducing the fresh perspective of the next generation of postfeminists. Like her unifying mission to include men and women in the New Holdfast, the narrative is structurally framed by Sorrel's prologue and epilogue. Weaving the various plot strands and unresolved conflicts together, *The Conqueror's Child* presents a more balanced polyphony. Alternately told in the first and third person subjective from the male, female, a new generational, the Riding Women's, Setteo's mythical *and* the postcolonial point of view— with the character Sallali the previously oppressed subaltern voice also enters the narration—the last book of the tetralogy most resembles a postmodern narration.

In accordance with the narrative structure, the series expands from "only one significant female character" (Jones 184) and three male characters to a variety of female and male characters, now being given various choices of gender roles.[16] Captain Kelmz, Eykar Bek, and Servan d Layo start out as stock characters, "the cynical old warrior, the son seeking confrontation with his father, and the cheery young rogue" (Charnas 1981, 103–104). Apart from Alldera, we get, Charnas admits, the stereotypical female triumvirate of the almost virginal "Man-Hating Bitch [Sheel]," "the Controlling Mother [Elnoa]," and "the Slinky, Treacherous Sex Goddess [Daya]" (Cavalcanti 12). While Charnas successfully widens the spectrum of richly characterized, distinct female characters, the characterization of minor male characters, for instance, Servan's Ferrymen crew, remains flat and their voices are interchangeable. Eykar and Servan, however, attain the status of round characters, and with Setteo and Veree the range of masculine portrayals diversifies.

Moving from the background and the societal margins of Book One to the center(s) in Book Two and Three, female characters eventually share the narrative platform with men in *The Conqueror's Child*, drifting in turn from their liminal status back into the narrative. It takes until page sixty-six of *Walk* for the first female character, unnamed and with "downcast eyes" (*W* 66) to appear, and another hundred pages before Alldera

---

[16]*Addressing a long-standing core issue of feminist sf, the creation of strong literary female role models, Charnas explicitly wants to "remind readers that half of the real world really is [populated by] women" (Mohr 1999c, 10).*

speaks up and uses the narrative "I." Alldera develops from "the least memorable character" (Lefanu 154), from a tabula rasa "inscribed [with] the myths, dreams and nightmares" (ibid. 147), to a complex character. In a similar reverse motion, two out of the three original male characters recede to the background, or vanish altogether. Captain Kelmz dies, and Servan who dominates *Walk*, disappears, then prowls the narrative borderlines of *The Furies* only to put in a fleeting, but ominously anachronistic appearance in the last book. As the sole character present in all four novels, Alldera emerges as the unifying narrative link (a role that Sorrel inherits)—similar to Nazareth Chornyak's presence as unifying narrative link in all three *Native Tongue* novels that Nazareth also passes on to a female inheritor, Delina—turning the tetralogy into what some critics call the "Alldera cycle" or "Alldera series" (cf. Clemente 1999, 2004). In *Motherlines* Alldera becomes the "outsider observer narrative device" (Miller 1983, 193). She is not only a narrative "bridge between the two groups" (ibid. 193), but also our utopian guide travelling "not through time ... but between histories and identities" (Bartkowski 96), and between societies.[17] In Book Four Sorrel takes on this narrative role of the guide, but she is the guide from utopia who gives us a tour of dystopia. In Charnas's view, Alldera is "both of another world ... and definitely of our own world" (Clemente 1999, 64) with her "anger ... rooted right here in America" (ibid. 66) and thus links fiction and reality.

Charnas maintains a balance between alienating male and female readers with, at times, unpalatable ideas, on the one hand, and challenging readers to disrupt ingrained patterns of thought, on the other hand; and in the process she invites men and women to assume different perspectives, which is a paradigm shift inherent to the feminist utopian/dystopian genre. Undoubtedly, the series is a tour de force for readers of both sexes, as both experience incongruous and dissolving gender roles that do not correspond to customary patterns of reader identification. Female readers may recoil from identifying with the victimized fem slaves and feel the urge to disassociate themselves from this part of female reality. Identification with the equally strange but strong Riding Women, especially with their mating ritual, is hardly easier. The vengeful and violent mastery of Free Fems may further alienate female readers, but this difficult identification also catapults them into a gender role opposed to everyday experience. The reconciliatory process of *The Conqueror's Child* leaves female readers with a new sense of empowerment

---

[17]*Like many literary utopian guides before her, Alldera falls into a healing sleep. In contrast to her literary predecessors, she falls asleep not in her own society, traveling in her dream to other worlds, but in utopia.*

and with plenty of roles from which to choose. Male reader response may vary from rejecting the homoerotics of *Walk* to disliking Servan d Layo's machismo, to increasing discomfort with Eykar Bek's hesitancy, introspection, and victim's role. *Motherlines* offers male readers of the series, otherwise not very likely to pick a book about an all-female world, the new experience of absent male characters; this role reversal climaxes with the men's victim position in *The Furies. The Conqueror's Child* requires male readers to identify against both male slave and master roles; and even though Eykar in his weakness and heroic despair personifies a new father/hero model, the novel dismisses male readers with the realization and knowledge that men need "to begin answering their own set of questions about defining masculine natures and ideals" (Clemente 1999, 64), as Charnas puts it. Because each book is open-ended the reader's imagination is allowed to roam freely. *Walk* ends with Alldera poised to run uphill, *Motherlines* with the Free Fems ready to return to the Holdfast, *The Furies* with conflicts unresolved between the sexes, and *The Conqueror's Child* leaves readers to speculate about the Holdfast's future. In a way the form thus suggests what the narrative content displays: history does not end, and there is no closure to time; it continues to unfold while we remake whatever circumstances in which we happen to live. This illusion of endings is perhaps best summarized in Sorrel's musings about the death chamber of the Old Holdfast: "Endpath had the word 'end' in it, but I have learned how rare true endings are ... since new things come bursting out of them almost at once" (*CC* 415).

4.3. The Past—Truth(s) and Memory

To create a better future, present conditions must be changed. To forge the present, it is crucial to know one's past. In league with truth, such knowledge is, in the words of the Nobel prize winning Nigerian author Wole Soyinka, commenting on the South African situation, "a social virtue that carries a potential for prevention or social alertness" (9). Charnas clearly details the power of the past and rejects the exclusive patriarchal and colonial representation of the past by aptly describing the firm grip that this one-sided version of the past, as Holdfasters know it, has on them. A past that dominates the present and precludes any future change by eternally perpetuating itself in the present, Charnas argues, leads eventually not only to the destruction of the colonial and sexual other, but virtually to *self*-destruction; any closed society must fail. Significantly, male survivors give the name "Holdfast" to their settlement in *Walk,* indicating their desperate clinging to old ways and resistance to change: "They call their land the Holdfast, after the anchoring tendril by which seaweed clings to the rocks against the pull of the current" (*W* 4).[18] In much the same way as their original culture was wasteful and hence brought on the destruction of their world, the Holdfast society is depleted of most natural resources. Holding fast to bygone bipolar hierarchical structures, their society comes to a standstill, a deadly interlocking of past and present negating any future.

A necessary part of human life, the past is contained in cultural and personal memory, but it is ambiguous and distorted. To this end, central issues of the *Holdfast* series include the mediation of reality, the construction of truth, and the dubious nature of the past as it is collectively and personally remembered in the invariably intersecting stories of dreams, myths, religions and history. These different ways of interpreting and (de)constructing reality describe major tools of memory manipulation in the novels. The remembered and monopolized past functions as the decisive factor of what constitutes reality and the present, and forms a foundation for shaping the future. Remembrance, Charnas reminds us, is another way of ensuring the survival and continuity of one's culture. By denying and distorting different perceptions and memories of reality, a culture can be altogether muted and erased. Memory and past are thus intricately intertwined with truth. Contrary to the beliefs inherent in the logic of epistemology and Western science, truth can be neither acquired nor possessed; in the Foucauldian sense the "regime of truth" (1979b, 46) is the product of a societal hegemonic discourse. As Robert Scholes writes:

> If we have no Truth with a capital *T*, we must stop using the notion of such Truth—in whatever guise—to measure what we then take to be our failure to attain it. But we must not give up distinguishing between truth and lies within whatever framework we can construct to make such determinations [1989, 154].

There is then no essence of truth inherent to objects and the world. Rather, like a mystical experience, it flashes through the mind and is therefore always the truth of the one who seeks and finds it *at that very moment*. Truth is not only, in Charnas's words, "vulnerable to chance" (Mohr 1999d, 20), but the more moments of truth can be collected, the more likely it is to form an approximation of something that resembles truth as distinguished from lie. The vindication of truth is the precon-

---

[18]*Bartkowski notes that a character in Le Guin's novel* The Eye of the Heron *(1978) is named "Holdfast": "LeGuin's emphasis in the name differs from Charnas's. Whereas Charnas's usage comes to be seen as a name given by men clinging to control and fearful of change and what lies beyond their territorial borders, LeGuin's character is one who continues against great odds to struggle against tyranny and domination" (Bartkowski 174n2).*

dition for reconciliation, as Soyinka points out in relation to the South African Truth and Reconciliation Process:

> Truth, the very process of its exposition becomes part of the necessity, and, depending on the nature of the past that it addresses, the impact it had made on the lives of the citizens ... it may be regarded as being capable of guaranteeing or foundering the future of a nation. Indeed, it may be seen as a therapy against civic alienation.... *The Truth shall set you free?* Maybe. But first the Truth must be set free [12–13].

Past truth presupposes memory, but memory is short and to err is human. Since memory is by nature selective, truth cannot be monolithic, as Alldera explains: "Everybody's got only part of the truth. And people do tell lies, or they are mistaken or forgetful, no matter how much time they spend *figuring*" (*CC* 402). She too has experienced the tricky treachery of distorting memory attentuated by time. In the opening section of *Motherlines*, when Alldera has just escaped from the confusion of the fallen Holdfast and is subjected to the solitude of the Wilderness, she suddenly reaches past the very real memory of slavery that she carries in the form of the "rape-cub" in her body to the new and distortive memory of the dystopian Holdfast as "homeland" (*M* 3). Eykar likewise gladly deserted his hateful job as official poisoner at Endpath and seeks comfort in the memory of the solitude and security of "homelike" Endpath, "a shelter he never should have left to venture into a senseless world" (*CC* 374–375).

This necessity to recognize the plurality of truth(s), to include multiple perspectives, and to learn from one's history the tetralogy advocates. Soyinka exhorts us that memory plays an important role in our responses to present conditions, but he also implies that memory and truth are "social strategies" that ultimately "seek the cathartic bliss, the healing that comes with closure" (20). *The Conqueror's Child* demonstrates exactly this healing process, but also argues that closure in terms of forgetting the past implies the danger of repeating it, while being cognizant of history indicates at least the possibility of using the knowledge to transform the present and thus to shape the future. Charnas argues for a historiography that promotes not the victors but rather the remembrance of the victims. A culture with varied and diversified means of memorizing the past is an essential ingredient for a utopian society inclusive of different ethnic, gender, generational, and religious views.

4.3.1. Polarizing Religion and the Wild Element of Spirituality

Religion provides one way of interpreting reality, of knowing and defining personal and cultural origins. By definition, religion externalizes human responsibility and projects it onto a superhuman controlling power that in turn legitimizes its secular representatives. Religion as an essentially hierarchical, dualistic, and oppressive control mechanism that propagates the physical/spiritual exclusion of the *other* is criticized by Charnas. Her representation of religion in the Holdfast consists of a degenerated and distorted version of half remembered Christianity, ritualized drug-induced manna dreaming, and its illegal counterpart Dark-Dreaming. Religions primary function is to instill a masculinist ideology, dividing the sexes and the generations. This Holdfast version of Christianity privileges the vindictive, archaic, and authoritarian patriarchal God of the OT altered to fit the ideology of the Seniors, conveniently linking women with the Wasting, and thus reproducing "the original Biblical fall of humanity" (Cranny-Francis 186). The two, hardly original animistic nature religions of fems and of captive men are equally dualistic and polarize the sexes. Applying the age-old anthropomorphism of the Moon and Sun/Bear, fems worship Moonwoman, and the men the Sunbear. With Setteo's shamanism, Charnas does suggest a different and personalized spiritual approach of inclusivity, yet her descriptions of Setteo's transgressive spirit/matter flights remain too elusive; no other character, moreover, can take up this narrative strand after Setteo's death to open up new avenues of spiritualism.

Like language, religion is "a system of signs, whose meaning is relational" since "a specific social usage gives a sign any meaning" (Loomba 35). The meaning of religion as an assemblage of rituals and signs is replaceable, and is always subjected to the definitions of the ruling social group. For instance, the original meaning of making the sign of the cross, symbolizing in Christian theology the acknowledgement of the Holy trinity, the unity of God's three divine forms of being (Father, Son, and Holy Spirit), is reversed into the recognition of discord and division, signifying "the opposed wills of Father and Son" (*W* 20).[19] Of the Christian gesture of prayer and blessing, in the Holdfast version of the sign of the cross retains only the Catholic use as protection. Although Christianity as such has been "discredited, the *sign* had survived as a recognition and acceptance of its *one great truth*" (*W* 20; emphasis added). Monolithic, God-given truth is in reality a human political decision. The Seniors decide what the true message is. Similarly, the crucifixion, formerly a Christian symbol of obedience, sacrifice, resurrection and forgiveness, is reinterpreted as the just punishment of a disobedient son "challenging his Father's authority" (*W* 83), therefore justifying the Seniors' rule over Juniors, because the latter, incited by women, also

---

[19]*In like manner, the Moon priestess Fedeka redesigns the fems' spiral sign of resistance into a "circular sign ... to signify the blessing of Moonwoman" (F 19).*

rebelliously challenged their fathers' authority. With Setteo's macabre offering of an upside down, crucified and "contorted corpse"—with the once threatening phallus turned into an impotent "shrivel of blackened flesh" (*F* 36)—crucifixion changes into a man-made proleptic image of the ensuing downfall of patriarchy and of Holdfast Christianity. Intending "to bring back 'Christ,'" peace and "the salvation of the Holdfast— the 'Second Coming'" (*F* 47), Setteo hails the Free Fems as "The Blessed," and female "Christs." Yet these messiahs, along with the message of change, bring also one of continued violence. Crucifixion devoid of any further meaning but violence is also captured in the horrific image of the three impaled Newly Freed in *The Furies*. Setteo recognizes in "this current manifestation of that timeless paradigm ... a response to the sign he himself had made, when he had raised his single Christ as signal for these Blessed to come. Here now were three Christs, in answer" (*F* 191).

Like signs and symbols, the Bible is also subjected to reinterpretations. In Charnas's representation, the Bible is a collection of *human* stories, a piece of influential literature, or as Charnas phrases it, "[a] pretty, poetic, fraudulent old novel" (Mohr 1999d, 20). The NT is reinterpreted and rejected by men as "[a] porridge of unmanly soft-headedness, mushy morals and anti-hierarchical sedition" (*W* 83) feminized by "God's own son ... preaching femmish softness" (*F* 47), undermining the masculinist notion of a once "manly creed" (*W* 84). In effect, it is a women's religion, since "most of the worshippers ... had been fems" (*W* 83),[20] and Christ is an effeminate man, a non-man. When Beyarra and Eykar as the representatives of both sexes move to jointly burn the Bible in *The Conqueror's Child*, they symbolically negate patriarchal religion: "[H]ad they not, men and fems, had enough of tyrannical fathers" (*CC* 186). Instead of rewriting or deconstructing the Bible, as Elgin does, Charnas simply opts for removing it altogether. To build a new Holdfast free of the primacy of Christianity, its written source must be demolished.[21]

In the Holdfast philosophy, woman as the repressed *other* is associated with carnality, lack of soul and spirit; in short, women are the contagious transmitters of evil. The Holdfast fems and men embody the "dystopian projection of the logical extreme of the ways in which spirit and matter are currently conceptualized" (Sargisson 161). Men are spirit, soul, sun, and light. Fems are associated with everything men fear, everything beyond their control. 'Woman' is insubstantial, unclean, closer to

---

[20]*Although resenting the Bible as a fraud, Charnas grants that the NT is "an attempt to restore humane values ... perverted by 'Saint' Paul into just another version of the old story; hypocrisy, sexism, subjugation of dissent, bribes, threats, and politics" (Mohr 1999d, 20).*

[21]*Interestingly, the fact that the creation of a new philosophy necessitates the actual and thus symbolical destruction of religious relics does not yet occur in the manuscript of* The Conqueror's Child *that mentions neither the Bible nor its destruction.*

the body, and thus animality. Hers is the night, the moon and the void, with the moon channeling "the forces of the void" (*W* 58). Women are absence without "souls, only inner cores of animating darkness shaped from the void beyond the stars" (*W* 57). Charnas demonstrates here what Irigaray later formulated so poignantly: "the female sex is defined as a lack, a *hole*" (Irigaray 1976, 63). In the patriarchal paradigm, the female sexual organ, the vagina, mirrors the spatial/spiritual void, and both voids terrify men as expressions of cyclical and uncontrollable nature,[22] reflecting the inner hollowness and emptiness of patriarchy.[23] The men feel they must be able to contain, control, and know nature as the *other*. Captain Kelmz, for instance, prefers "the night tamed into neat rectangles between compound rooftops" (*W* 20); and out in the generally much feared and mythologized Wild, men go rogue in "the stillness of the void" (*W* 142).[24] For fems, the openness of the sky represents how men limit their freedom; therefore, Alldera is frightened by "this open sky ... [because] it was hers to enjoy only by the whim of the masters" (*W* 141), whereas the enclosed space "of the Rendery [where she worked] ... belonged to fems" (*W* 141). When Alldera returns from the vast and unclaimed Grasslands, the Holdfast's narrowness "with margins so poignantly ragged" (*F* 24) stuns her. Geographically, the Holdfast has shrunk in correlation with her experience of inner and outer freedom in a land with no margins and no center. Living in balance with nature, the Riding Women do not fear uncontrolled nature, the open land and sky, but in turn resent the confinement of human settlements: "Out in the open they grew more confident ... even though the sky was an alien sky" (*F* 64). They feel the spiritual void, the violence, bitterness, and fear being engulfed by that "hungry emptiness. It has swallowed the Free Fems and now it is swallowing us" (*F* 67).

In the Holdfast, spiritual enlightenment and inner emptiness are glossed over by ritualized drug taking, so-called Dreamings, an obvious reference to the 1960s and 1970s drug-taking counter-culture. The

---

[22] *The spiral, the fems' symbol of resistance, is greatly feared as "the sign of the void, of fems, of everything inimical to the straight line of manly, rational thought and will" (W 119).*

[23] *The very name "Wasting" and the imagery of wasted barren land, food shortage, and a spiritual void associate the Holdfast with the old literary motif of the Waste Land. Charnas's postmodern version of the spiritual and physical desert/death of humanity's own making recalls pagan beliefs of the insulted Mother cursing the land with barrenness; Grail stories of land going to waste because a great lady/priestess/goddess has been offended and nature was plundered; and T.S. Eliot's famous multidimensional poem* The Waste Land *(1922)—drawing on Western and Eastern mythologies and religions—that characterizes the disillusionment of modern postwar society, emptied of any belief, devoid of sensibility, and lost in sterility.*

[24] *In American literature "the wilderness has been an exclusively masculine domain" (Showalter 243), whereas in the Holdfast series, by repopulating the wild with women—it is patrolled by Riding Women to prevent men from detecting and entering the Grasslands—the masculine zone is changed to the wild zone of women, literally a no-man's land where men are not welcome.*

manna drug is used for controlled mental escape. The private, individual experience of dreaming turns into a collective public event. At the Boyhouse Juniors are taught, for example, to center their dreams around "heroic themes ... of victorious battles ... [and] of power" (*W* 47). The drug is also used to seduce and control certain young men, so-called Rovers, into unquestioning obedience and executing violence. While the Biblical manna is a divine food supplied by a merciful and benign God, keeping his promise to lead his chosen people out of Egypt,[25] the Holdfast manna is a non-food produced by humans and does not represent a spiritual link. The Biblical manna provides in addition for body *and* soul and symbolizes sacramental and spiritual nourishment, the reconciliation and abolition of the divide between God and humans. The Holdfast manna, however, does not symbolize physical and spiritual liberation but psychological imprisonment and even death. It is used, moreover, as a necessary population control for this society threatened by starvation. Seniors "ripe for release" (*W* 80), but in reality death-seekers driven by "[c]ancer," "madness" (*W* 80), and desperation, flock to the aptly named Endpath, where the poisonous drug locks men into their very last dreams.[26] In DarkDreaming, Servan "open[s] the dark core" (*W* 47) of the soul and guides illegally drug-induced dreams. Like a postmodern Morpheus, he orchestrates the dreamer's dream, manipulates the psyche, and supplies the necessary mythology for opting out of the Official Myth. The "insidious lure of DarkDreaming lay partly in this deliberate abolition of hierarchy ... the void of their hidden selves, where any mad chaos was possible" (*W* 47).[27] DarkDreaming thus channels suppressed aggression and "potentially anti-social desires" (Lefanu 153). By keeping young men compliant, therefore, DarkDreaming and the outcast DarkDreamer Servan are essentially supportive of the system.

Charnas moves on from her criticism of patriarchal Christianity to criticizing ecofeminist positions, most prominently those expounded by Daly who aligns revalued femininity once more with nature. Albeit Daly's work—in particular her analysis of the mental colonization of women by patriarchal language and religion—is, in Sargisson's words, "disruptive

---

[25]*Today it has been identified as thick sweet liquid produced by scale insects living on tamarisks.*

[26]*The architecture of Endpath equates death with the return to the female womb, in that the "central chamber of Endpath is a domed circle" (*W* 27). Like a fetus brought to life in amniotic fluid, in a reverse motion the corpse is "born" into death by the sea water flooding the chamber and pulling the corpse with the current. The cyclical nature that men cannot escape from is epitomized by the Endpath's mutation from a fortress of death to a place of healing for Alldera after the assassination attempt, and back to a place of murder and rape in* The Conqueror's Child.

[27]*Dreaming is also associated with femininity and the body. One ferryman darkdreams of bodily and sexual metamorphosis, "he melted, he was a fem" (*W* 47), and Raff Maggomas dismisses dreaming as "[m]ind melting" (*W* 196) unworthy of men of action.*

of the mind/body divide ... [i]t stops short ... of being fully transgressive because Daly ... remains within a dualistic conceptual framework" (140). In *Gyn/Ecology*, Daly replaces, for example, phallogocentrisms with gynocentrisms, and her "universal woman" is predominantly white. With the Moonwoman cult, Charnas depicts exactly these inverted dualisms of ecofeminist positions and reintroduces with the Sallah cult, and with the Grasslanders, the women of color on whom cultural feminists such as Daly have not focused. Although the Moonwoman and Sunbear cults, congruent with the separatist motion of *Motherlines* and *The Furies*, represent a desirable step towards religious differentiation, both are nevertheless essentialist religions that underwrite a dualistic order by privileging female or male-centered nature deities. Father/God and Mother/Goddess cults prove equally destructive. The inherently palimpsest nature of religion, effacing or incorporating older religions and deities, is stressed by the appropriation of Setteo's spiritual bears by the Sunbear cult and by Fedeka's claim on Setteo's spirituality, that "[t]he mad belong to Moonwoman" (*F* 41). In captivity, the men incorporate and remake Setteo's private bear mysticism into a political religion that compels men to revolt. Unwittingly, Setteo provides "out of the world of his madness, a ritual of hope and aspiration ... Setteo's Bears ... replaced the gods ... of the Old Holdfast" (*CC* 186). In fact, the cult's central element, the Sunbear Dance, is a ritual of degradation and an outlet for repressed sexuality and aggression. It is a dance of sexual prowess and collective rape, a "drunken hate session" (*CC* 70). In the ritual, for instance, two rapists dressed as bears violate a victim, cheered on by voyeuristic onlookers chanting "power, power, power" (*CC* 187). In effect, they need Setteo's visions to legitimize their ritual rape as a transfer of the Sunbear's power to the participants. As a prophet, however, Setteo is difficult to manipulate. He lives according to his own rules, or rather his visions appear according to the rules of his "personal, illusory hell" (*CC* 143) and might predict "failure, destruction, and death" (*CC* 185) instead of victory.

Both cults also re-interpret events. Daya's and Fedeka's stories likewise reappropriate all actions as heteronomous and superimpose larger divine patterns on individual deeds. For instance, in one of Daya's stories Eykar is degraded to "Moonwoman's instrument" (*F* 18)—repeatedly he is described as "pale and cold" (*F* 18), associating him with the Moon—and as Moonwoman's minion he kills Raff. When he sets Alldera free, Daya narrates, he also acts under divine orders, "with the Lady's [Moonwoman's] own silver light in his pale eyes" (*F* 21). In a similar fashion, the men re-adapt the fems' slave stories of runaways who will come and liberate them: "[a] brave man risked his life to go exploring in the Wild ... to help us" (*CC* 190). In this sense, Servan represents Alldera's evil male alter ego. But unlike her, he does not return successfully, and just as Eykar is linked with the moon and femininity, the men's stories associated Servan with the sun and masculinity, "a hot, cruel, golden lad as greedy and merciless as the sun itself, and as beautiful" (*F* 18). He impersonates the Sunbear and is the "saviour" (*CC* 351), a perverted Christ figure.

Alldera, Eykar, and Sorrel oppose the attribution of divine power to nature and the resulting postponement of political and autonomous action. Alldera heretically objects that Moonwoman is an "ally of masters" (*M* 137), originally "invented by the Matris [the female slave overseers] to keep fems docile in their bondage" (*F* 48). For her, the Moonwoman cult is "a slave religion" (*F* 48), just as Eykar resents early on the first stirrings of a sun cult, scorning the childishness of "[a]ppealing to a sun god for power against a moon witch" (*W* 124). Sorrel questions the need for the imaginary and transcendent. She grounds herself instead in the present and tangible reality: "[W]hy ... *believe* in something? Besides yourself, your line, your friends and relations" (*CC* 160). Religion at its best may serve as a utopian model to be striven for, as Beyarra notes, "Most fems' experience of humanity hasn't been very encouraging.... We seek the reassurance of something more" (*CC* 160). Religion's intention might be to give ethical guidelines, Charnas accedes, but she insists that its "implicit purpose is ... always to divert energy and attention away from the search for true human intimacy, person to person, and to substitute the promise of intimacy with a non-being (God) or a kind of mass-intimacy with other believers" (Gordon 462). The only ones lacking any religious system, or a deity, and practicing self-responsible ethics of one-to-one intimacy are the Riding Women. "[T]heir society and their biology place each person so securely in relation to everybody else that they don't need to appeal to an outside force" (ibid. 463). Their approach to the world is a holistic one, acknowledging their link to nature and animality, for instance, most plainly during mating.

With the Holdfasters moving towards a multireligious society at the end of *The Conqueror's Child*—Sorrel works "with Eykar on a study of the connections between the moon, symbol of the Lady, and the sea, the Encompassing Heart of Sallah, in hope ... to find common ground" (*CC* 421)—the series suggests that the human need for religious compensation cannot be abolished, but acknowledges the exigency of at least tolerating different faiths in order to thwart fundamentalism. Only for this reason of religious diversification, it seems, has Charnas included the otherwise sketchy Sallah religion of the Pooltown people, an anthropomorphic worshipping of the Sea and a thinly disguised allusion to the Muslim god Allah.

Carefully distinguishing between religion and spirituality, Charnas suggests with Setteo's twisted shamanism that true spirituality is not external and controlled, but internal and uncontrollable, in her own words, a not unwelcome "wild element" (Gordon 464) that can only be experienced by a human "spirit-door" (ibid. 464) as a momentary existence between worlds. As shaman, Setteo can access various realities; the dead and the living are indistinguishable or rather are two modes of existence for him (cf. *F* 41). He encounters the animated spirits of all elements. His spirituality transcends moral judgements and rationality, and does not differentiate between human and animal. Where religion reinscribes a social status quo, Setteo's spirituality—a transreligious conglomerate of Christianity, Native American mythology and shamanism, all of a repeatedly erratic symbolism—has no societal aim. Charnas claims that he is "the concrete sign of ... openness" (Gordon 464), which a society needs to remain dynamic and open to change. Transgressing the spirit/matter and madness/sanity divide, Setteo is much less an "impotent Christ-figure" (Jones 190), as Jones argues, than, in Charnas's own view, a male Cassandra, a "crazy Tiresias ... [a] weak and fallible prophet" (Gordon 463) and a "trickster—Coyote, Raven, Loki ... in chains" (ibid. 464).[28] Like Shakespearean fools, he tells truth in his madness and forges lies in his sanity. For Jones, he is therefore "the most reliable observer" invoking "a nemesis" (190), since his narrations testify to atrocities and madness of the gender war. He is the first, for instance, to perceive what his fellow men repress: "The clearest truth was that the reign of men was over" (*F* 114).[29] It is, after all, not the shaman's task to save society, Charnas insists, but to provide visions and "questions with no answers, the immense creativity of mystery and untamed human energy" (Gordon 463). Therefore, once Setteo learns to master the written wor(l)ds and its prescribed truths, his visions stop and he realizes that "[y]ou can't have *all* the kinds of knowing in the world" (*CC* 69). Here visions, whether they stem from shamanism/fantasy or science/literacy, have parity as two different but equal ways of knowing. The fact that Setteo looses his dreamworld, after having acquired literacy, emphasizes that unilateral rationality may supersede and erase fantasy yet might not necessarily provide an all-encompassing wisdom.

The poetical passages of Setteo and his mystical Bears stand out among the harsh and realistic language Charnas uses. The metaphorical language is ambiguous about whether Setteo's elusive bears are real

---

[28]*Other minor tricksters are the mad Riding Woman, Grays Omelly, in* Motherlines *and Servan.*

[29]*Premonition takes him to the assassination scene where he helps to save Alldera, and he correctly predicts the return of the Sunbear/Servan with "death power in one finger of his right hand" (CC 184), the Pooltown gun.*

or illusory monster-spirits, personifications and catalysts of (human) violence, or shamanic/totemic Native American nature spirits.[30] Perhaps Setteo creates them in his madness, or perhaps he is the only one with an affinity to perceive them. The relations between Setteo and his Bears are unstable and changing; sometimes he is prey and sometimes a "strong spirit traveller" (*F* 324). The bears likewise inhabit the imaginary cold country, "the world of the Dead" (*F* 115), as opposed to the warm world of the living. Signifying that violence and death are inherently parts of and eternal laws of nature, the bears thrive on violence, nourished by human aggression and killing; but they also silently grieve about the killing of nature as such, about "the loss of everything that had lived ... before the Wasting" (*F* 117). Allegorically, the rule of violence is epitomized by the image of an ice bridge composed of "whole men, frozen in twisted postures.... Bear dancers were here, faces distorted with terror. Their fingers clawed, their fists pounded at the enclosing ice.... They screamed—inaudibly—for help" (*CC* 239).

This image of men frozen in their violence, however, is inconsistent because the fems' rule is equally brutal. The only man half-daring to reach beyond violence is Eykar. He is the *keystone* of the ice bridge, "curled with one arm over his eyes and the other thrust out ... fingertips already free, in a dimpling of melt-water" (*CC* 240). He is the central stone keeping the artificial, static male system intact, but he has also partially freed himself.[31] If he breaks free of the frozen bridge, male violence will fall apart. To prevent the loss of their food cache, the Bears need to thaw the ice on their terms: "One warm body can melt all this wealth of food so that we can reach it ... children burn very warm, and to be given these men by children would ... make us laugh" (*CC* 239). To maintain the circle of violence, the sacrificial death of a child is needed, and therefore Setteo is to bring "the hottest one [Veree] to the lowest step ... called 'Sunbear'" (*CC* 240). The moment that Setteo, torn between his love for Veree and fulfilling the Bears' request, and thus being accepted as their "true younger brother" (*CC* 320) and as men's equal, succumbs fearfully: he transforms into a Bear. "Setteo saw his own reflection in the child's pupils: there were yellow fangs pushing out his upper lip" (*CC* 242). On his way to sacrifice Veree to the "Sunbear" Servan, water is given twice to Setteo. The cairn that Sorrel built as the

---

[30]*His very name—Set is a Kiowa word for "bear"—associates Setteo with Bears and a Native American context. His affinity with animals also turns him into a mutated/resurrected version of Captain Kelmz, as he re-introduces the beastly animals Captain Kelmz longed for.*

[31]*The symbolic significance of the keystone as wedge, keeping a structure* in place, *is further stressed when Eykar inspects Sorrel's cairn and suggests adding a keystone to build a stone vault, a suggestion Sorrel objects to because a keystone would arch the roof upwards (Old Holdfast style) instead of downwards, her preferred tent-roof (Grassland) style.*

monument to a better future for Veree and all men "shed[s] tears for him" (*CC* 316) and quenches his thirst. When he encounters the Pooltown people, they also offer him water. These acts of compassion, "the debt of water given" and received, and the water's "reflection of the curved moon" (*CC* 321), remind Setteo of Moonwoman and the fems, and that it is truly his own decision whether he acts out of love or fear. Given the choice, he finds the courage not to turn Veree over to be made into another Servan. With his act of love, Setteo announces the 'Second Coming,' the new "time of love" (*F* 118) that he has foretold and that simultaneously leads to his death as the climax of his existence. At the very moment of his death, accidentally killed by Sheel, he transcends the extremes that threatened to crush him. The Bears warned him that escape from the war of the sexes is nearly impossible: "The Country of Anger has no boundaries once you stand upon its burning lands. The only way out of it is by flying into the quiet sky above. But to fly high enough to see beyond its borders takes the power of more than one wing" (*F* 326). To rise above separatism and to step over the boundaries of destruction, the sexes must unite their factions.[32] By heroically cutting the pattern of violence and sacrificing himself to his own gods in place of Veree, Setteo symbolically gains wings and freedom: "he soared, into a clean and tranquil sky" (*CC* 323).[33]

4.3.2. The Distorting and the Truthful Character of Myths

Myths identify another form of culturally shared memory. Like religion, myth describes a collective interpretation of reality.[34] Myths and the re/deconstruction of mythmaking are, if not always key elements, an essential part of the background in many sf novels, particularly in feminist sf, but also of feminist theory. The double-function of myth can potentially empower and limit us, as Sargisson explains: "if myth has (historically) embodied ideological values and aspirations, re/deconstructed myth perhaps can embody or at least inscribe different values" (217). In the *Holdfast* series, mythmaking and its deconstruction in relation to ideology occur in several instances. All point towards the ambiguity and arbitrariness of events that may end up as integral parts of history, reli-

---

[32]*Exactly such a momentary union of the sexes occurs when Setteo guides Beyarra to the Watchtower to save Alldera.*
[33]*The manuscript explicitly stresses the act of liberation: "he flew free" (ms. CC 450).*
[34]*E.g., formerly extant and now vanished parts of reality such as technology and animals acquire the status of myths.*

gion, or myth. Like truth, inherently, myth does not conform to either/or categories. As prehistoric, pre-scientific consciousness, myth means "telling a story" that might be grounded in facts, but myth also refers to a piece of fiction which again might convey a psychological truth. Generally speaking though, myths are fabricated stories, often involving the supernatural and dealing with creation. Myth and mythologies are akin to religion in their primitive attempt at explaining nature and the cosmos and in their reliance on belief. Myth can become part of religions and literature; and myth often indicate repressed desire and the unreal. Charnas takes a very critical stance towards myths and mythologies and exposes myth, like religion, as an artifact, created by humans and consequently often structured around political content. In the series, we witness the distorting and the truthful character of myth, and the utopian use as well as the dystopian abuse of myth. In Setteo's private mythology, for example, the Riding Women figure as other-worldly Angels and mentors, "great dead heroes of the past, remade by the Bears to be guides for the Blessed [the fems] in modern times" (F 114). Both Setteo's private bear mythopoeia and the author's mythopoeic re-appropriation of the Amazon myth illustrate the intersections between myth and religion/spirituality, while Daya's stories provide an example of turning history into myth.

The strong warrior physicality and the harmonic relation to nature has rendered Amazons the "favorite romantic images of feminist sf" (Jones 185). Following Greek mythology, women writers often presented Amazonian characters as anomaly and utopian exception, geographically removed to an island and hence cut off from "real" woman's role in society.[35] Haraway has described this essentially supportive function of Amazon tales: "Monsters have always defined the limits of community in Western imaginations. The centaurs and Amazons of ancient Greece established the limits of the centered polis of the Greek male human by their disruption of marriage and boundary pollutions of the warrior with animality and woman" (180). In like manner, representations of the subaltern woman underpin such notions of alien femininity:

> The non–European woman also appears in an intractable version, as "Amazonian" or deviant femininity. The Amazons are located by early colonial writings in virtually every part of the non–European

---

[35] *Batya Weinbaum offers a thorough, although at times slightly muddled, but nevertheless very insightful study of mythical, archetypal, historical, textual, and cultural manifestations of Amazons (for twentieth-century literary representations of Amazons, see especially 47ff.). According to Weinbaum, classical and medieval literature developed from depicting Amazons as a collective horde of warriors to showing the Amazon as "individuated anima figure" (xix), while contemporaneous literature "revitalizes," "reacts," and "reclaims" Amazons, focusing primarily on the Amazon as dying, as wild femininity, and as initiation rite.*

world, and provide images of insatiable sexuality and brutality. Thus female volition, desire and agency are literally pushed to the margins of the civilised world [Loomba 154].

Using Amazons as "concept rather than historic reality,"[36] Charnas revises and appropriates the Amazon tale for altered ends, and thereby challenges and corrects the gender stereotype embodied in the Amazonian myth. Profoundly changing the stereotypical Greek myth of mutilated femininity and of androgyneous females becoming more like men—etymologically the Greek word *a-mazos*, translated as "breastless," transports the erroneous belief that Amazons destroyed their right breast—Charnas virtually re-members the Amazons with two breasts and depicts how fems and men strive to become more like Riding Women (who are never called "Amazons").[37] The Riding Women of multiracial descent fit only into the patterns Haraway and Loomba describe insofar, as they live on the cultural margin in the uncharted desert, a geographical metaphor for their "otherness" and in that their admittedly strange, but hardly uncivilized, sexual and cultural practices differ vastly from the "civilized" Holdfast practices such as rape and anthropophagy. Yet they represent female agency, desire and volition as *positive* features of the *other* woman. Unlike the Amazons of Greek myth, moreover, they do not legitimize the status quo, but subvert it. Their femininity, independent of generic man, questions and their existence destablizes rather than fixes the essentialist universal of male/female. From the moment they take Alldera in, and later on when they allow the Free Fems to claim kinship, up to the actual journey of a small delegation to the Holdfast, the Grasslanders are affected by the Holdfasters. Their society is infused with the Holdfast's societal rules and norms, thus undercutting the Riding Women's function as outsiders. Moreover, unlike Amazons and despite being characterized as fierce warriors, the Riding Women never actually join the fems' war against men. Like Elgin's Aliens, they merely observe and comment on the battle and the building of a new society.

Through her reformulation of the traditional Amazon, in part, Charnas reshapes the feminist idea of "a less distorted past,"[38] a lost, actual feminist past, into the fictional future society of the Riding Women, a

---

[36]*Interview with Charnas. See the appendix.*
[37]*Following Robert Graves's claim that Amazon means "moon-woman" (379), the Riding Women could also be read as the incarnation of divine Moonwoman that both Fedeka and Daya prophesied.*
[38]*Interview with Charnas. See the appendix. Charnas dismisses "feminist theory about ... real Amazons, not just mythical ones" as "dreams revising the past," but is intrigued by the "idea of an Amazon culture" (Mohr 1999c, 8). To her the Riding Women represent not "a vaguely unnatural female threat to the hegemony of Greek men," rather they signify what she desires for "our real past" (Mohr 1999d, 16).*

potential future model for the Holdfasters that coalesces in the fictional present with their own mythical/historical past. While the Amazonian myth is exclusively anchored in our past, the Grassland society exists at the same time as the Holdfast. Myth can turn into reality, Charnas seems to maintain; myth functions to modify our reality and affects our world. Although seemingly coming from myth and returning to myth, the Riding Women are part of the Holdfast history and not part of its mythic lore, and thus exemplify perhaps most notably the transgressive element of myth. With the Riding Women, mythical and historical time merge; time as such becomes relative, as the Riding Women are rooted in history as well as myth, in the past as well as in the future. In this sense, myth signifies that ignored or wilfully forgotten part of a society which recedes not into historic but mythic past. For the Riding Women, for example, men are elements of "history-become-myth" (Bartkowski 95). This link between history and myth is further stressed by Alldera's departing, much like King Arthur's departure to Avalon (cf. also Mohr 1999c, 11), together with the Riding Women to where they have come from: the blurred realm of myth and history. Alldera has shaped Holdfast history, yet as much as her disappearance from the Holdfast's present gives the next generations, represented by Sorrel and Veree, physical and psychological space, her absence leaves space for myth to trail her. In fact, the myth-making process actually begins before she leaves.

The Riding Women's reproductive habits stresses their timeless existence even further. Parthenogenesis turns the Grasslanders into replicated "identical pairs, trios, or even more" (*M* 48), forming a postmodern "immortal feminist community" (Barr 1987, 7) that exists outside of time, as with each replica past, present, and future merge. On the one hand, this eternal recreation of the self presents an element of stasis in their culture; on the other hand, parthenogenesis creates a bond of continuity with the past as well as with the future. After her death, as one Riding Woman explains, "I'm still part of my motherline, with women of my flesh before me and behind me" (*M* 74). This concept of the self transgresses temporal and body boundaries, keeping them "in touch with strong currents that hold all the things and beings ... in balance" (*M* 150).

Charnas demonstrates the actual *making* of myths with the storyteller Daya. Daya mythologizes and valorizes Alldera into a secular mythical figure. Daya also politicizes that myth for her own schemes. In one episode, Daya reshapes her own inglorious participation in the assassination attempt. Her role mutates from inciting the murder to having prevented it. Daya retells the assassination story her way until fiction replaces reality, "until people thought that was how it had happened" (*F* 379), and her reputation changes. She is "if not a hero, at least not a villain"

(*F* 379). She claims, "I stopped the attack. I sent for help" (*CC* 61), when in fact it was Beyarra. In Daya's stories, Alldera acts under the orders of Moonwoman. For instance, Daya ascribes religious/mythic meaning to Alldera's return with wild horses from her solitary sojourn into the desert, when Daya remakes the desert episode into Moonwoman calling Alldera to the desert and sending Alldera back with horses the colors of sun, night and moon (cf. *F* 22). At the same time that Alldera is intrigued by "all the color and ornament" (*F* 32) that Daya adds, the messenger Alldera who values "accuracy in a message" (*F* 319) resents Daya's myth-making, that turns Alldera into "a stranger to myself, a myth instead of a person" (*F* 32). Because "[p]eople can believe anything of a legend" (*F* 348), Alldera is perceived as an overpowering threat by some who then attempt in fact to assassinate this mythic *image*. Alldera is increasingly confronted with this distortion of reality and self-estrangement.

Mythic embellishments literally represent Alldera as larger than life.[39] Upon first encountering Alldera, Beyarra objects: "We have songs about you. But they say you are very tall." (*F* 78). Although Alldera denies immortality and divinity in their last talk, Alldera and Eykar are acutely aware of this danger of myths turning them into gods. They are the stuff myths are made of, as Eykar remarks: "Someday they'll decide we were gods. Well, their descendants will.... We'll be long dead.... We won't care. Not even if they decide we were lovers, a divine pair coupling to bring forth the moon and the sun and all good things" (*CC* 410). That only Alldera vanishes from the story is significant. Sent out by the Matris on the pretense of finding the mythical Free Fems, the runner Alldera returns with the myth turned true. Her message has been delivered and her mission of liberating the fems has been completed. Whether she will be remembered as Moonwoman's representative although she never was a mooncult worshipper is therefore irrelevant. In contradistinction, the captive men's fantasy about free men roaming the Wild turned out to be as true, but it has not liberated them. For this reason, Eykar must stay behind. He is still needed as a role model for men trying to figure out how to be good fathers, how to explore manhood in different ways. By remaining in the New Holdfast, he can control his own myth to prevent others from twisting him into a symbol for machismo.

---

[39]*Captain Kelmz is another example of being mythologized into a "walking legend" (*W* 38). The Juniors know his "life better than he did himself" and revere him "like some mythical paragon of the manly virtues" (*W* 37).*

4.3.3. Piecing Together History's Truths: Language and Written and Oral History

Unlike religion and myth, by popular definition history studies the past and tries hard not to distort historic reality. The monopolization of history, the restriction of voices heard in the discourse of history, and the selection of events, however, leads inevitably to misrepresentations. Essentially, myth and history show different glimpses of reality, but, Charnas insists, "both are fiction, because none is the whole story, the real truth" (Mohr 1999d, 20). Nevertheless, in contrast to her scathing critique of myth and religion, Charnas stresses the need to know history: "Without history you are ... reduced to political infancy ... to victimhood, because you don't know any better than to submit ... [and then] reinvent the wheel of collective action yet again" (Gordon 461–462). However critical she remains of history as truth, written history is to her "a tool for curbing the excesses of myth and preserving *something* of past reality for the future" (Mohr 1999d, 20). Charnas takes a poststructuralist and feminist approach to history, suggesting "that the lives of various oppressed peoples can only be uncovered by insisting that there is no single history but a 'multiplicity of histories'" (Loomba 13). Her portrayal of the Holdfasters' changing take on history and the inclusion of the subaltern voice in Book Four demonstrate this necessity to get various "angles of vision on the past to see ... something that resembles its truth" (ibid. 19).[40] Various ways of inscribing and recording history are presented, such as orality (songs and stories), literacy (books, ledgers), inscriptions on the body (tattoos, memory marks), and the land (architecture, monuments, roads). Charnas emphasizes orality and literacy equally, for both are "carriers of truth" (Gordon 462); but both methods of memory storage are faulty by nature, even if an accurate representation of reality is desired. Manipulation and distortion are, in Charnas's view, not gender but power related. The monolithic, monocausal, and androcentric version of written and oral revisionist history in *Walk*—what Daly has termed "monodimensional reality"—that privileges male values and actions and excludes female and ethnic experiences as deviant, is mirrored in Elnoa's, the matriarchal leader of the Tea Camp, deliberate manipulation of the secret ledgers she keeps. Orality is no less distorting and revisionist. Men's chants exclude fems, and Daya's oral canonization of history in her stories manipulates male as well as female roles. With the individual songs of the Riding Women, the

---

[40]For instance, fems, Riding Women, and Sallali add their versions to the dominant version of the "Wasting."

importance of interrelating personal and public history is stressed and is picked up again by the acknowledgement of the indispensable multiplicity of written and oral history composed of a mosaic of personal subjective voices in *The Conqueror's Child*. As the storyteller's (Daya) and the librarian's (Eykar) pupil, the character Beyarra links literacy and orality, and she epitomizes the move towards historic decanonization, multidimensional reality, and multiperspectivism.

Language as the medium of written and spoken discourse and as the element that structures our perception of the world reflects an individual's or a group's societal status as well as one's perspective on reality. Both sexes identify the *other* in sexual and animal terms, creating a negative semantic space for the *other*. Men apply semantic derogation, following the rule that "words which are marked for females ... used in association with females ... [or] are marked female are marked negative" (Spender 16). Here, women are referred to as "fems," "dams," and "cunts," and the term "dirties" is used for people of color.[41] Already in the 1970s, Charnas had extended feminist criticism of patriarchal concepts of difference that construct woman as the sexual *other*, as "non-man" with reference to the male self, to the inclusion of the ethnic/racial category. Both people of color and women are linguistically excluded as "unmen" in the Aristotelian sense of impotent males on the grounds of race and sex. Masculinity and white skin determine human status. White man is the universal human, the norm against which women and people of color are measured. Fems, however, apply the same linguistic standard declaring themselves the norm. Disparagingly they speak of the Riding Women, deviant from *their* norm, as "mares." Once in power and now occupying the public domain, however, the Free Fems use similar derogatory terms such as "stick," "muck," and "cockie" for men.

The absence and presence of silence and sound is intrinsically linked with language. One presupposes the other; a speaker needs a listener and vice versa. In the Old Holdfast, silence is not contemplative richness, but is associated with nothingness, zero, femininity. Men fear the absence of sound, the oppressive silence of the void of the wilderness and the deathlike stillness of a nature devoid of animals, and desire silence at the same time. The figuratively silenced *other* is literally a muted group, as men sometimes cut fems' tongues out.[42] Language acquisition is a question of gender and status, and silence is the price fems pay for mere survival:

---

[41]*"Dirties" reflects a colonial discourse grounded in "medieval and religious associations of blackness with filth and dirt" (Loomba 71) that considered people of color, specifically Africans, as unclean and bestial.*
[42]*The anthropologists Edwin and Shirley Ardener (1975) were the first to use the terms dominat and muted group in relation to men and women. See also Spender (1980; esp. chap. 3) and Elaine Showalter (1985).*

female messengers and speakers such as Alldera are an exception. Male speech, on the other hand, is hard-edged, whereas the fems' indirect, submissive, and formulaic "softspeech" (*W* 60) corresponds with their repressed, low status. At the same time, their slurred guttural speech and submissive body language disguises their subculture. Whenever men approach, fems shield their world from further audio-visual male penetration. Suddenly, they "acquired a slight stoop or cringe," faces go "slack and foolish" (*W* 53). If needed, fems practice code-switching; Fossa, the leader of the Bayo fems, for instance, responds in male speech. Unlike the female linguists of Elgin's *Native Tongue* series, the fems do not have a language of their own; but they devise their own secretive use of language. Language, Charnas argues, needs speakers and listeners willing to share and understand. Usually a fem is required to speak in formulaic responses such as "this fem feels" (*W* 55) obliterating the self and her subjectivity. When Eykar asks Alldera for her version of events, for example, she denies using the voice he offers her, because as messenger she is "a brute with a memory for others' words" (*W* 151) and used to articulating only what the listener expects to hear. In this instance, ordered to speak, her silence becomes an act of defiance, and Eykar is unnerved by the eloquence of her silence.[43] However, she too nurtures the "prime fantasy of all speaking fems—that of becoming the one who, by sheer eloquence, drove through the barrier of men's guilt and fear" (*W* 152). When she finally speaks up, Alldera fulfills this dream, using her *own* words. Language becomes here a "symbol of integration" (Lefanu 156); sharing language and perspectives humanizes both Eykar and Alldera. The Riding Women's "singing drawl" (*M* 29) and "liquid speech" (*M* 55) contrasts sharply with the "hard-edged, barking speech" (*M* 30) of Holdfasters. Nenisi, for example, talks "like a musical instrument" (*M* 32). Free of interruptions and free to speak anytime, the Riding Women talk *with* rather than *at* one other. Speech and intonation reflect, therefore, the difference between hierarchical and communal communication systems: "the way the men—and fems, imitating men—had decided things, quickly, by command. Here, anyone ... could speak.... Their ease at speaking their mind still awed her [Alldera] ... she sought to share their free flow of conversation" (*M* 64).

Literacy and written history are primarily criticized as measures to exclude the *other* and to discipline and brainwash the (male) self. Literacy plays no major role. Only as the Holdfast universe grows increasingly complex in Book Four is literacy reintroduced as a way to store what Charnas calls "extended memory" (Gordon 461). Originally a locus of knowledge, the library, used as the Boyhouse in *Walk*, now conceals

---

[43]See also Chapter 4.4.2. for a further discussion of this scene.

information.[44] Here, chunks of history, the "[i]mages and records of the unmen" (*W* 112), are literally kept in darkness. The Seniors decree reality and history. Teaching a thus altered history turns into a matter of mindless memorization: "the books of the Ancients ... were read aloud ... until each boy could repeat what he had heard word perfect" (*W* 107). Historic distortions and misapprehensions of words no longer signifying existing signs are desired.[45] From early childhood on, Eykar is a "fanatical and gifted memorist" (*W* 107), infatuated with learning and history. Unlike his fellow pupils, however, the truth-seeker Eykar cannot ignore the "discrepancies of content" and realizes that the Boyhouse is not to "teach the truths" but to "impose discipline" (*W* 108). Distrusting the handed-down past eventually triggers his desire both to experience and question reality, the present, himself *and* to desire the inclusion of the *other's* point of view. Knowing that "[w]ords are power" (*CC* 149), his interest in Alldera's "own experience" (*W* 166), her story of Holdfast life, also marks the first step towards sharing that power and breaking up the male monopoly. Later he becomes the librarian and scrivener, a keeper of knowledge, the "guardian of the relics of civilization" (Jones 189).[46] For him, knowledge is a (mental) food, "to be harvested, like nourishing grain" (*F* 158), that a literally starved society should crave. On the other hand, on the pretense of "simply [being] a salvager of tattered books, a harmless and hopeful gleaner of knowledge" (*F* 200), he momentarily escapes from reality, the making of history in which he strives to partake.

As feminist historiography has criticized, those in power write history. Charnas reminds us that female written history, however, is equally manipulative and exclusive if used as a tool of power. The otherwise silenced voice of Elnoa, one of the fems whose tongue has been cut out, speaks in her secretly written ledgers, keeping history/herstory as she wants to remember it. Elnoa's writing is unreliable and subjective. Not interested in an accurate chronicle of reality, she deliberately misrepresents reality according to memory passed off as truth: "I write ... what I *remember*.... In my ledgers the *facts* are written" (*M* 129; emphasis added). The illusionary objectivity and the durability of writing obliterates and eradicates oral memory because Elnoa's ledgers "will outlast all your [the fems'] loud talk, your whispers, your singing of songs" (*M* 130).

---

[44]*Potentially, it is also a place of subversion. At the library Captain Kelmz sees pictures of beasts and here Setteo first encounters his Bears "smiling at him from the ... faded pages"* (F 145).

[45]*E.g., ironically feminist bra-burning literally mutates into the destruction of patriarchal weapons: "Since 'bra' was a word in an old language meaning 'weapon,' clearly 'bra-burner' meant a fem who ... destroyed the weapons of her master"* (W 58).

[46]*His role as knowledge seeker of the microcosm is foreshadowed by his astronomer's interest in the macrocosm. As Endtendant he "made maps of the heavens"* (F 367).

Orality and literacy, placed in opposition here, one trying to block out the other, are presented as complementary. Neither is immune to manipulation; neither can claim objectivity. Both can be used for integrative or exclusive purposes. Unlike in some feminist theorizings, from the start orality is not exclusively linked to women. Men, fems, and Riding Women use songs, chants, and storytelling; all forms take considerable part in history making. Stories, whether fictional, mythical or historical, are unreliable. Like Elnoa's rewriting history in her ledgers, both Daya and Servan, using the same sly and manipulative type of oral storytelling, reinterpret Alldera's and Eykar's lives. Servan conjures "transmutation[s] of the reality" (*W* 126), wilfully insinuating what is not and eradicating what is, presenting his relationship with Eykar in ever-changing ways. Daya reshapes and falsely glorifies the fems' Holdfast history, casts stories of the future and reconstructs Alldera's (past) reality into myth (cf. *CC* 39). Retrospectively, Daya even remakes Alldera into the active central character of *Walk* that she is only in retrospection of the whole series. As the preceding example suggests, perspective constitutes and changes reality. Even though Daya refrains from putting down her own name to give the impression of objectivity—"part of the storyteller's true art [was] to hold herself out of the tale and leave the glory to others" (*F* 172)—Daya's opinion and point of view are only thinly veiled. Her highly ambiguous storytelling art consequently vacillates between truth and lies. Daya falsifies the immediate history of the reconquest, arbitrarily obliterates the names of the bond fems who participated in their liberation, and omits Alldera's disquiet about the fems' cannibalism (cf. *F* 167). Daya's pupil Beyarra vacillates between fascination with the magic tales about the Tea Camp and the Grassland and disquiet over the arbitrary construction of Daya's concoctions. Daya acts out her authority of selection, "You remember more clearly than I do?" (*F* 168), and suppresses the objections of Beyarra, who becomes all the more determined to *"find out the names ... I will include them all, when I tell the tale"* (*F* 169). Alldera, too, reproaches Daya for glossing over Holdfast slavery and concocting plans of recovering the Holdfast as an oral sedative for the Free Fems at the Tea Camp: "Your romances of the past are as false as your romances of the future.... We were slaves. That's our real history" (*M* 140). Daya's fabrications immobilize and pacify fems just as the Matris's stories of escapees do. Both are stories of token resistance and "substitute dreams of the future for present action" (Lefanu 152). On the other hand, Daya truthfully keeps alive the memory of slavery as well as that of the Tea Camp. These are "tales of the truths of the old life" that help the fems to "remember straight" and to refrain "from making it ... romantic" (*F* 139). In this sense, Daya embodies the fems' living memory, "our singer, our poet, the keeper of our story for the future generations" (*F* 185).

Daya's stories are hybrids with specks of reality and a large chunk of fiction, selectively depicting a utopian and dystopian New Holdfast. She designs elaborate stories about the fems' future conquest of the Holdfast. Some are role-reversal stories about fems subjugating men as pet men (cf. *M* 182). Others are intricately linked with Moonwoman, just as her stories form "like a white stone at the bottom of a bowl of water" (*M* 100) and anticipate a future beyond the war of the sexes. In her version of the future, nature and time come to an almost Biblical standstill: "earth and sky are bound in a great stillness ... clouds hang in the sky without changing shape ... the sea itself lies still" (*M* 100) awaiting the change fems *could* bring. In Daya's allegorical fairy tale, the Holdfast stasis is symbolized by a "huge wheel of white stone" (*M* 100) that Moonwoman, in the form of an old fem, tries to move in vain. In succession three fems encounter the old fem. The first fem declines to help because she has returned "to conquer, not to work" (*M* 100); the second fem refuses "to follow anyone's orders, I've come to give orders" (*M* 101). In both instances the white wheel, the Holdfast stasis, blocks their way, and Moonwoman disappears. Only the third fem abjures this masculine representation of hierarchy and subordination. She emphatically recognizes herself in the old fem and cooperatively offers help. Together they can move the stone, instigate social change, and the third fem is rewarded with finding many fems alive. To instigate social change requires cooperation, the recognition of the self in the *other*, and a lot of painful work. Simply following the old roads paved with new stones, Daya warns, will not change the chosen route.

Daya wields the power of the word without ever quite realizing this considerable power. Instead, she envies Alldera her active heroic deeds and, indeed, shies away from taking any active part in the conquest; as Alldera remarks, "*only your stories are heroic*" (*F* 308). The real punishment for Daya the traitor is thus silencing her as storyteller: "nobody heard her words anymore. All her stories were suspect now. That was why she no longer told them" (*CC* 114). Even her death is a brilliant piece of staging, the last story she accomplishes. On her deathbed, she weaves the story of her own enigmatic heroic action. She claims the attack on Servan at Endpath as hers; her lover Galligan acted merely as "her weapon" (*CC* 397), as Beyarra correctly perceives. After Beyarra has recorded her version of the Endpath showdown, Daya is at last "done with words" (*CC* 400).

Songs are an important means for assigning the self a place in history and in the respective society of the Old and New Holdfast, and of the Grassland society. The men's formulaic *collective* songs primarily serve the purposes of instilling a *collective* masculine memory, of inscribing masculine history, and of claiming possession of land, glory, and achievements.[47] The Chant Protective cements the belief in male greatness and swears men to brotherhood (cf. *W* 9), the Boyhouse songs instill "manly virtues: pride, courage, strength, patience, reason, loyalty" (*W* 122) and the Chant Commemorative provides a linguistic memorial tomb for dead men. While the men sing for leisure, fems sing to ease their slave labor. Fems use double-voiced songs. Covering the true content, other seemingly wordless sounds always mask their real songs: "under the camouflage of gutturals and trills set up ... to mask the sense of the song from the men" (*W* 159).[48] Theirs are songs of protest and rebellion, a way of recalling their painful history and of remembering their dead. Their riddle-songs with titles such as "Why is a raven like a writing-desk?" (*W* 143), referring to the Mad Hatter in Carroll's *Alice in Wonderland*, effectively disprove the supposition that they are capable only of limited speech. Although the meaning and the memory of the literary allusion might be lost, it implies that once fems were literate.

For the Riding Women, *self*-songs are expressions of their *individual* stories that assert their contributions to their society's history. They practice exactly what Cixous has postulated: "Woman must put herself into the text—as into the world and into history—by her own movement.... Women should break out of the snare of silence" (1976, 875, 881). A Riding Woman sings "a personal song" (*M* 58) about "her own personal history" (*M* 66) and her origins; she sings of her accomplishments and heroic deeds that identifies her to other women and it helps her to understand herself. I would contest Jones's critical interpretation of the self-songs as potentially subversive of the society's cohesion, for the "common cultural heritage is [hence] ephemeral, disparate, ready to fly apart" (185). Rather in these songs of the *self* the individual voice is reconciled with the collective composed of selves. These self-songs celebrate a Riding Woman's ancestry of share-mothers, and as tool of memory storage they provide each woman with a sense of female historical continuity. When Alldera practices her own self-song for the first time, her song "is all about fems" (*M* 71) and not about herself. Expressing individuality when she has been denied subjectivity and always been grouped in a collective is problematic for her. By rejecting Alldera's self-song, Nenisi ignores what Alldera's past is about: fems in the plural. Historically, whether personal or collective, her subject status and her subjective point of view have never been an issue. Alldera asserts the importance of not blotting out the Holdfast reality: "It is part of my past,

---

[47]*Numerous chants regulate male social life. There are chants thanking the multifunctional hemp plant, chants preparatory of DarkDreaming, celebratory chants for men who dare "the borders of the Holdfast" (*W* 35), even if it is only for the profane purpose of obtaining wood.*

[48]*Men are ignorant of this double voicing. Significantly, only Eykar is early on disturbed by the songs (cf.* W *29).*

part of my life.... The first life was real too" (*M* 71). The different contents of fems' and Riding Women's songs are plainly recognizable at Sorrel's naming ceremony. The Riding Women sing of "cherished memories" (*M* 211) and the Free Fems contribute "songs of pain" (*M* 211).

The opposition between orality and literacy in relation to history is increasingly resolved in *The Conqueror's Child*. By reclaiming the library—before only subversive female writing, in form of spirals on the walls, signalled female presence—the fems take repossession of literacy. Several fems wrongly dismiss literacy as a masculine tool (cf. *CC* 45)—Daya opposes literacy as an "insult to the storyteller's art" (*CC* 191)—with a biased perspective. Sorrel's accusation that the Riding Women's "songs are truths about their foremothers' lives.... Your books are full of men's lies" (*CC* 108) is partly invalidated insofar as the fems discover books by female authors, much like feminist literary historians and historiographers did.[49] The transgression of oral and written history is specifically symbolized by the character Beyarra. As previously stated, the new historian Beyarra, former pupil of Daya the storyteller and now the student of Eykar the scrivener, merges orality with literacy. The correlation of both, and the avoidance of either one being the central source of truth, is captured in the image of Beyarra transcribing the oral stories of "eyewitnesses" (*CC* 48) into written accounts. In contrast to Elnoa's secretive and selective writing and Daya's ornamental orality, Beyarra writes "to spread knowledge around" (*CC* 50). With Beyarra "a new history with women as the makers and recorders of tales" (Bartkowski 94) evolves, and the content includes now "new stories, stories of the Free" (*CC* 50). Aspiring to tell truths in the plural, she takes care to get as many dissenting perspectives as possible on Holdfast history in the making: "Anybody can lie about the past.... Without records of others' experiences, who could correct the lies?" (*CC* 46). In contrast to history formerly told from an exclusive white male point of view, Beyarra's records include multiple her/his-stories of fems and, eventually, of men and of the Pooltown people. In a bow to postcolonial literature and criticism, Charnas embraces the cultural memory that was eradicated and blamed on women and people of color in the Wasting and allows the previously silenced and excluded subaltern a voice. Readmitted to literacy and the recording of history, men such as the young man Payder recognize the importance of plurality. He relishes the "piecing together of history's *truths*" (*CC* 421; emphasis added) in the book room.

History as lived reality is also inscribed as physical memory onto

---

[49] The reference to the autobiography *West with the Night* (cf. *CC 109*) by Beryl Mirkham, who was a pioneer aviator in British East Africa in the early twentieth century, stresses the existence of strong female role models.

the body and the land, and is expressed by architecture. Men redefine tattooing and use tattoos to visualize their social status within the Holdfast hierarchy. Each mark identifies company rank, bravery, and heroism, and distinguishes men from one other, but more importantly, from fems. The much abhorred "femmish"/feminine mark of birth is thus replaced and overwritten by a mark of masculinity. Although rejecting the ornamental as feminine—the "proper purpose" of tattooing is "to imprint rank-signs on the shoulders of men, not designs on the skins of fems" (*W* 99)—the scarred male body becomes eroticized. The acquisition of corporeal marks hierarchizes Juniors who "vied for standing on the basis of scars" (*W* 36). Significantly, when Servan undermines the system and their hierarchy by descending into DarkDreaming, the Seniors cauterize Servan's tattoo in order to erase his identity.

Previously inscribed in body and psyche with narrations of subordination and mutilations such as the cutting off of tongues, the Free Fems reclaim authorship of their own bodies and eventually learn to value "the integrity of ... any human body" (*CC* 92). In *The Conqueror's Child* Alldera witnesses, initially appalled by this "loathsome custom of the masters" (*CC* 91), how a young Bayo-born woman is tattooed without any anaesthetics. Watching the inscription of the woman's body, however, triggers memories of her own visible and invisible body scars; and she comprehends that these "memory marks" are far from ornamental and signify neither brutality nor submission but remembrance. The Bayo-born carry these body inscriptions as a reminder of the past and as an affirmation of their willingness "to bear the pain it may take in future to keep our freedom" (*CC* 94). Sharing marks by choice equals here the sharing of painful memories. Unlike her mother who has "scars of bondage, scars of war" and "the history of my people [the fems] sharp and lamentable in my heart" (*CC* 99), Sorrel is a tabula rasa in terms of a history of subjugation. This scarlessness was, after all, Alldera's choice at Sorrel's naming ceremony. Pressed by the Free Fems to claim her daughter as fem by giving her a femmish name, Alldera "declines to impose her own cultural identity on her child ... [and] name[s] the child, but not according to any cultural convention" (Sargisson 163). Therefore, the daughter of Alldera the Conqueror has no inscribed and no actual experience of objectification and patriarchy. All she knows of the fems' past is from their songs. She is ignorant of battle, oppression, submission, and bodily as well as psychological violation. Although the offspring of sexual violence, Sorrel carries no memory of slavery and subjection. She can only take a "glimpse into the vast distances between my history and theirs" (*CC* 57). Naturally, she lacks the fury, the anger, the vengeful hatred of the fems; she can, as a result, feel more lenient towards men who are, after all, an alien myth to her. Threatened with rape or death by Servan, Sorrel learns the hard way the dire need to be cognizant of history, which may otherwise repeat itself. She has to learn personally about the fems' past to understand the dangers of slavery. However, her different history allows her to see past the anger that hampers the onset of change in the present and puts the future into limbo: "Didn't harking back always to ancient wrongs distort perspective, distracting from more recent happenings" (*CC* 41).

Road and map imagery come to symbolize the conflicting "ways" of the history the Holdfasters come from, the present they live, and their search for better future ways. The past human inscriptions onto the land no longer provide a map. The old ways are dysfunctional and lead literally nowhere: "The roads of the Ancients ... were now only fragmented remnants of the broad, smooth, legendary ways and sketched connections between mere patches of rubble" (*M* 4). In contrast to finite human history, the restricted scope of human-made roads, Alldera experiences the infinity of nature: "This desert was a seemingly *limitless* stretch of dark earth, all rucked up into long rows ... as if the fingers of a giant hand had been drawn parallel through loose dirt" (*M* 7; emphasis added). Where the history of human roads limited her choice of ways before, she now experiences an endless desert with any direction to choose from and only an alien path of "[m]onster tracks" (*M* 3) to follow. Alluding to the perhaps most famous literary footprints in the sand—in Defoe's "history of facts," as he claims in the preface of *Robinson Crusoe*, the footprints lead to the discovery of cannibalistic *others*—these footprints of Women mounted on horseback lead Alldera not back in time, but forward out of her own self-destructive and cannibalistic society. Initially fulfilling the prophecy of revenge—Eykar recognizes in their wall-paintings in the labor fems' gallery passages "a map of the fems' rage and pain.... He read his own kind's future there" (*F* 334)—the Free Fems merely reinvent old ways, turning a cul-de-sac into a roundabout: "their road came from destruction and led to destruction" (*M* 63). The concept of roads, of linearity, and of mapping, is alien to the Riding Women. "It was as if the Holdfast people had been so afraid of getting lost in their ... country that they had had to mark its trails permanently with rocks" (*F* 67). As nomads in a harsh environment, their concept of life and nature is one of non-permanence and of change. Their sense of history and belonging is not grounded in the possession and marking of land; instead a Riding Woman symbolically "gives" a representation of the plains, in their relation to herself and her personal history, to her adult daughter in the form of a provisional map sketched into the sand. Immersed in the Grassland society, Alldera is "fortunate to be on another path" (*M* 63) that she will eventually introduce to her society. Upon her insistent request, the fems draw a map of the Holdfast into the sand and metaphorically give themselves their land in the tradition of the Riding Women. The Holdfasters thus learn to follow what Charnas has described as "the road of no-road, of improvisation and exploration ... the most open road there is, maybe the only open road" (Charnas 1988, 162). The tentative construction of the future as it develops means "making a road for yourself, out of questions" (ibid. 162) and not pregiven answers.

As cultural signs and tactile texts of material reality, architecture expresses ideology and stands as a silent testimony of the past. Holdfast architecture mirrors the bipolar social oppositions. Masculine architecture epitomizes hierarchy and phallic domination—"pyramidal men's compound reared up overlooking everything"—whereas the fems' living quarters "comprised the eeeecurved center" (*W* 52) and are associated with the feminine. The schizophrenic marginalization of fems and simultaneous preoccupation with femininity are also perceptible in the spatial arrangement. Enclosed by men-build architecture, the fems' quarters form the center of the Holdfast. With the reconquest, architectural artifacts of patriarchy are destroyed. Of the great Dreaming Hall only a flight of "shallow steps" (*CC* 112) remains that is instantly occupied by fems "claiming ownership of the ceremonial center of the men's world" (*CC* 112). Other buildings also change what they signify with the events of history; the Watchtower, for instance, becomes "a cairn marking the death" (*CC* 264) of one of the assassins. And the fems raise cairns as monuments of remembrance. These landmarks of slavery make the history of fems visible, marking the place where a fem was "killed in slavery or in the war" (*CC* 40). The cairns are reminders of suffered subjection and violence and monuments of the past and the dead, a tactile text replacing the oral, a "substitute for a proper memorialization in the self-songs" (*CC* 216).

The cairn Sorrel builds, however, significantly breaks several of these conventions. Her cairn is a monument for Veree, for a *boy* and not for a fem. It is not to remember history, but to indicate the future, "his future, his freedom, his life ... my hopes in bringing him here" (*CC* 164). Her cairn commemorates not the dead, but addresses the living. Shaping her cairn as "stone tent ... a Grassland tent" (*CC* 197), moreover, Sorrel also joins the oppositions between stone and tent, between Holdfast and Grassland, between static and dynamic.[50] The actual stacking of stones turns from a personal into a political act, becoming "a prolonged gesture of protest" (*CC* 195) against the exclusion of male children and eventually of men in general. When Sorrel realizes that she herself refuses

---

[50]*Opposed to materialism, the Grasslanders live in tents and equate permanent architecture with death and an unhealthy focus on objects, as Sheel remarks: "People should bring life into the world, not things"* (CC 223).

to include the other sex—Eykar asks her in vain to add a flake in memory of his friend Captain Kelmz—the cairn turns into "a monument ... to my failure of Veree" (*CC* 205).[51]

4.4. The Present: Domination and Possessive Relationships

Material conditions are the major focus of the novels. In the Holdfast, institutionalized hatred, domination, suppression, possessiveness, competition, aggression, violence, and abuse characterize all relations. Charnas asserts that the values of "possessions ... possessing and being possessed" (Mohr 1999d, 18) lead to destruction, and the series chronicles the slow path towards creating cooperative, non-violent, and non-possessive cultural, social, familial, and sexual relationships. Once more, women instigate change, but once again not because of their sex. The answer to Jones's rather sceptical remark about *Furies*, "[W]hat's so special about 'women' after all?" (190) is, therefore, "nothing," apart from their victimization. According to Charnas, human psychology, not moral superiority, will compel whoever is most oppressed to rebel against the current power structure. Oppressed men such as the Juniors, for instance, revolt at the end of *Walk*. Charnas argues that the world is driven by power, but the world does not necessarily need to be structured by the physical and sexual shape of our bodies. The position of slave and master can be taken by both sexes in various manifestations and roles. How to redefine these destructive interpersonal and intercultural relationships, how to create a society without reimplanting and replicating patriarchal and colonial, societal and familial structures, is the major focus of the novels. The stories focus on coming to terms with familial relationships, accepting one's biological ties, *and* defining the psychological ties of affinity by choice. Specifically, the relationships of Alldera, Eykar, Servan, and Sorrel, and in a broader sense of Raff Maggomas, Captain Kelmz, Setteo, Daya, Beyarra, Nenisi and Sheel, stand symbolically in place of the generational, familial, and gender relations between fems and men, mothers and daughters, and fathers and sons. Where *Walk* foregrounds father/son relationships and the outcome of patriarchal colonialization, the sequels push mother/daughter and father/daughter rela-

---

[51]*In fact, the cairn serves as a life-saver. When Setteo kidnaps Veree to offer the boy to the Sunbear, he passes the cairn. In Setteo's dreamstate the cairn first transforms into "an altar to the moon" (*CC* 316) and then magically changes into a stone horse, "the moon's creature ... making the Warm World's humble, wordless argument by its presence" (*CC* 320). Both transformations metaphorically remind him of acts of love.*

4.4.1. Families of Affinity: From Biological to Psychological Ties

In the Holdfast, origins are obliterated, and parenthood is unknown to eliminate Oedipal patricide as a preemptive attack against the fathers. The nuclear family as a potentially subversive unit is abolished in an "inversion of the conventions of patriarchy, where the name of the father must be known, the primary taboo question in the Holdfast is to ask, 'who is my father?'"(Bartkowski 84).[52] With female and male offspring raised separately in the kitpits and the Boyhouse, no familial relationship whatsoever develops between parents and children. Cementing "certain structures of fraternal kinship" (ibid. 94) by leveling all males, "[a]ll men were brothers," is supposed to ward off "the fated enmity of fathers and sons" (*W* 24). The Law of the Father is renamed the "Law of Generations," and the age units of a gerontocracy replace the smaller family unit. The assumed personal diametrical opposition between father and son gets shifted to a factual Senior/Junior enmity, a generational distrust. "I'm a man, not a boy. You can't trust me" (*W* 29), Captain Kelmz consistently warns Eykar. Boys are raised as an "anonymous mob" (*W* 42) in the Boyhouse and are sporadically raided as well as individually raped as a reminder of the older men's authority. The uprising of Juniors against Seniors, the "final drama" of *Walk*, Frances Bartkowski observes, reenacts "in reverse" (86) the scenario Freud describes in *Totem and Taboo*. In a cannibalistic ritual, the patriarchal horde—modeled on Darwin's primal horde—ruled by an overbearing father who monopolizes women, kills and feeds on the father and eventually kills one other to gain the patriarchal power. *Walk* ascribes to men a high "innate" potential of aggression that the rigid generational hierarchy is meant to control, as Sargisson notes: "these various controlling mechanisms and structures implicitly acknowledge a "natural" tendency towards aggression [within the society of men], compounded by the association of the body with weakness" (162).[53] With *The Furies* Charnas demonstrates that women possess an equally high potential for aggression.

---

[52] *We get to know little about the life of the Pooltown people. Presumably, they lived in intact traditional families, perhaps reflecting the fact that African Americans have "historically been denied the privilege of forming family units" (Loomba 165), and for them the institution of the family consequently represents an achievement.*

[53] *Eykar engages in such a battle with his weak and fallible body that allows others to inflict physical pain and hence take control over him.*

By marking his son Eykar as his possession, the Senior Raff Maggomas undermines the principle of parental anonymity, not to reintroduce the nuclear family, but to re-establish the name of the father and patrilinear "blood ties." Maggomas is an overbearing father presence *in absentia* for Eykar, who carries the stigma of an outsider for knowing his identity. Driven by the question as to why he was singled out, Eykar embarks on his quest. Yet when father and son finally meet, megalomaniac Maggomas does not recognize the fragile and pensive Eykar as his son, and instead instantly identifies the sly and predatory Servan as his son. Servan is the spiritual son of Maggomas if not the biological one, as both ruthlessly instrumentalize people as pawns and lust after the absolute power of a god-creator; Maggomas even claims to have shaped himself, "I was born to shape myself" (*W* 201).[54] He desires to form Eykar in his own monstrous image, saying: "[y]ou were born to be shaped to your capacity" (*W* 201).

Like Maggomas, Servan wants an inheritor of his own making. He molds the young Pooltown boy Shareem into his image, after having murdered Shareem's biological father Gaybrel. Servan tries to corrupt Shareem into becoming one of them: "This is *our* sea, now ... *Yours*, when you learn to be one of *us*" (*CC* 172; emphasis added), and initiates Shareem to "the rites of Holdfast manhood" (*CC* 378). Under Servan's influence, Shareem learns dominance and violence, and he not only accepts his new spiritual father's heritage, but also accepts it when Servan rapes Shareem's two younger sisters. Entering the schizophrenic mind set and psychic dislocation of colonial identities that the psychoanalyst Frantz Fanon has described in *Black Skin, White Masks*, Shareem emulates the white men by literally adopting the white man's mask as he uses white ash for "aping the New Men" (*CC* 74). As split subject, Shareem identifies with the master and not with the slaves. Brainwashed, Shareem claims, "I'm with d Layo," and buys into the sexist paradigm; now he perceives his mother as "coward," his sisters are "only girls," and Free Fems are "unnatural" females and should be "back in chains where they belong" (*CC* 376).

For Servan and Maggomas, utility is the only reality, in contrast to Eykar who is eager "to see what it [a thing or a person] was, rather than what use it might be to him" (*W* 198). Maggomas sees himself as creator of a future kingdom with Eykar as his successor, the "Crown Prince" (*W* 191), a ready-made, and deadly future path that Eykar repudiates—"I accept nothing from you: not your name, not your place, not your future" (*W* 199)—and Servan readily accepts: "They would be gods" (*W*

---

[54]*Early on the fascination of pottery links Servan with the god-creator theme, "to draw form from a lump of moist earth and to fix it permanently"* (W 85).

188). In Alldera's subsequent refusal of a predestined future, of survival at all costs, Eykar recognizes their mental kinship: "We seem to be kin of some sad and foolish kind" (*W* 212). By killing Maggomas and thus rejecting his patrimony of destruction and exploitation and a predetermined future, limping Eykar, a postapocalyptic "swollen-footed Oedipus" (Vasey), seemingly repeats history and fulfils the very Oedipal revenge the fathers fear. The patricide remains ambiguous, however, since half of the Holdfast population carries the same birthmark—as the ferryman Hak discloses to Servan, "[Maggomas] had been tricked ... into thinking somebody was his son who really wasn't" (*CC* 297)—implying also a notion of already existing interrelations and kinship among Holdfasters. If Eykar is not Maggomas's son, the patricide is really a homicide, and Eykar is not biologically programmed, but truly revolts against a future of cannibalism.

Captain Kelmz and Eykar, on the other hand, provide positive father figures. As spiritual father surrogate, Kelmz teaches Eykar integrity and friendship, and the courage to transgress borders. By not taking the insignia of a Senior, Kelmz refuses to cross the age line and thus rejects the hierarchy of Seniors and Juniors. Kelmz also reintroduces a principle of equality and mentoring among men: "The appropriate attitude of an older man towards a younger was wary concern, not lust. A man could hardly have a relationship of equals with one less mature than himself" (*W* 38). And he meets Eykar "on his own ground without pulling age-rank" (*W* 84). Eykar, who confronted Maggomas in his role as Endtendant within the rules of the Holdfast, steps out of the Holdfast's rules for Kelmz who saved his life. When Kelmz dies, Eykar refrains from saying "the words of the Endpath offering" because "it wasn't as Endtendant that he had travelled with Kelmz" (*W* 132) but as friend. Eykar acknowledges Kelmz as his true father in spirit when he compares Maggomas and Kelmz: "how small Maggomas stood next to the memory of the dead Rover officer" (*W* 204). It is Alldera, however, who explains to him the nature of his feelings, when she comments, "What you expressed was grief for a lost friend," and Eykar comprehends that his grim life has conditioned him "to know Maggomas for a monster" but not to know the concept of friendship: "I still couldn't see something as simple as Kelmz and myself until you showed me just now" (*W* 213–214). Eykar finds in his ambiguous love and parental relationship with Setteo another same-sex friendship, encompassing more than physical and/or sexual attraction. Their strongest affinity is mental and spiritual. Setteo admires Eykar's more rational approach, "you are my mind" (*CC* 72), while they both can "speak that language of madness" (*CC* 143). Upon Setteo's death Eykar feels "*'selfless' ... I am left without my self. He took with him the self I had even begun to love a little*" (*CC* 348).

The ambiguous paternity of Sorrel (both Eykar and Servan raped Alldera) stresses the uncertainty of biological fathership, the irrelevance of parental possession, but also the importance of men learning how to be fathers. Setteo's absurd speculation that Sorrel, linked by her name with the Riding Women, might have been birthed by the Grasslanders, because she "smelled rather like Sheel" (*CC* 130), points towards the move beyond possessive progeny that Charnas claims. Fathers (and mothers) and sons and daughters need to disregard genetics and choose their paternal (parental) role model. Eykar alternates between desiring that Sorrel be his biological child and fearing the resultant consequences and responsibilities. Searching for a psychological familiarity which he detects in her honest rejection of the honorific "Hera" that now replaces "Heroes" (besides alluding to the Greek myth of gods), and in her mutinous spirit, he concludes that she is perhaps, after all, his daughter with promising "[p]otentialities destroyed or closed off in both of them [Alldera and Eykar] now lived ... in this young person" (*CC* 148). Now, he can *think* positively of the term 'father,' associated with hate and abhorrence in the past, but he still fears commitment. If Sorrel would touch him, "he would lose himself in some way that could never be remedied" (*CC* 148). Eykar perceives Sorrel's self-determination, that she is "full of desires of her own" (*CC* 146), and he refrains from his initial impulse to teach her reading and writing. If he accepts his fatherly role, he will not dictate her future as his father did.

At first Sorrel also resents the concept of a father, stating "it was nothing to me" (*CC* 111), and this attitude ties Sorrel to her Holdfast heritage. When Sorrel can let go of her preconceived notion of a father as monster, she perceives the psychic similarity between the Riding Women and Eykar, who talks like "another of my share-mas" (*CC* 200). Physical contact, touching him, now "seemed perfectly natural" (*CC* 202). Sorrel identifies with Eykar, and thus his denied humanity outrages her. She, too, experiences "fury that this *father* of mine ... should be sitting bowed at my feet, begging. No grown person should be in such a position; no share-ma of mine" (*CC* 291), a fury very different from that of the fems. In captivity she demands the same, the treatment as equal, of Servan: "Untie me if you want ... a human conversation" (*CC* 382).

Acting as a father in terms of caring is far more difficult for Eykar. Tricked by Servan into believing that Sorrel killed Setteo, Eykar denies their bond and helps Servan to abduct Sorrel. Betrayed by Eykar and threatened by Servan with rape, Sorrel is reduced to a mere object in the men's game of love and power: "my two fathers, were about to destroy me" (*CC* 388). In an effort to prevent the rape by allying Sorrel with Servan, Eykar reveals Sorrel's "red birthmark" (*CC* 384) and declares her Servan's daughter. Horrified, she fears Servan's heritage, a dormant, destructive biological streak within and consciously *decides* against him as role model (cf. *CC* 383). Only at the very last moment does Eykar realize that an act of revenge will cancel out his love for Setteo, and so he chooses between abusive love for Servan and protective love for Sorrel. He finds the courage to act out his father role, as he kicks the gun away from Servan. Determination of biological paternity is not the issue, as Alldera points out—"she has what's best of Servan ... she has what's best of you [Eykar]"—but choosing responsibility is the real task: "She's yours ... by your own choice" (*CC* 411). Eykar learns to disregard biological paternity and slowly takes on the role of a father, a new role he just begins to redefine. In Alldera's words, "a father must be a sort of male sharemother" (*CC* 401). Sociobiological activities like caretaking, Charnas emphasizes, can be degenderized without eliminating physical differences. Making "a different fatherly pattern"[55] not modeled on competitive possession, but aimed at communal posterity, Eykar becomes both the spokesman on behalf of men as an integral part of human society and a new father figure or male role model for the younger generation of men. He struggles to achieve—for Sorrel and for a whole new generation of men—what Peter Fitting has noted as a developing new theme in several other feminist utopias: the invention of "new roles for men, who should learn caring and nurturing skills and ... parenting" (1985, 175). These alternative roles men, however, have to design for themselves. Therefore, the young man Payder longs to meet the Grasslanders in vain, since they are the fems' metaphorical alternative. Through the story's twist of Galligan's attacking and Eykar's killing of Servan instead of Daya or Sorrel, Charnas directs our attention to the fact that it is men's task to redefine masculinity and widen their narrow choices of roles, as Alldera analyzes: "Men generally want someone to do it for them—us ... but in the end it's their own job.... Drawing the line between what a man may do and what he may not do and still have other men call him a man" (*CC* 401–402).

Women also have to learn to be effective mothers. Forced previously into biological maternity, fems are reproductive machines and "powerless mothers" (Barr 1987, 131) ignorant of the social exertion of motherhood. The Free Fems need to define "how to be a 'mother'" (*F* 282), as the warrior Kobba remarks. Alldera's and Sorrel's mother/daughter relationship towers over any other. Not a natural mother, Alldera feels very ambivalent about maternity. Initially, she comes to the Grassland with the message of the raped body, the perpetuation of the Law of the Father, and only at the end of *The Conqueror's Child* can Alldera relate to her daughter. As Sheel observes, it is much harder to love the *other*

---

[55]*Interview with Charnas.* See the appendix.

than the replicated self: "Without the pull of identically patterned minds and bodies ... it might take unusually long for Alldera and Sorrel to meet" (*M* 239). Rejecting the pregnancy in a Darwinistic fight for survival, Alldera tries to abort the foetus, the "efficient little parasite" (*M* 4). In contrast to the unnaturalness, sterility, and pain of giving birth in the Holdfast, Alldera experiences giving birth as a natural, joyful, and creative communal event in the Grassland.[56] The Riding Women support her physically through touch and accompany her contractions with songs. "Their song took its rhythm from her breathing and reinforced it. She surged over the pain on their music" (*M* 25). Birth thus becomes an exuberant moment "full of power" (*M* 25) and connectedness. As the offspring of rape, Sorrel is primarily a constant reminder of this violation. Alldera refuses to bond with the infant, rejects breastfeeding, and leaves the mothering to the Riding Women, who are the "*better mothers*" (*CC* 367).[57] In the Grasslands, Alldera slowly learns positive interrelations and bonding, "a collectivity of sisterhood and kinship" (Bartkowski 94) among women. The Riding Women also teach her a new concept of "rich connectedness," of ancestry and posterity: "[here] your relations stretched back through your entire life" (*M* 49).

Sorrel, on the other hand, has an "instant affinity" (*M* 197) with her Grassland mothers and "no spark of special feeling" (*M* 200) for Alldera. During her childhood and adolescence, Sorrel is overshadowed by her overbearing, though mostly absent, heroic mother and resents being identified merely as "Sorrel Alldersdaughter [sic]" (*CC* 236), a struggle underscored by the very title of the last book. Sorrel reacts with anger at being abandoned by Alldera the Conqueror, who is "more a mother to the rest of the Free Fems" (*CC* 21) than to Sorrel. The adolescent Sorrel vacillates between wanting to gain her mother's recognition and the desire to be independent, to be her "own person" (*CC* 59). She grapples moreover with a sense of leading a life of "trashings and boilings that led nowhere," compared to her mother's life "like an arrow shot high ... a true heart shot" (*CC* 103), only to discover that she is "a couple of inches taller" (*CC* 232) than the real Alldera. Sorrel's and Alldera's adult/child relationship, negotiating dependency and independence, is reflected in the negotiation of cultural kinship between Grasslanders and female Holdfasters. Claiming kinship, the Free Fems become part of the extended Grassland families and their futures interlock; but they do not share the same history. Culturally, the Free Fems assume the status of

---

[56]*Here,* Motherlines *reflects feminist criticism of the treatment of childbirth in patriarchy in the 1970s aptly circumscribed by Rich as "the fragmentation of body from mind ... the sense of abandonment, of being imprisoned, powerless, and [being] depersonalized" (176).*

[57]*Sorrel's physical resemblance to Servan or Eykar is of great importance to Alldera's ability to love or not to love her daughter (cf. CC 95).*

children until the Riding Women—as they do in their naming act of mothers when a child emerges from the childpack and joins the community of the adult women—give in absentia their history and a map of their land to the New Holdfast society, now emerging from childhood towards adult status.

Sorrel's hybrid identity, raised as a free Riding Woman and born as a fem without a fem's past, sharing origins but not history, alienates Alldera further from "this stranger-child of mine" (*CC* 97). As the offspring of sexual violence, Sorrel also carries her mother's memory of slavery and subjection, but the daughter does not share the debilitating experiences of objectification and patriarchy. Taking a shared history of slavery as the yardstick for affinity, Alldera feels closer to the pet fem Daya. In *The Conqueror's Child*, mother and daughter cautiously learn to accept their differences and negotiate "*whether we can love each other or not*" (*CC* 369). A natural, inbred maternal instinct is just another myth, as Alldera comments: "*You don't have to love someone just because they've come out of your body. There is no obligation either way*" (*CC* 96; cf. also *CC* 416). Love for one person, however, should not overrule the common good. Servan, for instance, holds the children of Sallali hostage and blackmails Sallali into entering the New Holdfast. Under the pretense of the shared experience of slavery, she insinuates herself into the confidence of the Free Fems only to betray them. Resisting such blackmailing of emotions, Alldera refrains from surrendering the New Holdfast to Servan to save Sorrel, despite the fact that the possibility of her daughter's death tears Alldera apart: "She hurled away the water gourd.... It shattered ... that was her soul, splintered apart and scattered forever" (*CC* 369).

Charnas undercuts the romantic family myth that only blood relations can answer one's needs and stresses generational and psychological rather than familial bonding. The non-hierarchical culture of the Riding Women is structured around non-possessiveness, communality, cooperation, sharing, and tribal kinship. Their children are sharemothered, and children choose heartmothers of affinity who are not necessarily their biological or "bloodmothers." The disruption of the traditional mother/child dyad and the Grasslanders' open, non-possessive sexual relationships lead to the "dispersion of intimacy in adulthood and childhood" (Bartkowski 101) and create close bonds without exclusive ties.

Charnas's concept of sharemothering intersects with feminist psychoanalytic investigations of the pre–Oedipal phase and psycho-sexual differentiation, namely with the thesis Nancy Chodorow formulates in her highly influential study, *The Reproduction of Mothering* (1978). Children learn to differentiate between self and *other* in relation to a primary caretaker who is in most cases the mother. Woman is hence the *other* for both sexes. A boy identifies negatively and a girl positively with the mother. Upon entering the Law of the Father with its inherent negative value of woman as no-man, femininity becomes a negative value. Chodorow suggests shared parenting, and Charnas extends this notion to communal childcare, stressing the importance of fathers and men as additional primary caretakers. Children will then develop with a different sense of gender identity and a more balanced set of values in relation to gender roles. Choosing from more than one parental model also stresses psychological rather than biological ties. Charnas believes that the practices of caretaking of the next generation are crucial in avoiding competitiveness. A cooperative culture needs to reject progeny in terms of social Darwinism and possession, as Charnas suggests—"*my* genes, *my* bloodline, *my* property"—and move towards "families of affinity" (Mohr 1999c, 11). This relationship describes exactly what the Holdfasters have to learn: to be mothers and fathers in terms of collective progeny instead of possessive genetic progeny and to unlearn what Setteo so aptly describes as "this matter of one person owning another" (*CC* 131). If children are to be raised as humans and not as animals, Charnas opines, they will need new and different role models. In the end, some Holdfasters share households, moving towards the "extended family" (Mohr 1999d, 21) that Charnas advocates.

Given her special background, Sorrel symbolizes the transgression of the dualism of nature and nurture. With Sorrel the Grasslanders want to start "the first new Motherline" (*M* 62) through nurture, feeding their new daughter "the milk of their bodies ... and the love of their hearts" (*CC* 22). In turn, Alldera claims the nature of the child's conception, "a Holdfastish cub, with dam and father" (*M* 62), yet Sorrel's behavior proves to be more Grasslandish. In the end, neither "nature" (whether Eykar or Servan fathered Sorrel) nor nurture prevail, but both are important. Physically incapable of starting a new biological motherline, Sorrel sets Veree up as her daughter and, entering the Holdfast as "trickster" (*CC* 51), temporarily passes herself off as the mother of a new line. Sorrel fosters a new transgressive or hybrid human line by introducing the Grassland's ethics she has internalized to the New Holdfast; there she also adapts it to include men. Mother and daughter share the desire for social innovation. Alldera liberates the fems, but early on her concern is the future "creation of the truly 'free' fems: the children of the conquerors" (*F* 312). Coming around "*full circle*" (*CC* 210), Sorrel advances the inclusion of men and shifts the focus towards the next generation and the future. Sorrel's link with Veree turns her into the advocate for the reintegration of men: "someone must speak sanely on behalf of Veree's sex" (*CC* 118). Sorrel identifies with Veree because they have both experienced being an "unwanted child" (*CC* 124). Where Sorrel sees a neglected human being, others see Veree as a member of the opposite sex. As a male Holdfast child, Veree is as much a rejected, social misfit and outsider as Sorrel was among the all-female childpack of the Grasslands, "me and Veree, the two outsiders" (*CC* 53). Sorrel adopts Veree for reasons of psychological affinity: "Holdfast-bred but Grassland-born, he was more like me than any other living person" (*CC* 32). Because she has never experienced masculine supremacy, she can see Veree as a human regardless of his sex. Sorrel takes him to the New Holdfast "so that he would not live as a freak" (*CC* 31), only to recognize that she has given him "to his worst enemies" (*CC* 103). She wants to extend the freedom she has experienced to the male sex: "I'm going to pass it [the gift of freedom] on to Veree" (*CC* 153). And she dreams of a society where Veree can be a full member, otherwise, as Sorrel warns, "half of your own children ... [will] be slaves forever" (*CC* 122). It is not enough to raise one sex in freedom, only to let a male child "suffer the sins of its fathers" (*CC* 205). On the contrary, it is time to "focus on the next generation of men instead of their elders" (*CC* 210), as Beyarra notices. A shift in phraseology indicates the fems' altered thinking, as the fems no longer call these children of their bodies *and* their emotional desire "cubs." They acknowledge the risk of perpetuating inequality if girls are raised to be "free people" and "boys to be their slaves" (*CC* 102), leading to discussions of "partial freedom" (*CC* 121) for boys, because "Slavery should not be something boys were born into, but a punishment for crimes against the Free" (*CC* 205).[58] As the generational dedication of the last book indicates, utopian hope begins with showing concern for posterity and raising *all* children of the future in freedom.

4.4.2. Of Lovers, Sexuality, and Reproduction

According to Sargisson, "Charnas's dystopia is transgressive of the dominant norms of sexual behaviour of our present" in that "[h]eterosexual penetrative intercourse is despised" (162). The transgressive sexual aspect incorporates, I believe, more than an inversion of heterosexual practices, as Charnas rejects a dualistic view of biology and suggests a natural diversity of sexuality.[59] In the series, sexual practice encompasses heterosexuality, lesbianism, homosexuality, homosexuality as pseudo-

---

[58]*In the manuscript this "idea of changing slavery for the little boys from something they were born into to punishment for crime" (ms.* CC *397) is Beyarra's. Sorrel is characterized as far more inclined towards considering men as "half-formed creature[s]" (ms.* CC *797).*

[59]*On the naturalness of a wide variety of sexualities in nature, challenging human notions of, and arguments by analogy about, natural heterosexuality and unnatural homosexuality in the animal kingdom, compare Bruce Bagemihl (1999).*

heterosexuality, and bisexuality, all functioning according to principles of exclusivity and sexual violence. These destructive sexual practices are juxtaposed with the Riding Women's alternative practice of a non-exploitative sexuality free of power structures and possessiveness. With regard to the Grassland society, Barr correctly notes that an "absence of sexual violence coincides with the absence of men" (1983, 64). Yet Barr's and Wolmark's claim (cf. Wolmark 1994, 84) that Charnas argues for a gender-specific innate male violence is easily disproven by the sexual violence of the Free Fems in the Tea Camp. The sexual violence perpetrated by fems in the sequels further corroborates the argument that sexual violence is linked to power. Non-reproductive homosexuality/lesbianism and enforced and violent reproduction are crucial issues in the Old and the New Holdfast. The predominantly abusive love relationships of the Holdfasters are contrasted with the monosexual relationships of the Riding Women, whose sexuality is not organized around reproduction, since they conceive parthenogenetically and by choice. Charnas argues against a false dichotomy of natural and unnatural sexuality, and for sexual and gender variance, regardless of reproduction. To develop a different polysexual and polygendered system, reproduction must be removed from the center of sexuality to a peripheral position. The utopian society that Charnas imagines moves beyond the perception of two distinct genders to a society where non-procreative heterosexuality and procreative homosexuality/lesbianism can be practiced between equals who respect each other.

In the homosexual Holdfast culture, sexual orientation is not a matter of choice, but it is artificially designed; this society, Charnas comments, "drives itself into homoerotic patterns by defining women out of the arena of human eroticism and into ... demonism" (Mohr 1999d, 21). Similar to Atwood's *The Handmaid's Tale*, women in Charnas's dystopia are reduced and compartmentalized according to their body functions. Pet fems are objects of beauty who provide heterosexual service that is considered perverse; dams are for breeding; labor fems do manual work. What Sargisson values as a transgression of the heterosexual norm is really heterosexuality disguised as substitute homosexuality, with the division of age replacing the homosexual taboo of heterosexuality. Therefore, the pet fem Daya, who in her boyish slimness supposedly embodies the male idea of femininity as androgyny, really is a substitute boy, offering "male and female beauty both at once" (*M* 43). Within this "super-masculine economy" (Sargisson 162), Western society's idealization and valorization of man is brought to its logical extreme. Junior men function as substitute women, an arrangement that leaves heterosexual superior/inferior oppositions intact.[60]

[60]*In interviews Charnas stresses that this is not "about the society that gay men would construct*

Sexual interaction commonly takes place as the institutionalized rape of both sexes, with the perpetrator generally being male. In the dystopia of the Old Holdfast, rape is a non-event. The Boyhouse/library is the primary location of enforced homosexual sex across age boundaries. The Boyhouse is a place of humiliation and violence.[61] Here Eykar first learns "to differentiate between his treacherous, lascivious and vulnerable body and the outraged spirit trapped inside" (*W* 111). This violation of bodily integrity leads to a body and mind split that Eykar struggles with all his adult life, attempting to resist his weak body and to eradicate the body inscriptions of rape. This dualistic struggle between mind and body, masculinity and femininity, passivity and action, is captured in the two diametrically opposed male protagonists, strong and masculine Servan and his weak and feminized lover Eykar.

Their abusive and ambiguous love relationship that Lefanu has peculiarly described with "tentative tenderness" (156) illustrates this homoerotic "prison sex." Servan is associated with external action, dominance, destruction, competition, and the lust for power; Eykar is introspective, inquisitive, thirsty for knowledge, and questions Holdfast propaganda. At first they are attracted to each other because each is an outsider; Eykar for knowing his father, and Servan for his recalcitrance. Eykar also finds in Servan a sparring partner for discussions. For opposite reasons, they both reject submission—Eykar questions the validity of the very power Servan desires—and, because during their First Dream Eykar falls ill and Servan almost dies, both are thus considered "borderline cases" (*W* 77). Servan's descent into unguided (Dark)Dreaming results in their expulsion from the Boyhouse: "one to become Endtendant at Endpath, and the other ... to his presumed death in the Wild" (*W* 22). This similar past sets the abusive pattern of their interwoven lives, of Servan's bullying, seducing and compelling Eykar into reluctant complicity. On the one hand, Eykar is simply the ticket to power for Servan, the puppet he can work, a blank onto which he can inscribe his dreams: "That was the aura surrounding Eykar's wiry figure in Servan's mind: the potentiality for mythical action" (*W* 86).[62] Repeatedly, Servan tries to tempt Eykar into usurping power, modestly announcing, "You'll be the ruler; I'm only ... Kingmaker, not king" (*CC* 352), a temptation that Eykar resists several times. As a true impersonation of Maggomas, Servan urges Eykar to "regain what's lost ... take what's ours" (*CC* 348) and to recreate the

---

[continued] *for themselves," but a homosexual "world created by straight men which allows homosexual behavior because women are so degraded" (Mohr 1999d, 21).*
   [61]*The library is also the place where Eykar and Kelmz recognize their shared experience of sexual victimization and transgress the age taboo; suddenly "the years that stretched between [them] ... seemed not to be a barrier but a spectrum which included them both" (*W* 112–113).*
   [62]*Servan drugs the oversensitive Eykar with manna and parades him as "the Oracle."*

Old Holdfast. Eykar, however, recognizes the crown Servan offers for what it is, Servan's "*chance for revenge*" (*CC* 352). On the other hand, as much as Servan is Eykar's "maker and master" (*CC* 345), Eykar also wields power over Servan because Eykar represents absolution and integrity:

> Eykar still stood in his mind like a rock in deep water, offering nothing, yielding nothing, dividing the current nevertheless.... The right image came at last: Eykar was a comet, blazing with the effort to hold together through the aching void long enough to win the right of surcease—aware, alone, and desperate. Servan was enraptured with Eykar's brightness; to embrace Eykar was to bathe in fire [*W* 86–89].

Servan's love is conditional. He only feels a temporary obligation to Eykar, a tie "Servan had always broken at will" (*CC* 168). His idea of love is to "torment ... and still remain beloved" (*CC* 350), a vicious circle of submission and degradation that Eykar can only escape by destroying Servan in the end. The price that ethereal Eykar pays for loving Servan is confronting his own carnality, for his "carnal being became more real; the farseeing and austere soul gave ground" (*W* 112).

The representation of lesbian love relationships—equally structured by power, control, competition, domination, submission, and abuse—contests Cranny-Francis's argument that for Charnas only "male sexuality is *by nature* almost uncontrollable and extremely violent" (188).[63] In the series, sexual violence is not gender specific, but is related to power. In the Holdfast economy, fems compete for the attention of the masters, and they frequently abuse and betray each other. At the Tea Camp, for example, the fems retain their passive object status as Elnoa's "playthings or drudges" (*M* 140). Elnoa's "sexual appetite, nourished on power" (*M* 94) denies other fems a subject status.

The ambiguous relationship between Alldera and Daya mirrors that of Eykar and Servan. Unlike the men, Alldera and Daya start out as opponents and develop from antagonists to lovers, and from friends to foes. As newcomer to the Tea Camp, Alldera, sensitized by her experience of Grassland relationships to the mechanisms of repression and dominance, refuses to adapt to the Tea Camp system; and hence she poses a threat to the fragile power system. Both Daya and Alldera measure the other in terms of a masculine economy of feminine beauty. Alldera is contemptuous of Daya's past as a pet fem. Daya likewise considers Alldera plain and a realist lacking imagination. Daya's intrigues

---

[63] *The father/son and love relationship between Eykar and Setteo, and Galligan's devotion to Daya, are admittedly sketchy examples of non-violent male sexuality.*

lead to the physical maiming of Alldera, a pain with which the disfigured pet fem identifies: "The sight of the runner's pain-cramped body brought back the pain of her own maiming" (*M* 119) and eventually to the expulsion of them both. At Fedeka's Camp they become reluctant lovers. When their love affair fizzles out, Alldera offers Daya friendship, an alien concept to the pet fem. "Daya had never been a friend before" (*M* 171). Conditioned to attract with beauty, concoctions, and intrigues, Daya does not know *how* to be a friend. Because she feels inferior, moreover, Daya simultaneously admires, envies, and resents Alldera's courage and heroism; "I'm not strong Alldera the runner, proud Alldera ... tough Alldera whom women respect and fems learn from. Look at me: Daya that was a man's pet, a man's toy, good at games" (*M* 216–217). Like Servan, Daya is a "possessive partner" (*F* 15) and schemes "to be close to power ... and Alldera was power" (*F* 19). Her jealous passion eventually turns her against Alldera, love becomes hate, and, significantly, "the only blood Daya ... [is] able to shed [is] ... Alldera's" (*F* 342). Alldera's heroism and bravery contrast sharply with Daya's own cowardice and incapability to overcome her fear, for which the pet fem can never forgive Alldera: "I shake when I see a man ... you are a hero, nothing scares you! Well, I'm only human, and I'm afraid" (*F* 186). Daya's dilemma is that in times of war actions are required, whereas she is a woman of words. "I trusted in cleverness, skills and tales. But what are words ... when deeds mean everything" (*F* 246). Daya accuses Alldera and fems at large of devaluing the femininity she represents: "softness, flexibility, imagination—talents of slaves" (*F* 247).

The exploitative same-sex relations of the Holdfast also contrast with the same sex relationships of the Grasslands that are not located within the paradigm of homosexuality/lesbianism, replicating heterosexual dominance patterns. Free from male restraints and heterosexual pressures, the Riding Women have created a non-dominance oriented monosexual culture—often misinterpreted by critics as a community of lesbian separatists—that does not imitate the opposite sex behavior, but rather uses the behavioral repertoire of both sexes. Unlike present-day lesbians who are forced to define themselves against a dominant heterosexist patriarchy, none of the Grasslanders has known such strictures. Therefore, Charnas maintains, the Grasslanders practice an alternative rather than a lesbian sexuality (cf. Mohr 1999d, 17), because the Riding Women do not need a reference to an opposite or complementary *other* to define the self.[64] Drawing on the full scale of human characteristics

---

[64]*Charnas view of lesbianism as defined against heterosexuality contrasts sharply with Wittig's and Gearhart's definitions of lesbianism. Exactly because a lesbian is self-defined without reference to man, Wittig has defined lesbians as third sex, a definition Gearhart surpasses by*

undivided by feminine or masculine categories, they are both: strong quarrelling warriors *and* caring mothers, tender *as well as* fierce lovers. Here, "No one is master of the other" (*M* 67). This concept, however, also includes the notion of choice and sexual liberty. Nenisi, who nursed Alldera like a mother, is Alldera's Grassland guide to utopia and her "female mentor" (Barr 1993, 55); and she eventually becomes Alldera's lover. On the one hand, sharing love with Nenisi integrates Alldera into the Grassland society—"[s]he was a woman now" (*M* 68)—and gives her the feeling of connection. On the other hand, Nenisi's sharing of love with other Riding Women is for Alldera an act of "unfaithfulness" (*M* 69) that follows the Holdfast paradigm of exclusivity. In the Grasslands, sexuality is "an extension of community feelings" and "sensual intimacy" (Miller 1983, 195), a physical contact free of possession. Exclusivity in the sense of owning one person, however, denies this inclusivity and "keeps everyone else out," as Nenisi explains, "as if ... only I and my lover are true women" (*M* 69–70). How, Nenisi asks, can one lover "be all the women in the camp" (*M* 70)? In an allegoric gesture, Nenisi compares their non-possessive concept of love to pebbles: "Look, here is womanness. Why should we separate from each other two by two? What makes it right for two to be alone, when it is not right for one to be" (*M* 70). According to Nenisi, it is less the physical sharing of the body that has led to their estrangement than the lack of shared words. "Making love is much the same for all, but each person speaks only her own words. I have few of your words" (*M* 244–245). Alldera, the messenger of a master's words, caught in the dominant body politics of the Holdfast, has to learn this idea: the importance of her *own* words, the intimacy of mind-sharing, and the aberration of the exclusivity of the body. Perhaps an amalgam of both, the transgression of either possessiveness or liberal sharing, will heal the destructive relations of fems and men. Of all the characters, the Riding Woman Sheel, a vehement critic of the Holdfast's "notion that any two people should be permanently sealed together by any act of sex" (*F* 110), has to concede that "it can make people [strong], to stick with each other as a couple" (*CC* 256).

The Holdfast symbol of power, the phallus, becomes an object of ridicule and anatomical absurdity among Grasslanders, where phallo(go)centrism is deprived of its mystique. For Sheel, for instance, the penis is a "ludicrous, dangling nuisance and hardly capable of the brutalities recounted" (*M* 9). In this culture, celebratory of the vagina, where "male sexual organs are thought to be aberrant, threatening, encumbering, and ridiculous" (Barr 1993, 46), a Freudian concept of penis envy is non-exis-

---

[continued] *alleging that lesbians are an altogether different species. In the light of their theories, the Riding Women are a third sex, or even another species.*

tent. The Riding Women separate sexuality from reproduction, possession, and domination. They also conceive by choice. Genetically altered by male scientists to procreate parthenogenetically "with a double set of traits" (*M* 60), their no longer natural reproduction disrupts the dubious concept of "naturalness," i.e. nature/culture dualism, and becomes "the natural that is not, and the cultural which is derived from it [the natural]" (Sargisson 164). Refining their reproductive biology, originally designed for "a masculinist war culture" (Mohr 1999d, 18), the Riding Women transform from experimental objects into subjects creating their own non-violent culture.

The question Charnas poses here about sexuality and reproduction is, what exactly do we define as natural and what as cultural practice? The Riding Women replace the artificially triggered gestation process with ritual mating with horses, often misread by critics and readers as actual insemination and ultimately as a symbolic affirmation of the necessity of penetration. The mating, however, not only transgresses the sexual human/animal opposition, but also symbolizes their rich bond with nature. This carnivalesque celebration of life affirms the "balance of all things [that] includes us ... and animals" (*M* 150). Here, neither nature nor humans become objects of exploitation, but function as part of the organic interrelation of all forms of existence, the "kinship of creatures" (*M* 155). In comparison to the "natural" Holdfast method of reproduction *cum* rape, the "unnatural" mating seems "[s]imple and clean" (*M* 61) to Alldera. In the light of the libidinal excess and sexual brutality of the Holdfast, however, their mating seems less deviant. Yet, the Free Fems' and Sorrel's attempt at copying this androgynous way of reproduction fails. Bartkowski argues that the successful establishment of a new motherline would indicate "a future resolution of the conflict between those who have not known men and those who have escaped their rule" (97). More importantly, Charnas directs our attention here to the necessity for a reconciliation between the sexes. Charnas exhorts that reproductive separatism, like parthenogenesis, cannot be the solution for an inherently gonochoric people of dual sex. *Motherlines* is therefore not a "dialectical reply" (Bartkowski 91), a utopian antithesis to the dystopian thesis of *Walk*, but a postulate—further explored in the integrative synthesis of Book Three and Four that we are two sexes of many genders—for the interaction and cohabitation of the sexes. Consequently Sheel, who denies the Holdfasters the right to exist within the Grassland's ecological system of balance, stating "you can't put in balance something that never belonged at all" (*M* 150), concludes in Book Four that Holdfasters must and can create their own balance. Detecting a surprising degree of similarity in behavior between Sorrel and Alldera, Sheel admits that Holdfasters breed "true to line after all, these double-blooded people" (*CC* 224).

Otherwise considered perverse, heterosexual contact occurs solely as dutiful rape for reproductive purposes in the Holdfast breeding rooms. Driven by an egomaniacal interest only in the self, Servan arbitrarily rapes Alldera simply to confirm his superiority. For similar reasons, Servan rapes Salalli, after having killed her husband Gaybrel, the leader of the Pooltowners, to assert his position as new leader and "pale imitation of Gaybrel" (*CC* 76); and he rapes Daya at Endpath to test Galligan's submissiveness.[65] Eykar rapes Alldera out of frustrated jealousy of his unfaithful lover Servan and fear, as well as out of his attraction to the *other*. Servan rapes Alldera for power and uses feminine ways of pleasing, taking "endless time with stroking and touching that were plainly modelled on the gentle practices of fems among themselves" (*W* 146). He arouses her not to give but to ascertain that he controls both the pain and the pleasure of his sexual object, a "violation far uglier than any common assault" (*W* 146) that Alldera successfully undermines by faking arousal. Afterwards, Servan desires to eradicate the moment of contact with the *other*. As a reminder of Alldera's non-human position as well as to implement "his god-like unpredictability" (*W* 147), Servan then forces her to eat mud.

The relationship between Eykar and Alldera is the only heterosexual relationship characterized in depth. Their ambivalence is representative of the possibility and impossibility of a rapprochement between the two sexes. Eykar's rape of Alldera takes a somewhat different direction than Servan's. To cut Eykar's clumsy violation short, Alldera, in fact, helps him to "carry through his assault" (*W* 163). In contrast to Servan's raping her, the union describes a moment of brutality for them *both*. In an attempt to cancel out the psychological injuries, Alldera matter-of-factly takes stock of her physical injuries, feeling nevertheless "hollow in body ... hollow in mind" (*W* 164). Eykar does not rape by the Holdfast rules. Realizing that, contrary to Holdfast myth, physical contact with a fem neither contaminates his body nor his soul, Eykar seeks a way beyond rape and towards truth.[66] He encourages Alldera to break the silence and speak: "words, her only weapon" (*W* 166). At the very moment that Alldera expresses the forbidden pronoun "I," "the equalizing name for the self" (*W* 166), she claims subjectivity and humanity.[67] Coming into

---

[65]*Servan also rapes Sallali's eldest daughter Lissie to ensure his position as leader by claiming "Lissie for himself" (CC 171).*

[66]*An earlier scene links the male gaze with penetration and foreshadows not only the rape, but indicates Eykar's desire to break the wall of silence. Perceiving that Alldera disguises her thoughts behind "a face like a round shield," expressing a "willed stupidity," Eykar wants "to penetrate this smoothness" with "the lance of his keen sight," wondering "what sort of being would be found hiding" (W 104)?*

[67]*This rape scene, where Alldera claims her subjectivity on the individual level in relation to Eykar, is mirrored by her arrival in the Holdfast. There, she "hurls a stone out into the air" and yells "I, Alldera, I am here!" (F 25), now claiming her rightful place in society.*

touch with her identity, she takes back her autonomy.[68] In the realm of language, they can meet as equals: "It gave her an extraordinary feeling of power, of reality. That was the danger" (*W* 172). Alldera verbally retaliates against Eykar's physical violence, by denying his desperate desire that "fems ever [could] love masters" (*W* 172), and continues their talk on her terms. Alldera remains silent *by choice*, until Eykar invites her to speak again, "his bending to her unspoken rule filled her with ... power" (*W* 174).[69] Their talk has changed nothing with regard to the societal realm. Alldera is still a non-person, a slave: "You're not speaking to a person ... only to a fem" (*W* 178). Desperate to meet an equal in dystopia at last, Eykar insists that talking has changed them from master and slave to individuals: "where do you see 'men,' where do you see 'fems' in here? There's nobody but us," but realizes then that mere words do not annihilate power relations: "[I]t's worth nothing while I have the power of death over you.... Nothing that passes between us can be anything but rape" (*W* 178). To "heal up the horror between men and fems—or just between us two" takes more than this fragile verbal negotiation; therefore, Eykar cannot permit Alldera "to be a person" (*W* 178), but sets her free upon the downfall of 'Troi.[70]

Significantly, the only person Alldera meets from her past is a man—Eykar. With "the unique history the two of them shared" (*F* 360), Charnas emphasizes that the two sexes come from the same, a shared, past. In *The Furies*, Alldera and Eykar re-encounter each other in reversed societal and gender roles and in another moment of illusory equality. This time Eykar "needs to speak" (*F* 152), and Alldera is eager "*to meet— that other*" (*F* 153). Both Alldera the strong conqueror and Eykar with his maimed and failing body feel joy as they meet as scarred survivors: "*We did not die ...* incredulous, exultant laughter brimm[ed]" (*F* 156) in both of them. Alldera is moved by a "riot of impermissible feeling" (*F* 156), because Eykar represents her only link to the past. Their shared history, having lived "as closely as any pair of femmish cubs," emotionally binds them closer to one other than to anyone else: "Such proximities could not be cancelled" (*F* 156; cf. also *F* 228, *F* 314). The moment of equality slips away as "the drumming of hoofbeats and the cries of

---

[68]*Similarly, Beyarra takes on subjectivity in both realms at the very moment she switches from speaking of herself in the third person, "she would not know where to aim," to "this fem thinks—I think ... I could learn to make arrows" (F 82–83).*

[69]*A similar moment of desiring Alldera to judge him occurs when he confronts his father. Eykar searches Alldera's gaze for the confirmation that he is not a monster like his father, but Alldera denies an absolution and defies him with laughter.*

[70]*Misreading the end of* Walk, *by stating "it is significant that [Eykar] Bek dies," Cranny-Francis wrongly argues that Eykar rightly dies because he is "unable to reject the exploitative capability conferred on him" (204), and that Alldera survives because she can renegotiate her subject position.*

alarm" (*F* 158) remind Alldera who her people are, for what purpose she came, and that she has to cope with the present and not the past. Paying "an old debt: a gift of life for a gift of life" (*F* 159), Alldera saves Eykar's life in return, thus reaching "through the wall of icy air between the two of them" (*F* 189). She declares that the "truth-teller" (*F* 194) Eykar and Setteo are witnesses, and hence designates them as male eyes and male memories.

In contrast to Jones, who comments that the sexual attraction between Alldera and Eykar is "bizarrely out of place in the past and equally irrelevant now [in *The Furies*]" (187), Charnas demonstrates with this relationship that heterosexual attraction on the individual level can be imagined, experienced and felt, but not externalized in action and lived in a polarized society. In *The Furies*, the sexual attraction between Alldera and Eykar is no longer defined by sexual violation. Alldera imagines cautious physical contact with Eykar, "to touch that pale skin" (*F* 228). Eykar daydreams of gently exploring her body that he formerly feared, "to try the weight of her breast in the palm of his hand, to test with his lips and tongue the soft skin" (*F* 267; cf. also *F* 272, *F* 332). But the potentiality of an interpersonal relationship is again instantly overshadowed by their reversed societal roles of master and slave. Their sexual intercourse still would not describe an encounter of equals. Furthermore, the "singular connection" (*F* 231) between Alldera and Eykar enables them both to hold more than one vision of the *other*. Focusing on "*the present and not the past*" (*F* 230), Alldera moves beyond memories of hate, of seeing in Eykar the former master, towards seeing the interlocutor, scholar, and advisor in Eykar the slave. Eykar struggles with reconciling the "two visions" (*F* 202) of Alldera, the feminine role of the healer who tended his wounds, and her masculine role as leader of an army. In retrospect, he comprehends that "the inner truth of his journey west to meet his father ... was about Eykar and a fem, after all" (*F* 202).

Alldera and Eykar undergo a painful process of recognizing their shared humanity and the need for forgiveness if there is to be hope for an alliance between the sexes. Both are pained by the ugliness, brutality and bloodshed of the conquest. Alldera had hoped that, through knowing Eykar, they "all [could] do better together," but she now believes him to be a deviant among his own kind, "a freak among your own sex" (*F* 277).[71] Eykar reproaches Alldera that without "forgiveness, ever" (*F* 277) there will be no peace, only eternally bitter relations between the sexes.

---

[71]*Intimate knowledge of the other, of Alldera as representative of her sex, "the only one of these people he had ever really known"* (*F* 339), *propels Eykar to protect Alldera or die with her at the assassination scene.*

In a gesture of sad understanding, Alldera brushes his lips with her fingertips, the closest they ever get to a kiss. Another moment of physical intimacy occurs after Alldera has been badly wounded in the assassination attempt. Eykar's body, which previously inflicted sexual violence on Alldera, now gives her comfort and warmth without any sexual overtones. Holding her protectively in his arms, "[t]heir two heartbeats thumped like the footsteps of people running together" (*F* 340).

This image of running and of synchronized heartbeats captures their shared dissatisfaction with the status quo of savagery and betrayal they both want to flee. Cognizant of the intertwining of their personal fates with that of their sexes, Eykar knows they need to "find a way to soothe and heal each other" (*F* 383). Pondering whether they are "joined at the soul," Alldera can now perceive "their essential likeness to each other" (*F* 383). At the end they are attracted to each other by psychological closeness and can forge a relationship that is not grounded in sexual contact, as Alldera notes, "without actual sexual coupling, Eykar and I matter to each other" (*F* 391). Virtually like a first mother and a first father of the New Holdfasters, they have learned to respect each other's humanity and exchange a "frankness" on which they build their "unlikely alliance" (*CC* 214). Romance is never part of their relationship. The only "true love" Alldera has is Nenisi, while Eykar loves Setteo.

With the Free Fems in charge, however, heterosexuality and reproduction remain tied to violence. The fems use the men as studs, thus reversing roles of subject/object, and are therefore equally guilty of turning the opposite sex into a commodity. In a satricial feminist rewriting of stereotypes where the return of males to an all-female society turns any "Amazon into a mewling sex kitten" (Mohr 1999d, 17), a Newly Freed secretly rapes/mates with a drugged male slave who experiences heterosexuality as pleasurable. "I loved it," (*F* 266) he asserts. Alldera's claim that "a fem riding a man to orgasm ... is [not] the same as a man raping a femmish slave" (*F* 275) holds true only insofar as now fems can produce offspring by choice. In its present form as described earlier, the sexual act remains rape. The survival of the Holdfasters depends on the ability of the two sexes to step out of this spiral of violence. "They shared sex for the making of progeny, but they didn't share love" (*F* 17). The deadly intersection of cultural violence and heterosexuality is captured in the linked images of the captive men's violent act of vindictiveness— they impaled three Free Fems—and the fems' perception of the sexual act as a violent penetration: "[to be] impaled on this hairy fellow's sex" (*F* 213).

Hence the pressing question remains: How can the sexual act be reimagined as "something ... other than an ugly necessity" (*F* 148–149)? With the doctrine of homosexual orientation removed and inequal power relations eased, several passages hint at such a future heterosexual reconciliation. Back in the Old Holdfast, some fems, in fact, recreated heterosexuality and phallic penetration, using a wooden phallus "to root in her body with it like a man" (*M* 68).[72] Beyarra is sympathetic with the raped male slave, feeling an "unexpected tenderness" (*F* 216) towards him; and Daya and Galligan genuinely appear to like each other. In *The Conqueror's Child*, the young man Payder confesses to Eykar, although sternly denying any "romantic" (*CC* 65) infatuation with the female sex, that he enjoys heterosexual intercourse, but more importantly the act of "laugh[ing] together" (*CC* 65) with one fem in particular. Eykar's advice is a credo for individual choice that flies in the face of societal dogma: "Don't let anyone ... tell you who you do or don't love. You are the only authority on that" (*CC* 65). In the future, sexuality will become a matter of choice, with heterosexuality accounted for only one option among many.

At the end of the last book, Charnas outlines a society with a plurality of multifaceted sexualities incorporating a mixture of feminine and masculine behavior without either partner copying heterosexual gender roles. Blurring the categories of nature and culture, reproduction and sexual orientation are combined in new ways. The New Holdfasters will not choose either heterosexuality or homosexuality or lesbianism, but they will participate in a transgressive sexuality subject to changes of preferences. Some are lesbian fems who procreate—Sorrel, for example, conceives her daughters by inseminating herself with a syringe—some are non-reproductive homosexuals and other heterosexual partners presumably reproduce. A fluctuating number of members of both sexes share hearths for a period of time, interacting in various relationships and sexualities, raising offspring as caretakers, biological and non-biological mothers and fathers in multisexual, polygendered communities, or Holdfast versions of families of psychological affinity.

4.4.3. The Ontology of Slaves and Master: "But what is slave? What humanity is it?"

Charnas fictionally explores the ontological question that Soyinka has poignantly formulated in relation to the African condition, "But what is *slave*? ... what humanity is it?" (Soyinka 69), and has concisely answered, "The condition of 'slave' is a denial of the freedom of action, of the freedom of choice. Bondage, be it of the body or of the human

---

[72]*Daya is one of these pets who feel that penetration had gratified her "in some inexplicable way" (F 152).*

will" (ibid. 70). In this sense, Charnas represents women as slaves. The nature and the abolition of bondage and slavery, on whatever grounds, are the overriding issues with which the texts deal. Intermingling her critique of sexism/patriarchy with racism/colonialism, Charnas shows patriarchy's treatment of women as a conquered sex. They are colonized subjects with a psychosexuality similar to that of colonized people, an analogy that risks the replacement and annihilation of the colonized colored woman by white women, of "erasing the specificity of colonialist and patriarchal ideologies, besides tending to homogenize both 'women' and 'non-Europeans'" (Loomba 163). The prologue of *Walk* reveals the linked patriarchal and colonial concepts of otherness and difference: "They [the men] remember the evil races whose red skins, brown skins, yellow skins, black skins ... marked them as mere treacherous imitations of men, who are white ... and most of all the men's own cunning, greedy females. Those were the rebels ... men called them 'unmen.'" (*W* 4–5). Wolmark criticizes that in *Walk* and *Motherlines* class and race differences between women "are subsumed into the universal category of woman" and consequently "reproduce those patriarchal ways of thinking that they set out to critique" (1994, 82). Although Charnas definitely foregrounds gender issues, it is problematic, as Wolmark alleges, that the series does not separate "gender from other forms of institutionalised oppression" (ibid. 83). However, for feminism and the feminist sf novels of that time, the inclusion of race issues was unusual, and any explicit mentioning of racism, as *Walk* does, was rare. By representing women in the role of slaves and modeling the Free Fems' regime on neocolonial systems, Charnas achieves a fusion of the categories of gender and race that risks the obliteration of ethnic specificity. This threat she tries to amend by stressing the ethnic diversity among Riding Women and the reintroduction of women of color to the narrative in the last book. This representation of men and women caught in perpetuated patterns of domination and submission, in power hierarchies of colonial *other* and colonial oppressor that renders them both master and slave, will be examined in the following section.

To move from the violence necessitated by an uprising and the escalation of war towards a peaceful utopian cooperation, Charnas argues, the collective trauma of slavehood, the dichotomy of oppressor and oppressed, needs to be lived. It is a necessary part of the liberation struggle that everybody experiences the flip side of dominance to gain a dual consciousness and thus fully understand the need for change. Victimization is no guarantee of not turning into oppressors, and to believe that dehumanizing the *other* leaves the self unharmed is a misapprehension. On the contrary, the objectification, or in the terminology of the Martiniquan Marxist critic Aimé Césaire, the colonial "thingification" (21), of the *other* degrades both colonizer and colonized subject, and damages the subjectivity of master and slave, as Fanon has pointed out in *Black Skin, White Masks*. Holdfasters of both sexes must cease to collude in a slave system and abandon their roles as willing slaves and masters. Charnas illustrates that the mere attempt to escape the discourse of repressive opposites, of male/female, white/black, masters/slaves, good/evil, leads to the inversion and perpetuation of binarism, just as the structure of the New Holdfast society constantly provokes memories of past wrongs and inflicts new atrocities, because its structure inherently continues an unexpiated past.

But how are we to transcend iniquities and retribution, and initiate a process of reconciliation and social regeneration? Can slavery and oppression be expiated and is doing so expedient? Mitigation, Charnas proposes, must be achieved by forgiving without condoning the past wrongs. Neither the perpetuation nor the negation, or the extinction in the sense of leveling, of opposites will transform society; but the seizure of the slippage of pluralities in between opposites will create a new sense of being. Defining a new society presupposes defining the subjects participating in it. This process of decolonization, the restructuring of subjectivity, begins with the recognition that internalized sexist and colonial dichotomies must be demystified. A collective peace of mind necessitates first a mental reconciliation (e.g., Alldera and Eykar), a healing of the psychological and the physical mutilations, which then allows a peaceful physical cohabitation and social cohesion, to ensure that everyone benefits from this new society.

The series also addresses the questions of survival and resistance. Is survival a legitimate tool of resistance? And under what circumstances is death preferable? Is survival possibly supportive of an oppressive system? Charnas warns that survival at all costs, understandable as it is on the individual level, can be counterproductive on the collective level. At the time of the Wasting women refrain from taking action and decide to "do what they [the men] say for now" (*W* 3). Similarly, the Matris' line of resistance is basically to stay alive and thus collaborate to maintain the system. But survival, Alldera scornfully retorts in response to Eykar's suggestion she should flee with Servan "is an overrated achievement" (*W* 212) if it means future enslavement by Servan. Faced with the threat of the return of patriarchy in *The Conqueror's Child*, the fems have learned their lesson and are no longer ready to comply and sacrifice for survival: "Better no men than masters again" (*CC* 265).

To ensure survival, Salalli tolerates the abuse of her daughters, the alienation from Shareem and allows Servan to blackmail her into becoming his emissary to win the fems' confidence. She takes pride in her position as Servan's "chosen woman" (*CC* 263), which is not "some sort of voluntary slavery" (*CC* 263), as Sorrel suspects, but *because* she assumes doing so will give her and her children the greatest chance of survival. Confronted with the choice between following Servan or Alldera, the opportunist Salalli decides according to "who was going to win" (*CC* 293) and which way better guarantees the future of her and her children (cf. *CC* 299). As much as she resents Servan, "a land of women living free and forthright with no men above them" (*CC* 292) seems unimaginable to her, and furthermore she does not want her daughter to be a "master of slaves" (*CC* 340), as Sorrel observes.

In the series, male and female rule are represented as variations of patriarchy and matriarchy; both can also be read as colonial systems grounded in the enslavement of the other sex. On an axis measuring patriarchy, the modified patriarchal structure of the Pooltowns is placed on the lower end, the Holdfast patriarchy and Servan's anachronistic threat of re-newing the Holdfast structure in the middle, only surpassed by Maggomas's extreme masculinism and cannibalism. He envisions "building a new, better and truly rational society" (*W* 188), subsisting "primarily on the meat, skins and muscle power of a mass of down-bred fems" (*W* 205). This final instrumentalization and commodification of humans—an allusion to Swift's satiric *A Modest Proposal* that suggests eliminating starvation and overpopulation in Ireland by using children as food—is the outcome of masculinity defined as "violence and insensitivity, *machismo*" (Cranny-Francis 189), a masculinity that ultimately enslaves the male self, earlier on symbolized in *Walk* by the sub-class of Rovers, the instrumentalized slaves trained to kill at a commander's will. As "vengeful ghosts of their fathers" (*CC* 406), men caught in patriarchal thought undermine true change. In Charnas's line of thought, the "competitive dominance drive" is, however, not restricted to the male sex. Rather, she sees it as "a potentiality in *people*" (Mohr 1999d, 19; emphasis added) and a relic of our primate origins. In Charnas's view, aggression is only one aspect of "masculinism tied to biology" (ibid. 20) that the reactionary Servan embodies most prominently, a behavior the human race needs to transcend. Charnas warns postfeminists that machismo is a continuous inner threat lurking within both sexes, easily revivified and far more likely than invasion from outer space. Postpatriarchal society is not (t)here yet and the state in-between is fragile.

Female rule is equally caught in subjection. In the Holdfast, the female overseers, the Matris, oppress members of their own sex, and fems practice "sly politicking" (*W* 167).[73] Any attempts at resistance are instantly quelled. Observing how Sorrel fights being ritually cleansed in

---

[73] *The name "Matri," of course, indicates a kind of matriarchal rule. Similar to the Aunts in* The Handmaid's Tale, *the Matris exemplify submission turned into complicity.*

a bath and how the Riding Women encourage her resistance by praising her strength and obstinacy, Alldera notes that back in the Holdfast this sign of individuality and rebellious independence would have been suppressed; or Sorrel might well have been killed outright by the Matris. The obviously oppressive rule of despotic Elnoa at the Tea Camp, physically established by her wagon "holding the center of the yard, dominat[ing] everything" (*M* 93), contrasts sharply with Wolmark's listing of *Walk* and *Motherlines* as examples for nature/culture and masculine/feminine essentialism, claiming that women achieve freedom only upon their escape into the wilderness (cf. 1999, 231)[74] and interprets both the Tea Camp and the Grassland society as "utopian alternatives" (Wolmark 1994, 84). On the contrary, incapable of decolonizing their minds to invent a new life, the fems at the Tea Camp are still driven by internalized hierarchical and possessive thinking. Despite signs of marginal freedom—they now, for example, wear their hair long, growing it for their "own pleasure rather than for the profit of a master" (*M* 94)—they simply re-establish patriarchal patterns in a matriarchal society, rebuilding and perpetuating the known social system of mastery and slavery.

Alldera instantly recognizes the Free Fems as the unchanged fem slaves. She sees the Tea Camp for what is is, "a big femhold with Elnoa as master" (*M* 106). They re-create dystopia with the only difference being that so-called "Free" Fems now assume the roles of masters *and* slaves, making "one of themselves master and serve her" (*M* 139). Only Alldera questions Elnoa's rule: "Who are you to give me orders?" (*M* 115), and she is bitterly punished for her insubordination. Unlike the Riding Women, the Free Fems cling to external controls. Lifting external oppression, Charnas warns, will not automatically change us, if our internal programming remains untouched. Imitating the only form of power they have experienced, the Free Fems reverse roles and install a neocolonial system, turning exactly into what they hated most. Matriarchy as inversion of patriarchy and its binary order leaves the space of domination intact. Power is a corrupting force, and both sexes are prone to it.

To unlearn the behavior of a slave and/or a master is painful on both sides. According to Fanon, the necessary stage of essentialized identities and of usurping the now vacant role of masters is part of the decolo-

---

[74]*Wolmark, like a number of other critics, stubbornly resists the temptation to extend her criticism to the whole series. The essay I am referring to, "The Postmodern Romances of Feminist Science Fiction" (1995), has been republished in the anthology* Cybersexualities: A Reader on Feminist Theory, Cyborgs and Cyberspace *(1999) edited by Wolmark. At the time,* The Furies *was published and clearly the fems' return to the Holdfast, their use of its technology and their struggle to build a freer culture in the Holdfast transgress this nature/culture and feminine/masculine essentialism.*

nization process, but should not be consolidated for too long, or a new form of repressive nationalism and neocolonialism, or sexism in the case of the Holdfast's analogy, will settle in. The Holdfast development takes a similar course. First, the fems take freedom, usurp the role of "masters in the men's place" (*F* 98), and then begin to realize that to gain full humanity, they must stop being slaves and masters, stop domination and subordination in personal, sexual, and cultural relationships. To claim humanity, they must refuse being victimized and victimizing. The act of taking "free names" not ending on the femmish "a," provides one example that signifies this decolonizing process and taking on subjectivity. Freedom not only necessitates a refusal of being victimized, but it also requires claiming humanity for oneself *and* for the *other*. To build a truly postpatriarchal, postmatriarchal society, the New Holdfasters must break out of the vicious cycle of violence and walk in this newly created, fragile space.

Liberty also implies the danger of leadership and the corrupting influence of power. Alldera assumes the role of the reluctant leader. Although distrusting power as such, she is nevertheless perceived as powerful and is resented for it. Allegorically, the failed assassination symbolizes also the sacrifice of an effigy representing, in the minds of some, the old system of leadership. Only after being without a leader—Alldera withdraws from the fems to Endpath—are the Fems capable of building a new power system and distributing leadership among themselves. New structures need new leaders, and Alldera who has been maneuvered into leadership wants to pass on her leadership as a warrior because she dislikes power but also because it "may not be so good for peacetime" (*CC* 258). She wants to make "space for new leaders" and, logically consistent, her unspoken question silently addressing Sorrel as bringer of peace for all is: "*Will you one day lead these people?*" (*CC* 258). Yet passing on matrilinear power conflicts with what Alldera has learned from the Grasslanders: freedom is not guaranteed by the leadership of one, but by power-sharing. In the Whole Land Council, each person takes on responsibility in exerting power. In the end, she gives her role up for love, to be with Nenisi.

With the ensuing rivalry among the Free Fems, between the Free Fems and the Newly Freed, and the frictions between Fems and Riding Women, Charnas illustrates the historical infighting within feminism and the frictions of leadership. From *Motherlines* on, the ambivalent relationship between Free Fems and Riding Women develops from hostility to cautious, increased contact, from the reluctant claiming of kinship and the recognition of shared relations in the past, to the acknowledgement of some common causes and aims. In *The Furies*, the Free Fems, having been brutalized all their lives, are faced with the difficult task of establishing and learning humanity, first of all among themselves, as Eykar realizes: "the central matter of the femmish conquest was ... the relations of the fems to one another, among themselves, and to the Wild Women" (F 360). Only with these frictions settled can "the forging of a new relationship" between the sexes with Eykar as "intermediary"(F 360) begin. The Newly Freed, however, resent the freedom and the establishment of the neocolonial rule of the victorious Free Fems they perceive as "invaders" (F 92) and, absorbing the male gaze, as "renegades" (F 110).[75] The Free Fems likewise accuse the Newly Freed of being "too cowardly to run away to freedom and now ... too cowardly to fight for yourselves" (F 180), and, aping the Riding Women, assume the role of know-all adults towards these "childish people" (F 209). Quickly, the fems' rule verges on a hierarchy of victors where "some ex-slaves are more equal than others" (Jones 187).

While the Grasslanders are born to freedom, the fems have to win it from men, but now they carry a notion of what freedom is inside, as Alldera reflects: "*I return a free person*" (F 27). On the one hand, the conflict between Newly Freed and Free Fems deals with the necessity of actively *taking* and not just receiving freedom. On the other hand, it addresses the problem of liberation by invasion or intervention according to one's own ideology, and hence incapacitating the inhabitants.[76] Having experienced a marginally improved male rule, because the remaining fems "were gradually bettering their situation without violence" (Jones 187),[77] the Newly Freed are reluctant to participate in the violent act of throwing off their masters to become, as they fear, the commodities of female masters. Being liberated from (sexual) colonizers is not quite the same as having chosen and fought for freedom. Here, Charnas harshly comments on the conservative retreat of many women during the backlash of the 1980s, but also portrays postfeminist attitudes of rejecting any fight because equality is considered won, a "perceptual

---

[75]*Interestingly, the Matri Mayala even denounces the Free Fems as "savages" and Alldera as "Wildrunner" (F 100) gone rogue or native in the wild.*

[76]*It is also a variation of the conflict between Grasslanders and Free Fems who are, as Bartkowski notes, after all "freed women" in contrast to the "free women" (93). In Motherlines, Sheel cannot understand that women allow others to turn them into slaves, i.e. "fems," especially since her "first ancestors shaped their own freedom" (M 17; emphasis added). In a typical paraphrase of 1970s feminism, Sheel, who totally underestimates the complicated nexus of domination and submission, wonders why fems never simply united to overthrow their masters.*

[77]*Apart from one fem's claim that they were "working toward our own betterment, we didn't need you" (F 107), there is no further textual evidence to support Jones's assertion that the remaining fems actively worked towards their empowerment. Rather, the battle between Seniors and Juniors left both ranks diminished and Juniors became more lenient with fems, "because they were fewer and so more valuable" (F 80). However, the Newly Freed have a different attitude towards men, knowing each "by name" (F 93). Due to the scarcity of fems, gender relations were eventually less characterized by brutality.*

difference that is linked to generation" (Mohr 1999d, 21). Setteo pinpoints exactly this problem with his question: "How can the Meek [the Newly Freed] ... inherit the earth if they rush to serve their old masters again?" (*F* 324), while the "old masters" may literally refer to the male masters, or to the old gods of violence. As ubiquitous entities, the Bears wisely answer that freedom and equality cannot be given: "The Meek already own the earth and always have. No one can give them what has always belonged to them; they must claim it for themselves" (*F* 324). *The Furies* and *The Conqueror's Child* explore thus what Charnas describes with "the difficulty of learning what being free is if you've never known it, even if you have a living, functioning example right in front of you" (Mohr 1999c, 8),[78] i.e. the beginning of the attempt to bring home the Grassland utopia: "At home, what we find and what we make will be ours" (*M* 225).

Significantly, on their return to the Holdfast, the first men the Free Fems encounter are "one dead man and one mad one" (*F* 42). Symbolically, men as they knew them are dead, or must die out, and madness is what will follow. The fems' reconquest begins with the capture and then mutilation and even cannibalization of men, and thus, as Jones notices, "the Free Fems have already matched the level of barbarism the men achieved at the final climax of *Walk*" (186). In this sense, *The Furies* presents "a reworking of *Walk to the End of the World* with a female cast" (Jones 189). Caught in masculine colonial behavior, the fems take revenge, "giv[ing] the pain and anger to our masters" (*M* 225). Yet how can they invent a future without the anger of the past unspent, how to "make a new, whole self without spending ... old poisons first" (*F* 277)?

Alldera argues that fems have to learn to stand up: "Fems who never dared speak up to a master must find the courage ... to kill him in battle" (*F* 275), first of all to show themselves, but also the men, that they are capable of violent resistance. Only then the "world was altered" (*F* 104). Hence slavery, humiliation, and violence are used to purge their anger and to break the arrogance and superiority of men. In contradistinction to Daya's claim, "An ex-slave is a wise master" (*F* 150), the fems turn into cruel slavers with slightly changed motives. Men enslaved women for being the weaker sex; fems enslave men for revenge. Ironically, the same fems who as slaves fought the distortion of the soul, holding on "to their human decency" (*F* 183), now turn themselves into bloodthirsty monsters. In one of their discussions, Eykar sadly points out to Alldera that history repeats itself only in reversed roles. Fems lost their humanity the moment they killed men and now show the "same blindness" and "same excesses" (*F* 275) that men did. Dismissing

---

[78]*Salalli objects too when Servan sets her free; she does not know what freedom is.*

Alldera's objection that men turned them into what they are now, Eykar retorts that mere reaction and destruction instead of action and creation is not enough: "Haven't you come back to be something else than *our* creation? Something new, something of your own...?" (*F* 276; emphasis added).

The creation of something different from "master and slave" in whatever inversion or reversed roles is the issue with which the New Holdfasters are faced. Now since both sexes and black and white have lived both roles, perhaps a third space can be created. A new concept unsettling the master/slave concept of domination is named by Setteo: taking "care of children required natural slaves ... with an inclination to serve those smaller and weaker" (*CC* 125) than oneself. Such a self-chosen role of submission, where the stronger person serves the weaker, does not follow the rules of exploitation. Setteo is thus a new role model for "how a man may fit himself to the role of a human being" (*CC* 416). Also exempt from the cycle of domination and submission, from any oppression at all, is the Grassland society. Their "[c]ulture is derived from shared life experience" (Sargisson 163) and is not shaped according to race, class, or sex. Here, natural and cultural life are not perceived as hierarchical but cyclical: "Nothing came in 'firsts' and 'lasts' here, but as 'another' or 'again.'" (*M* 40). Among the Riding Women who do not possess anything or anyone and are "always free," since they "bow to no one, for any reason" (*CC* 368), Alldera learns "how not to be a master" (*M* 225). Here, the fems experience a non-hierarchical system without positions to be gained, but with fluid relations between equals: "You don't need a position when you have kindred" (*M* 160). Horse-riding is perhaps the ultimate metaphor for independence, empowerment, and mastery *without* domination. When rider and horse commune in body and mind, do they succeed in forming the harmonious unity that at first led Alldera to perceive the Riding Women as one being: half human, half animal.

Only when both sexes begin to rehumanize themselves will the master/slave dichotomy end, as Sorrel stresses: "Better a human being, man *or* woman, than a master of slaves" (*CC* 151). Sorrel's feelings for Veree are a constant reminder that "men must be made human again" (*CC* 156), as Beyarra states. Representative of the "reconciliationists" (*CC* 136) amongst the Newly Freed, increased contact with men, especially with Eykar, Beyarra wants "*something better than rage and hatred and contempt between women and men*" (*CC* 49).[79] Daya's motive for changing the fem-men relations is, on the one hand, fed by her belief in divine calling—making "human beings of them ... with her [Moonwoman's]

---

[79]*In the manuscript of* The Conqueror's Child, *Beyarra even calls Eykar Bek her "friend" (ms. CC 214).*

help our healing will begin" (*CC* 116)—that is closely tied to the aim to rehabilitate herself. On the other hand, Daya's own preference for heterosexuality inspires her desire to craft "the greatest gift of all, a true, sound peace" (*CC* 136). The victory Alldera achieved Daya wants to top with "the crown of the Conquest: wiping slavery from the face of the Holdfast" (*CC* 194). To demonstrate the possibility of cooperation between the sexes, she makes her lover Galligan an accomplice of her attempt to avert the threat Servan poses to the New Holdfast: "we'll make a path of cleansing for all men ... you good lads and our own boys growing to manhood need a way to step out of your chains" (*CC* 193). In contrast to Elgin and Atwood, Charnas explicitly calls on men's need to rehumanize themselves or, in Alldera's words, "to learn to carry their honor for themselves" (*CC* 405–406). Analogous to feminism, she argues, men need to be cognizant of masculine issues. Victimization is then a necessary step to recognize the importance of injustice and equality. Only male characters such as Setteo, Eykar, and Veree, who are in some way disabled and have been victimized or mutilated by other men, and who do not participate fully in the masculine power structure are willing to change. Their lack of sharing the "masculine privilege" gives them the ability "to empathize with other people who are not privileged" (Mohr 1999d, 19).

4.5. The Slow Way to the Future

4.5.1. Borderwalkers

The Holdfast society is ruled by a notion of homogeneity grounded in binary oppositions in which the self is defined against an *other* that the self strives to exclude and exterminate. Gender and culture differences function to discriminate, subordinate, and eliminate the other sex, ethnic groups, and animals, and hence to legitimize the power and domination of the (white, male) self. Within this cult of sameness, any visible reminders of differences are suppressed. Females are excluded from the public sphere, and people of color as well as animals are eliminated. This obsession with homogeneity drives men to create ever finer lines of difference and sameness within their own sex group. Yet whatever has been defined and excluded as the *other* is found inside the self. Total sameness equals self-destruction, because parts of the *other* are part of the self, rendering binary oppositions impossible and necessitating a reconceptualization of difference in relation to the self. Clear-cut binary oppositions become diffuse as various binarisms are transgressed, as the self discovers the *other* within without that *other* ever being analogous. The self is not the *other* and the *other* is not the self, but each contains and reflects aspects of what was formerly defined as opposite. Identity is experienced as situational as the characters inhabit cultural and sexual states inbetween the either/or logic. The boundaries of opposites are thus transgressed.

An element of the bestial can be found in humans, males display feminine and females masculine qualities, certain traits and behavior of the Holdfasters resemble that of the Grasslanders, and the Grasslanders detect something Holdfastish within themselves. Masculinity, femininity, animality, they all become points of reference for both sexes, and for the Riding Women. Therefore, a paradigm shift is required to redefine these exclusive binary concepts of difference as the interdependence of self and *other*, the location of internalized differences within the self, surface. Only the creation of a new view of non-hierarchizing and homogenizing self and *other* relations, grounded in recognizing and valuing difference as non-threatening and practiced as a constant interplay and negotiating shifts between self and *other*, will potentially liberate Holdfasters, allowing them to establish a mode of coexistence.

Here the ethnographic term "transculturation," used for the cultural process that takes place when cultures meet, proves valuable. As explained earlier in Chapter 2, transculturation means, according to Pratt, that the subordinate group incorporates parts of the culture the dominant group transports. As much as transculturation is part of a culture clash, it is also a "process of inter-cultural negotiation and selection" (Loomba 68). This social interactive space, where cultures meet, Pratt has termed the "contact zone." Despite sexual and racial segregation, the inevitable nuances of contact in this contact zone require first that individuals learn new ways and then introduce the new knowledge into their own society. If we go on the assumption that analogous to cultural transmission, there exists also a process of transportation between what we are used to thinking of as binary categories, then several characters acquire not only the status of borderwalkers between cultures, but also between other binary poles.

Alldera and Sorrel, for instance, are both fems and Grasslanders; even Sheel, who is alienated from her own culture and lives for the most part with fems, comes to at least acknowledge Holdfast ways. Veree is a Holdfaster and a Riding Man, thus crossing cultural and sexual divides; Eykar personifies the dualistic struggle between mind and body and adopts Grassland behavior, such as sharemothering. He and Servan also draw on masculine as well as feminine traits, while the cutboy Setteo defies any sex or gender role classification. Captain Kelmz transgresses the age line and desires to re-introduce a positive (human) animality—a link between animal and human that the Riding Women celebrate—

into an animalized and brutalized world of predatory animality that Servan embodies. As I discussed earlier, Setteo walks the knife edge between reality and dreams, hovering between madness and clairvoyant sanity, and Beyarra transgresses the literacy/orality divide.

All these borderwalkers, being in one way or another simultaneously insiders and outsiders, move on the edge between societies, sexes, and gender/age roles. Their liminal status as marginal persons rooted in more than one culture, or one sex, or one ascribed role, allows them to learn individually and then to instigate change. The double vision, the consciousness of being simultaneously inside and outside, of being complicit and subversive, and the cultural crossovers produce hybridity and ambivalence. Transgressed oppositions lead to a new nomadic consciousness and an indeterminate hybrid identity that is no longer bound by Cartesian dichotomies; and the meeting of disparate cultures, entering multifarious connections, produces new cultural constellations.

The transgression of boundaries also enables the characters to gain a changed view of the self, of other cultures, and to incorporate parts of what was previously termed *other* into the self. This permeability of the self and the experience of the *other* from inside trigger the paradigm change necessary to obtain a broader perspective. Their borderline position makes them catalysts of Bhabha's aesthetics of liberation. Transforming themselves, their capacity to assuage differences between opposites transforms society. Stepping out of one's own society and becoming a borderwalker, Charnas stresses, is thereby an irreversible process: "You walk the borders of your own society forever after, unable *not* to look outward as well as inward, and to compare. You can never rest easy in the unthinking, uncritical center again" (Mohr 1999d, 20).

The most important borderwalker between cultures is, of course, Alldera.[80] Her physical/geographical journey from the Holdfast to the Grasslands, back to the Holdfast, and her return to and disappearance from the Grasslands, matches her spiritual journey. In *Walk*, Alldera keeps apart from the other fems; even though she is an insider of the fem society, right from the beginning she is presented as an outsider and a borderwalker. She is neither a pet fem for lack of beauty, nor a labor fem, but a trained fast runner and messenger of men's words. Although she is a slave, her intellectual training, her "protofeminist consciousness" (Bartkowski 87), drives her to question the social structure and, for instance, masculine concepts of beauty and disfigurement. In a way, she becomes a Riding Woman before she even meets the Grasslanders, when

---

[80]Charnas explicitly stresses the importance of hybridity and borderwalkering that Alldera signifies: "to stir people together, mixing ideas and customs, in hope of provoking new insights into old problems" (ms. CC 86).

she chooses to actively shape her life over "waiting ... like a slave" (*M* 11). At the Tea Camp, Alldera is instantly an outsider because she refuses to wear "a slave smock" (*M* 115), the attribute of slavery, and keeps to her own ways. Alldera's first journey takes her symbolically to a country of female authenticity and liberation that fascinates and repels her. After an initial resentment of the different cultural and sexual practices—analogous to the historical anxiety about going native, usually accompanied with descriptions of the dangerous seductiveness of the *other* and the European's regression into madness and primitivism as in Joseph Conrad's *Heart of Darkness*—Alldera "goes native" as she gets accustomed to the Grasslanders, who are no longer "alien and forbidding but familiar" (*M* 34).

Alldera neither assimilates completely to the Riding Women's psychic difference, nor is she absorbed by the Tea Camp society. Yet the reassurance of her own cultural background at the Tea Camp allows her to search and find a third way that neither adopts Grassland nor Holdfast culture completely. While Alldera's first journey into the wilderness and inhospitable desert is an involuntary escape from destroyed 'Troi, her second wandering into the desert, the literary trope for the fictional journey of identity, is deliberate and willingly chosen. Alldera enters what in the Holdfast mythology was synonymous with the unknown, the uncharted landscape where the potentially dangerous *other* may reside, and comes to terms with the unknown. Where the Riding Women's nursing provided her with a rebirth into a dream-like country, she now shapes her own metaphorical rebirth. In pursuit of the wild horses in the desert, Alldera willingly sheds her human identity and after becoming one of a band of horses gradually becomes human again.[81] As the tamed wild horses that she brings back from her second journey into the desert indicate, Alldera will shape the future of her people.

After this period of complete isolation and renewal, Alldera reenters both societies on her own terms. Rather than adapting to the Tea Camp or to the Grassland, she forges a new way. Both insider and outsider, slipping in and out of the two societies, Alldera provides the missing link between the cultures, remaining always on the edge. As Nenisi comments "Alldera doesn't fit in with her own people any better than she did with us" (*M* 149). This liminal status permits her to forge a kinship between the two female communities—a fusion embodied by setting up a Holdfaster tent in the Grassland camp—that privileges neither

---

[81]Unlike Gulliver in Gulliver's Travels, *who is forced to recognize his animality exactly because the aroused Yahoo "females had a natural propensity to me as one of their own" (Swift 315), Alldera is reminded of her humanity among the wild horses: "I never gave off the right odours to rouse the stallion" (M 147).*

culture. Every time Alldera joins the fems "behind the divider" (*M* 180) put up by fems in the Holdfaster tent, she literally crosses the line between Women and Fems, but refuses to take sides as the Free Fems demand of her at Sorrel's naming. Both Nenisi and Alldera stress the similarities and connections between the cultures despite their obvious differences. To Nenisi the fems are an "outland Motherline made up of lots of cousins instead of mothers and daughters" (*M* 184), and Alldera extends the notion of relation to both Holdfast sexes: "Are not the men and fems beyond the mountains elements of the world" (*M* 201)?[82]

Daya's cultural transgression is less obvious than Alldera's. Despite being a vehement advocate of Holdfastish culture, Daya is also intrigued by the Grassland. Otherness in the sense of the exotic eroticizes and appeals to Daya, who muses about how it might feel "to be touched by a woman as black as char and to stroke a creature [a horse] that was not even human at all" (*M* 110). Unsurprisingly, Daya is irresistibly drawn to the muscular, alien Alldera, who has just returned with tamed horses from her journey into the desert. Of the Free Fems at the Tea Camp, only Daya loves the plains. She is a "natural rider" (*M* 157); and while Alldera loves the "mastery" of the horses, Daya is attracted by "the joining of her own meager strength to their power" (*M* 158). The new skill of horse-riding offers Daya a new valuation of herself, a new aspect of physicality besides beauty, a new range of freedom and a sense of power. Approaching her own people while mounted on a horse shifts her perception. Now Daya can see the fems and their "closed, defensive masks" (*M* 162) through the eyes of a Riding Woman. Where the pet fem was an outsider because of her sex in the Tea Camp, she returns as a cultural outsider because of her new ability. The alien experience of horse-riding also familiarizes Daya with the Grasslanders: "Now that she rode a horse herself the idea of staying a while among the Mares seemed less alien" (*M* 164).

As her mother did, Sorrel borderwalks between cultures and questions given patterns and rules. Her name aligns her instead with a "sorrel mare" (*M* 207); she is neither culture's property. Repeatedly identifying with Grassland customs and perception, she is nevertheless attracted to the "exotic possibilities" (*CC* 22) of the Holdfast, but cannot totally identify as either fem or Woman. Additionally, Sorrel links men with fems and Grasslanders, as she pushes the male question into the

---

[82] *This question of difference and sameness is also addressed earlier in the aforementioned fems' riddle-song "Why is a raven like a writing desk?" (W 143), taken from the tea party episode in Carroll's* Alice's Adventures in Wonderland, *where the Mad Hatter's question remains unanswered. In the Holdfast context, the long lost signs "raven" and "writing-desk" no longer signify the actual animal and object, but serve to question the Holdfast "concept of likeness" (W 143), of forcing sameness onto disparities.*

foreground. She and Veree are the first hybrid children raised in or by the two cultures. Despite her tendency to compartmentalize, "seeing everything as black and white" (*CC* 400), and being "split apart, a person with 'two shadows'" (*CC* 159)—that of her mother and the fems' past and that of a future including Riding men—Sorrel represents the reconnection between fems and women, females and males, past and future, children and parents. She introduces a new element, something that does not fit the dualistic pattern, in Setteo's words, Sorrel is "not a Bear or a carrier of Bear spirits ... but something else" (*CC* 132).

Cultural change begins on the individual level, then resonates in both societies: "Alldera had wanted to make changes, first in herself and then in the Free Fems, but never in the lives of the women. Now change had followed her to Stone Dancing Camp" (*M* 203), as the Free Fems introduce "qualities that the Riding Women lack: versatility, adaptability, perseverance and patience" (Lefanu 163–164). Transculturation works here both ways. The fems unlearn "their slavish ways" (*M* 238) and learn bonding, but they also add their knowledge to the Grassland, for instance, by building a granary. Negative change occurs too, however, as Sheel comments: "We're not immune to corruption" (*F* 394). As the Riding Women's initial rejection of everything Holdfastish yields to curiosity in *The Furies*, some attend the moonwoman rituals, one takes to drinking beer, and another catches the Holdfast cough. The fury and pain of the Holdfast literally infects the Riding Women, driving two of them to self-destruct. Even Sheel, otherwise skeptical of anything new and the keeper of unchanging Grassland traditions, unwittingly instigates change when she sends a pregnant fem to the Grassland and gives the female Grassland name Veree to the yet unborn child. Instead of being "a daughter of both lands" (*F* 127), Veree becomes the first Riding Man of the Holdfast.

Within the dualistic paradigm, the sexual and cultural *other* is invariably perceived as non-human and animalized human, as beast and as monster. After having witnessed the bestial murder of his lover, "with his throat torn out by a rogue Rover" (*W* 47), Kelmz, for instance, sees beneath the veneer of civilized man and perceives the beast(iality) in men. The "gleaming skin of the ferrymen" reminds Kelmz "of insect armor" (*W* 35) and to him Servan, who is frequently characterized as a human "prowling predator," is "an actual beast" (*W* 9).[83] In turn, Ser-

---

[83] *To Alldera Servan stands outside of human society. He is a "hungry beast, one of those amoral instinctual creatures," a "hunting predator" (W 125). Throughout Servan is characterized as a slick human animal. He is the predecessor of the male protagonist Dr. Weyland of the novel* The Vampire Tapestry (1980) *that Charnas wrote after the completion of* Motherlines. *In* The Vampire Tapestry *Charnas depicts vampires if not exactly as human siblings then at least as our cousins, as an almost extinct branch of humans. Dr. Weyland is a professor of*

van describes Salalli as "good-looking creature in a[n] ... animal-like way" (*CC* 312), while for Pooltowners "light-skinned people were not fully human" (*CC* 419), and the fems insist on calling the Grasslanders "mares." Having defined the actual beast out of the arena, men redefine themselves as subhuman beasts and ethnically different, forcing Juniors to live naked in the dorms "to be reminded of how like beasts and Dirties they were" (*W* 108), and thus men turn into what they desired to exclude; they become "all that they hated" (*W* 161), as one fem song concludes. Treating the *other* as beast implies acting like one.

Maggomas is perhaps the ultimate human monster. When Eykar warns Alldera that the wilderness may be populated by monstrous beasts, Alldera retorts: "I am experienced ... at handling monsters" (*W* 213). Therefore, upon meeting the mounted Riding Women, she perceives them as monsters. However, Cranny-Francis's assertion that males "act like monsters" and females "are treated like monsters" (203) does not exempt fems from bestial behavior and the "predatory look" (*M* 56). The closing scene of *Walk* captures this animality of humans in a primeval scene where essentially the Holdfasters, united in their Darwinistic struggle for survival, are "all hunters, all quarry" (*W* 215).

Although I agree with Lefanu's assessment of Kelmz as "the most traditional and unquestioning" (154) male character in *Walk*, he is the only man who questions the beast/human polarity. It seems to me that his infatuation with the animal *other* that he truly desires to meet, "to see real beasts ... scented alien beings" (*W* 48)—a wish he is granted in a manna-dream that allows him to unleash his unconsciousness and experience *himself* as beast—indicates less a confirmation of the bestial core of man than a close connection between humans and animals and the rightful place of animals in the human world. In contradistinction to Cranny-Francis's reading of Kelmz as desiring a logic of *machismo*, I argue that Kelmz rather admires a natural animality and desires the return of beasts to escape the bestial behavior of the Holdfast. His ability to see the animal in humans and to imagine the humanity of animals indicates the reciprocal bond between humans and animals, a bond both Alldera

[continued] *anthropology and not "a supernatural creature ... but rather the sole member of another species, a product of evolution" (King 1993, 80). Differing vastly from conventional vampire stories that serve to cement the status quo of human/animal and dismiss the reader into a well-ordered world of bipolarity, Charnas's representation uses "the figure of the vampire to challenge rather than reinforce the binary oppositions—such as good/evil, human/alien, and masculine/feminine" (ibid. 75). Dissolving the demarcation between human and other, Weyland's only obstacle to full humanity is that his prey are humans whom he does not even kill, but only feeds on. Maureen King's observation about the recast vampire figure Weyland holds equally true for Holdfast men and Servan in particular: "As the vampire is a beast, so too is the human" (80). Yet Dr. Weyland, in many other ways a matured Servan, is driven by instinct and is not ambitious, malicious and power-hungry as is Servan. While Weyland is also hunted and victimized, Servan is the feline hunter, playing with his prey for his own amusement.*

experiences when she adapts to an animal/horse identity in the desert and the Riding Women celebrate in their mating. Their transgression of the human/animal opposition is the most explicit one. However, a logical break in Charnas's argument that the Grasslanders exist outside of the heterosexual paradigm reveals itself in their adherence to the dualistic paradigm of men as bestial enemies. Strictly speaking, men who are, after all, utterly marginal to their society should be a mere curiosity in the Grassland. Instead, the Riding Women treat men as bestial "semi-human" (*F* 292) *other*, where their own transgressive bond with horses should connote at least animal maleness positively. Calling men vermin (cf. *CC* 40) just as men refer to fems as vermin (cf. *W* 4), the Riding Women apply the same logic that denies the *other* human status.[84] Thus, "a male child was no more a 'little person' than a litter of sharu-get were 'persons.'" (*CC* 220).

Eykar, Setteo, and Veree, the three male characters transgressive of the male/female sex and gender roles, undergo a feminization and are denounced as "effeminate" by other men. The cutboy Setteo inhabits a space between sexes and gender roles. We first meet him as a male female, dressed like a "house fem" (*F* 41) and bowing in femmish manner. When Daya claims his capture, he slips her rein and, "standing on his hands, comically inverted," his upside down skirt reveals that he is a "fake fem and no man" (*F* 39). From his own hybrid sex status, he knows that "[o]ther states, between the extremes, must exist" (*F* 114). Men and fems are repeatedly forced to revise their automatic association of a certain display of behavior with one sex.

Incapable of separating gender roles from sex and because of the Grasslanders' natural ease, their physical strength and mastery of horses, Alldera and later on the Newly Freed initially perceive the Riding Women as men. Only upon touching one Riding Woman's body is Alldera convinced of the stranger's femaleness. Similarly, the Free Fem's violent and self-assertive behavior leads the Holdfast men to take them for men.

Especially male characters undercut the totality of masculinity that patriarchal ideology propagates. The male body enters an economy of the ornamental and is displayed for the male gaze. The ferrymen, for instance, wear "earrings, pendants, anklets" (*W* 37). In this economy of the ornamental, Servan, the Machiavellian machismo character par excellence, is also characterized by a seductive beauty. Servan embodies a destructive masculinity in terms of machismo, animality, body power

---

[84] *At the same time, the reference to "vermin" recalls the King of Brobdingnag's sweeping conclusion that humans are "the most pernicious race of little odious vermin that Nature ever suffered to crawl upon the surface of the earth" (173) in Swift's* Gulliver's Travels.

and external action, which is complemented by Eykar who struggles with an emergent feminized masculinity that no longer fits the artificially constructed dualism of male/female, mind/body, rationality/irrationality, sanity/madness.

According to the Holdfast paradigm, the exercise of reason allows the male/mind to conquer the taint of the female/body. Suffering from this body/mind divide, this "split into opposites" (*W* 105), Eykar tries to overrule the increasingly failing body brute, his "bestial enemy" (*W* 96), a physical frailty that feminizes him and allows others to victimize him. This experience of victimization allows him to sympathize with fems. The more Eykar recognizes the disparity between ideology and reality, the more he learns to respect women, the more he can accept his body. By killing Maggomas and then Servan, he twice rejects the traditional masculinity of aggression and domination they represent. Eykar's reconstructed, albeit flawed, model of masculinity is characterized by internal agonizing, questioning intellectuality, and the belief in the power and justice of words, "words, not mindless violence" (*W* 24), and the desire to "heal up the horror between men and fems" (*W* 178). Like Setteo, the increasingly vision-impaired Eykar is a mutilated visionary and truthteller. Yet while the former uses his inner eye of vision/spirituality, the latter unblinkingly absorbs everything with the cold eye of rationality. But although Eykar is a prophet to whom men blind to reality do not listen, he becomes the inventor of a new masculinity and a spokesman for the younger men, trying to "change their thinking" (*F* 275). Being on the margins of the male society, he is also cognizant of the chance for change. Eykar has "the courage to learn from his 'enemies'" (Mohr 1999d, 17) and, consequently, the Free Fems represent "the first infusion of life" and "the only hope ... for a future" (*F* 146) to him. The new pattern of masculinity he designs is that of "a builder, a helper ... a creator" (*CC* 151–152).

The hopes for a truly new definition of the male sex, however, are pinned on Veree. Physiologically a male Holdfaster and psychologically a feminine Grasslander, he is "raised free" (*CC* 132). His experience of gender-bending and cross-dressing as female, used to "being called 'her' and 'she'" (*CC* 35), renders him psychologically and culturally hybrid. He cannot identify with a masculinity grounded in slavery; Veree and the captive men are no longer of the same kind. He links the male body with feminine experiences. Born a man, he is nevertheless a "pretty fair woman" (*CC* 418) and perhaps the image incarnating what wise Alldera summarizes in a nutshell: "We aging warriors ... [of] both sexes, are more alike than not" (*CC* 208). Like the Grasslanders, the Holdfasters should not let biology restrict their humanity. Everyone can be "a full human being with all of the human potentiality ... with the exception of a few biological specifics."[85] Instead they learn to be "not equals of sameness but potential partners of equal worth" who "use their imagination ... [and] stop treating artificial boundaries as absolute."[86]

4.5.2. "The Only Reality for Us Is Here": The Women and Men of the New Holdfast

Charnas envisions a future of reconciled sexes and of "negotiated tenderness" (Mohr 1999c, 12), of what the South African writer Bessie Head has called "a compromise of tenderness."[87] With their return to the Holdfast, the Free Fems also return from utopia to the reconstruction of what will be their reality for which they seek pragmatic solutions to the serious problems that confront them. To return to a settled daily routine after the war, the New Holdfasters, both women and men, must break out of the vicious cycle of violence: "Something had to be imagined besides ... brutality, pain, danger, and degradation; or how would they ever be able to bring themselves to create the future they had come home for...? It must be different. They would make it different" (*F* 149). The Holdfasters, "who had no society even now, only an army" (*F* 183) as Sheel comments, have to define the concept of a "society" and then learn how to build it. With the abolition of mastery and slavery, the Holdfasters now have to learn the freedom of choice. The central question of *The Conqueror's Child* is, therefore, the question of freedom: "*When do we become truly free?*" (*CC* 97). Only if both genders reject dualistic thinking and go beyond separatism and war and share power by empowering everyone will their exclusive societies evolve into a postpatriarchal, multicultural society, affirming difference and equality by allowing everyone the full range of human traits and rights. In contradistinction to Jones's gloomy forecast that "the cycle of abuse will never be broken" (191) and, therefore, no solution can be offered, the New Holdfasters pave the way for utopia in *The Conqueror's Child*. Charnas refrains from depicting a New Holdfast utopia, but scatters several hints that point towards the making of a better society.

Turning away from sexual, cultural and familial/generational separatism and war, the Holdfasters negotiate various new alliances. Several passages indicate a change of perception, acknowledging differences that

---

[85] *Interview with Charnas. See the appendix.*
[86] *Interview with Charnas. See the appendix.*
[87] *With the phrase "negotiated tenderness" (Mohr 1999c, 12) Charnas refers somewhat misleadingly to Bessie Head's story "Heaven is not closed" where Head talks of the necessity for "a compromise of tenderness," as Bill Clemente pointed out during one of our discussions at the ICFA conference in 2001.*

cut across binary poles and altered relations between the sexes. A future reconciliation between the sexes is hinted at by, for instance, some captive men's argument that fems "are mostly like us, some straight, some crooked" (*CC* 182) and by some fems' positive attitude towards men, allowing men to join their hearths unchained and respecting "the integrity of the human body, any human body" (*CC* 92). The fems now want to give the men the "*choice* whether to be people or not" (*CC* 396; emphasis added). After all, Alldera broods, the goal cannot be "permanent enmity between us and the men ... and our own sons," but "peace, not war; brothers, not slaves" (*CC* 45). This new alliance is indicated by an image of cooperation between the Pooltown woman Melnie and the former ferryman Blix, a member of Servan's renegade band: "Blix caught Melnie's elbow to steady her.... They walked close together and *shared their loads*" (*CC* 301; emphasis added). The possibility that traditional binary oppositions are soon to be transgressed is also symbolized by the name of one of Sorrel's daughters: Allda-Tamann, an amalgam of the victim Alldera and her assassin Tamansan-Nan.

Charnas's allegory of the building of a new world moves from one patriarchal society in *Walk* to a plurality of five societies, from a white supremacist society to the inclusion of other ethnic groups and a multicultural, multi-ethnic, multireligious society in *The Conqueror's Child*. According to Charnas, the last book of the series is thus a completion of the revolution, a necessary "reconnection to the rest of the world" (Mohr 1999c, 11). The proliferation of various cultures and societies stresses the emergence of cultural change and adaptation and the acceptance of different ways of life. Acknowledging multiculturalism, the series enlarges the scope of societies to include the Riding Women, the New Holdfast, the Pooltowns, the all-female community of Breakaways who create "their version of Grassland freedom" (*CC* 417) by adopting the Grassland culture in the South—"to take some horses ... and live like Riding Women ... to be away from men altogether and to live truly free" (*CC* 55)—and the Bayo-born of the Swamps, escapees from the former fem quarters. The fact that hierarchy and old patterns of superiority are persistent is illustrated by the Bayo-born society that reinserts the female as the dominant universal category: "all humans were conceived female, but some were necessarily cursed with carrying the poison of male seed" (*CC* 92). They take to castrating men after they have fulfilled their "procreative duty" (*CC* 92).[88] The psychological and geographical broadening of the Holdfaster's garrison mentality—focusing before their vision

---

[88] *The manuscript explicitly stresses the essentialism of the Bayo-born society, where castration is equivalent with a return to "full, female humanity" (ms. CC 89). Alldera rejects essentialism and biologism, an absolution of atrocities on the grounds of genes: "It would mean that*

only on the male self and the Holdfast—is signified by the construction of boats. On the one hand, the boats can only be constructed with the help of the Pooltowners, on the other hand, the New Holdfasters' very reason for wanting to set sail is the now no longer heretical assumption that there *are* other cultures beyond the Holdfast and that contact with other cultures is desirable.

Racial prejudice works both ways. Although initially applying a concept of sameness on the grounds of skin color, Alldera then perceives the cultural differences between Sallali and Nenisi. Unlike Sallali, Nenisi has never been "any man's 'chosen woman.' The two dark people might as well have come from different planets" (*CC* 272). The Pooltowners also adhere to an inverted but nevertheless dualistic view of other cultures determined by skin color. To them the Holdfasters are "evil whites" (*CC* 75). Exactly because he rejects dualistic compartmentalizing, their leader Gaybrel, who does not want to attack the invading strangers just because "their skin is pale" (*CC* 73), dies for believing in utopia, "the ideal of a new, fair world" (*CC* 75).

Sallali also privileges race as the common denominator when she asks Alldera "[W]hy would I tell *you* our secrets? White, you are white, like him [Servan]" (*CC* 274). At another occasion, however, she considers sex the decisive factor when she weighs up the chances of the fems' defeating Servan: "*They will fall as we fell*" (*CC* 292). Yet again, among the Free Fems, among her own sex, Sallali feels "unalterably set apart, an alien shocked by the outlandish ways of her hosts" (*CC* 408). While Sallali is alien because of her skin color, she is obversely appalled by the Holdfast practice of homosexuality and lesbianism as well as the idea of fems as masters of male slaves. In a moment of mutual recognition, Sallali and Alldera see in each other fragments of the (Holdfast) past and the (Pooltown) future. Because of her past, Alldera can relate to Sallali's subordination as a way of survival. When Alldera advocates ethnic diversity, clearly favoring the reversal of the effects of the genocide, she also pinpoints the mental paradigm shift that the Holdfasters need to put into practice:

> I hope all her [Sallali's] people are dark-skinned.... Do you believe those Holdfast lies about evil nigs and blackies helping to bring on the Wasting...? [We are] hardly anything but blonde hair, brown hair, light skin, light eyes. We're free, but our bodies are still cut to the pattern our masters chose for us.... I want a wider world for my daughter than the narrow one his [d Layo's] kind tried to lock us into [*CC* 267].

[continued] *all the horrors men had committed had been inevitable, and in no way their own responsibility: not their choice but their chemistry" (ms.* CC *91). For her, castrated sexuality is synonymous with asexuality, incapacitation, and a return to an "artificial pre-pubescent state" (ms.* CC *91).*

In *The Furies* and *The Conqueror's Child*, the similarity of behavior and appearances is repeatedly pointed out between the cultures of the Holdfast, the Pooltowns, and the Grassland. Fems are "as dangerous as Women of the Omelly line" (*F* 104); Eykar resembles "an elder of the Soolay line" (*CC* 106) and talks tersely like Sheel; even Servan looks like "*a shorter, meaner version of the Jargasonna line*" (*CC* 384). A Riding Woman assumes that Sallali and her people are "some lost cadre" (*CC* 323) of her own line. Exposing the illogicality of racism in an allegory taken from the animals, Alldera asks: "Do you look at our horses and see bays and grays and sorrels and say, get rid of all the bays, they don't belong" (*CC* 268)?

What Charnas presents us with is not a blueprint for utopia or radical change, but rather the fluid process leading towards the building of a new and better place consisting of different cultures and social systems. The negotiations between fems and men towards a society of parity with differences offers no solution insofar as infinite imperfections are implied. To Sheel's abhorrence these negotiations are fragile and keep changing; she complains, "Then nothing you have done here will ever be secure!" (*F* 390), for the Holdfast society will keep evolving, because "[e]verything's in motion all the time, people and events and ideas shifting about like bubbles on a running stream" (*CC* 227). The Holdfasters are not nomadic in the geographical sense but sexually, politically, and culturally, as Sorrel explains: "We are as restless a breed as the Riding Women, in our own way" (*CC* 417).

Charnas reminds us that this process is not only a long but also a very hard and difficult way that depends largely on the individual in his and her function as societal shaper and transformer. What the New Holdfasters struggle with is the creation of a better society without rules laid out beforehand, but inspired by the example of the Riding Women's culture. For that reason, Sheel remains as a living model, "our teacher" (*F* 103), until the Holdfasters have begun building their own future: "We need a person without the taint of this place's history to help us choose new pathways" (*F* 395). With the disappearance of Alldera and the mythical Riding Women and the wild zone they inhabit—both represent the new element "of the independent, powerful woman who is subject to no one and nobody's object either" and who lives "cooperatively and in an exploitative but nondestructive relationship with nature" (Mohr 1999d, 17)—the abstract values remain to be recreated as part of Holdfast reality.

The vanishing of the Riding Women also signals what we knew all along: we are not Riding Women, and their way of life cannot be simply transferred. For once the notorious liar Daya has told the truth: "The only reality for us is here ... not over the mountains in another country"

(*CC* 360). The future lies not in implementing a false concept of sameness, in adopting a preconceived model, since the Holdfasters will never be the same as the Grasslanders. Alldera's uncertainty about what exactly the Holdfasters will be—"Fems aren't Riding Women.... I'm not sure we're fems anymore, either. We were slaves.... Are we Women, if we're free? Can we be Women of the Holdfast...?" (*F* 396)—is answered by her daughter Sorrel: "if there are to be *women* like those *Women*—riders and fighters and lovers and true-speakers, making their lives from day to day with all their powers—it seems they will be ourselves and our daughters, or no one" (*CC* 428; emphasis added). By decapitalizing "Women" into "women," Sorrel stresses the necessity of creating their own future. This Holdfast future may remain unnamed and unpossessed, but only the creation of a new hybrid culture celebrating and negotiating difference and equality on a daily basis will result in truly free women and men of the Holdfast.

5

The Poetic Discourse of the Split Self
Margaret Atwood's The Handmaid's Tale

A word after a word after a word is power.
—Margaret Atwood, True Stories (64)

The trouble is all in the knob at the top of our bodies. I'm not against the body or the head either; only the neck, which creates the illusion that they are separate. The language is wrong, it shouldn't have different words for them.
—Margaret Atwood, Surfacing (81)

Margaret Atwood, Canada's most prominent and prolific novelist, poet, critic, and essayist and winner of numerous awards and literary prizes—including two Governor General's awards for *The Handmaid's Tale* and for the poetry collection *The Circle Game* (1966); her novel, *The Blind Assassin* (2000), won the prestigious British Booker Prize in 2000 for which Atwood had been shortlisted in 1987, 1989, and 1996—has ventured so far only once into the dystopian genre. Her futuristic dystopian novel *The Handmaid's Tale* (1985) instantly brought Atwood international acclaim.[1] Considering Atwood's long-standing interest in

---

[1] The Handmaid's Tale *also won the Arthur C. Clarke Award for the best sf novel in Britain, the Los Angeles Times Fiction Prize, and was shortlisted for the Booker Prize. Apart from making the* New York Times*'s bestseller list, it was also nominated for the Ritz-Paris Hemingway Prize in France and was* Time *magazine's book of the year in 1986. Volker Schlöndorff adapted* The Handmaid's Tale *into a film in 1990, starring Faye Dunaway, Robert Duvall, and Natasha Richardson; the screenplay was written by Harold Pinter. Schlöndorff's and Pinter's film version, however, turns the novel into a trite, conventional melodrama with an unconvincing finale in which Offred heroically kills the Commander and escapes the system.*

power politics on all levels and in social and gender issues, however, this excursion into dystopia is not surprising.

With Elgin and Charnas, she shares an interest in the subversion of genre literature from a feminist perspective, drawing on classical as well as popular mythologies, and—despite her well-known literary characterization of duplicity and doubles—a distrust of binary logic. Compared to the *Holdfast* tetralogy and *The Native Tongue* trilogy, Atwood describes the most classical dystopia and is the least interested in sf, despite her latest satiric turn to sf in *The Blind Assassin*. Of the dystopias under discussion, Atwood's dystopia defamiliarizes us the least, as the setting and the dystopian practices are so easily recognizable as the 1980s extrapolated into a near future. Atwood has repeatedly emphasized that "[t]here is not a single detail in the book that does not have a corresponding reality, either in contemporary conditions or historical fact" (Schreiber 209). While, unlike Elgin's *Native Tongue* trilogy, *The Handmaid's Tale* lacks distinct utopian projects and subthemes, the novel shares with Elgin's dystopia the privileging of language as a dystopian and utopian tool; as opposed to Charnas's *Holdfast* tetralogy, open war between the sexes plays no part in Atwood's narrative that lacks both war and reconciliation. Rather, two major themes of Atwood's oevre, victimization and survival, dominate the poetic narrative discourse of mental liberation—unsurprisingly, among the novels on hand, the Canadian poet's dystopia uses the most poetic language—in terms of a psychological struggle for sanity and survival.

Exploring the psychological landscape of a woman dehumanized in dystopia, *The Handmaid's Tale* demonstrates a certain affinity with the inner-space fiction of the New Wave authors of the mid–1960s and their predominant concern with the exploration of the psyche rather than with outer space. As an act of defiance, the narration of the story itself becomes the utopian subtext of *The Handmaid's Tale*. As with her literary predecessors in Atwood's fictional universe, the female protagonist/narrator Offred becomes in this context—despite the indubitably feminist focus of the novel—what Frank Davey wrote about the mutilated and repressed female protagonists of Atwood's earlier novels: a "symbol of common humanity brutalized by instrumental language and rationalist phallic technology" (108), and, we might add, brutalized by an all-pervasive binary logic. Psychologically, Offred escapes dystopia by holding onto desire, that potentially utopian notion, "that talent for insatiability" (*HT* 3).[2]

Much has been written about Margaret Atwood's work, and critical commentary on her best-selling novel *The Handmaid's Tale* has been stag-

---

[2]*Page references to* The Handmaid's Tale, *cited as* HT, *are given parenthetically in the text.*

gering. Critics have focused on, among other issues, the classical dystopian (Malak; Ketterer)[3] and the feminist content (Miner; Rubenstein; Bouson; LeBihan; Dopp);[4] the Historical Notes (Foley), the Biblical content (Kaler; Larson; Filipczak); the framing epigraphs and the dedications (Carrington 1987b; P. Murphy; Evans; Stein 1996); narrativity, postmodern theories, and the mind-style of Offred (Kauffman; Finnell; Caminero-Santangelo; Garlick; Nischik, Staels); literacy and orality (Andriano; Klarer 1990, 1995), and the possibilities of teaching *The Handmaid's Tale* (Burack).[5] *The Handmaid's Tale* has also been the object of various comparative studies.[6]

The duality that marks Atwood's poetry and novels, the opposition between male and female, rational and irrational, technology and nature, the USA and Canada, manifested in the doubleness of female characters and in mirrors as a prevalent symbol, has been much commented upon.[7] As Jessie Givner writes, "[o]ne of the most persistent arguments in Atwood criticism is that her works are structured by duality and binary opposition" (56). Such readings, valid as they are, reduce Atwood to a writer preoccupied with pinpointing, explicating, illustrating, and replicating the multifarious underlying dualisms of our Western cultures. Only a few critics have marginally touched on the disruption of the dualism inherent in Atwood's work. Coral Ann Howells, for instance, claims *The Handmaid's Tale* as a "critique of feminism ... a double-edged one which rejects binary oppositions" (1996, 131), but she does not elaborate

---

[3]*Ketterer labels* The Handmaid's Tale *a "contextual dystopia," since the inclusion of the Symposium presents an, albeit potentially circular, "discontinuous context, and historical development" (213), but obviously fails to notice the continuity of sexism in the Historical Notes. Patrick D. Murphy also launches a dissatisfaction at Ketterer's reading (cf. 31–33).*

[4]*Atwood has defined her version of feminism as "human equality and freedom of choice" (Brans 142) and "as part of a larger issue: human dignity. That's what Canadian nationalism is about, what feminism is about, and what black power is about. They're all part of the same vision" (ibid. 102).*

[5]*This list of topics and critics refers only to a selected choice of works. No doubt, critics will find further worthwhile angles; any quick run of the MLA database on* The Handmaid's Tale *will display an ever growing number of entries.*

[6]*The novel's similarities and differences have been traced with regard to Wells and Orwell (Caldwell; Ingersoll), Bradbury's* Fahrenheit 451 *(Wood), Timothey Findley's* Not Wanted on the Voyage *(Keith), Bersianik's* The Eugélionne *(Bartkowski), Nadine Gordimer's* July's People *(Bazin), the mother theme in Piercy's* Woman on the Edge of Time *(Hansen), Shelley's* Frankenstein *(Hollinger),* The Butcher's Wife *by the Chinese author Li Ang (Chen), and Margaret Laurence's short story "A Gourdful of Glory" and Sarah Murphy's* The Measure of Miranda *(Howells 1989), to name just a few of the various comparative avenues critics have taken.*

[7]*Duplicity in Atwood's art, though not in* The Handmaid's Tale, *which had not been written at that time, has been most notably discussed by Sherrill E. Grace (1980; 1981) and Robert Lecker (1981). Grace basically situates Atwood not only within a dualistic framework, but also claims that Atwood advocates "the need to accept and work within" (1980, 134) the binary oppositions. In a later article, Grace somewhat refocuses her former analysis, instead looking at Atwood's negotiation of the spaces between the breakdown of those boundaries "separating victor/victim, mind/body, self/other, and culture/nature" (1983, 7).*

on this important theme. For Eleonora Rao, the subjection of female characters to self-division represents a "female strategy" (xviii) of duplicity aimed at survival, which I would call "multiplicity" because the term duplicity remains within binary boundaries; and at least in *The Handmaid's Tale*, Atwood supplies her heroine with more than one double.

Although Rao initially notes that "Atwood's texts partake of a logic of 'both/and' rather than 'either/or'" and that binary oppositions are not necessarily "mutually exclusive" (xviii) in Atwood's fiction, her actual analysis of Atwood's novels remains unsatisfying inasmuch as she investigates and focuses on the coexistence of but not on the dissolution of dichotomies.[8] And while Raffaella Baccolini reads *The Handmaid's Tale* as a critical dystopia, because the dystopian narration encapsules utopian hope in "the choice of time setting, the personalities of the protagonist's mother and Moira (her lesbian friend), Offred's thoughts, the use of the epistolary genre, and the open ending" (22), she fails to note the transgressive function of Offred's poetic discourse of survival, although she thus recognizes the subversive resistance of Offred's narration. Insofar Baccolini's and Rao's cogent analyses, however, come perhaps closest to noticing that Atwood's dystopia partakes less in traditional dystopian narration than standard readings suggest. After all, even Tom Moylan classifies Atwood's novel as "one of the last 'classical' dystopias" (2000, 105), an assessment he somewhat revokes in a later chapter, stating that Atwood's dystopia presents a "continuation and challenge to the classical dystopia" (ibid. 163) or might constitute an "ambiguous dystopia" (ibid. 166).[9] *The Handmaid's Tale* can be read as a transgressive utopian dystopia, since a utopian subtext is interwoven into the dystopian narrative of *The Handmaid's Tale* and because there are various hints in the novel pointing towards a transgression of binarisms that critics have so far overlooked. By extension, it might be fruitful to examine Atwood's other novels from this perspective of transgression, focusing on Atwood's "breaking [of] imprisoning circles" (Grace and Weir 13) rather than on the polarities described.

First, I briefly look at the postmodern narrative structure and what I call the "generic palimpsest" rather than generic hybridity that Atwood creates by drawing on a variety of genres we catch glimpses of under the

---

[8] *Cf.:* "*Dichotomies such as subject and object, fact and fiction, conscious and unconscious body and mind, are scrutinized the narratives privilege their coexistence*" *(Rao 99).*

[9] *In Moylan's (mis)reading, the non-totalitarian states of Canada, Britain, and Brazil embody a "utopian horizon" beyond Gilead's borders and the "Underground Femaleroad" as a potentially utopian path which, however, he considers failed in the light of the "anti-utopian triumph" (ibid.) of the Gileadean system that renders Offred's tale, and thus* The Handmaid's Tale, *a tale of resignation. Although he acknowledges the patronizing attitude of the academics, he claims that the Historical Notes "constitute a potential 'utopian' gesture," signifying a "relatively more utopian world" (ibid. 165), because this future society is discontinuous of Gilead.*

veneer of dystopia. I then examine how the concepts of duality and *otherness* lead to forms of fragmentation on the geographical (Canada/U.S.), on the sociopolitical (female/male), and on the psychological level (self/other). Here, the analysis focuses on the creation of worlds apart for the sexes and cultures and on the two failed male attempts at subverting the system that men created; I also outline how the internalization of binary concepts leads to a self-destructive fragmented (feminine) consciousness. The last section investigates how this potentially self-annihilating dichotomous discourse can be subverted. Breaking the silence ascribed to women, the fragmented fictional self, Offred, achieves transgression through narration. She creates polyperspectives, offers multiple versions of reality, rather than a monolithic depiction of reality, and probes language for *multiple* rather than either singular or dualistic meanings. With the creation of a fictive narrative alter ego within and beyond the text, Offred desires and incorporates the otherwise excluded *other*. Her subversive use of language as a liberating discourse moreover deconstructs the either/or patterns of thought; and as she becomes increasingly cognizant of Gilead's patriarchal perspective, she balances it with her own and other's contrary discourses.

Exploring the concepts of self and *other*, Atwood illustrates what psychoanalytic theories suggest, namely that there is a fundamental division not only between the sexes, but also within the individual consciousness. *Otherness* is then not exclusively an external category. On the one hand, Atwood underscores how the existence of an all-defining center dominated by the masculine subjective self's view of reality—that constructs and posits everything alien to it as *other*, and hence pushes women to the margins of (patriarchal) society, denying them the fulfillment of selfhood—ignores and represses the *other's* values to stabilize this center. In other words, reality and values are perceived as universal, but are truly contingent upon a specific gendered (masculine) perspective. On the other hand, Atwood suggests with Offred's narration that, although dualities may exist, they should not necessarily be considered as mutual exclusives, but can rather be united without leveling the differences. According to Atwood, the human capability of assuming *another* perspective can destabilize the presupposed internal polarization of self and *other*. To allow the coexistence of more than one reality and perspective, perhaps even to view these as constituents, may not erase but bridge this mental split. Offred's narration, for instance, allows Offred exactly this: multiple perspectives and various realities, and telling her story as well as other's stories thus saves her from psychological fragmentation.

5.1. The Tale, Its Narrative Structure, and Its Generic Palimpsest

Criticizing sexism and marginalization, Atwood's dystopia focuses mainly on progeny and on class and gender division as legitimized by patriarchal religion; her fictional state Gilead is founded on the literal interpretation of the Old Testament (cf. Gen. 30). The novel is set against the background of the rise of neoconservatism, of the Moral Majority, and of Christian fundamentalism of the 1980s; and it extrapolates from the right wing's backlash against the feminist and gay movements as well as the Vatican's doctrinal edicts against any deviances from heterosexual marriage. On a larger scale, "Atwood apocalyptically foresees the failure of humanism, liberalism, individualism, feminism, and capitalism" (Kauffman 222).

Projected into the near future, Atwood's feminist dystopia is set in what was formerly Cambridge, Massachusetts, in the U.S. After a rightwing, religious fundamentalist *coup d'etat*, the Republic of Gilead is thus founded in the heart of puritan colonization. Gradually, women are stripped of all constitutional rights: their bank accounts are cancelled, and they lose the right to work, to own property, and to vote. Gilead shifts the relation between the sexes towards one of inequality, imbalance, and possession, as the female protagonist Offred reminisces with regard to her changed relationship with her former husband Luke: "We are not each other's, anymore. Instead, I am his" (*HT* 171). Pushed to the margins, women can no longer move freely in public.

The totalitarian theocracy, suffering from depopulation due to rampant sterility caused by chemical pollution and nuclear radiation, uses the few, still fertile women, the so-called Handmaids, as breeders. Focusing on women as inferior *other*, only the women's unique capacity to reproduce is scrutinized, blamed or celebrated, whereas the male sterility remains unquestioned. While the totalitarian system's doublethink idealizes maternity as the "ultimate" female achievement, women are, in fact, dehumanized and objectified. Restoring the "natural order" of female obedience to man depicted in the OT legitimizes the total political, economic, and biological subjection of women. Biological sex and gender converge; and a woman's social role is determined by and reduced to her biological sex.

The rigid class system, the segregation of the sexes, surveillance, media propaganda, and ceremonialized public rituals of violence against state offenders (including executions and hangings) maintain a system of terror. The male monopoly on literacy, however, describes a far more insidious and perfidious measure of control. The media are censored

5. The Poetic Discourse of the Split Self   235

and books are banned; and even among males, access to literature is hierarchized and monopolized by Gilead's elite, the Commanders. With the exception of the Aunts rewarded for their collaboration—they control and train the Handmaids—women are banned from reading and writing: reading is punished with "a hand cut off, on the third conviction" (*HT* 259). Hence, women are not only almost invisible in this dystopia, but they are also effectively silenced. In Gilead, politics are truly sexual/textual body politics and, as in *Fahrenheit 451*, reading and possessing books become heroic and subversive acts.

Against this totalitarian, misogynist, and monological system the first person narration of *The Handmaid's Tale* fights. Ellipses and analepsis, narrative disruptions, gaps, and non-chronological fragments characterize Atwood's postmodern novel. The non-linear narrative form, the personal first-person narration of the Handmaid Offred, who retrospectively recounts her story, therefore defies the patrilinearity Gilead superimposes on the content level, and this structure likewise deconstructs Gilead's monolithic truth. In alternating chapters, divided into "Night" and "Day" sections, Offred reflects on the pre–Gileadean period, the past Gilead wants to erase, and describes her life in Gilead. She reminiscences about her feminist mother, her life with her husband Luke and her daughter, their failed attempt to flee across the border to Canada, her arrest, and her life as a Handmaid in the household of Commander Fred and his wife Serena Joy. The Commander entices Offred to partake in illegal activities such as playing a game of Scrabble and takes her to the illegal brothel called Jezebel's. Because the Commander might be sterile, Serena Joy arranges for Offred to meet in private with their chauffeur Nick. Although these sexual encounters are devoid of romantic overtones, Offred enjoys this physical intimacy. The novel concludes on an ambiguous note, and Offred's fate remains uncertain: Nick pulls up in a police van and takes Offred away. Yet we never get to know whether he is in fact a member of the secret Underground organization Mayday and saves her, or whether he is a member of the secret police, the Eyes, and betrays her.

Appended to the novel are the "Historical Notes" from the academic "Symposium on Gileadean Studies" of the year 2195. These reveal that Offred's story is a recollection, an oral text taped on audiocassettes labeled as music, and that the story we just read is filtered, possibly no longer an authentic text. By desiring to establish *the* text, Professor Piexoto tries to construct a definite authorship, *one* history, *one* "objective" truth, and therefore *one* reality that Offred's fragmented narrative has just disrupted and rejected. Offred is not even responsible for the story's title, a sexist pun combining "humor and denigration" (Freibert 281), but also subversively indicating that "the issues of genre (tale) and gender (tail) are joined" (Kauffman 224):

> The superscription "The Handmaid's Tale" was appended to it by Professor Wade, partly in homage to the great Geoffrey Chaucer ... I am sure all puns were intentional, particularly that having to do with the archaic vulgar signification of the word *tail*; that being, to some extent, the bone, as it were, of contention, in that phase of Gileadean society of which our saga treats [*HT* 283].

The Professors have transcribed and presumably edited and rearranged Offred's subjective oral story, turning her-story virtually into an object of his-story. On the one hand, this change stresses the orality/literacy dichotomy; on the other hand, Offred's story is thus, strictly speaking, neither oral nor written. By taping her story, Offred combines orality (female) and technology (male) to form a kind of secondary orality, since she is not directly connected with her auditors. Thus, her spoken text is as much removed/distanced from audience as a written text is at the moment of production.

Although the Gileadean regime is a matter of the past, the speech of the keynote speaker Professor Piexoto reveals that sexism exists in a latent form even in this future society. He makes sexist jokes about the Chair, Professor Maryann Crescent Moon, downplays Gilead's sexist and totalitarian politics and, refusing to pass judgement—"Our job is not to censure but to understand" (*HT* 284)—expresses a general affinity with Gilead's misogynist system: "its genius was synthesis" (*HT* 289). Piexoto marginalizes and trivializes Offred's story moreover by wishing for "twenty pages or so of print out from Waterford's [the Commander's] private computer" (*HT* 292), and he condescendingly apologizes for Offred's bad style and muddled mind. This framing story thus repeats Gilead's sexist dystopia: once more women are dehumanized and belittled and Offred's life is reduced to an academic question.

The two dedications, the three epigraphs, and the Historical Notes add yet other perspectives. Thus framed by a metafictional metatext, context, and metacriticism, the text cannot be fixed and remains open to multiple interpretations. The narrative, the epigraphs, and the Historical Notes combined with the two dedications—to Atwood's "favorite ancestor" (Atwood 1982, 331) Mary Webster who, due to a tough neck, survived being hanged as a witch in 1683 and, because of the law of double jeopardy, could not be executed twice for the same crime[10]; and to Perry Miller, Atwood's former professor of early American Literature at Harvard—produce "a text which comments on itself, on the act of authorship, and on the act of reading" (Bergman 847). Fiction, reality,

---

[10] *In interviews Atwood has repeatedly commented on the obvious parallels between the early settlers' puritanism and the puritan theocracy of Gilead: "the mind-set of Gilead is really close to that of the seventeenth-century Puritans" (Lyons 223).*

history, and Biblical history mingle. The dedications suggest that if the historical Mary Webster had told *her* real story, she could very well have become the object of a real academic historian; in this sense the historical perspective mirrors Professor Piexoto's fictional condescending probing of Offred's personal experiences. Both the Historical Notes and the dedications thus serve as reminders of the need to be aware of history's bias. The dedications also link Atwood's personal history and ancestry with the founding history of the U.S., specifically with the hypocrisy of historical puritanism that her former teacher Perry Miller so bluntly expounded. As much as Mary Webster can be read as Offred's *real* narrative double beyond the text, Perry Miller could be seen as the counterbalancing, positive pendant to the fictional character of Professor Piexoto.[11]

The epigraphs add further "layers of inference" (Stein 1996, 57) and a framing lens through which we read the novel. The first epigraph establishes Gilead's explicit link with the Bible, since "the polygamy of the Old Testament provides the sanction" (Malak 9) for the institutionalized abuse of women as breeders. The second epigraph, taken from Swift's *A Modest Proposal*, "predicts the political depth" (Freibert 284) and "suggests the ironic method of Atwood's argument" (Carrington 1987b, 127). Furthermore, Karen Stein notes that Swift's and Atwood's texts "establish metaphorical links between women/animals/procreation/food" (1996, 64). The third epigraph, the paradoxical and even nonsensical Sufi proverb, may allude "to Atwood's criticism of audiences content with stones, readers who refuse to read serious literature" (Carrington 1987b, 127); yet it more distinctly foreshadows, as Nancy V. Workman explains, the discursive mode Offred uses when she muses about Gilead's paradoxes and language's multiple meanings.

Similar to the chapter epigraphs drawn from various official discourse and contrasting with the chapter content in Elgin's trilogy, the Historical Notes describe an official male discourse, a *patrius sermo* in the form of an academic lecture that examines and (almost) dismisses Offred's story, the *materna lingua* of the private female discourse. Feminine and masculine text, orality and literacy, parataxis and hypotaxis are juxtaposed, reflecting the "traditional definitions of 'feminine' speech versus 'masculine' writing," the feminine being "subjective, disordered, associative, illogical," the masculine being "objective, orderly, controlled, logical" (Kauffman 228). Offred's text is charged with the usual

---

[11]*On the corresponding aspects of the narrative content of* The Handmaid's Tale *and the historical reality alluded to by the dedicatees, see Mark Evans (1994). Among other issues, Sandra Tomc also elucidates the dedications, but focuses on their ironic connotations. In contrast to Evans, Tomc portrays Miller as a scholar celebrating puritanism as essentially American (cf. Tomc 80).*

reproaches: it is full of gaps, inaccurate, too personal, and lacks facts. Yet the very narrative structure of *The Handmaid's Tale* illustrates the illusion behind so-called facts, accuracy, and completeness by drawing attention to the gap between women's history and "official" male history, to the "(female) testimony plus (male) commentary" (Larson 37), when Piexoto attempts "to analyze history on the basis of male biography, and thereby *mutes* the woman's voice" (P. Murphy 35). Piexoto's failure to deduce Offred's real name "June" reveals his inability to read between the gaps, to perceive what is hidden.[12] His discourse virtually transmutes June; she becomes in effect the gap in history that she anticipated: "I am a blank, here, between parentheses" (*HT* 213).[13]

Consequently, both the Historical Notes and Offred's story are told by unreliable narrators, and both share a limited perspective. Because Offred is denied choice and because of her restricted access to media and any other written sources, her narrative is incomplete, whereas blinded by the system in which they work the academics *choose* to limit their perspectives. Stripping off the myth of textual objectivity, Atwood thus draws attention to the dubious nature of authenticity. With the revelation that the text we just finished reading is a mediated, second-hand account, readers are jerked into suspicion and distrust. What is true and how much has been edited in *The Handmaid's Tale*, in history, in any text at all? Moreover, the framing "creates a gap between our initial, heuristic reading of the book, a reading in which the narrator's authority is valorized" (Deer 225), especially since Atwood omits an "initial pseudo-documentary device" (P. Murphy 33) and lures the reader into taking the novel at face value. Although the Historical Notes, relegating Offred to the background, may have a distancing effect on some readers, far more importantly, they allow readers to witness how Offred's tale is placed into a new, yet again defamiliarizing and distorting context, echoing Offred's repeated incantation: "Context is all" (*HT* 136).

Toying with the tropes of classical dystopia and clearly aiming at a believable and realistic near-future scenario, Offred's tale is very subtly contextualized. Where Elgin's and Charnas's series are recognizably hybrid on the generic level, incorporating, amongst others, sf elements and utopian strategies, the generic transgressions of *The Handmaid's Tale*

---

[12]*Harriet Bergmann, Constance Rooke, and Ketterer were the first to point out that Offred's real name is probably June. Bergmann notes that "Offred never tells us her name directly, but the list of names at the beginning of the novel indicates that it is probably 'June,'" since every other name in the list is assigned to a character" (853). Rooke supports her view that "[t]he Handmaid's name is June" (175) similarly, but also points out the various textual hints that link "June" with moon and love (cf. 176–179). Arguing along the same lines, Ketterer adds that the Symposium takes place in June which might indicate a "cyclical process" (214) of history.*

[13]*For further analysis of the Historical Notes, see also Deer, Lacombe, Rubenstein, LeBihan, and Foley.*

are much harder to pinpoint. The book definitely lacks any of the sf tropes such as highly advanced technology, aliens, gadgets, and space opera. The few technological devices such as Compudocs, Compucounts, Compuphones, and Compuchecs merely underwrite Atwood's argument that advanced (computer) technology will facilitate the incapacitation of any group labeled as *other*. Atwood instead focuses more on "a very different kind of technology ... the technology of power" (Hammer 45) rather than on technotopia. The novel's transgressive utopian subtext, Offred's discourse of survival on which this chapter focuses, has mostly been ignored. Undoubtedly, its sociopolitical and feminist content (subjection of women, surveillance, totalitarianism, and near future setting), its focus on "two of the major topics of contemporary dystopias: the aftermath of nuclear war and women's oppression" (P. Murphy 27), the framing device of a "contextual dystopia" (Ketterer 213), and its narrative status as a found manuscript place *The Handmaid's Tale* quite firmly within the classical (feminist) dystopian tradition; or, as Larson ironically suggests, the novel presents otherwise a "Christo-fascist utopia" (40). Privileging the novel's narrative mode, some critics have classified *The Handmaid's Tale* as satiric dystopia (Deer, Freibert, McCarthy) or as satire (Hammer). Atwood has also commented that *The Handmaid's Tale* is "not science fiction of the classical kind. There are no martians. There are no space machines. I would say instead that it is a dystopia, a negative utopia" (1985, 66). If we presuppose that Moira exclusively takes on the role of the actively rebellious character, Moira's failed escape attempts suggest the classification of Atwood's novel as classical dystopia, where rebellion usually fails. Yet if we foreground Offred's inward discourse as active rebellion, and, since there is no textual evidence to prove whether Offred/June survives or not, it is debatable whether *The Handmaid's Tale* can be subsumed under the label "classical" dystopia.

Underneath this seemingly definite classification of the novel as dystopia (whether classical or transgressive) lurks "a palimpsest of unheard sound, style upon style" (*HT* 3). This quotation from *The Handmaid's Tale*—within the text, it refers to the gymnasium where lingering music is faintly heard by the desperate ear, straining for memories of a brighter past—could just as well be read as Atwood's *modus operandi* for writing this novel. What can be heard is then a polylogue rather than a "dialogue of inter-texts" as Rao argues (cf. xv). Although the overwritten genres (apart from the Biblical subtext) are less obvious than in Elgin's and Charnas's novels, critics have pointed out a number of generic transgressions, stressing the postmodern breakdown between genres.

The Handmaid's Tale has been placed in close proximity to the postmodern feminine discourse of private letters, transporting "the dominant motifs of epistolarity into the twenty-first century, transforming the heroine's 'letter' into a tape recording.... The medium changes, but the mode remains the same" (221–222), as Linda Kauffman writes; she traces the tale's origins "to the *locus classicus* of epistolarity, the *Heorides*, for like Ovid's heroines, Offred narrates from exile" (Kauffman 222). Similarly, Michele Lacombe reads *The Handmaid's Tale* in the "confessional mode of the spiritual autobiography" (5) probing "beyond the paraphernalia of science fiction" (9) and discovers various palimpsestial examples in the novel.[14] For Anne K. Kaler, Atwood's "theocratic dystopia ... synthesizes Northrop Frye's four forms of prose fiction into one, combining an autobiography in a confessional journal mode, an anatomy of how a dystopia works, a futuristic fantasy with romance elements, and a novel with horrific detail into a full-fledged satisfying satire" (43).[15] The latter assessment is also emphasized by Stephanie Barbé Hammer, who understands Atwood's novel as almost "a satiric text-book case" (39). Underneath the layer of the satiric text, Hammer detects a plot that "unfolds ... weirdly reminiscent of popular gothic romances" (41), wherein the passive heroine patiently awaits her rescue by the young, dynamic hero.

Mary McCarthy, Madonne Miner, Sandra Tomc, and Dorothy Jones, who even likens Offred's status as Handmaid to the "socially ambiguous position of a Victorian governess" (32), share a similar perspective on the novel. Against enthusiastic readings of *The Handmaid's Tale* as positioning love as the sole subversive force (cf. Ehrenreich 34; Malak 15), Miner cautions that the romance plot "follow[s] decidedly conservative narrative forms" (150). Because of the romance plot, Tomc disputes Atwood's feminist critique, since the plot "translates into an advocacy of traditional femininity" (74), a notion seconded by Chinmoy Banerjee, who otherwise unconvincingly reads *The Handmaid's Tale* as an uncritical "pseudo-dystopia" (90) not grounded in "a close analysis of [contemporary] history" (79).[16] For Banerjee, the novel provides a "parody of the [costume] Gothic" (84), aimed rather at naïve consumption than feminist or dystopian critique. Susanna Finnell estab-

---

[14]*For example, besides the obvious reference to the gymnasium, Lacombe lists "the substitution of pictures for words on store-fronts" with "traces of former names under the script," the "semiotic layering [of] the manuscript itself as artifact and as text" (4), and the environment in general "as a new language to be decoded" (9).*

[15]*Kaler refers here to Frye's well-known study* Anatomy of Criticism *(1957). Frye taught at the University of Toronto when Atwood was there.*

[16]*In relation to other, earlier novels by Atwood, Lecker and Davey have raised the point that Atwood consciously uses and subverts the romance plot by refraining from the "happily ever after" ending or, in Davey's words, the "romance patterns are themselves patriarchal second-order constructions from which, to be "free" in any meaningful way, Atwood characters will have to escape" (62).*

lishes in *The Handmaid's Tale* the quest pattern that has been examined in other Atwood novels such as *The Edible Woman* and *Surfacing*. For Finnell, *The Handmaid's Tale* tries "an old form (the quest based on a journey motif) on a new model (the female)" (200), where Offred "struggles with the antagonist, who, mythical in proportion, does not have a face, but is the repressive Gileadean society itself" (202). Offred's rescue (or rather unknown destiny), Finnell argues, turns the novel into an "anti-quest," where the journey "becomes a lost trace, a lacuna, a negative space" that takes place "in the blank pages" (204) between Offred's story and the Historical Notes. In her study on fairy-tale archetypes and sexual politics in Atwood's oevre, Sharon Rose Wilson moreover traces resonances of the Red Riding Hood intertext and the Triple Goddess myth in *The Handmaid's Tale* and elucidates how Atwood subverts and reverses these archetypes into "an anti-fairy-tale" (293).

By dissolving, overwriting, and subverting generic boundaries, Atwood creates a narrative chimera of immediacy and by resisting closure, she rejects sentimentality, the easy cop-outs of traditional popular genres—such as the romance plot, the Gothic narrative, the fairy-tale, and to some extent the redeeming resolution of the quest theme—to which her dystopian palimpsest alludes. Undercutting conventional reading patterns, the ending that is none urges the reader—whom Offred repeatedly invokes and whose forgiveness and understanding she implores: "remember that forgiveness too is a power" (*HT* 126)—to begin again, to pay special attention to the gaps and blanks.

Whereas the Aliens and earth colonies in the *Native Tongue* trilogy and the mythical Riding Women in the *Holdfast* tetralogy serve as *defamiliarizing* foils for the *other*, the generic interrelationships of the romance plot, the fairy tale, and the autobiographical features of *The Handmaid's Tale* serve the very opposite function by *familiarizing* us with the defamiliarized *self*. Invited to identify with Offred and her tale, the reader is urged to recall similar plots in other novels and genres; and thereby Atwood ultimately drives home a message of urgency and the pivotal realization that we need to question our own readiness to comply with dissatisfactory, dystopian circumstances.

5.2. Forms of Fragmentation

5.2.1. More Than Two Solitudes: Geographical Splits

As Catherine Stimpson notes, *The Handmaid's Tale* describes Atwood's "first foray into an extended representation of America" (qtd. in Tomc 75). Atwood's well-documented Canadian nationalism situates the U.S. and Canada in terms of dichotomies of oppressor/victim and as masculine/feminine from a gendered position.[17] Atwood's view of the U.S. as the imperialistic (male) aggressor to Canada's (female) victimization becomes clearer if one takes into account that the relationship between the two states and their two literatures has indeed been a gendered one, marginalizing the latter: "Canada is not the fifty-first state of the United States, nor is Canadian literature part of American literature, rather it is the *other* North American literature" (Pache 3; emphasis added).

Writing as a Canadian female author from the *other* perspective about the sociopolitical status quo within the U.S., Atwood places Gilead in the U.S., while the escape route leads to Canada. For Atwood, the U.S. is more prone to dystopia, since its national theme is, in her estimation, the conquest of the West and it lusts after a utopia, based on "the model for all the world postulated by the Puritans" (Atwood 1972, 32). Atwood explained why she chose the States as the setting for Gilead:

> America is a tragic country because it has great democratic ideals and a rigid social machinery.... But Canada is not tragic, in the classical sense, because it doesn't have a utopian vision. Our constitution promises "peace, order and good government"—and that's quite different from "life, liberty and the pursuit of happiness" [Sandler 57].
> I set it in the States because I couldn't fly it in Canada.... Could this happen in Montréal or Toronto? ... it is not a Canadian sort of thing to do. Canadians might do it after the States did it in some sort of watered-down version.... The States are more extreme in everything. Our genius is for compromise. It's how we make our way on the French/English front.... Canadians don't swing much to the left or the right, they stay safely in the middle [Lyons 223].

Similarly, the fictional Canada in *The Handmaid's Tale* compromises and attempts to stay "safely in the middle." Its role remains ambiguous. On the one hand, Canada functions as a sheltering haven; on the other hand, like the Aunts (or like the Matris in the *Holdfast* series) who collaborate, Canada becomes complicit: "the Canada of that time did not wish to antagonize its powerful neighbour, and there were roundups and extraditions of such refugees" (*HT* 292), as Professor Piexoto notes. The Historical Notes thus suggest that Canada, as it neither opposed its neighbor nor intervened, has once more taken the (feminine) victim position.

---

[17]*In general, Atwood's Canadian nationalism has not gone unchallenged. Given Atwood's opinion on nationalism, her view of the gendered relations between Canada and the U.S., and her continued "promotion of Canada's cultural autonomy from the States" (Tomc 74), it is perhaps not surprising that Tomc declares the feminist critique in* The Handmaid's Tale *as a essentially conservative one, "advocating traditional femininity" (74).*

5. The Poetic Discourse of the Split Self

In *Survival* (1972), her seminal study of Canadian literary themes, Atwood formulates the thesis that Canadians perceive and often represent themselves as victims and that, in contrast to the frontier for the U.S. and the island for England, the "central symbol for Canada ... [is] survival, *la Survivance*" (32).

In dystopia, fictional Canada once more tries to survive, this time near the Republic of Gilead. Because Offred's main concern is survival, she can perhaps be seen as a disguised *Canadian* female hero whose objective is not heroism but "hanging on, staying alive" in a social wilderness, where survival means an "awful experience ... that killed everyone else. The survivor has no triumph or victory but the fact of his [sic] survival: he has little after his ordeal that he did not have before, except gratitude for having escaped with his life" (Atwood 1972, 33). In the light of Atwood's analysis in *Survival*—namely that many "representative Canadian literary figures ... have been 'ordinary' people" (165) and not necessarily heroes or heroines fighting on behalf of society—Offred's failure as a conventional heroine renders her even more Canadian.

If we apply Tomc's reading of Offred's narration as a "form of [mental] border patrol" (75), then *The Handmaid's Tale* mutates into border or inner space fiction, where the American frontier moves inward and metamorphoses into the internal border of what justifies physical/spiritual survival. The Canadian wilderness theme metamorphoses into Offred's exploration of the unknown territory of her alienated body and the wilderness of human psychology, the juggling of various branching and conflicting wild stories.[18] In short, Offred is confronted with the ultimate Canadian question, "[W]hat price survival?" (Atwood 1972, 33). Unsurprisingly, Offred's physical escape route leads her north, if not as far as the wilderness, then to Canada. The blank spaces of Offred's narration thus metaphorically merge with what Atwood has labeled the Canada of American popular imagination: "that blank area north of the map" (Oates 78).

In this context, it is important to note that the Historical Notes from the distant future displace this geopolitical dualism by opening up a third space, the far north. After all, Gilead has contributed to a substantial "redrawing [of] the map of the world, especially in this hemisphere" (*HT* 281), as the Chairperson Professor Maryanne Crescent Moon points out. Possibly, Bergman speculates, the "Third World ... [has] taken over"

---

[18]*Cf.*: "*I sink down into my body as into a swamp, fernland, where only I know the footing. Treacherous ground, my own territory. I become the earth I set my ear against, for rumours of the future. I'm a cloud, congealed around a central object. Inside it is a space, huge as the sky*" (HT 69).

(852)? The "Twelfth Symposium on Gileadean Studies" takes place at the University of Denay in Nunavit. It has generally been acknowledged that—apart from a literal reading of "Denay" and "Nunavit" as Atwood's tongue-in-cheek innuendo to 'deny none of it'—Nunavit is the Inuit name for a Northern territory in Canada, and consequently Denay may allude to the Indian Déné Nation.[19] Furthermore, the names of the two professors from the University of Denay, Professor Maryann Cresent Moon and Professor Johnny Running Dog, also suggest native origins and ethnic diversity.[20]

Inserting the North as a third territory, the appendix hints at the increased importance of the First Nations of the Americas and their perspectives that challenge the dualism of the North American continent, of U.S.-Americans and Canadians, and within the Canadian context, the myth of the two solitudes: the two founding nations England and France.

This fictional geographical shift implies a changed (socio)political balance of power, possibly due to the "plummeting Caucasian birth rates" (*HT* 286). Moreover, the existence of a Department of Caucasian Anthropology indicates the dwindling influence of the Caucasian race, if not a reversal of hierarchies. Hence, "Moon's and Piexoto's narratives provide not only necessary information but a postcolonial perspective" (Wilson 291) in that marginalized Caucasians are now the object of academic study.

5.2.2. Male and Female Worlds Apart

Gilead adheres to endless binary oppositions such as public/private, men/women, self/other, literacy/orality, and power/submission. The social structure is strictly hierarchical, marginalizing, excluding, or eliminating women, people of religious faiths other than Christianity, and non-white ethnicities; in short, whoever is not identical with the white, male subject. African-Americans are forced to return to Africa, and the "Children of Ham" are forced into resettlements for farming purposes in less hospitable "National Homelands" (*HT* 79). While followers of other

---

[19]*See also Kaler, who deciphers Denay as "deny-none-of-it" (9), and Ketterer (cf. 212), who suggests that the names might imply an indigenous setting. Both explanations indicate Atwood's feminist and postcolonial criticism.*

[20]*Even the name of Professor James Darcy Pieixoto, a curious mix of Jane Austen's hero of* Pride and Prejudice *and an Aztecian name, indicates a certain hybridity. As a Professor from Cambridge, England, he is, on the one hand, linked with the colonial Empire; on the other hand, he is connected with Gilead's setting, Cambridge in Massachusetts. Both allusions explain his condescending behavior.*

faiths are stigmatized, if not executed, those Jews who refuse to convert to Christianity are shipped to Israel:

> [T]hey were declared Sons of Jacob and therefore special, they were given a choice. They could convert, or emigrate to Israel. A lot of them emigrated, if you can believe the news ... some people go out that way, by pretending to be Jewish.... You get hanged for being a noisy Jew who won't make the choice [*HT* 188–189].

Just as contact with other ethnic groups and religions is virtually impossible, any personal interaction between the sexes, and even within the same gender group is severely restricted, if not totally prohibited; and contact between the classes is limited. In fact, men and women live completely segregated lives. Since men exert all social control, monopolize power, and occupy the public sphere, women are essentially powerless and relegated to the domestic sphere. Some women, however, foster the *illusion* of power; a power restricted to the subjugation of the female sex or the female self: the Aunts indoctrinate the Handmaids, who "control" reproduction, while the Wives dominate the domestic sphere. "Woman" participates in the dystopian system and upholds its norms that objectify and exclude her.

Within the male social hierarchy of this authoritarian oligarchy, where the Commanders hold the top position, followed by the Eyes (secret police), the Angels (military), and the Guardians (police), there is a certain social upward mobility, whereas women are downgraded. Guardians can only marry if promoted to the status of Angels; only after acquiring the rank of Commander, who are alone allowed to procreate with Handmaids, are Angels "allotted a Handmaid of their own" (*HT* 22).

Color-coded uniforms divide women into eight groups according to their reproductive functions and their social status: sterile Wives (blue); post-menopausal, unmarried Aunts (brown); fertile Handmaids (red); elderly, sterile servants called "Marthas" (green); lower-class Econowives wearing red, blue, and green striped dresses indicating the combined functions they provide; widows (black); and Handmaids who fail to reproduce after three chances or rebellious women are declared "Unwoman" (grey) and deported to the Colonies to clean up toxic waste.[21] Officially, the lowest group of women, the prostitutes—former intellectuals, prostitutes of the pre–Gileadean era, or rebels—at the state's brothel Jezebel's does not exist. Gilead's patriarchal paradigm defines

---

[21]*Interestingly, just as Charnas refers to women and non-whites with the term "unmen," Atwood also uses the prefix "un" to linguistically denote the exclusion of woman as non-man and the implicit denial of femininity for those women who do not comply to or fit into the masculine definition of femininity as passivity and fertility.*

womanhood and femininity as reproduction, whereby all non-reproductive women are given ersatz occupations. Wives substitute biological procreation with gardening and knitting scarves, and thus symbolically express their felt lack in "stiff humanoid figures, boy and girl, boy and girl" (*HT* 13). The pious Aunts condition and indoctrinate the Handmaids at the Rachel and Leah Re-education Center and supervise the prostitutes at Jezebel's. A Martha's kingdom is the household. Only the Econowives "are not divided into functions" (*HT* 23).

In accordance with Gilead's policy of division and segregation, contact between the women of different classes is especially discouraged. Each class either considers the other morally inferior—for example, the Marthas look down on the Handmaids: "it's the red dress she [a Martha] disapproves of, and what it stands for" (*HT* 9)—or begrudges the alleged power, privileges, and possessions of the other class: "we all envy each other something" (*HT* 45). To maintain this rigid compartmentalized system, Gilead oppresses the autonomy of the individual and makes social life uniform. Apart from a technological system of surveillance, Gilead enforces obedience through abduction, torture, deportation, and execution, thereby preventing any rebellion.

This isolated, segregated condition of the Gileadean individual is perhaps best captured in the image of the Handmaids, either isolated in their breeding service at the Commander's household or forced to walk "in twos" (*HT* 19) whenever in public. Subjected to such an extreme form of collectivism, the originally positive image of "two walking as one" is thus turned into a metaphor of ultimate isolation and total control, and epitomizes Gilead's fear of individuality and its dogma of dualism. Additionally, forced to wear identical red, nun-like uniforms and suffering the indignity of having their names obliterated with patronymics composed of the possessive preposition "of" and the first name of the respective Commander, indicating ownership, the Handmaids' identities are effectually erased.

The only point of contact between men and women outside the "family" compound occurs during public rituals of controlled violence that effectively further the segregation and polarization of the sexes. These ceremonies also ensure obedience and progeny by centering around alleged offenses against religion or sanctioned procreational sex. Unlike the *Holdfast* series, *The Handmaid's Tale* does not contain gruesome scenes of sudden outbursts of violence such as crucifixion and anthropophagy. Like a literary enactment of Foucault's *Discipline and Punish* (1979) in which Foucault traces the changing methods of punishment to control social deviance, Gilead mixes corporeal punishment that seems medieval with modern disciplinary methods of internalized self-control, not the least achieved by public confessionals. Gilead's rigid penalty system instils terror and submission by regular and publicly sanctioned violence that are common and televised, with amputations for minor convictions and the death for more serious offences. This system simultaneously turns the citizens into accomplices by coercing them into active as well as passive participation in these collective atrocities. Testifying and Prayvaganzas foreground verbal obedience. The former describes a form of brainwashed, self-accusatory confessional of imaginary sexual crimes (such as rape and abortion) that Handmaids are forced to practice at the Rachel and Leah Re-education center. At the latter one, a futuristic version of sectarian mass weddings, the Commanders' adolescent daughters give their wedding vows of subservience to their husbands, the Angels. Salvagings (a sarcastic word play on salvaging and savage) and Particicutions (a very apt amalgam of participation and execution) secure physical obedience.

At Men's Salvagings, "offenders" allegedly undermining the Republic's monopoly on sexuality and progeny or its religious faith—for example, gynecologists practising illegal abortions, homosexual "gender traitors" desiring the (male) self, and members of other faiths such as Jews or Jehovah's Witnesses—are publicly hanged to exterminate any rebellion and feelings of or attempts at solidarity against Gilead's "us and them" polarization.

At Women's Salvagings, the Handmaids function as Gilead's female executioners and in a communal act hang "rebellious" women, convicted of crimes such as adultery, attempted escape or abortion. As passive but jubilant accomplices of the cruel killing, Wives witness these spectacles, whereas the Aunts supervise the killing. While only the Handmaids actually pull the rope that hangs the culprit, Aunts and Wives thus symbolically partake in the execution. Moreover, by punishing a member of the female sex, Aunts, Wives, and Handmaids symbolically punish themselves. By hanging a woman who has rebelled against heteronomy and stepped out of her role as object, women effectively ensure that their own guilt causing complicity will keep them in the passive victim and object position.

At the so-called Particicutions, a mob of Handmaids is manipulated into rechanneling all their repressed aggression against men, namely against their officially legitimized and socially sanctioned rapists, the Commanders. In blind rage and with bare hands, the avenging Handmaids virtually tear Gilead's male political rebels apart, falsely accused of rape or infanticide. Again, the Handmaids collaborate with the totalitarian system as they participate in Gilead's atrocities, and they execute the very men and women who might have become their potential liberators.

Perversely, the executions grant them an illusion of choice and freedom, as Offred sarcastically remarks: "we are permitted anything and this is freedom" (*HT* 262). To kill, the Handmaids need to reduce the male subject to an object and hence participate in the same dehumanizing dualism that oppresses them. The annihilation of the *other* presupposes the dissociation of the self from the *other*, the negation of humanity: "He has become an *it*" (*HT* 263). Killing the *other* also affects the self, because this violence first requires the self to eliminate feelings of empathy, sympathy, compassion, and respect for life. Offred remembers having noticed this psychological detachment in her husband Luke before he killed their cat:

> I'll take care of it, Luke said. And because he said *it* instead of *her*, I knew he meant *kill*. That is what you have to do before you kill, I thought. You have to create an it, where none was before. You do that first, in your head, and then you make it real. So that's how they do it, I thought ... that snuffing out of love.... That's one of the things they do. They force you to kill, within yourself [*HT* 180–181].

Focusing on progeny, two additional rituals enact the ultimate display and degradation of the female body and its sexuality. Although both the Ceremony (a communal Bible reading followed by coercive copulation) and the Birth Day (a communal gathering on the occasion of a Handmaid's giving birth) take place in the private sphere and deal with inherently private events, they nevertheless attain the status of public rituals or collective acts. These initially celebratory events, associated with bonding, intimacy, and connectedness, turn into the illusion and/or abhorrence of bonding and eventually into acts of isolation. These rituals in particular set women against one another. With the Ceremony, the Birth Day, and the illegal state brothel Jezebel's, Gilead thereby separates the body from emotions: sexuality from erotic desire, the legal, but non-erotic, basically asexual mechanical act of reproduction (Ceremony) from illicit, non-reproductive sex (Jezebel's), and biological from psychological motherhood (Birth Day). While the male subject actively participates in various of these sexual activities, women are limited to one role: that of receptive object and victim.

Despite the mingling of female classes on Birth Days, the class and gender segregation is maintained, if not strengthened: Wives and Handmaids painstakingly avoid one another, and the Commander of the household is absent. While the Wives celebrate downstairs, upstairs the Handmaids symbolically share the child labor of Ofwarren/Janine in a state of trance, in an illusion of sisterhood: "we can feel it [the baby] like a heavy stone moving down, pulled down inside us, we think we will burst. We grip each other's hands, we are no longer single ... we're the same as her [Janine], we're drunk" (*HT* 118). Only at the very moment of birth, does the Wife of the household rush into the bedroom full of Handmaids. Imitating Janine who is held by two helpers, the Wife too is held by two Wives and frames Janine on the Birthing Stool. By naming the newborn baby, the Wife takes possession of the infant as a status symbol, although the respective Commander legally retains the property rights over the child.

Similar to the rechanneling of aggressive emotions at the Particicutions, Birth Days serve as an outlet for repressed positive emotions. Following the instructions of the Aunts, all Handmaids identify with the pregnant Handmaid's giving birth: "it's a victory, for all of us. We've done it" (*HT* 119). Subtly, Gilead uses the Birth Days—the mental and physical participation in the birthing, the sharing of the birth pangs, and the anticipation of motherhood—to remind the Handmaids of their own "failure" of childlessness. Exhausted from the emotional strain, Offred addresses her absent feminist mother with bitter irony:

> we're without emotions now.... We ache. Each of us holds in her lap a phantom, a ghost baby. What confronts us now ... is our own failure. Mother, I think. Wherever you may be. Can you hear me? You wanted a women's culture. Well, now there is one. It isn't what you meant, but it exists. Be thankful for small mercies [*HT* 120].

The idea of a "sisterhood"—a society of subdued women that the Aunts so fervently believe in establishing: "For the generations that come after, Aunt Lydia said, it will be so much better. The women will live in harmony together, all in one family.... Women united for a common end! ... each performing her appointed task.... Your daughters will have greater freedom" (*HT* 152)—turns into a frightful parody of empowering female networks of the past. Moreover, sisterhood is perverted into an enforced, compulsory all-female community built on sorrow, loss, envy, and *angst*. Subtly turning the notion of freedom on its head, women's freedom of personal liberty is cut; as Aunt Lydia appreciatively remarks, now women are being "given the freedom from" (*HT* 24) competition and gender equality. Overlooking the important fact that women lack any choice, the Aunts believe in "a spirit of camaraderie among women" (*HT* 208). As Gilead demonstrates, this compulsory "sisterhood" isolates and disempowers women, precluding any potential solidarity among women.

The monthly Ceremony likewise precludes any emerging solidarity in the form of sexual love and bonding between members of the opposite sex; and it thus serves to reinforce Gilead's central metaphor of control. Fully dressed except for the reproductive body parts, the Commander and his assigned Handmaid, who is doubled by the Wife framing the Handmaid, have intercourse in a perverse imitation of the "licensed" marital act of dutiful procreation advocated by patriarchal Christianity:

> My red skirt is hitched up to my waist.... Below it the Commander is fucking. What he is fucking is the lower part of my body. I do not say making love, because this is not what he's doing. Copulating too would be inaccurate, because it would imply two people and only one is involved. Nor does rape cover it: nothing is going on here that I haven't signed up for [*HT* 88].

Although taking place within the realm of intimacy, the sexual act is turned into a degrading, procreational public act of utter separation devoid of emotions: "It has nothing to do with passion or love or romance ... [or] sexual desire" (*HT* 89). While the Commander performs in "a state of absence" (*HT* 150), Offred dissociates herself from her body, which is also reflected in her switch from first person subjective to third person objective: "If I were to open my eyes.... I would see his open eyes.... Kissing is forbidden between us. This makes it bearable. One detaches oneself. One describes" (*HT* 89).

The prohibition of touching and kissing creates an illusory, additional distance of interacting objects rather than of involved subjects. This obsession with purifying sex of all *desire*—let alone the threat of compassionate love—and, consequently, of exterminating the self's desire for acceptance by the *other* as well as for the momentary rupture of isolation through the very act of physical (and ideally emotional) contact, indicates the potential danger sexuality as fulfillment of bonding presents to Gilead's rigid system, based as it is on total polarization, isolation, and anonymity. Consensual sexuality, love, and erotic desire as momentary transgressions of dualism are exactly what Gilead has tried to eliminate and must continue to repress at all costs—as Aunt Lydia remarks: "*Love* is not the point" (*HT* 206)—not taking into account desire's immense and irrepressible force as the following dialogue between the Commander and Offred reveals:

> What did we overlook?
> Love, I said.
> Love? said the Commander. What kind of love?
> Falling in love, I said [*HT* 206].

Whether love really represents the subversive force in *The Handmaid's Tale* eventually leading to Offred's rescue, as several critics (cf. Malak; Ehrenreich) have claimed, remains unclear.

Atwood takes a critical though ambiguous stance towards romantic love as, on the one hand, a potentially liberating force that enables humans to value the *other*. On the other hand, romantic love specifically traps women in the victim position (cf. *HT* 211–212). Offred's relation-

5. The Poetic Discourse of the Split Self 251

ships with the three male characters of the novel, her husband Luke, the Commander, and her illicit love interest Nick, illustrate love's ambiguity. Linking past and present male adherence to masculine superiority, the Commander and Luke patronize Offred (e.g. both translate Latin; Luke explains the etymologies of words such as "Mayday" and "fraternize") and support patriarchal, hierarchizing difference between men and women. Luke, for example, maintains that "[t]here are some differences" (*HT* 59) between men and women; a claim echoed by Offred's feminist mother who asserts that men lack something (cf. *HT* 114-115) women supposedly have. Luke's statement that "women were incapable of abstract thought" (*HT* 115) resounds in the Commander's smug remark that for women "one and one and one and one don't make four" (*HT* 174).[22] By treating women as interchangeable commodities instead of as singular individuals (substituting their respective wives with the younger, fertile Offred), Luke and the Commander practice exactly the abstraction that Offred challenges: "One and one and one and one doesn't equal four. Each one remains unique.... They cannot be exchanged, one for the other. They cannot replace each other. Nick for Luke or Luke for Nick" (*HT* 179-180).

The sole male character not subscribing to this hierarchizing binarism is the Commander's chauffeur Nick. Nick is unmarried, ignorant of Latin, and in a way closer to the female's position. Asked by the Commander's wife Serena to impregnate Offred because Serena suspects that her husband is sterile, Nick initially functions as a male Handmaid/prostitute. Given that some sort of human bond, if not love, is established between Nick and Offred—although Offred stresses that "[n]either of us says the word *love*, not once. It would be tempting fate; it would be romance, bad luck" (*HT* 254)—their secret physical relationship clearly transgresses Gilead's segregation of the sexes. While the Commander and Luke do not oppose Offred's repressed object status, Nick risks his life for Offred if we read the end as a successful rescue attempt. At the same time, the subversive potential of love is undercut. Repeatedly, Offred is paralyzed by her love relationships. When Gilead renounces all constitutional rights for women, Offred does not join the protest marches but follows Luke's advice "to think about them, my family, him [Luke] and her [their daughter]" (*HT* 169). Similarly, she loses all interest in the underground organization when she teams up with Nick and chooses once more the personal over the political. For this reason, Miner labels

---

[22]For Miner, Luke and the Commander are "structurally twins" (160) because in both cases Offred is the other woman, and these extramarital affairs even take place in the very same hotel. Luke cheats on his first wife with Offred, and as Handmaid, she is the sexual/procreational double of the Commander's wife.

the novel as a statement "about love's tendency to follow decidedly conservative narrative forms" (150), and Tomc dismisses Offred's "self-protective passivity" as a "refusal of a politics of emancipation" (73).

Just as the relationship between Offred and Nick contains some disruptive but not quite transgressive elements, Atwood describes, with the eroticized, pornographic display of women as objects at Jezebel's and the sexual tease of literacy at the Scrabble game, two failed (male) attempts at transgression of the very polarities men created. Both involve the setting up of an otherwise prohibited (sexual) intimacy in new spaces of secrecy and privacy, yet both actually perpetuate binary oppositions.[23]

Although Gilead's seemingly "ascetic" society both negates sex as an act of physical and emotional communication between lovers in a deeply involved human relationship and condemns and suppresses desire, eroticism, sexuality, and any positive compassionate emotions as inherently feminine and thus hostile to the patriarchal system, desire and erotic sexuality thrive illegally in the brothel Jezebel's. Access to the recreated erotic desire in this secret world of illusionary intimacy is, however, restricted to (selected) members of the male elite. At Jezebel's, the sexual act changes solely for men and only insofar as men's physical lust is attended to without being on public display and without the duty of procreation. Jezebel's does not interfere with but reinforces Gilead's dualistic positioning of male subject and female object. The male subject does not desire the female *other* in its difference, but constructs "woman" once more as the object of male sexuality and desire, as the Commander's staging of Offred as dressed up pre–Gilead date clearly indicates. Woman therefore remains in the humiliating victim position. As with the Ceremony with its emphasis on reproduction, Jezebel's privileges physical sexuality, separating body from mind and emotion, a split that Offred, cognizant of body, mind, and emotions as components of sexuality and ultimately love, tries to mend: "nobody dies from lack of sex. It's lack of love we die from.... Can I be blamed for wanting a real body, to put my arms around? Without it I too am disembodied" (*HT* 97).

The Scrabble game that Offred and the Commander secretly play in the Commander's study is doubly illegal, since it demands and promotes literacy, and takes place in private. Distinct sexual overtones turn the game into "linguistic foreplay" (Lacombe 15), a new kind of voyeurism, vividly connecting power with language and literacy: "I read quickly, voraciously, almost skimming.... If it were eating it would be the

---

[23]At the Scrabble game, consciously playing with the pun on pen/penis to which Susan Gubar first drew attention, Atwood emphasizes the connection between writing and intercourse as two discourses of power. As Offred notes: "The pen between my fingers is sensuous, alive almost, I can feel its power, the power of words it contains. Pen is Envy" (HT 174).

gluttony of the famished, if it were sex it would be a swift furtive stand-up in an alley somewhere" (*HT* 172–173).[23] Yet although the Scrabble game as such "suggests the free interplay and interchange of ideas between equals," it creates "only the illusion of a true exchange" (Andriano 93). On the one hand, pretending an interest in Offred's mind, the Commander once more desires her body. On the other hand, since, as Amin Malak writes, "the victimization process does not involve Offred and the Handmaids alone, but extends to the oppressors as well" (13), he also tries to regain his own sense of individuality and elicit an image of himself as human rather than as procreational machine. At the Ceremony after these private meetings, his attempt to touch Offred's face betrays his need to express (or experience) something other than impersonal physical copulation. Yet the Commander's successful establishment of himself as subject—now the Commander is no longer "a thing" from which Offred can dissociate—merely shifts the former balance of two objects performing intercourse into a subject/object hierarchy in which the Ceremony now signifies a "breach of propriety" (*HT* 151) for Offred, who remains in the object position. The power politics between the Commander and Offred never change: he is master and she is his sexual slave.

5.2.3. "Gilead is within you": Women's Fragmented Inner Worlds

The political and social division into (male) self and (female) *other* expands into the enforced psychological fragmentation of women. Gilead's concept of the self constructs everyone outside the realm of the male self as *other* and cultivates a hostility to all other worldviews. "Woman" is difference, an aberration measured against the male self, as Aunt Lydia explains: "God made ... you different" (*HT* 43). Within the patriarchal economy woman is consequently indoctrinated either to submit to man's view of woman as alienated *other*, or to annihilate herself.

In the first case, according to Atwood, women involuntarily as much as voluntarily participate in their own subjugation by collaborating with the ruling system in the oppression of the female self. To this end, the Aunts and Wives assume the roles men have scripted, and in return are rewarded with the top positions within the limited female hierarchy. In this respect, women function as the correlative of man in a position of superiority. In her actions and expressions, Aunt Lydia "who was in love with either/or" (*HT* 8) epitomizes this internalization of binary hierarchies. Women in effect turn women and themselves into objects. The Handmaids exemplify this paradoxical self-image of the fragmented female self: a Handmaid is as much despised as she is needed for her reproductive capacity. She is the "good/bad woman, the saintly prostitute" (Bouson 140); she is both private property and public commodity, rendered invisible by her uniformizing habit and visibly on public display; at long last, she is a "vessel" (*HT* 128), a purely objectified body without a mind.[24]

In the second case, the dividing line between self and *other* moves inward, causing a psychological split. Defining oneself as *other* and object, negating one's own self and subjectivity, results in psychological fragmentation, destabilization, and schizophrenia, as in the case of the Handmaid Ofwarren/Janine. At the "Testifying," a form of brainwashing and self-accusation that epitomizes the Foucauldian confessional mode in which the act of confession simultanesouly constructs the very compliance the subject admits to, a Handmaid must charge herself as a perpetrator of sexual "crimes" in the past (e.g. rape or abortion) to which she was in fact *subjected*. Janine who had been gang-raped and who subsequently aborted the foetus, must not only give testimony against herself, but she is also denied victimhood. Subtly using psychological repression to force the Handmaids into line, the Aunts' question "But *whose* fault was it?" turns the female object position into that of acting subject, supported by the chorus of indoctrinated Handmaids blaming Janine as culprit, chanting: "*Her* fault, *her* fault, *her* fault" (*HT* 67).[25] Forced into psychological self-censorship, negating herself, wiping out her memory, and altering her perceptions, Janine splits her consciousness when she accepts guilt for a crime that she herself is in fact innocent of: "It was my own fault.... I led them on, I deserved the pain" (*HT* 68). This programming of the Gileadean ideology into the unconscious elucidates the frightening totality of the system: Gilead constitutes "an integral part of the self" (Filipczak 173).

Slipping over the edge with her eyes "come loose" (*HT* 263), Janine withdraws into madness and turns into an automaton spewing out the formulaic phrases expected of her. Soon the verbal madness requires a physical outlet, and at the Particicution her blood-smeared mouth (pre-

---

[24]*Recurring mirror imagery as well as allusions to various* doppelgängers *underline this fragmentation of the female self. Repeatedly, Offred catches glimpses of herself doubled and of her identity obscured in the mirror: "a distorted shadow, a parody of something, some fairytale figure in a red cloak"* (HT 9). *For example, Offred perceives herself and Serena in the hall mirror: "I see the two of us, a blue shape, a red shape, in the brief glass eye of the mirror. Myself, my obverse"* (HT 243). *Similarly, the Handmaid Ofglen doubles Offred: "She's like my own reflection, in a mirror from which I am moving away"* (HT 42). *Other doubles are the dead Handmaid who formerly lived in Offred's room, Serena Joy, Moira, and various fairy-tale figures (e.g. Red Riding Hood) to which Offred alludes. Ultimately, her patronymic Gileadean name that overwrites her former identity with a new one signifies a Handmaid's double identity and her schizophrenic existence.*

[25]*Imagery links the true believers; Janine and the Aunts are characterized as rodents: Aunt Lydia's "front teeth were long and yellowish her mouth [that] of a dead rodent"* (HT 52) *and Janine resembles "a newborn mouse"* (HT 68).

sumably, she has gorged herself on the unfortunate male victim) and wild stare indicate her progressing insanity. Significantly, Janine gives birth to an "unbaby," a girl. Metaphorically speaking, Janine rebirths herself; but the outcome, the product of the annihilated, psychologically disintegrated female self is another incomplete, damaged female self.

5.3. Storytelling as Psychological Means of Transgression

While male characters mostly adhere to a unified self and a Cartesian logic, Atwood's heroines enter fragmentary selves composed of multiple subjectivities. These female protagonists, Nora Foster Stovel writes, often embark on quests "for identity, as each Janus-headed heroine struggles to integrate her splintered personae" (qtd. in Mycak 10). Offred's quest, however, is for her remembered identity as well as an invocation and anticipation of other personae inside (characters as readers/listeners) and outside (us readers) of the text. Where other protagonists suffer from self-division, descending into "dysfunctional behaviours, multiple personalities, and complete psychological disintegration" (Mycak 10–11), Offred gains psychological balance and sanity from imagined *doppelgängers* and alter egos. In contrast to Bartkowski who sees Offred as a split subject by necessity—"in order to live with contradiction you pay the psychic cost of any shred of a coherent sense of self, identity, integrity" (149)—I argue that, for Offred, self-division is perhaps less a process of disintegration than a wilfull and simultaneous balancing of at least two modes of consciousness. Paradoxically, her fractured identity gains a notion of coherence from the "discontinuity and contradictions [that] can be constitutive parts of subjectivity" (Rao xvi). In agreement with Rao, I argue that the inconsistencies of the ego are central to "Atwood's poetic vision [that] lays stress on metamorphosis and change" (xvii). To remain sane, the self needs the *other* as a mirror reflecting the self, as Atwood describes in her poem "Marrying the Hangman": "[t]o live in prison is to live without mirrors. To live / without mirrors is to live without the self" and if the physical *other* is denied, another *voice* can provide this Lacanian speculum; "[t]his voice / becomes her mirror" (1978b, 48). Imprisoned in Gilead, Offred creates such a speculum, another voice, with her narration: this is Offred's act of defiance, her means of rebellion.[26]

---

[26]Hilde Staels also identifies narration as Offred's form of resistance. Staels's analysis, however, focuses primarily on the mind-styles of Offred, of the totalitarian regime, and of the Professors of the Historical Notes and disregards the transgressive nature of Offred's poetic discourse.

Indubitably, polarization is the denounced basic structure of dystopian Gilead and reality is most likely *presented* as duality to us. Yet, besides the well-documented recurring features of dualism, character doubling, self-division, and the split voice that critics have identified in *The Handmaid's Tale* and in other novels by Atwood, there is also an element of transgression, of multiplicity, and of polyvalence in Offred's narrative.[27] Significantly, Offred gives three, not two, contrasting versions of her initial encounter with Nick and of her fantasy about what might have happened to her husband Luke. In addition, Offred is not only doubled by Moira but also by several alter egos (Ofglen, Serena, the dead Handmaid, the reader). Offred desires the ability to enter various discourses and viewpoints, fragmented as they are, more than she desires a coherent and unified self. Offred's narration expands Sherrill Grace's contention that Atwood advocates an acceptance of duality; the tale also challenges Linda Hutcheon's notion that Atwood's "art derives its power and meaning from those very postmodern contradictions" (157) in the sense that Atwood's art depends on polarities. Offred exposes, combines, and accepts binarisms as being of equal value and as simultaneous occurrences rather than opposed modes of existence: "The shell of the egg is *smooth* but also *grained*.... It's a *barren* landscape, yet *perfect*" (*HT* 104; emphasis added).

5.3.1. Storytelling as Resistance

Critics have identified Offred as a passive, non-confrontational antiheroine who vacillates between the pros and cons of collaborating with the system, unsure which one guarantees survival, and who each time prefers survival to rebellion: she merely tells her story rather than effecting change. This criticism concurs with Atwood's own statement that Offred's "voice is that of an ordinary, more-or-less cowardly woman (rather than a heroine)" (qtd. in Cooke 276). For Jamie Dopp, this "guise of an Everywoman" (54) signifies a "devaluation" and a demonstration "of the impossibility of female heroes" (55); but she concedes that the portrayal of an ordinary woman rather than a heroine facilitates reader identification with Offred, whereby Atwood acknowledges the very difficulty of being heroic and the necessity for everyone to act according to her or his means. Moreover, Offred's insistence on survival—so easily and self-righteously dismissed as cowardliness from the safe dis-

---

[27]Mycak lists the various approaches critics have taken towards the split self in Atwood's novels: "the perfunctory use of the divided self"; the "dynamics of division between characters;" a character's "inner dualism [as] resolution of Atwood's own conflict"; the "split voice" and narrative dichotomy as "organizing principles"; and the integrative approach of restructuring the fragmented self into a unified self (cf. 11–14).

tance of being snuggled into an armchair—drums home the uneasy question of how the majority of readers would act in dystopia? What heroic acts are actually available in Gilead?

Resistance in the form of heroic deeds "is not condemned by the text—it is merely seen as useless" (Caminero-Santangelo 24). Physical resistance against Gilead fails, as Offred's own escape attempt, to some extent her mother's feminist fight in the pre–Gileadean era, Moira's failed flight and subsequent life at Jezebel's illustrate. Moreover, physical resistance might ultimately lead to self-destruction, as Ofglen's suicide demonstrates. In this sense, her mother, Moira, and Ofglen are Offred's active doubles; Moira in particular embodies what Lorna Sage has called the typical Atwoodian protagonist's "best friend who's wild, irreverent, swaggering" (162).[28] Moira and Ofglen represent what Atwood has described elsewhere as complementary figures: "your complement is someone who supplies those elements that are lacking in you" (Kaminski 32). Moira, Ofglen, and to a certain extent Offred's mother, who was an active member of the Women's Liberation Movement, provide Offred's narration with what she lacks: an aspect of active physical rebelliousness.

Offred is in fact well aware of her own passivity: "I wish this story were different.... I wish it showed me in a better light ... at least more active, less hesitant, less distracted by trivia" (*HT* 251); and she recognizes her own lack of heroism: "I don't want her [Moira] to be like me. Give in, go along, save her skin.... I want gallantry from her, swashbuckling, heroism, single-handed combat. Something I lack" (*HT* 234). As positive alter egos on the intra-textual level, these courageous self-assertive women thus triple rather than double Offred, and thus *The Handmaid's Tale* diverges from the usual narrative constellation of "ghosts, doubles, and/or guides" (Carrington 1987a, 41) who accompany Atwood's female protagonists.

Criticism of *The Handmaid's Tale* conventionally considers Moira as a positive, heroic "role model: a radical feminist heroine who inspires the narrator" (Banerjee 85). This perspective overlooks, however, the significance of contrasting Moira's resistance with Ofglen's altruistic resistance. While Moira only takes action to liberate herself—twice she

---

[28]*In her latest book,* The Blind Assassin, *Atwood picks up this theme of the passive, non-heroic Everywoman and her active, deviant other with the two sisters Iris and Laura Chase. While the latter represents the* other *within, "perhaps Laura wasn't very different. Perhaps she was the same as some odd, skewed element most people keep hidden but that Laura did not" (Atwood 2000, 89), the former ensures survival by being a conformist, but learns to fight back. In the light of Iris's equation of the first letter of her name with the first person singular—"I was everybody's letter" (ibid. 89)—Offred's first-person narration can indeed be read as everybody's story.*

tries to escape from the training center for Handmaids, an audacity that turns her into a collective "fantasy" (*HT* 125) of rebellion—and Offred is preoccupied with her own individual survival, Ofglen is a member of the Mayday Underground resistance, and altruistically and heroically engages in the rescue of others. At the Particicution, Ofglen unhesitatingly kills the political rebel, falsely convicted as a rapist, before the enraged Handmaids get to attack him. Ofglen spares *him* a painful torturous death, and thereby endangers herself; indeed, this act of mercy leads to the discovery of her membership in the underground organization. To prevent incriminating others, Ofglen then commits suicide.

By choosing Moira over Ofglen as a role model and internal judging authority, Offred once more chooses individual survival over altruistic heroism and, therefore, the past and not the present.[29] In the end, while Offred perhaps survives, Moira doubly fails: physically she is entrapped at Jezebel's, and psychologically she ends up verging on indifference and resignation.[30] Moira's last act of subversive defiance, secretly acting out her lesbianism and thus only surrendering part of her body to men at Jezebel's,[31] is hardly the heroic ending Offred would have liked to imagine for her friend: "I'd like to tell a story about how Moira escaped, for good this time. Or ... I'd like to say she blew up Jezebel's.... I'd like her to end with something daring and spectacular" (*HT* 234).

Witnessing the failure of heroic physical action in dystopia, Offred chooses narration as a less obvious means of insubordination. Janine's descent into madness illustrates that to resist the internalization of the psychological mind-set of Gilead while outwardly complying with it invites the risk of psychological disintegration and schizophrenia. In Janine's case, an alien subjectivity controls and erases or splits off her own subjectivity. For Offred, storytelling presents the possibility of storing in her consciousness, but not necessarily internalizing, various view-

---

[29]*Afraid of torture, Offred is also ready to surrender her body like Moira, "I resign my body freely, to the uses of others I am abject" (HT 268; emphasis added), yet she knows she is incapable of giving up oppositional thinking: "I'll obliterate myself I'll empty myself I'll abdicate. I know this can't be right but I think it anyway" (HT 268).*

[30]*Although I agree with Rao's view that Moira "survives intact the programme of conditioning into the acceptance of female guilt" (20), Offred's account of meeting Moira at Jezebel's indicates that Moira has lost the mental drive compelling her to escape or to openly resist. Rather, she has now arranged herself with Gilead.*

[31]*Moira's lesbian inclination undercuts the heterosexual polarity of Gilead and its focus on progeny. (Ignoring lesbianism as a possibility, the regime penalizes only homosexuality as a non-productive form of sexuality and thus non-legitimized "abnormality.") Yet Moira also falls into the trap of dualistic categories when, arguing for separatism, she presupposes automatic equality between women in an all-female utopia, "because the balance of power was equal between women" (HT 160). Offred rejects the notion of separatism, "if Moira thought she could create Utopia by shutting herself up in a women-only enclave she was sadly mistaken" (HT 161), because it does not deal with the reality of two sexes. On lesbianism and lesbian visions in sf, see also Tucker Farley (1984).*

5. The Poetic Discourse of the Split Self

points. Where Janine succumbs to the "either/or" of Gilead, therefore Offred's subjectivity is never endangered, because as narrator she can juggle disparate and conflicting perspectives, including her own, without privileging one over the others.

Likening Offred to a muted Scherazade, Stein asks, however, whether "discourse itself [is] an adequate form of political action" (1991/1992, 278). Regardless of whether one answers this question in the positive or negative, the narration does indicate, however, Offred's emerging political consciousness. Yet as Caminero-Santangelo argues, the "direction of resistance in the postmodern [sic] consequently changes from a one-directed struggle against the dominant order to a more flexible resistance that is context-specific (and, therefore, contradictory: what is resistant in one context could be seen as complicit in another)" (24). Offred finds herself exactly in such a "condition ... of compromised resistance" (Howells 1996, 138). For Caminero-Santangelo, this "resisting position would be one *outside* the symbolic order" (24) and implies that Offred can only resist from what Kristeva aligns with the preverbal. As much as Offred repeats the dominant patriarchal discourse, she counteracts the monologic dystopian discourse when she speaks from the gap, the slippage point of being inside and outside Gilead's dominant phallogocentric discourse, as, for instance, her perception of the subtly but significantly shifted meanings of proverbs illustrates. In a context where women's silence and absence is desired and effectually promoted, the female narration expands the Handmaids' conspiratorial whispering, their form of verbal rebellion.[32] Offred's act of resistance is, then, her narration: the audacity to acquire a (female) narrative voice and presence, to name and probe language, to disrespect, contest, and decenter the official, public, patriarchal discourse with the secret subtext of her own, private, and individual story and the various stories she relates. At the same time, storytelling enables her to establish and counterbalance her fragmented voice against the male discourse, and ultimately to position herself as a "creative non-victim."[33]

---

[32]*Cf.: "We learned to whisper almost without sound. We learned to lip-read" (HT 4). The Handmaids resort to reducing their oppressors by "whispering obscenities. It is like a spell of sorts. It deflates them, reduces them to the common denominator where they can be dealt with" (HT 208).*

[33]*In Survival, Atwood outlines four categories of victimization/victimhood: denial of victim experience; acknowledgement of inferior victim role and thus unchangeable victor/victim position; repudiation of victim role; creative non-victim (cf. 36–39). In contradistinction to Dopp who argues that Offred and hence the reader occupy position number two—since "the text offers readers not a position of active resistance to patriarchy, but a position of abjection that shares the fatalistic passivity of the protagonist. In this sense the dominant subject-position offered by The Handmaid's Tale is a victim-position" (44)—my reading suggests that Offred in her role as a creative storyteller occupies position number four.*

Narrative resistance therefore replaces physical heroism, and the speaking subject subsequently surmounts the failed acting subject. As narrator and storyteller, Offred represents the paralyzed, mutilated, and (almost) muted artist isolated and cut off from her audience, who successfully tells a powerful tale of emotional, artistic, psychological, and physical survival. By scrutinizing language and its formative power, by decoding Gilead's monolithic code, by desiring a textual *other*, and by creating multiple realities, Offred rebels verbally against Gilead, its monomania and binarisms. In the end, Offred embodies both: Everywoman, anti-heroine, and passive victim as well as defiant, rebellious narrator. Atwood's portrayal of female narrative resistance, however, undeniably borders dangerously close to traditional, stereotypical associations of femininity with passivity, since the novel lacks any suggestion of where—beyond survival—this poetic discourse leads Offred. Nothing in *The Handmaid's Tale* indicates how Offred's individual discursive practice could translate into a larger disruption of the dystopian society, since Atwood's examination of the discursive relation between subject and society ignores the political implications on a larger scale.

5.3.2. "I Tell, Therefore You Are": The Reader as Narrative Alter Ego

On the extra-textual narrative level, Atwood introduces another form of the mirroring self with the *other* that Offred conjures: someone who legitimizes her own existence within the realm of language, someone who witnesses her witnessing Gilead. Just as Offred creates her own self through language by linking physical with imaginary existence—"I compose myself. My self is a thing I must now compose, as one composes a speech" (*HT* 62)—she also invents the reader: "By telling you anything at all I'm at least believing in you. I believe you're there. I believe you into being. Because I'm telling you this story I will your existence" (*HT* 251). By imagining an alter-ego, an opposite, in the form of a reader or listener, Offred transgresses the solipsism of recording/writing as she implodes the divide between narrator and reader. With the subtly twisted Cartesian incantation "I tell, therefore you are" (*HT* 251), Offred invokes the *other* self, the reader or rather the *readers*, and simultaneously "she affirms her faith in survival" (Kauffmann 223) if we follow the logic of the text. As Lorna Sage states, "the important thing is to trade with the world outside" (1992, 168). Dissolving the opposition between reality and fiction, the reader/listener becomes Offred's double beyond the text, beyond fiction, whom Professor Piexoto also invites with his last remark—"Are there any questions?" (*HT* 293)—aimed at his academic audience in the Historical Notes to enter the narration as extra-textual *other*.

Only if Offred's story finds a reader or listener will she at last be remembered and raised above anonymity as an individual. By communicating with an *other*, Offred first of all shifts "the center from the 'I' to 'you,' decentering the Cartesian subject" (Givner 72); and she then destabilizes the dualistic I/you, narrator/speaker, and reader/auditor structure by anticipating a plurality of listeners: "'*Dear you*,' I'll say.... *You* can mean more than one. *You* can mean thousands" (*HT* 37–38). On the extra-textual level, this 'You' can include any number of future readers; on the intra-textual level, these multiple readers/auditors could be Moira, Luke, her mother, her daughter, or anyone of her contemporaries. Although her story is a monologue, the frequent invocations of a listener/reader indicate a desire for reciprocal communication, a dialogue, an exchange of stories. Offred narrates "because after all I want you to hear it [her story], as I will hear yours too ... if I meet you or if you escape, in the future or in Heaven or in prison or underground, some other place" (*HT* 251), and thereby acknowledges that her fate is by no means singular.

5.3.3. *Offred's Poetic Discourse of Survival*

Narration enables Offred to move from the position of a staged object to that of a performing subject, from silence to eloquent verbosity. Offred's silent inner "multilogue" proves what she notes about Serena's subversive, fecund garden: it conveys "a sense of buried things bursting upwards, wordlessly, into the light, as if to point, to say: Whatever is silenced will clamour to be heard, though silently" (*HT* 143). With Coral Ann Howells, I argue that Offred's storytelling is the "primary means for her psychological survival" (1996, 127) or, in Lacombe's words, it signifies her "insistence on psychic survival" (10). In short, this Handmaid's tale provides what Howells has called "a woman's survival narrative" (1996, 126). The inner discourse of protagonists who come to question the dystopian system they live in is a well-known narrative twist. Literary predecessors in this respect include Winston Smith in *1984* and Montag in *Fahrenheit 451*. Offred's discourse differs, however, in that, first, her inner opposition to the dystopian system is (retrospectively) already existent at the novel's opening.

Despite Offred's initial claim that "[t]hinking can hurt your chances, and I intend to last" (*HT* 7), she constantly contemplates, interrogates, and examines language and its signs and signifiers; she likewise refuses to take anything at face value. Offred's heightened awareness of the dubious nature of knowledge makes her an accessory and complicit. This is reflected in her desire for absolution when a new Handmaid replaces Ofglen: "All I did was know. All I did was not tell" (*HT* 267). Precisely for noticing the changes and *not* telling in pre–Gileadean times and during the coup d'etat, Offred became implicated in Gilead's system, and this initial, evasive silence she retrospectively remedies by telling what she knows. Second, Offred inserts a *poetic* discourse, investigating language at its linguistic roots. She retrieves and links multiple meanings of words and sayings whereas Gilead imposes only one, a totalitarian measure of monopolizing language that Atwood has described elsewhere: "The aim for all suppression is to silence *the voice*, abolish the word, so that the only voices and words left are those of the ones in power" (1982, 350). With its word shift and pun, Moira's sarcastic rephrasing of the Gileadean hymn "There is a Balm in Gilead" as "There is a Bomb in Gilead" (*HT* 205) signals the subversive use of language, revealing the disruptive potential of the retrieved voice, that Offred has in fact discovered with her poetic discourse of survival: the subversive use of words, language, and its construction of reality are the linguistic bombs attacking Gilead and simultaneously the healing balm left for the systems' opponents.[34]

Decentering Gilead's singularity, its monological, monosemous, and hierarchical official discourse, its one voice, Offred creates a polysemous aesthetic discourse, a plurality, a polyphony, and cacophony of voices— filtered through and mediated by her consciousness *because* of her constant awareness of alternative points of view and of reality in the plural— by giving us various reconstructed perspectives: of the past, of the present, of male and female voices, of Gilead's patriarchal mind-set, and of her mother's and Moira's feminist views.[35] Speaking from the locus of the gap, Offred can insert her associative/feminine worldview into the official, patriarchal discourse. This position of being inside and outside allows her to vacillate between both world(view)s and generates her transgressive discourse that consequently negates a dualistic choice of either/

---

[34] *In the Bible the rhetorical question of the prophet Jeremiah, "Is there no balm in Gilead" (cf. Jer. 8:22), refers, on the one hand, to the miraculous balm from Gilead said to heal wounds and, on the other hand, to the deplorable condition of the Jewish state, and whether there is any medicine that could heal "the diseased organism of the country" (Filipczak 173). Whereas in Edgar Allan Poe's famous poem "The Raven" the speaker, ecstatically imploring the laconic raven that might bring his deceased Leonore back, refers with his hesitant, morbid question "Is there—is there balm in Gilead?" (945) to the medical Biblical balm, this future Gilead turns the Biblical question with a slight twist of phrasing into an affirmation: Gilead has a medicine, i.e., an ideology, that will heal everyone from the disease of freedom and choice.*

[35] *Offred's awareness of filtering, impersonating, and approximating other's viewpoints is illustrated, for instance, by her remark that she can only try to "make it sound as much like her [Moira] as I can" (*HT 228*).*

or. Where Gilead thus speaks from a center, Offred supplies the focalizing perspective yet not the narrative center. Rather, she "circles" around her own perception, speaking from various positions as she negotiates her own view and the perspectives of other characters. Like the speaker of Atwood's poem "The Circle Game" who situates herself on the margins—"I live / on *all* the edges there are" (1978a, 24; emphasis added)— Offred juggles the blanks and the cutting edges from where she speaks: not the Empire writes back, but women, rejecting the colonization of their minds, talk back from the peripheries to which society relegated them.

Speaking as a suffering and passive victim, mourning the loss of husband and child, and as a defiant survivor, reducing her oppressors with sarcasm, Offred's narration is double-voiced: "her very sophisticated, ironic, and poetic voice is paired with a somewhat naïve, marginally informed, and apologetic one ... one is allusive, elliptical, and dense, while the other is garrulous, cliché-ridden, and filled with redundancy" (Banerjee 86–87).[36] The former voice cites "Marlowe, Shakespeare, and Tennyson" (ibid. 87); the latter remains ignorant of the etymology of words. Banerjee claims that a lack of communication between these two voices, "one of a poet and the other of a normal heroine," indicates "a hierarchical relation, since the literary competence subsumes the feminine, while the latter remains blind to the former" (88). No textual evidence, however, supports this "hierarchizing" and "non-communicative" relation; rather, Offred frequently slips in and out of her voices of the poet and of an Everywoman in the very same paragraph. At the same time that we witness Offred's inner monologue, the narrative thus becomes dialogic. This shift in tone and topic thus indicates indeed Offred's fragmentation: her multi-level thinking, acting a part to survive, her tendency to question and to dissect certain words and situations.

Caught in the ongoing dialectic between Gilead's discourse, her personal view, and the memory of other point of views, the narrating "I" is constantly displaced, but nonetheless continually seeks yet another, a third perspective beyond dualism: "What I need is perspective.... Perspective is necessary. Otherwise there are only *two dimensions*" (*HT* 135; my emphasis). On the one hand, the various versions of truth liberate Offred from binary thought; on the other hand, multiple perspectives allow Offred to distance herself from the fictional reality: "Otherwise you live in the moment. Which is not where I want to be" (*HT* 135). As Sisk

---

[36] *For Arno Heller, Offred's nightly retrospection, though a "vitally necessary counterpole" ("lebensnotwendiger Gegenpol"), provides merely "internal psychic escapism" ("innerpsychisch realisierte Fluchtmöglichkeit" 196). Despite recognizing that Offred's story "signifies a form of resistance," Rao argues along similar lines: "Offred's fictional fabrications bring an alternative world into existence and create a refuge from the painful reality of her own life" (78–79).*

writes, Offred's story and the interwoven stories of other characters counteract the reality imposed by Gilead:

> Offred understands that the act of telling inscribes a reality and that the teller therefore controls reality through her language and the story she tells.... But unlike the Gileadean regime she also understands that telling cannot silence other stories and that her telling a story is only an attempt to create a different reality [118].

In opposition to the circumscribed, predetermined life that Offred leads, nothing is finalized or fixed in her narrative. Emphasizing "the artificial order that fiction imposes on reality" (Deer 226), she allows interpretative variety by giving us various approximations of events, because *language* can only approximate events and emotions.

Stressing that memory distorts, Offred emphasizes that all reality as mimetic representation transcribes a mediation and a reconstruction: "All of it is a reconstruction.... It's impossible to say a thing exactly the way it was, because what you say can never be exact, you always have to leave something out, there are too many parts, sides, crosscurrents, nuances; too many gestures" (*HT* 126). Significantly, Offred juxtaposes three rather than two different versions of what might have happened to her husband Luke, stressing that *all* versions, despite the insufficiency and relative reality/fictionality of each version, are *equally* real for her: "The things I believe can't all be true.... But I believe in all of them, all three versions of Luke, at one and the same time" (*HT* 100). She likewise narrates three versions of her first night with Nick: "I made that up. It didn't happen that way. Here is what happened.... It didn't happen that way either. I'm not sure how it happened; not exactly" (*HT* 245–246). For lack of any other textual evidence, readers cannot determine which version might approximate the truth, and are ultimately required to recognize the impossibility of labeling truth and untruth. The polarization of "true" and "false," fact and fiction, is fictionally dismantled. Indeed, Offred's refusal to believe in the binarism of either/or, in choosing and, consequently, monopolizing reality or truth, refutes the assertion that Offred arrives at what Jill LeBihan calls the "rigid third term ... or the stasis of indecision," although LeBihan grants Offred the rejection of being the "subordinate half of the binary" (102). For Offred, truth is *part* of her story—"whatever I have left, which is not much but *includes* the truth" (*HT* 252; emphasis added)—which she is unwilling to pinpoint. Instead of choosing sides, Offred balances her versions of truths.

With biting sarcasm Offred's abounding associations parody and enlarge the narrow and limiting use of words in Gilead. Drawing attention with multilevel puns to the slipperiness of words, to the duplicitous meanings, the etymology of words, and to language as such, a closely knit metaphorical network and wordplay, Offred "transforms an unbearable assigned empty space into a space of self, a fiction of a self being projected into space, or inscribed on the 'blank'" (Finnell 209). Offred counterbalances the isolation and restricted physical movement she is subjected to with a widening heterogeneous inner space that she narratively explores in the "effort to maintain freedom of imagination" (Reesman 6), which Gilead tries to repress. In fact, metaphorically Offred's story thus reunites the Gileadean split of the physical and the mental, the numbed body and the muted mind. Through storytelling, Offred (re)creates and (re)produces a mental space that Gilead denies her by exclusively defining woman as a reproductive body, reducing the Handmaids to "two-legged wombs," "sacred vessels, ambulatory chalices" (*HT* 128). Where Gilead ascribes the sphere of the rational, literacy, and logos to masculinity, Offred associates the realm of words, the textual feminine story, with the physical, likening her story of the war of the sexes, her "limping and mutilated story" to "a body caught in crossfire or pulled apart by force" (*HT* 251) and the exchange of "clipped whispers" of the muted Handmaids to "amputated speech" (*HT* 189).[37]

Like other Atwoodian heroines, for instance, such as Laura in *The Blind Assassin* whose deviant behavior partially stems from taking words and sayings quite literally, Offred examines words and given definitions, where the Gileadean use of language limits women and "fence[s] in the self" (Finnell 209). Challenging a uniform society with a uniformizing language, Offred unearths the multiple meanings of words and the multiplicity of language, as Sisk writes: "Offred remembers old words that are now proscribed or whose meanings have been rendered obsolete or heretical by the revolution, like *free ... sheepish* (when describing men) ... *job* (something women no longer have) ... *networking* (which women no longer do) ... *romance* ... and *normal*" (110).[38] Where Gilead adheres to monolithic meaning, Offred's figurative and associative use of language, her frequent use of similes and metaphors, reconnects words and their meanings in new ways.[39] Using metonymy and synaesthesia, as

---

[37]For a further discussion of the connection between the representation of the fragmented body and text in relation to the self in The Handmaid's Tale, see Roberta Rubenstein (1988). In Rao's view, the anthropomorphic and the actual "corporeal disintegration" indicate a "dissolving ego" (83).

[38]For example, recalling the time when all women lost their jobs, Offred ponders the word "job": "having a job. Job It's a job for a man. Do a jobbie, they'd say to children, when they were toilet-trained. Or of dogs: he did a job on the carpet. The Book of Job" (HT 162). Cf. also: "Household: that is what we are. The Commander is the head of the household. The house is what he holds. To have and to hold, till death do us part. The hold of a ship. Hollow" (HT 77).

[39]Obsessively, Offred associates and compares, for example, the hanged men on the Wall "look like dolls like scare-crows as if their heads are sacks. The heads are zeros. The heads are the heads

Hilde Staels points out, Offred "connects the concrete and the abstract ... the visible (the 'true' and 'real') and the invisible (declared 'unreal' and 'irrational')" (165).[40]

Offred notes the phallogocentric construction of language, for example, the subtly twisted content of Biblical quotes, but remains strangely dependent on the language she criticizes: "Although Offred uses the oppressor's language ... [she] fits it to her needs" (Freibert 288). Unlike Elgin's women linguists in the *Native Tongue* trilogy, Offred never considers the creation of new words or another language.[41] Where Elgin contests phallogocentric language with the insertion of a women's language expressing the female perspective, Atwood approaches language the other way around. Atwood instead situates Offred along the borderlines of Gilead's phallogocentric discourse to probe, to reclaim and to restructure our existing contemporary language as a locus of change and linguistic resistance. Mental liberation or decolonization requires then, according to Atwood, not the creation of a new language, but a subversive reflection on language.

In this context, it is important once again to note Offred's repeated statement that "[c]ontext is all" (*HT* 136). On the content level, this statement refers to the Scrabble game and the Commander's demand that Offred kiss him; two non-spectacular events if considered isolated, but absurd in this context. On an abstract narrative level, as I have argued previously, this statement can be read in the light of the appended Historical Notes that place Offred's story in a new temporal and authorial context. From a linguistic perspective, or more precisely a Kristevan semiotic approach, Offred's remark can be perceived as the liberating linguistic strategy of the decentered subject. According to Kristeva, if language is a heterogeneous process rather than a fixed structure or system, where "*all* meaning is contextual" and "isolated words or general syntactical structures have no meaning until we provide a context for them" (Moi 157), a changed context can deconstruct and change the constructed sexist meaning of language.

[continued] *of snowmen" (*HT* 31); the hanged women look "like chickens strung up by the necks in a meatshop window; like birds with their wings clipped, like flightless birds, wrecked angels" (*HT* 260) "like dead butterflies or tropical fish" (*HT* 266); Ofglen's initially pious behavior seems to Offred "as if she's voice-activated, as if she's on little oiled wheels, as if she's on top of a music box her meek head, bowed as if into a heavy wind" (*HT* 41). The irises in Serena's garden are "like blown glass, like pastel water momentarily frozen in a splash" (*HT* 143).*

[40]*E.g.: "Sun comes through the fanlight. I step into it briefly, stretch out my hands; they fill with flowers of light" (*HT* 46); "Time as white sound" (*HT* 65).*

[41]*McCarthy charges Atwood for this lack of linguistic innovation, whereas Ketterer objects that the use of contemporary language has the advantage of not dating Atwood's dystopia so quickly (cf. Ketterer 215). Either view neglects that Atwood thus achieves an* examination *of contemporary language.*

From this perspective, language as such is not sexist but its use is, since the dominant group in power determines the *meaning* of the sign. Thus, a sign is rather "'polysemic' rather than 'univocal'" (ibid. 158). Kristeva suggests that poetic language, which she associates with prelinguistic experience, is inherently disruptive of the paternal Symbolic Order and generates new meanings: "The poetic word, polyvalent and multi-determined, adheres to a logic exceeding that of codified discourse and fully comes into being only in the margins of recognized culture" (65). Although Kristeva argues in favor of avant-garde writing, her and Atwood's poetic strategies converge insofar as both privilege metaphorical language. If metaphors are closely related to or originate in the Imaginary Order, or in Kristevan terms, in the semiotic, then Offred's insertion of poetic language stems from such a semiotic pulsation and destabilizes the Symbolic Order of phallogocentric discourse. By interrogating Gilead's mental boundaries and shifting between discourses, Offred transgresses the propagated divide between the Imaginary and the Symbolic order and reinserts the semiotic in the symbolic.

Perhaps the most obvious transgressive narrative aspects of *The Handmaid's Tale* are its resistance to closure and the rupture of the opposition of fiction and reality, inasmuch as Offred's story as well as the Historical Notes refute an ending: "I would like to believe this is a story I'm telling.... If it's a story I'm telling, then I have control over the ending. Then there will be an ending, to the story, and real life will come after it.... It isn't a story I'm telling" (*HT* 37). Since Offred has no control over the events—"I have given myself over into the hands of strangers" (*HT* 276–277)—and therefore the ending, readers are meant to deduce that she indeed tells a real story. Furthermore, Offred's story ends on an ambiguous and transgressive note: "Whether this is my end or a new beginning I have no way of knowing.... And so I step up, into the darkness within; or else the light" (*HT* 276–277). This ambiguity is reflected by Professor Piexoto's closing of his academic paper with a question, although the appended masculine text criticizes exactly the inconclusive moment of the feminine narration.

Offred's last words seemingly posit a duality of darkness and light, of death and survival, of her nightly reminiscences and the daily tortures—a duality that is further mirrored by the two Eyes who stand "one on either side" of the "double doors" (*HT* 276) of the van—but they also leave space for a third reading (version).[42] Campbell Reesman, refer-

---

[42]*For Kaler, Offred's final words, the "omission of a preposition with the word 'light,'" merely indicate "the nebulous ending Atwood intended" (59). Offred's dark/light imagery is ironically juxtaposed with Piexoto's misleading, self-righteous belief that "the past is a great darkness," a darkness he intends to illuminate with "the clearer light" (*HT* 293) *of his own day, although he*

ring to Wendy Barker's study of Atwood's and Emily Dickinson's imagery, maintains that in both authors' works "sun and light [are] identified with male values ... while darkness and even confinement are settings for these women speakers' healing dialogue with readers" (qtd. in Reesman 9). Evidently, Offred escapes from the penetrating daylight gaze of men when she steps out of the rationale of Gilead and into her secret discourse of the night: "I tell time by the moon. Lunar, not solar" (*HT* 187). But by juggling both discourses her narrative voice also "escape[s] from these categories altogether, from the polarities of light and dark" (Reesman 9–10). Offred upends the bipolarity Gilead upholds. Depending on perspective, polarities become fluid; outside resembles inside, and darkness might signify light: "Out there or inside my head, it's an equal darkness. Or light" (*HT* 182). Her use of dark and light imagery illustrates that Offred connects rather than hierarchizes existing opposites, emphasizing the impossibility of distinguishing, for example, between darkness and light. The very difference produces and creates a compository, fluid polarity: "there can be no light without shadow; or rather, no shadow unless there is also light" (*HT* 99). Her discourse stresses the interdependency of dualities, not their exclusory nature, and achieves a synthesis, a "dialectical unity of opposites" (P. Murphy 33), without leveling the contradictions.[43] Offred's closing remarks, referring to the end of her life in Gilead, may, however, imply a new life in freedom, just as the darkness within the van may signify the light at the end of the Gileadean death tunnel. Offred is left in a transitory position where darkness is not the opposite of light, and an ending is not the negation of a beginning. Each may contain the other. It all depends on the much implored "perspective" (*HT* 135). Context is everything.

Offred's story thus ambiguously signals her physical survival and a potentially utopian change of the individual in that she persists in a state of psychic plurality, of a mind transgressive of binary logic; yet the actual outcome of her changed consciousness is projected beyond the boundaries of the novel. The juxtaposition of fictional past, present, and future—Offred's memories of the past (our past/present), her remembered account of her present life in Gilead (our potential future), and the retrospective gaze of the future casts on Gilead in the form of the Historical Notes—emphasizes that without an imagination of the future and an acute awareness of history, we are left without desire and conse-

[continued] *obviously overlooks various allusions and hidden clues in Offred's narration (e.g. her real name, June). The "echoes" (HT 293) resounding in this historical darkness are really the perpetuation of Gilead's sexism in the academic discourse.*

[43]*For the interchangeability of dark/light imagery, see also Atwood's poem "Interlunar": "The lake, vast and dimensionless, / doubles everything, the stars, / the boulders, itself, even the darkness / that you can walk so long in/it becomes light" (Atwood 1992, 122).*

5. The Poetic Discourse of the Split Self

quently fall victim to life in a disconnected, eternal present. Without the temporal continuum, the idea of resistance wanes and resignation dominates: "Time's a trap ... I must forget about my secret name and all ways back. My name is Offred now, and here is where I live" (*HT* 135).

The core of Atwood's argument seems to be that the logic of dualism—ostensibly inherent in our consciousness and thought only because we are conditioned to structure both according to binary patterns—the univocal meaning of language and of discourse first have to become unfixed to enlarge the conceptual universe. If we move towards polyperspectivism, multiplicity of meanings, and allow various subjectivities to reside simultaneously in the self, if we challenge any notion of a unified discourse, then Aunt Lydia's dark and intimidating proclamation—crudely paraphrasing as well as twisting Jesus' alleged words "the kingdom of God is within you" (Luke 17:21)—that "The Republic of Gilead ... knows no bounds. Gilead is within you" (*HT* 23) would come undone and Gilead would have no dominion.

Conclusion

> *I promise you, you can do magic with words.... You can change the world with words.*
> —Kate Wilhelm, *Juniper Time* (7)

As the previous close readings demonstrate, the texts of Elgin, Charnas, and Atwood are feminist transgressive utopian dystopias that dislodge our binary logic concerning the generic, formal, and content level in that they describe various forms of transgression and hybridity. Taken as examples from a larger body of feminist dystopian texts that present utopian alternatives and suggest transgressions on various levels, the textual analysis of these narratives discloses the degree to which contemporary feminist dystopias constitute indeed a new genre, one characterized by the interweaving of dystopian and utopian narrative strands bound by the distinctive feature of transgression. The resulting "dystopian" fiction is, however, less a literature of despair than a literature of moderate hope.

Dystopian from the outset—whether by a military coup as in *The Handmaid's Tale*, a legislative cutback as in the *Native Tongue* trilogy, or an ecological catastrophe as in the *Holdfast* series—these feminist texts describe the development of oppositional utopian movements or strategies. Narrating the point of transition from dystopia to utopia, these narratives illustrate the process of individual and societal transition towards a better yet imperfect and, therefore, dynamic society less riven by dualisms and potentially grounded in new conceptual spaces that suspend binary logic. Since utopia can no longer be fixed, the texts never claim utopia and the utopian dystopian texts hover in the in-between, the dynamic interstitial space between classical dystopia and utopia.

While all the works under discussion provide momentary and often vivid glimpses of disruption, transgression, and hope, Charnas paints the most dismally graphic picture of the grim individual and societal process towards this better and alternative world. With Nazareth's desperate recital of Encodings and other instances of the soothing influence of Láadan on women, with the alliance between the women linguists and the men of the PICOTA (the founding of the Meandering Water Tribe), and with the spreading of Audiosynthesis, Elgin punctures her dystopian Terran universe with small instances of individual and societal transformation. Elgin refrains, however, from detailing the actual process. Atwood, on the other hand, shows no societal transformation; but we witness Offred's narrative unfixing of the dystopian reality, and her story demonstrates an individual's process of enlarging the conceptual universe by creating for herself new utopian conceptual spaces.

Both Atwood's and Charnas's dystopian scenarios (and also, in the case of the *Holdfast* novels, the transformation process towards utopia) include gruesome physical violence, whereas Elgin focuses less on overt physical violence than on intense and often debilitating psychological verbal and non-verbal violence. For Elgin, non-violence ought to be not only the result but also the means of societal transformation. Charnas, on the other hand, sees no way to avoid a violent confrontation if positive change is to follow. And if we take Offred's poetic discourse of survival as exemplifying the individual's transformational process, then Atwood presumably would opt more for a non-violent process. Since *The Handmaid's Tale* does not focus on societal change, however, a conclusive Atwoodian position cannot be ascertained.

Significantly enough, Charnas's and Elgin's initially dystopian texts end not merely on a positive note and thus rewrite the traditional dystopian conclusion (the death or defeat of the rebel), but they also signal the emergence of a better life. Since utopia is no longer conceptualized as a blueprint but rather as a dynamic and continuous movement towards the improvement of society, this pragmatic utopia can never be attained. Such a progressive utopian vision belies specific description in that such a vision describes always future and ongoing projects. Consequently, all novels discussed resist closure: with the envoy of the PICOTA sending the message of evolutionary hope out into the cosmos, the future of the earth and of Earth's space colonies remains uncertain; Alldera and the Riding Women disappear from the Holdfast; and stepping "into the darkness within; or else the light" (*HT* 276–277), Offred's fate is indeterminate.

As I have outlined in the preceding chapters, the utopian dystopia is by definition a generic hybrid that takes as its foundation the unraveling of classical utopian and dystopian narratives and then incorporates other genres. The *Native Tongue* series, for instance, recognizably draws on sf elements, and the *Holdfast* series likewise uses predominantly the nexus of mythical/quest, but also fantastic, epic, and adventure tale elements; and both series insert distinctly perceptible utopian subtexts.

In contrast, the generic transgressions of *The Handmaid's Tale* are more subtle. Not only is the utopian element of Offred's narrative act well-disguised—and has therefore gone largely unnoticed—but Atwood's novel also differs from the other two works insofar as she does not *re*write specific generic tropes. Rather, she *over*writes—thus my suggestion to take the palimpsest as Atwood's generic *modus operandi* for *The Handmaid's Tale*—the genres of epistolarity, autobiography, romance, and fairytale. One must recognize, however, that while the hybridizing of dystopia and utopia denotes a key element of the subgenre of utopian dystopia, the cross-fertilization of genres is, generally speaking, a literary phenomenon that informs much of postmodernist fiction.

Similarly, some of the manifold narrative transgressions are indubitably related to the use of postmodern narrative strategies. Although all of the analyzed texts are postmodern, *Walk* and *Motherlines* are the least so; and *The Handmaid's Tale* and the *Native Tongue* trilogy, *Earthsong* in particular, represent the most postmodern, episodic, fragmentary, and non-linear narratives that call attention to the text as a construction and mediation. Additionally, Atwood and especially Elgin mix various discourses that deconstruct and displace one other. Characteristic elements that all the discussed novels include are the fragmentary assemblage of a polyphony of conflicting voices and perspectives, and the female characters' move from silence to speech. Charnas and Elgin introduce multigenerational cluster characters or societal voices that disrupt our notion of a distinct narrative voice, but each author provides the narrative with necessary continuity by using Alldera/Sorrel and Nazareth/Delina as unifying narrative links. And Atwood conversely posits Offred as the central character—yet not as the narrative center—whose singular narrative voice filters and focalizes all perspectives.

Furthermore, all three authors create *female* heroes and through these specific characterizations, the texts simultaneously undermine and reconceptualize the conventional notion of the lone strong (male) hero and the (patrilinear) quest motif. Deconstructing the concept of a superior larger-than-life heroism, Elgin, Atwood, and Charnas relocate heroism in smaller, individual, and thus harder to recognize courageous deeds and acknowledge the difficulty of acting heroic. The female characters are often placed in contexts not traditionally seen as a locus for heroic effort. Traditonal quests would, in fact, be counterproductive for undermining these familiar narrative patterns conventionally seen as heroic. To this end, both Atwood and Charnas utilize an ordinary Every woman who develops, to use Charnas's phrase, into a "reluctant hero" who values survival as a crucial heroic act.

Charnas and Atwood, moreover, juxtapose and link passive and active female roles. Although Moira and Ofglen are active female characters not unlike Alldera, unlike Charnas's protagonist they both essentially fail in their endeavors to counteract physically the totalitarian system. Conversely, Offred successfully survives despite being more passive and hesitant to act. Offred shares with Daya, Alldera's passive alter ego, this role of the non-confrontational, passive survivor, the preoccupation with one's own individual survival, and the role of storyteller. Only Charnas, however, extends this ambiguous role of the passive hero, who by conventional measures is a "flawed" hero, to the male characters Eykar and Setteo. Far from being dashing heroes and encumbered by a mutilated body, Eykar and Setteo hesitatingly perform nonetheless heroic deeds. Elgin's two female heroes Nazareth and Delina are similarly characterized by a partially dysfunctional body. And while neither hardly plays the swashbuckling hero's role, Nazareth eventually stands up to her malevolent husband Aaron, and Delina defies Chief Bluecrane's attempt to keep her from her vision quest.

The concept of the new female hero is not only linked with the deconstruction of the conventional quest narrative, where the male hero leaves the community to accomplish a task and thus transformed returns to the community with a stronger identity. In contrast, Charnas's and Elgin's female heroes embark on quests that focus instead on the self in relation to communal goals. They even place themselves subordinate to "feminine" communal goals. The female heroes of the *Native Tongue* and the *Holdfast* series desire and achieve societal transformation only as members of and with the help of their (female) community. Nazareth's Encodings, for example, denote only part of the larger Láadan project; and although Audiosynthesis originates from Delina, who specifically seeks Chief Bluecrane's help for her vision quest, it is spread by the Meandering Water Tribe.

In like manner, the goal of Alldera's quest is the liberation of her people. Although she is the initial engine of the Free Fems' return to the Holdfast and the ensuing reconstruction thereof, only the combined effort of Free Fems, Newly Freed, "new men" such as Eykar and Payder, the Pooltown people, and the emerging new generation of New Holdfasters will gradually bring about the desired change. Unlike the male quest for the self that often leads to the alienation, isolation, or death of the hero, the hero of this female quest pattern achieves a transformed self by reaching out to others. The self and the community are thus no longer placed in opposition, but are perceived as intrinsically connected.

Essentially moving from a separatist to an integrationist approach, both Elgin and Charnas, however, presuppose a momentary separation of the female self from the male community in order to develop utopian projects or movements that then aim at societal integration. In the *Native Tongue* books, for instance, the separate female space of the Barren and the Women's Houses allows the women linguists to create Láadan; the nunnery and the Thursday Devotionals provide a secluded female space where the women linguists can disseminate Láadan; and from separate space habitats, the field chapels, the women linguists' order "Our Blessed Lady of the Star Tangle" popularizes Audiosynthesis. In the *Holdfast* series, the Riding Women develop in the secluded space of the Grasslands. The Free Fems and the Newly Freed need to keep the men as captives to establish their own societal rules. Alldera even needs to be separated from the Free Fems of the Tea Camp to fully immerse herself in the Riding Women's society.

According to Elgin, a paradigm shift that dislodges the binary logic can only be achieved from a momentary place of dislocation, from within a separate physical/geographical space. Yet, while for Elgin solely this spatial separation in turn allows the creation of a new mental space and the decolonization of the mind, Charnas's approach is more subtly diversified. Although the *Holdfast* books depict the most extreme spatial separation of all the novels by initially removing the Free Fems altogether from the patriarchal Holdfast, Charnas emphasizes that separatism provides only a temporary solution. The Free Fems at the Tea Camp, for example, live separately from the Holdfast men but fail to restructure their all-female society. As the final two novels of the *Holdfast* series underscore, separatism must be accompanied by the interaction and contact between disparate cultures and the sexes, to allow the necessary process of transculturation and the experience of borderwalking.

Unlike Elgin and Charnas, Atwood foregrounds individual resistance and the individual's psychological means that lead to a rejection of binarisms. Thus preoccupied with the survival of the self, *The Handmaid's Tale* does not address communal issues or does so through implication. Suffering from the totality of her isolation, Offred acts (or rather narrates) on her own by necessity, but desperately desires the (re)connection with an *other*, for example, with Nick and Ofglen; and she joyfully notices that Ofglen speaks in the plural: "there is an *us* then, there's a *we*" (*HT* 158). At the same time, Offred's remark signifies that the individual's resistance and survival alone is not a context that allows for sufficient progressive development. Not the opposition between self and society, these transgressive utopian dystopias argue, but the self situated within a larger community and, therefore, connected with communal action will successfully initiate utopian change.

Thematically, the three authors foreground different utopian movements or experiences to transgress in varying degrees the binaries of self/other, subject/object, male/female, center/periphery, human/animal or human/non-human, master/slave, nature/culture, mind/body or spirit/matter, and sanity/madness. While Elgin suggests two distinct utopian projects (Láadan and Audiosynthesis), Charnas proposes the involvement of all societal and personal areas, the individual experience of borderwalking, of slippage between cultures, norms, sexes, mentalities, and sexual orientation. As does Charnas, Atwood concentrates on the individual experience, but privileges exclusively the internal, psychological development: the utopian potential of storytelling, the ability to enter various perspectives, and to live in a state of mental flux, in a psychic state of plurality.

The textual analysis of the eight novels has shown that the suggested methods for the achievement of these moments of utopian transgression are cultural and linguistic hybridity, a nomadic and heterogeneous consciousness, the decolonization of the body and the mind, code-switching, transculturation, borderwalking, and a poetic discourse/narration. Significantly, such a transgressive utopian principle acts within what Cixous has described as the feminine libidinal economy that refrains from an economy of exchange and is instead driven by the desire to give without taking. Examples of such an economy include the Aliens, the women linguists, and the Riding Women. Key issues involved in the shaping of the transgressive utopia are the (re)construction of language; the participation of language in the construction of the past, present, and future reality; and language's various discursive disguises as religion, history, myth, literacy and orality; the necessity to free all forms of relations from notions of possession, violence, and a master/slave attitude; the question of how to involve men and the call to redefine not only femininity but also masculinity.

Language figures as a key tenet in all the works under discussion, and all the texts critique the exclusion of women and women's experiences from language. Each author, however, questions language from a slightly different angle. Atwood, for instance, takes the stance that language is not a linguistic system inherently masculine, sexist, and/or imperialist; she argues instead that the phallogocentric and restrictive use of language informs the sexist/racist meaning of signs. For Atwood, polysemic, polyvalent signs and metaphorical or poetic language in particular provide the means for the disruption of the dominant phallogocentric discourse. This approach perceives language as a heterogeneous process of constant permutations, where meaning is derived in relation to a specific context rather than a fixed system of signs and signifiers. A changed context, Atwood argues, can restructure and change the constructed sexist/racist meaning of language. The fact that the novel rejects closure suggests both the potential and the uncertain nature of the undertaking: its very flexibility and uncertain nature also makes language vulnerable.

Unlike Atwood, who critically examines our existing phallogocentric language and reclaims it as a locus of linguistic resistance and change, Elgin supports the standpoint that the structure of our language per se describes a phallogocentric discourse that can only be changed by the insertion of a women's language expressing the female perspective. Thus, while both Atwood and Elgin contest the phallogocentrism of language and the need to decolonize the mind, Elgin envisions a utopian change via the creation of a new language that must be inserted in the dominant discourse, whereas Atwood promotes the subversive reflection of language, the retrieval of the multiple meanings of signs, and the necessity to change the context in which language is used. While Charnas essentially concurs with Elgin (and Atwood) on language playing such an important part in the creation of reality and "on the centrality of words and their meanings,"[1] Charnas addresses less the linguistic aspect of language than the manipulative (ab)use of language in the creation of history, myth, religion, and storytelling. As does Atwood, Charnas criticizes the falsification or obliteration of cultural and personal history, the manipulation of the collective and individual memory as the repository of the past.

While the dystopian narrative strand of all eight novels focuses on material conditions, physical oppression, and dysfunctional interpersonal and intercultural relationships, of the three authors, only Charnas's *Holdfast* books chronicle the movement from possessive, oppressive, and violent relationships towards the creation of cooperative, non-violent, and non-possessive cultural, social, familial, and sexual relationships. According to Charnas, such a movement presupposes the human capacity for and the experience of borderwalking binaries that eventually results in a hybrid identity. Both Elgin and Charnas identify the need to differentiate between psychological and biological ties, and they likewise criticize the valorization of "natural motherhood." The Láadan word that signifies "love for the sibling of one's body but not of one's heart" (*NT* 276) thus provides the linguistic expression for what Charnas terms bloodmother and heartmother in the Grassland society. Yet Charnas not only postulates but also depicts new ways of cohabitation: the Holdfasters, for instance, adopt the Riding Women's practice of sharemothering and transform it into the co-parenting that both sexes will eventually practice.

Similarly, both Elgin and Charnas emphasize the necessity of cultural hybridization and the ensuing emergence of a heterogeneous, multicultural, multi-ethnic, and multireligious society. To this end, both authors use an essentially alien *other* (Aliens and Riding Women) as a foil for the cultural *other*—in the last book of the respective series both

---

[1]*Interview with Charnas. See the appendix.*

the Native Americans of the PICOTA and the Pooltown people are added on as cultural/ethnic *other* to be integrated into society—and the alien society as an alternative model or inspiration for the utopian restructuring of human society. Only the *Holdfast* series, however, describes the alien, the Grassland culture and the transculturation process in detail.

In comparison to Elgin's and Atwood's utopian dystopias, the *Holdfast* tetralogy provides with *The Conqueror's Child* an important addition to the feminist agenda: Charnas addresses the gender question not only from a feminist point of view, but asks what men can and must do to recreate masculinity and broaden the roles of men. How can men participate in the construction of utopia? This question plays no role in *The Handmaid's Tale*, and in the *Native Tongue* novels men participate neither in the construction of Láadan nor of Audiosynthesis. Only the PICOTA men are involved in the distribution of Audiosynthesis. By and large, the resonance principle on which the *Native Tongue* books are based envisions, on the one hand, a non-violent way of disseminating important utopian notions. On the other hand, the resonance principle diminishes men to the role of minors who need to be educated and manipulated into a non-violent version of humanity. In the *Holdfast* novels, however, men explicitly need to find their *own* way to rehumanize themselves, and they must redesign male stereotypes (e.g. destructor, explorer, and protector) and reinscribe new roles such as creator/inventor, caretaker, parent, and mentor. Men need new values and skills such as empathy and nurturing, qualities that patriarchy vilifies as feminine or as homosexual qualities if practiced by men.

This demand that men must *participate* in and contribute to the imagining and the creation of utopia renders *The Conqueror's Child* simultaneously the most transgressive utopia and the most realistic among the novels discussed; the concluding volume of the *Holdfast* series consequentially addresses what is perhaps one of the most pressing social question of the new millennium: how can men redefine masculinity? Charnas expands feminism not only to include men, but she also advocates a masculinism that no longer adheres to roles derived from bipolarity. The American journalist Susan Faludi proves in *Stiffed* (1999), her latest analysis of sex/gender relations, how we are very much in need of such a masculinism as opposed to a masculinity that "prevents men from thinking their way out of their dilemma" (14). In fact, it is amazing how much Faludi's sociopolitical findings overlap with the fictional sociopolitical analysis of Charnas's *Holdfast* series. A comparison of these two works, stemming from dissimilar discourses, would most definitely be a fruitful enterprise. In her attempt to analyze why postmodern American men are so angry and violent, Faludi ascertains a "crisis of masculinity" (1999, 7) that calls for new images of masculinity, "an alternative vision of manhood" (ibid. 41), not grounded in control and violence, but rather based on the retrieval of the nurturing and maternal qualities of masculinity.

Faludi's findings underline the realist bend of the *Holdfast* series. In fact, Faludi likewise assumes a basically transgressive stance with her assertion that men need to realize that they are not only the makers of history but are also the subjects (and the victims) of history. Faludi's analysis of American masculinity in the 1990s shows that the masculine mystique is shattered as an artificial cultural construct, analogous to feminism's earlier shattering of the feminine mystique: traditional masculine roles are no longer adequate in our media-fueled ornamental culture of vanity and glamor, because consumerism victimizes men *and* women. According to Faludi, the concept of masculinity is growing more feminine in the sense that masculinity is becoming increasingly defined as ornamental. As a result, men also become trapped in an obsession about their own bodies, just as women do. What Charnas describes in the Holdfast tetralogy—the Riding Man Veree, who cannot grasp traditional concepts of masculinity/femininity, epitomizes this cross-dressing—Faludi ascertains in our reality: femininity and masculinity can no longer be understood as opposites but as two cross-dressing phenomena. Essentially, Charnas's fiction chronicles what Faludi considers the future of our reality: only a combined effort of feminism and a new masculinism will lead to a successful restructuring of our societies. "Men and women are," Faludi believes, "at a historically opportune moment where they hold the keys to each other's liberation" (1999, 595). Transgressive utopian dystopian literature in particular generates visions that invalidate Faludi's lament that the "lack of maps" (1999, 606) cripples such a paradigm shift.

Bearing in mind that the very impetus of utopian and dystopian literature is fueled by a dissatisfaction with the sociopolitical status quo and the desire for change, the question remains, how can the telling of stories about the future transform the present? Utopian literature can influence our approach to reality insofar as the literary representation of a magically changed world or society catalyzes desire. By imagining the previously unimagined, the unheard, or the silenced, these literary texts both reflect how what we perceive as reality limits us, and such stories provide us not with blueprints but with visionary glimpses of how our real world could be changed. The new genre of transgressive utopian dystopia in particular distorts our bipolar picture of the world, questions in a unique way the current structure of our society and our relationships, and describes an imaginary new space. These texts compel us to filter our surroundings and to see those interstices of ontological reality that existed before, but which we chose to ignore. In many respects, these novels lift curtains, revealing exactly what the systems attacked have shrouded through various power politics, and renew the potential to desire a future that is not "a replica of today," as Russell Jacoby provocatively states.[2]

Transgressive utopian dystopias thus fulfil not merely an aesthetic function but also produce a valid social vision. They transport a (socio)political message, politicize, and initiate readers to a renewed awareness. Fern claims that utopian literature in general suffers from "its essentially hybrid nature" (1988, 454) and, therefore, produces neither a valid social vision nor an aesthetically fulfilling literary experience. Transgressive utopian dystopias contest Fern's claim. Hybrid by definition, it is exactly their multi-leveled transgressive approach that enables these texts to achieve both a political and an aesthetic impact. Instead of isolating politics and literature, it is the very tension between both that makes utopian, dystopian, and sf novels so very exciting and enriching. These dystopias engage the readers in utopia, because these novels do not give a guided tour of utopia but outline how a utopia transgressive of dualisms might be brought into existence. The reader thus becomes not an observer but a participating witness, and in his or her engagement with the literary text becomes a momentary member of utopia.

Precisely this engagement with the process of change produces in the reader a double perspective, a hybrid consciousness. As a hybrid literature, transgressive utopian dystopian fiction consequently demands of readers no less than an equally hybrid approach that by a leap of imagination displaces and suspends the normative worldview. We might not speak new languages, but we may approach words more critically. We might not become "sharemas" but can rethink the structure of childcare and the division of labor. Most of all, however, we can choose to leave behind the hierarchized binarisms that structure our lives and that more often than not give the short end of the stick to those who are deemed *other*. We can refuse taking the short end, or we can demand the possible: both ends and the middle part too. We can say, in the words of one of Russ's characters in *On Strike Against God* (1980), "I do not want a better deal. I do not want to make a deal at all. *I want it all*" (1980a, 18).

Transgressive utopian dystopian texts provide us with literary expressions of and reflections on cultural attitudes, our human potentialities, and social structures of the future. Such a literature dislodges binary logic, names and claims a *reality* of flux, of a continuum of different but equal aspects of a reality that we have so far not been able to perceive because we are conditioned to think in patterns of polarities. These books describe in literary terms what Daniel Singer advocates in

[2]*See the introduction (ii).*

terms of political agency: "our society contains the elements of its *potential* transformation, and in this interaction of the existing and the possible ... lies the burden of our responsibility and the mainspring of political action" (qtd. in Moylan 2000, 107). The aim of this new dystopian subgenre is, using Teresa de Lauretis's words, "the telling of new stories so as to *inscribe into the picture of reality* characters and events and resolutions that were previously invisible, untold, unspoken (and so unthinkable, unimaginable, 'impossible')" (11). It is a reality and a future that includes us all in a frame of difference and equality. Transgressive utopian dystopian fiction describes a vision that simply and effectively states, once more in the words of one of Russ's characters, "*Let's be reasonable. Let's demand the impossible*" (1980a, 107).

Appendix:
"First you are human"
An Interview with
Suzy McKee Charnas

At the 20th International Conference of the Fantastic in the Arts in Fort Lauderdale, Florida, in March 1999 I had the great pleasure to meet Suzy McKee Charnas and discuss my reading of the *Holdfast* tetralogy, a stimulating discussion that we continued via e-mail and at WisCon 24, Madison, Wisconsin, in May 2000, and again at the 22nd International Conference of the Fantastic in the Arts in Fort Lauderdale in March 2001, where I also had the opportunity to conduct an interview with Suzy. After an exhausting day, perched on a ridiculously uncomfortable chair in one of the stuffy conference rooms, Suzy patiently answered my many questions during a three-hour interview. The longer part of the interview has been published in *The New York Review of Science Fiction* (cf. Mohr 1999c, 1999d), whereas this previously unpublished shorter part of the interview, those questions that deal specifically with transgression and contain brief references to Atwood and Elgin, is printed here.

Contemporary feminist utopias, the British political scientist Lucy Sargisson argues, are transgressive. They resist closure and reject binary oppositions. These feminist utopias describe dynamic societies in the process and in the progress towards utopia. Transgressions involved are, for instance, self/other, human/animal, spirit/matter divisions. Would you consider the Holdfast *series or one of the books as feminist transgressive utopian dystopias, opting rather for* difference *and* equality than for difference *or* equality? *In contrast to what other critics wrote, I felt you were already opting to go beyond separatism and war with* Furies, *and emphasize that now in* Conqueror's Child.

CHARNAS: Certainly! I hope that is the culminating impression of the last book—that we have to get beyond simplistic dualism. We don't know how to deal with polarity. Every time we say here's an X and there's a Y and they are different from each other, we can't seem to resist saying also, X is *better* than Y, or vice versa. We can't seem to manage the idea of parity, let alone the parity among a number of different things rather than between two opposites or two degrees of the same thing. We gravitate toward seeing things in terms of the superiority of one and the inferiority of the other.

If you break down and destroy the definition that creates the polarity, maybe you have a chance of putting all that stuff out there on some plain of parity. Then you can see things not as better or worse than each other, yet not in equality either, if they aren't identical. Parity meaning that the two terms hold the same value, they are both valuable, one is not dominant over the other, or by definition better or worse.

I'd like my books to put into the readers' mind this idea: "Here are people trying not as equals but as potential partners of equal worth to make things come out better." They are indeed working towards this transgressive utopia, but haven't gotten there yet. At the end of *The Conqueror's Child*, the compartments that we put people into have not broken down. There are still men and women, there are some people in between, dark and light, young and old, people and animals, and they have not all merged to become the same thing. People reach across those boundaries, but they can't actually jump over and become the other.

When I started working on *Furies*, it took me a while to realize that it was really two books, not one. Before I could get to *Conqueror's Child*, which is about trying to get beyond separatism and war, as you phrased it, I would have to go through the separatism and war part, and that was *Furies*. By the end of that book some of the Free [Fems] are already reaching toward somewhere beyond separatism and war. They are tired of war. They fought hard, now they want the reward—which is something better than before and better than more war. In *Conqueror's Child*, they move forward a little bit, trying to attain this.

But I don't describe their utopia—I don't construct it but only hint in certain directions that they think might lead there—because I don't believe in perfection, not for human life. Only what's complete, what's finished changing, in other words what's dead is "perfect." And that's not much fun to write, or to read about. Of course that doesn't mean we shouldn't keep trying for improvement, once we see a way towards it. So my characters are left still dealing as best they can with what's left of the old ways, while trying to work out and create new and better ones. Maybe that is as close to utopia as a society like ours, one that values change, can actually come.

I read your novels as dystopias with a strong utopian undercurrent, a strife to create utopia without fixing it, with transgressions of the human/animal divide, self/other, male/female, master/slave oppositions, the mother/child dualism. Are these novels a clarion call to transgress all these dividing lines? A description of the intricately interwoven and linked rather than the clear cut and decisive?

CHARNAS: There is certainly an attempt to help people to blur the division lines, to take the energy we use in maintaining the division and use it for something constructive made by both parts that are being held apart by the barrier between them. It takes a lot of energy and resources to maintain those artificial boundaries over which you may not step because you are white or black, or a woman, or a man, or a person of one generation or another. The books attempt to show that if you can reach across some of those lines then you can reclaim that energy as a social and personal resource of great value and unimaginable potentiality.

I like to think that my work serves to encourage people to use their imaginations to see where in their real life they might be able stop treating artificial boundaries as absolute, suspend this mindset that on the one side is the superior, and on the other is the inferior, and see where that leads us.

You seem to call male and female humans to transgress supposedly feminine and masculine social gender roles and the connected behavior, to cut beyond the separatism, to be both, to be more to be truly human.

CHARNAS: Absolutely. There's no doubt about that. We've lost sight of the truly human. I think it's because there are so many of us, so we divide us into pieces to be able to deal with the sheer volume of contacts and connections. I can divide off some people into a category where I don't have to think of them much, because they're not-me, they're different; they're Chinese, or the very old, or silly yuppies or whatever, and I don't have anything crucial in common with them. So I don't have to deal with them one to one to one, which is exhausting; I make them into a category, and that immediately reduces their humanity, since to me I am the essence of "human" and they are not-me, they are "them." I think we all do this. You define other people away from you this way, until you reach a point where you're reasonably comfortable.

The basic division is along gender lines: men versus women. I'm not really sure we can dispense with that one ever, but we at least ought to think about where we can do without it; where we can consider ourselves as each one being a full human being with all of the human potentiality at their command with the exception of a few biological specifics in each case (although only two varieties of these doesn't even cover everybody).

I don't mean that each person expresses every human potentiality, but that each person has the potentiality to express everything, and they select what they will use and develop according to their character.

But everybody comes with the full complement: the aggression, the sentimentality, the lovingness, the fearfulness, the strength, you've got it all, whether you're male or female or something in-between. That's what I'm really after, that sense that a human being is a person first, and man and woman second, if not third or fourth. First you are human. If we could do that we'd be a lot better off.

Since I've left New York, I am very aware of the way we do face to face contacts, because when I grew up in New York City I had a couple of hundred contacts every day, of various levels of superficiality and depth. To be able to manage that, I decide that you are not a human being, you are the grocer from whom I have come to buy oranges. That way I don't have to deal with you as a person who comes with a whole panopy of concerns and possibilities and questions, fears, worries, and hopes. I can't deal with all that; if I had to do that with every single person I run into in a day I'll lose my mind.

So I push most people I meet each day aside, and I put them into a little box labeled with their function with regard to me, and I try to confine our interaction to what comes with that label, while the grocer is doing the same with me to preserve *her* sanity. We artificially put people in different places, denying their full humanity, because we can't deal with so many full humanities and still function ourselves. That's how we recognize a Messiah when he or she shows up—by their capacity to deal comfortably and fully with each person's humanity. Maybe it takes a God.

But I think we have to learn to do more of it than we do, especially across that first, basic line of sex and gender, if we're to reduce the most pervasive and destructive aspects of our behavior toward each other. It's not easy. It's not something that even fictional people—my fictional people, anyway—can accomplish fully and all the time even in one book. It takes four books just to achieve some glimpses, some moments of that kind of mutual recognition and respect.

In their complicity, the Matris of Walk *and* Furies *strike me as similar to the Aunts in* The Handmaid's Tale.

CHARNAS: Yes, both exemplify some women's complicity in the suppression of others so that they themselves can be a little less oppressed: the spectacle of co-optation. Cultural pressures are very strong to make you submit; where does submission become complicity? If a board comes down on my head and I fall down, am I being complicit in being knocked down, because I am not strong enough to let the board bounce off my head and stay standing?

But if I take the board from the oppressor's hand and turn around at his command and whack *you* over the head, that is sure as hell complicity. Yet it's hard to blame people for doing that (I am thinking of the Tibetan monks who were forced at gunpoint by invading Chinese soldiers to shoot and kill fellow monks) if the alternative is to be obliterated yourself. On the other hand, you'd better be aware starting out that your own people can be suborned to become not your allies but your enemies.

What about Suzette Haden Elgin's stance on language playing such an important part in the creation of reality?

CHARNAS: My version of that is my attention to the creation of history (and obviously I concur with her on the centrality of words and their meanings). All oppressed groups become very aware, I think, of the power of the language that is used to reduce and confine them.

Elgin has created the women's language Láadan. Do you think women need their own language?

CHARNAS: Well, if we conclude that we do, we'll have Elgin's creation to turn to; but I don't think it is likely to happen like that. Artificially created languages of any kind have a very hard time making it in the world even when the need seems to be great; look at Esperanto (so far, anyway).

Using the women linguists in the Native Tongue *series as her mouthpieces, Elgin claims that there are specific parts of reality have never existed because they have not been named. To make them visible and part of reality for everyone, we need to name them.*

CHARNAS: Well, that's what feminist writers are doing with the language we have, or trying to, anyway. Elgin is right, there are glaring omissions, but once such concepts are described and named for everyone, is that "women's language," especially? It becomes everyone's language; and I think the language I am most familiar with, English, is flexible and rich enough to fill the experiential gaps, if the will is there to do the necessary invention. But maybe someday we'll try the other route of a language for women only and see how that works out.

Do you consider the violence of the mind or of the body more immediate?

CHARNAS: I can't distinguish those except in specific circumstances. In Afghanistan right now physical violence seems to me to be more immediate than mental. If you go out without your veil the fanatics of the Taliban beat you, maybe even kill you.

In my own culture you get rude remarks if you walk around some places "inappropriately" dressed; you will *probably* not be beaten to death. But you may be shamed, or embarrassed or frightened, and that may seem just as painful because you start with the common assumption that you won't get beaten for letting your hair show. Where the violence of the body is prevalent, I think it's more immediate; where the violence of the mind is prevalent, then that is what's more immediate.

Bibliography

Primary Sources

Atwood, Margaret. *The Blind Assassin*. New York: Nan A. Talese, 2000.
_____. *The Circle Game*. 1966. Toronto: Anansi, 1978a.
_____. *The Handmaid's Tale*. 1985. Toronto: McClelland-Bantam, 1986.
_____. *Poems 1976–1986*. 1987. London: Virago, 1992.
_____. *Surfacing*. 1972. Toronto: General, 1983.
_____. *True Stories*. New York: Simon & Schuster, 1981.
_____. *Two-Headed Poems*. Toronto: Oxford University Press, 1978b.
Blake, William. *The Poems of William Blake*. Ed. John Sampson. London: Senate, 1995.
Carroll, Lewis. *Alice's Adventures in Wonderland & Through the Looking-Glass*. 1865. New York: Bantam, 1981.
Charnas, Suzy McKee. *The Conqueror's Child*. New York: Tor, 1999.
_____. *The Conqueror's Child*. ms. Private Collection Ron Larson. 1999.
_____. *The Furies*. New York: Tor, 1994.
_____. *Motherlines*. 1978. New York: Berkley, 1979.
_____. *The Vampire Tapestry*. 1980. Albuquerque, NM: Living Batch, 1994.
_____. *Walk to the End of the World*. 1974. London: Women's, 1989.
Elgin, Suzette Haden. *Earthsong*. New York: Daw, 1994.
_____. *The Judas Rose*. New York: Daw, 1987a.
_____. *Native Tongue*. New York: Daw, 1984.
Heinlein, Robert A. *The Moon Is a Harsh Mistress*. 1966. New York: St. Martin's, 1996.
Le Guin, Ursula K. *The Dispossessed*. New York: Avon, 1974.
_____. *The Left Hand of Darkness*. 1969. New York: Ace, 1972.
Poe, Edgar Allan. *The Complete Tales and Poems of Edgar Allan Poe*. Introd. Hervey Allen. New York: Modern Library, 1965.
Rand, Ayn. *Anthem*. 1938. New York: Signet, 1995.
Russ, Joanna. *On Strike Against God*. London: Women's, 1980a.
Wilhelm, Kate. *Juniper Time*. New York: Pocket, 1979.

Secondary Sources

Albinski, Nan Bowman. *Women's Utopias in British and American Fiction*. London: Routledge, 1988.

Aldiss, Brian, and David Wingrove. *Trillion Year Spree: The History of Science Fiction.* Rev. ed. New York: Atheneum, 1986.

Alridge, Alexandra. *The Scientific World View in Dystopia.* Ann Arbor: UMI, 1984.

Alva, Jorge J.K. de. "The Postcolonization of the (Latin) American Experience: A Reconsideration of 'Colonialism,' 'Postcolonialism' and 'Mestizaje.'" *After Colonialism, Imperial Histories and Postcolonial Displacements.* Ed. Gyan Prakash. Princeton: Princeton University Press, 1995, 241–275.

Anderson, Kristine J. "Places Where a Woman Could Talk: Ursula K. Le Guin and the Feminist Linguistic Utopia." *Women and Language* 15:1 (1992), 7–10.

———. "To Utopia via the Sapir-Whorf Hypothesis: Elgin's Láadan." *Utopian Studies III.* Eds. Michael S. Cummings and Nicholas D. Smith. Lanham, MD: University Press of America, 1991, 92–98.

Andriano, Joseph. "*The Handmaid's Tale* as Scrabble Game." *Essays on Canadian Writing* 48 (1992/1993), 89–96.

Ardener, Edwin. "Belief and the Problem of Women." *Perceiving Women.* Ed. Shirley Ardener. London: Malaby, 1975, 1–28.

Ardener, Shirley. "Introduction." *Perceiving Women.* Ed. Shirley Ardener. London: Malaby, 1975, vii–xxiii.

———. "Sexual Insult and Female Militancy." *Perceiving Women.* Ed. Shirley Ardener. London: Malaby. 1975, 29–54.

Armitt, Lucie. "Your Word Is My Command: The Structures of Language and Power in Women's Science Fiction." *Where No Man Has Gone Before: Women and Science Fiction.* Ed. Lucie Armitt. London: Routledge, 1991, 123–138.

Ashcroft, Bill, Gareth Griffiths, and Helen Tiffin. *The Post-Colonial Studies Reader.* London: 1995.

Asimov, Isaac. "Social Science Fiction." *Modern Science Fiction: Its Meaning and Its Future.* Ed. Reginald Bretnor. New York: Coward-McCann, 1953, 151–168.

Attebery, Brian. "Women Alone, Men Alone: Single-Sex Utopias." *Femspec* 1:2 (2000), 4–15.

Atwood, Margaret. "Margaret Atwood: 'There's Nothing in the Book That Hasn't Happened.'" *Quill & Quire* 51:9 (1985), 66.

———. *Second Words: Selected Critical Prose.* Toronto: Anansi, 1982.

———. *Survival: A Thematic Guide to Canadian Literature.* Toronto: Anansi, 1972.

Auerbach, Nina. *Communities of Women: An Idea in Fiction.* Cambridge, MA: Harvard University Press, 1978.

Baccolini, Raffaella. "Gender and Genre in the Feminist Critical Dystopias of Katherine Burdekin, Margaret Atwood, and Octavia Butler." *Future Females, the Next Generation: New Voices and Velocities in Feminist Science Fiction.* Ed. Marleen S. Barr. Boston: Rowman and Littlefield, 2000, 13–34.

Bagemihl, Bruce. *Biological Exuberance: Animal Homosexuality and Natural Diversity.* New York: St. Martin's, 1999.

Bailey, Richard W. *Images of English. A Cultural History of the Language.* Cambridge: Cambridge University Press, 1991.

Bammer, Angelika. *Partial Visions: Feminism and Utopianism in the 1970s.* London: Routledge, 1991.

Barnes, Myra Edwards. *Linguistics and Languages in Science Fiction-Fantasy.* New York: Arno, 1975.

Barnouw, Dagmar. *Die versuchte Realität oder von der Möglichkeit, glücklichere Welten zu denken.* Meitingen: Corian, 1985.

Barr, Marleen S. *Alien to Femininity: Speculative Fiction and Feminist Theory*. Westport, CT: Greenwood, 1987.
_____. *Feminist Fabulation: Space/Postmodern Fiction*. Iowa City: University of Iowa Press, 1992.
_____. *Lost in Space: Probing Feminist Science Fiction and Beyond*. Chapel Hill: University of North Carolina Press, 1993.
_____. "Utopia at the End of a Male Chauvinist Dystopian World: Suzy McKee Charnas's Feminist Science Fiction." *Women and Utopia: Critical Interpretations*. Eds. Marleen Barr and Nicholas D. Smith. Lanham, MD: University Press of America, 1983, 43–66.
_____, ed. *Future Females, The Next Generation: New Voices and Velocities in Feminist Science Fiction Criticism*. Lanham, MD: Rowman & Littlefield, 2000.
Bartkowski, Frances. *Feminist Utopias*. Lincoln: University of Nebraska Press, 1989.
Baruch, Elaine Hoffman. "Women in Men's Utopias." *Women in Search of Utopia, Mavericks and Mythmakers*. Eds. Ruby Rohrlich and Elaine Hoffman Baruch. New York: Schocken, 1984, 209–218.
Bazin, Nancy Topping. "Women and Revolution in Dystopian Fiction: Nadine Gordimer's *July People* and Margaret Atwood's *The Handmaid's Tale*." *Selected Essays: International Conference on Representing Revolution, 1989*. Ed. John Michael Crafton. Carrolton: West Georgia College, 1991, 116–127.
Beauchamp, Gorman. "Of Man's Last Disobedience: Zamiatin's *We* and Orwell's *1984*." *Comparative Literature Studies* 10 (1973), 285–301.
_____. "Technology in the Dystopian Novel." *Modern Fiction Studies* 32:1 (1986), 53–63.
Berghahn, Klaus L., and Hans Ulrich Seeber (eds.). *Literarische Utopien von Morus bis zur Gegenwart*. Königstein. Athenäum, 1983.
Bergmann, Harriet F. "Teaching Them to Read: A Fishing Expedition in *The Handmaid's Tale*." *College English* 51:8 (1989), 847–854.
Bergonzi, Bernard. *The Early H.G. Wells: A Study of the Scientific Romances*. Manchester: Manchester University Press, 1961.
Bhabha, Homi K. *The Location of Culture*. London: Routledge, 1994b.
_____. "Of Mimicry and Man: The Ambivalence of Colonial Discourse." *October* 28:1 (1984), 125–133.
_____. "Remembering Fanon: Self, Psyche and the Colonial Condition." *Colonial Discourse and Postcolonial Theory*. Eds. Patrick Williams and Laura Chrisman. New York: Columbia University Press, 1994a, 112–123.
Biesterfeld, Wolfgang. *Die literarische Utopie*. Stuttgart: Metzler, 1982.
Bleich, David. *Utopia: The Psychology of a Cultural Fantasy*. Ann Arbor: UMI, 1984.
Bloch, Ernst. *The Principle of Hope*. 3 vols. 1957. Oxford: Blackwell, 1986.
Blunt, Alison, and Gillian Rose. "Introduction: Women's Colonial and Postcolonial Geographies." *Writing Women and Space: Colonial and Postcolonial Geographies*. Eds. Alison Blunt and Gillian Rose. New York: Guilford, 1994, 1–25.
Bolinger, Dwight. *Language: The Loaded Weapon*. London: Longman, 1980.
Boltz, Carol J., and Dorothy U. Seyler. *Language Power*. New York: Random, 1982.
Booker, M. Keith. *Dystopian Literature: A Theory and Research Guide*. Westport, CT: Greenwood, 1994.
Bouson, J. Brooks. *Brutal Choreographies: Oppositional Strategies and Narrative*

Design in the Novels of Margaret Atwood. Amherst: University of Massachusetts Press, 1993.
Brans, Jo. "Using What You're Given." *Margaret Atwood: Conversations.* Ed. Earl G. Ingersoll. Willowdale: Firefly, 1990, 140–151.
Bray, Mary Kay. "The Naming of Things: Men, Women, Language and Reality in Suzette Haden Elgin's *Native Tongue.*" *Extrapolation* 27:1 (1986), 49–61.
Broderick, Damien. *Reading by Starlight: Postmodern Science Fiction.* London: Routledge, 1995.
Bronfen, Elisabeth. *Over Her Dead Body: Death, Femininity and the Aesthetic.* Manchester: Manchester University Press, 1992.
Brown, R. *Words and Things.* Glencoe, IL: Free, 1958.
Burack, Cynthia. "Bringing Women's Studies to Political Science: *The Handmaid's Tale* in the Classroom." *NWSA Journal* 1:2 (1988/1989), 274–283.
Butler, Judith. *Gender Trouble: Feminism and the Subversion of Identity.* London: Routledge, 1990.
Cadora, Karen. "Feminist Cyberpunk." *Science-Fiction Studies* 22:3 (1995), 357–372.
Caldwell, Larry W. "Wells, Orwell, and Atwood: (EPI)Logic and Eu/utopia." *Extrapolation* 33:4 (1992), 333–345.
Cameron, Deborah. *Feminism and Linguistic Theory.* London: Macmillan, 1985.
_____. (ed.). *The Feminist Critique of Language: A Reader.* London: Routledge, 1990.
Caminero-Santangelo, Marta. "Moving Beyond 'The Blank White Spaces': Atwood's Gilead, Postmodernism, and Strategic Resistance." *Studies in Canadian Literature* 19:1 (1994), 20–42.
Carrington, Ildikó de Papp. "Margaret Atwood." *Canadian Writers and Their Works.* Eds. Robert Lecker, Jack David, and Ellen Quigley. Vol. 9. Toronto: ECW, 1987a, 25–116.
_____. "A Swiftian Sermon." *Essays on Canadian Writing* 34 (1987b), 127–132.
Carroll, John B. *Language and Thought.* Englewood Cliffs: Prentice-Hall, 1964.
Cavalcanti, Ildney. "The Profession of Science Fiction, 52: A Literature of *Unusual* Ideas." Interview with Suzy McKee Charnas. *Foundation* 72 (1998), 5–19.
Césaire, Aimé. *Discourse on Colonialism.* 1950. New York: Monthly Review, 1972.
Charnas, Suzy McKee. "No-Road." *Women of Vision.* Ed. Denise DuPont. New York: St. Martin's, 1988, 143–163.
_____. "A Woman Appeared." *Future Females: A Critical Anthology.* Ed. Marleen S. Barr. Bowling Green: Bowling Green State University Popular, 1981, 103–108.
Chen, Zhongming. "Theorising About New Modes of Representation and Ideology in the Postmodern Age: The Practice of Margaret Atwood and Li Ang." *Canadian Review of Comparative Literature* 21:3 (1994), 341–354.
Chodorow, Nancy. *The Reproduction of Mothering: Psychoanalysis and the Sociology of Gender.* Berkley: University of California Press, 1978.
Cixous, Hélène, and Catherine Clement. "The Laugh of the Medusa." *Signs* 1:4 (1976), 875–893.
_____. *The Newly Born Woman.* Manchester: Manchester University Press, 1986, 80–81. Originally pub. as *La Jeune Née.* Paris: Union Generale d'Editions, 1975.
Clemente, Bill. "Apprehending Identity in the Alldera Novels of Suzy McKee

Charnas: Intersection of Feminist Science Fiction and Postcolonial Studies." *The Utopian Fantastic: Selected Essays from the Twentieth International Conference on the Fantastic in the Arts.* Ed. Martha Bartter. Westport, CT: Greenwood, 2004, 81–90.

_____. "Of Women and Wonder: A Conversation with Suzy McKee Charnas." *Women of Other Worlds: Excursions Through Science Fiction and Feminisms.* Eds. Helen Merrick and Tess Williams. Nedlands: University of Western Australia Press, 1999, 60–81.

Clute, John, and Peter Nicholls (eds.). *The Encyclopedia of Science Fiction.* New York: St. Martin's, 1995.

Cooke, Nathalie. *Margaret Atwood: A Biography.* Toronto: ECW, 1998.

Cortiel, Jeanne. *Demand My Writing: Joanna Russ, Feminism, Science Fiction.* Liverpool: Liverpool University Press, 1999.

Cranny-Francis, Anne. "Man-Made Monsters: Suzy McKee Charnas's *Walk to the End of the World* as Dystopian Feminist Science Fiction." *Science Fiction Roots and Branches: Contemporary Critical Approaches.* Eds. Rhys Garnett and R.J. Ellis. London: Macmillan, 1990, 183–206.

Daly, Mary. *Gyn/Ecology: The Metaethics of Radical Feminism.* 1979. London: Women's, 1987.

_____, and Jane Caputi. *Websters' First New Intergalactic Wickedary of the English Language.* Boston: Beacon, 1987.

Davey, Frank. *Margaret Atwood: A Feminist Poetics.* Vancouver: Talon, 1984.

Deer, Glenn. "Rhetorical Strategies in *The Handmaid's Tale*: Dystopia and the Paradoxes of Power." *English Studies in Canada* 18:2 (1992), 215–233.

de la Concha, Angelas. "The Female Body: A Resonant Voice in the Multicultural Scene." *Gender, I-deology: Essays on Theory, Fiction and Film.* Eds. Chantal Cornut-Gentille D'Arcy and José Ángel García Landa. Amsterdam: Rodopi, 1996, 55–72.

Delaney, Samuel R. *The Jewel-Hinged Jaw: Notes on the Language of Science Fiction.* Elizabethtown, NY: Dragon, 1977.

_____. *Starboard Wine: More Notes on the Language of Science Fiction.* Pleasantville, NY: Dragon, 1984.

de Lauretis, Teresa. "Feminist Studies/Critical Studies: Issues, Terms, and Contexts." *Feminist Studies/Critical Studies.* Ed. Teresa de Lauretis. Bloomington: Indiana University Press, 1986, 2–19.

Derrida, Jacques. "Signature Event Context." Trans. Samuel Weber and Jeffrey Mehlman. *Glyph* 1 (1977), 172–197.

Devine, Maureen. "*Woman on the Edge of Time* and *The Wanderground*: Visions in Eco-Feminist Utopias." *Utopian Thought in American Literature: Untersuchungen zur literarischen Utopie und Dystopie in den USA.* Eds. Arno Heller, Walter Hölbling, and Waldemar Zacharasiewicz. Tübingen: Narr, 1988, 131–145.

Dick, Philip K. *The Short Happy Life of the Brown Oxford.* New York: Carol, 1990.

Donawerth, Jane. *Frankenstein's Daughters: Women Writing Science Fiction.* Syracuse: Syracuse University Press, 1997.

_____, and Carol Kolmerten (eds.). *Utopian and Science Fiction by Women: Worlds of Difference.* Syracuse: Syracuse University Press, 1994.

Dopp, Jamie. "Subject-Position as Victim-Position in *The Handmaid's Tale*." *Studies in Canadian Literature* 19:1 (1994), 43–57.

DuPlessis, Rachel Blau. *Writing Beyond the Ending: Narrative Strategies of Twentieth-Century Women Writers.* Bloomington: Indiana University Press, 1985.

DuPont, Denise. "Interview. Suzette Haden Elgin." *Women of Vision*. Ed. Denise DuPont. New York: St. Martin's, 1988, 59–68.

Edwards, Lee R. *Psyche as Hero: Female Heroism and Fictional Form*. Middletown: Wesleyan University Press, 1984.

Ehrenreich, Barbara. "Feminism's Phantoms." *New Republic* 17 March 1986, 33–35.

Ehrlich, Susan. "Critical Linguistics as Feminist Methodology." *Changing Methods: Feminists Transforming Practice*. Eds. Sandra Burt and Lorraine Code. Peterborough: Broadview, 1995, 45–74.

Elgin, Suzette Haden. "Another Plea for Quality Control." *Linguistics & Science Fiction* 17:6 (1998), 1–2.

———. "A Conversation with Suzette Elgin." *The Monthly Aspectarian: The Magazine for the New Age*, Worldwide ed. Online. Internet. Jan. 1996. http://www.lightworks.com/MonthlyAspectarian/ [Accessed 28.9.1998]

———. "A Feminist Is a What?" *Women and Language* 18:2 (1995), 46.

———. *A First Dictionary and Grammar of Láadan*. Ed. Diane Martin. Madison, WI: Society for the Furtherance and Study of Fantasy and Science Fiction, 1988b.

———. *Genderspeak: Men, Women and the Gentle Art of Verbal Self-Defense*. Englewood Cliffs, NJ: Prentice-Hall, 1993.

———. *The Last Word on the Gentle Art of Verbal Self-Defense*. New York: Prentice-Hall, 1987c.

———. "Report on a Thought Experiment." *Linguistics & Science Fiction* 13:9 (1994), 17–20.

———. "Some Proposed Additions to the Glossary of Needed Lexical Items for the Expression of Women's Perceptions." *The Lonesome Node* 1:1 (1981). Online. Internet. http://www. [Accessed: 20.8.1998]

———. "Washing Utopian Dishes; Scrubbing Utopian Floors." *Women and Language* 17:1 (1992), 43–47.

———. "Women's Language and Near Future Science Fiction: A Reply." *Women's Studies* 14 (1987b), 175–181.

Elliott, Robert C. "Literature and the Good Life: A Dilemma." *Yale Review* 65 (1975), 24–37.

———. *The Shape of Utopia: Studies in a Literary Genre*. Chicago: University of Chicago, 1970.

Emberley, Julia. *Thresholds of Difference: Feminist Critique, Native Women's Writings, Postcolonial Theory*. Toronto: Toronto University Press, 1993.

Eschholz, Paul, Alfred Rosa, and Virginia Clark (eds.). *Language Awareness*. New York: St. Martin's, 1982.

Evans, Mark. "Versions of History: *The Handmaid's Tale* and Its Dedicatees." *Margaret Atwood: Writing and Subjectivity*. Ed. Colin Nicholson. London: Macmillan, 1994, 177–188.

Faludi, Susan. *Backlash: The Undeclared War Against American Women*. New York: Anchor, 1991.

———. *Stiffed: The Betrayal of the American Man*. New York: William Morrow, 1999.

Fanon, Frantz. *Black Skins, White Masks*. New York: Grove, 1967.

Farley, Tucker. "Realities and Fictions: Lesbian Visions of Utopia." *Women in Search of Utopia, Mavericks and Mythmakers*. Eds. Ruby Rohrlich and Elaine Hoffman Baruch. New York: Schocken, 1984, 219–232.

Fehlner, Gert. *Literarische Utopien als Reflexion und Kritik amerikanischer Wirklichkeit: Ausgewählte Beispiele seit den 60er Jahren*. Meitingen: Corian, 1989.

Ferns, Chris. "Dreams of Freedom: Ideology and Narrative Structure in the Utopian Fictions of Marge Piercy and Ursula Le Guin." *English Studies in Canada* 15 (1988), 453–466.

———. *Narrating Utopia: Ideology, Gender, Form in Utopian Literature.* Liverpool: Liverpool University Press, 1999.

Filipczak, Dorota. "Is There No Balm in Gilead?—Biblical Intertext in *The Handmaid's Tale.*" *Journal of Literature & Theology* 7:2 (1993), 171–185.

Finnell, Susanna. "Unwriting the Quest: Margaret Atwood's Fiction and *The Handmaid's Tale.*" *Women and the Journey: The Female Travel Experience.* Eds. Bonnie Frederick and Susan H. McLeod. Pullman: Washington State University Press, 1993, 199–215.

Firestone, Shulamith. *The Dialectic of Sex: The Case for Feminist Revolution.* 1970. New York: Bantam, 1972.

Fitting, Peter. "Recent Feminist Utopias: World Building and Strategies for Social Change." *Mindscapes: The Geographies of Imagined Worlds.* Eds. George E. Slusser and Eric S. Rabkin. Carbondale/Edwardsville: Southern Illinois University Press, 1989, 155–163.

———. "Reconsiderations of the Separatist Paradigm in Recent Feminist Science Fiction." *Science-Fiction Studies* 19:1 (1992), 32–48.

———. "'So We All Became Mothers:' New Roles for Men in Recent Utopian Fiction." *Science-Fiction Studies* 12:2 (1985), 156–183.

Florence, Penny. "The Liberation of Utopia or Note Why Feminist Science Fiction Is a Means to the End of the Possibility that Feminist SF in the Ideal Literary Form." *Plotting Change: Contemporary Women's Fiction.* Ed. Linda Anderson. London: Edward Arnold, 1990, 64–83.

Foley, Michael. "Satiric Intent in the 'Historical Notes' Epilogue of Margaret Atwood's *The Handmaid's Tale.*" *Commonwealth Essays and Studies* 11:2 (1989), 44–52.

Foucault, Michel. *Discipline and Punish: The Birth of the Prison.* New York: Random, 1979a.

———. "Of Other Spaces." *Diacritics* 16 (1986), 22–27.

———. "Truth and Power: An Interview with Alessandro Fontano and Pasquale Pasquino." *Michel Foucault: Power, Truth, Strategy.* Eds. Meaghan Morris and Paul Patton. Sydney: Feral, 1979b, 29–48.

Foust, R.E. "A Limited Perfection: Dystopia as Logos Game." *Mosaic* 15:3 (1982), 79–88.

Freibert, Lucy M. "Control and Creativity: The Politics of Risk in Margaret Atwood's *The Handmaid's Tale.*" *Critical Essays on Margaret Atwood.* Ed. Judith McComb. Boston: G.K. Hall, 1988, 280–291.

Friedan, Betty. *The Feminine Mystique.* 1963. Harmondsworth: Penguin, 1982.

———. *The Second Stage.* London: Sphere, 1983.

Friend, Beverly. "Virgin Territory: The Bonds and Boundaries of Women in Science Fiction." *Many Futures, Many Worlds: Theme and Form in Science Fiction.* Ed. Thomas D. Clareson. Kent, OH: Kent State University Press, 1977, 140–163.

Frye, Northrop. *Anatomy of Criticism.* Princeton: Princeton University Press, 1957.

———. "Varieties of Literary Utopia." *Utopias and Utopian Thought.* Ed. Frank E. Manuel. Boston: Houghton Mifflin, 1966, 25–49.

Fukuyama, Francis. *The End of History and the Last Man.* New York: Free, 1992.

Garlick, Barbara. "*The Handmaid's Tale*: Narrative Voice and the Primacy of the

Tale." *Twentieth-Century Fantasists: Essays on Culture, Society and Belief in Twentieth-Century Mythopoeic Literature.* Ed. Kath Filmer. New York: St. Martin's, 1992, 161–171.

Gearhart, Sally Miller. "Future Vision: Today's Politics: Feminist Utopias in Review." *Women in Search of Utopia, Mavericks and Mythmakers.* Eds. Ruby Rohrlich and Elaine Hoffman Baruch. New York: Schocken, 1984, 296–309.

Gilbert, Sandra M., and Susan Gubar. "Sexual Linguistics: Gender, Language, Sexuality." *New Literary History* 16 (1985), 515–543.

Givner, Jessie. "Names, Faces and Signatures in Margaret Atwood's 'Cat's Eye' and 'The Handmaid's Tale.'" *Canadian Literature* 133 (1992), 56–75.

Gnüg, Hiltrud. *Utopie und utopischer Roman.* Stuttgart: Reclam, 1999.

Gordon, Joan. "Closed Systems Kill: An Interview with Suzy McKee Charnas." *Science Fiction Studies* 26:3 (1999), 447–467.

Gough, Val. "Commentaries on *Native Tongue*." *Foundation* 79 (2000), 35–36.

Grace, George W. *The Linguistic Construction of Reality.* London: Croom Helm, 1987.

Grace, Sherrill E. "Articulating the 'Space Between': Atwood's Untold Stories and Fresh Beginnings." *Margaret Atwood: Language, Text and System.* Eds. Sherrill E. Grace and Lorraine Weir. Vancouver: University of British Columbia Press, 1983, 1–16.

──────. "Margaret Atwood and the Politics of Duplicity." *The Art of Margaret Atwood: Essays in Criticism.* Eds. Arnold Davidson and Cathy E. Davidson. Toronto: Anansi, 1981, 55–68.

──────. *Violent Duality: A Study of Margaret Atwood.* Montréal: Véhicule, 1980.

Graves, Robert. *The Greek Myths.* New York: Penguin, 1955.

Green, Michelle Erica. "There Goes the Neighborhood: Octavia Butler's Demand for Diversity in Utopias." *Utopian and Science Fiction by Women: Worlds of Difference.* Eds. Jane L. Donawerth and Carol Kolmerten. Syracuse: Syracuse University Press, 1994, 166–190.

Grossmann, Kathryn M. "Woman as Temptress: The Way to (Br)otherhood in Science Fiction Dystopias." *Women's Studies: An Interdisciplinary Journal* 14:2 (1987), 135–145.

Grosz, Elisabeth. "A Note on Essentialism and Difference." *Feminist Knowledge: Critique—And Construct.* Ed. Sneja Gunew. London: Routledge, 1990, 332–344.

Guha, Ranajit, and Gayatri Chakravorty (eds.). *Selected Subaltern Studies.* New York: Oxford University Press, 1988.

Hall, Stuart. "Cultural Identity and Diaspora." *Colonial Discourse and Postcolonial Theory.* Eds. Patrick Williams and Laura Chrisman. New York: Columbia University Press, 1994, 392–403.

Hammer, Stephanie Barbé. "The World as It Will Be? Female Satire and the Technology of Power in *The Handmaid's Tale*." *Modern Language Studies* 20:2 (1990), 39–49.

Hansen, Elaine Tuttle. "Mothers Tomorrow and Mothers Yesterday, but Never Mothers Today: *Woman on the Edge of Time* and *The Handmaid's Tale*." *Narrating Mothers: Theorizing Maternal Subjectivities.* Eds. Brenda O. Daly and Maureen T. Reddy. Knoxville: University of Tennessee Press, 1991, 21–43.

Haraway, Donna J. *Simians, Cyborgs, and Women: The Reinvention of Nature.* New York: Routledge, 1991.

Harper, Mary Catherine. "Incurably Alien Other: A Case for Feminist Cyborg Writers." *Science-Fiction Studies* 22:3 (1995), 399–420.
Haschak, Paul G. *Utopian/Dystopian Literature: A Bibliography of Literary Criticism*. Metuchen, NJ: Scarecrow, 1994.
Heller, Arno. "Die literarische Dystopie in Amerika mit einer exemplarischen Erörterung von Margaret Atwoods *The Handmaid's Tale*." *Utopian Thought in American Literature: Untersuchungen zur literarischen Utopie und Dystopie in den USA*. Eds. Arno Heller, Walter Hölbling, and Waldemar Zacharasiewicz. Tübingen: Narr, 1988, 185–204.
_____, Walter Hölbling, and Waldemar Zacharasiewicz (eds.). *Utopian Thought in American Literature: Untersuchungen zur literarischen Utopie und Dystopie in den USA*. Tübingen: Narr, 1988.
Hengen, Shannon. *Margaret Atwood's Power: Mirrors, Reflections and Images in Select Fiction and Poetry*. Toronto: Second Story, 1993.
Heuermann, Hartmut, and Bernd-Peter Lange (eds.). *Die Utopie in der angloamerikanischen Literatur: Interpretationen*. Düsseldorf: Bagel, 1984.
Hillegas, Mark R. *The Future as Nightmare: H.G. Wells and the Anti-Utopians*. New York: Oxford University Press, 1967.
Hockett, Charles F. "Chinese Versus English: An Exploration of the Whorfian Theses (II)." *Language and Culture: A Reader*. Eds. Patrick Gleeson and Nancy Wakefield. Columbus, OH: Charles E. Merrill, 1968, 120–142.
Hofstadter, Douglas R. *Gödel, Escher, Bach: An Eternal Golden Braid*. New York: Vintage, 1979.
Holland-Cunz, Barbara (ed.). *Feministische Utopien: Aufbruch in die postpatriarchale Gesellschaft*. Meitingen: Corian, 1986.
_____. *Utopien der neuen Frauenbewegung: Gesellschaftentwürfe im Kontext feministischer Theorie und Praxis*. Meitingen: Corian, 1988.
Hollinger, Veronica. "Putting on the Feminine: Gender and Negativity in *Frankenstein* and *The Handmaid's Tale*." *Negation, Critical Theory, and Postmodern Textuality*. Ed. Daniel Fischlin. Dordrecht: Kluwer, 1994, 203–224.
Howells, Coral Ann. "Free-Dom, Telling, Dignidad: Margaret Laurence, 'A Gourdful of Glory,' Margaret Atwood, *The Handmaid's Tale*, Sarah Murphy, *The Measure of Miranda*." *Commonwealth Essays and Studies* 12:1 (1989), 39–46.
_____. *Margaret Atwood*. London: Macmillan, 1996.
Hudson, Richard A. *Sociolinguistics*. Cambridge: Cambridge University Press, 1984.
Huggan, Graham. "Decolonizing the Map: Post-Colonialism, Post-Structuralism and the Cartographic Connection." *Past the Last Post: Theorizing Post-Colonialism and Post-Modernism*. Eds. Ian Adam and Helen Tiffin. London: Harvester Wheatsheaf, 1991, 125–138.
Hutcheon, Linda. *The Canadian Postmodern: A Study of Contemporary English-Canadian Fiction*. Toronto: Oxford University Press, 1988.
_____. "Circling the Downspout of Empire." *Past the Last Post: Theorizing Post-Colonialism and Post-Modernism*. Eds. Ian Adam and Helen Tiffin. London: Harvester Wheatsheaf, 1991, 167–189.
Ingersoll, Earl. "Margaret Atwood's '*The Handmaid's Tale*': Echoes of Orwell." *Journal of the Fantastic in the Arts* 5:4 (1993), 64–72.
Irigaray, Luce. *Je, Tu, Nous: Towards a Culture of Difference*. Trans. Alison Martin. London: Routledge, 1993.
_____. "Women's Exile." Interview. *Ideology and Consciousness* 1 (1976), 62–76.

Jackson, Rosemary. *Fantasy: The Literature of Subversion*. London: Methuen, 1981.
Jacoby, Russell. *The End of Utopia: Politics and Culture in an Age of Apathy*. New York: Basic, 1999.
Jameson, Frederic. *Postmodernism, or, The Cultural Logic of Late Capitalism*. Durham, NC: Duke University Press, 1991.
_____. "Science Fiction as a Spatial Genre: Generic Discontinuities and the Problem of Figuration in Vonda McIntyre's *The Exile Waiting*." *Science-Fiction Studies* 14:1 (1987), 44–59.
JanMohamed, Abdul R. "The Economy of Manichean Allegory: The Function of Racial Difference in Colonialist Literature." *Critical Inquiry* 12 (1985), 59–87.
Jones, Dorothy. "Not Much Balm in Gilead." *Commonwealth Essays and Studies* 11:2 (1989), 31–43.
Jones, Gwyneth. *Deconstructing the Starships: Science, Fiction and Reality*. Liverpool: Liverpool University Press, 1999.
Jones, Libby Falk, and Sarah Webster Goodwin (eds.). *Feminism, Utopia, and Narrative*. Knoxville: University of Tennessee Press, 1990.
Kaler, Anne K. "'A Sister, Dipped in Blood': Satiric Inversion of the Formation Techniques of Women Religious in Margaret Atwood's Novel *The Handmaid's Tale*." *Christianity and Literature* 38:2 (1989), 43–62.
Kaminski, Margaret. "Preserving Mythologies." *Margaret Atwood: Conversations*. Ed. Earl G. Ingersoll. Willowdale: Firefly, 1990, 27–32.
Kanneh, Kadiatu. "Feminism and the Colonial Body." *The Post-Colonial Studies Reader*. Eds. Bill Ashcroft, Gareth Griffiths, and Helen Tiffin. London: Routledge, 1995, 346–348.
Kateb, George. *Utopia and Its Enemies*. New York: Schocken, 1972.
Kauffman, Linda. "Special Delivery. Twenty-first Century Epistolarity in *The Handmaid's Tale*." *Writing the Female Voice: Essays on Epistolary Literature*. Ed. Elizabeth C. Goldsmith. Boston: Northeastern University Press, 1989, 221–244.
Kaveney, Roz. "The Science Fictiveness of Women's Science Fiction." *From My Guy to Sci-Fi: Genre and Women's Writing in the Postmodern World*. Ed. Helen Carr. London: Pandora, 1989.
Keinhorst, Annette. *Utopien von Frauen in der zeitgenössischen Literatur der USA*. Frankfurt a.M.: Lang, 1985.
Keith, W.J. "Apocalyptic Imaginations: Notes on Atwood's *The Handmaid's Tale* and Findley's *Not Wanted on the Voyage*." *Essays on Canadian Writing* 35 (1987), 123–134.
Kessler, Carol Farley (ed.). *Daring to Dream: Utopian Stories by United States Women: 1836–1919*. Boston: Pandora, 1984.
Ketterer, David. *Canadian Science Fiction and Fantasy*. Bloomington: Indiana University Press, 1992.
_____. "Margaret Atwood's *The Handmaid's Tale*: A Contextual Dystopia." *Science-Fiction Studies* 16:2 (1989), 209–217.
Khanna, Lee Cullen. "Women's Utopias." *Feminism, Utopia, and Narrative*. Eds. Libby Falk Jones and Sarah Webster Goodwin. Knoxville: University of Tennessee Press, 1990, 130–140.
King, Betty. *Women of the Future: The Female Character in Science Fiction*. Metuchen, NJ: Scarecrow, 1984.
King, Maureen. "Contemporary Women Writers and the 'New Evil': The Vampires of Anne Rice and Suzy McKee Charnas." *Journal of the Fantastic in the Arts* 5:3 (1993), 75–84.

Klarer, Mario. *Frau und Utopie: Feministische Literaturtheorie und utopischer Diskurs im anglo-amerikanischen Roman.* Darmstadt: Wissenschaftliche Buchgesellschaft, 1993.

———. "The Gender of Orality and Literacy in Margaret Atwood's *The Handmaid's Tale.*" *AAA—Arbeiten aus Anglistik und Amerikanistik* 15:2 (1990), 151–170.

———. "Orality and Literacy as Gender-Supporting Structures in Margaret Atwood's *The Handmaid's Tale.*" *Mosaic* 28:4 (1995), 129–142.

Kramarae, Cheris. "Present Problems with the Language of the Future." *Women's Studies* 14 (1987), 183–186.

———. *Women and Men Speaking.* Rowley, MA: Newbury House, 1981.

Kress, Gunther, and Robert Hodge. *Language as Ideology.* London: Routledge, 1979.

Kristeva, Julia. *Desire in Language: A Semiotic Approach to Literature and Art.* Ed. Léon S. Roudiez. Trans. Alice Jardine, Thomas Gora, and Léon S. Roudiez. New York: Columbia University Press, 1980.

Kumar, Krishan. *Utopia and Anti-Utopia in Modern Times.* Oxford: Blackwell, 1987.

———. *Utopianism.* Buckingham: Open University Press, 1991.

Lacombe, Michele. "The Writing on the Wall: Amputated Speech in Margaret Atwood's *The Handmaid's Tale.*" *Wascana Review* 21:2 (1986), 3–20.

Lanser, Susan Sniader. *Fictions of Authority: Women Writers and Narrative Voices.* Ithaca, NY: Cornell University Press, 1992.

Larson, Janet L. "Margaret Atwood and the Future of Prophecy." *Religion and Literature* 21:1 (1989), 27–61.

LeBihan, Jill. "*The Handmaid's Tale, Cat's Eye* and *Interlunar*: Margaret Atwood's Feminist (?) Futures (?)." *Narrative Strategies in Canadian Literature: Feminism and Postcolonialism.* Eds. Coral A. Howells and Lynette Hunter. Buckingham: Open University Press, 1991, 93–107.

Leblanc, Lauraine. "Razor Girls: Genre and Gender in Cyberpunk Fiction." *Women and Language* 20:1 (1997), 71–76.

Lecker, Robert. "Janus Through the Looking Glass: Atwood's First Three Novels." *The Art of Margaret Atwood: Essays in Criticism.* Eds. Arnold Davidson and Cathy E. Davidson. Toronto: Anansi, 1981, 177–203.

Lefanu, Sarah. *Feminism and Science Fiction.* Bloomington: Indiana University Press, 1989.

Le Guin, Ursula K. "American SF and the Other." *Science-Fiction Studies* 2 (1975), 208–210.

———. "Is Gender Necessary?" *The Language of the Night: Essays on Fantasy and Science Fiction.* Ed. Susan Wood. New York: Putnam, 1979b, 161–169.

———. "Science Fiction and Mrs. Brown." *The Language of the Night: Essays on Fantasy and Science Fiction.* Ed. Susan Wood. New York: Putnam, 1979a, 101–119.

Levitas, Ruth. *The Concept of Utopia.* London: Philipp Allan, 1990.

Lewis, Arthur O. "The Anti-Utopian Novel: Preliminary Notes and Checklist." *Extrapolation* 2:2 (1961), 27–32.

Loomba, Ania. *Colonialism/Postcolonialism.* London: Routledge, 1998.

Lorde, Audre. "An Open Letter to Mary Daly." *This Bridge Called My Back: Radical Writings by Women of Color.* Eds. Cherrie Moraga and Gloria Anzaldúa. Lathan, NY: Women of Color, 1983, 94–97.

———. *Sister Outsider: Essays and Speeches.* Trumansburg, NY: Crossing, 1984.

Lyons, Bonnie. "Using Other People's Dreadful Childhoods." *Margaret Atwood: Conversations*. Ed. Earl G. Ingersoll. Willowdale: Firefly, 1990, 221–233.
Malak, Amin. "Margaret Atwood's *The Handmaid's Tale* and the Dystopian Tradition." *Canadian Literature* 112 (1987), 9–17.
Mannheim, Karl. *Ideology and Utopia*. New York: Harcourt, 1936.
Manuel, Frank E., and Fritzie P. Manuel. *Utopian Thought in the Western Word*. Cambridge: Belknap, 1979.
McClintock, Anne. "The Angel of Progress: Pitfalls of the Term 'Postcolonialism.'" *Colonial Discourse/Postcolonial Theory*. Eds. Francis Barker, Peter Hulme, and Margaret Iversen. Manchester: Manchester University Press, 1994, 253–266.
McHale, Brian. "Elements of a Poetics of Cyberpunk." *Critique* 33:3 (1992), 149–175.
_____. *Postmodernist Fiction*. New York: Methuen, 1987.
Mead, Margaret. "Towards More Vivid Utopias." *Utopia*. Ed. George Kateb. New York: Atherton, 1971.
Meyers, Walter E. *Aliens and Linguistics: Language Study and Science Fiction*. Athens: University of Georgia, 1980.
Mezciems, Jenny. "Swift and Orwell: Utopia as Nightmare." *Between Dream and Nature: Essays on Utopia and Dystopia*. Eds. Dominic Baker-Smith and C.C. Barfoot. Amsterdam: Rodopi, 1987, 91–112.
Mihailescu, Calin Andrei. "Mind the Gap: Dystopia as Fiction." *Style* 25:2 (1991), 211–222.
Miller, Casey, and Kate Swift. *The Handbook of Non-Sexist Writing for Writers, Editors and Speakers*. Rev. ed. London: Women's, 1980.
Miller, Margaret. "The Ideal Woman in Two Feminist Science-Fiction Utopias." *Science-Fiction Studies* 10:2 (1983), 191–198.
Miner, Madonne. "'Trust Me': Reading the Romance Plot in Margaret Atwood's *The Handmaid's Tale*." *Twentieth Century Literature* 37:2 (1991), 148–168.
Minh-ha, Trinh T. "Writing Postcoloniality and Feminism." *The Post-Colonial Studies Reader*. Eds. Bill Ashcroft, Gareth Griffiths, and Helen Tiffin. London: Routledge, 1995, 264–268.
Moers, Ellen. *Literary Women: The Great Writers*. New York: Doubleday, 1976.
Mohanty, Chandra Talpade. "Under Western Eyes: Feminist Scholarship and Colonial Discourse." *Boundary 2* 12:3/13:1 (1984), 333–358.
Mohr, Dunja M. "Commentaries on *Native Tongue*." *Foundation* 79 (2000b), 38–39.
_____. "An Interview with Suzy McKee Charnas. Part 1." *The New York Review of Science Fiction* 12:1 (1999c), 1, 8–12.
_____. "An Interview with Suzy McKee Charnas. Part 2." *The New York Review of Science Fiction* 12:2 (1999d), 16–21.
_____. "Parity, with Differences: Suzy McKee Charnas Concludes the HOLDFAST Series." *Science Fiction Studies* 26:3 (1999b), 468–472.
_____. "Postkoloniale und feministische Kritik in Suzette Haden Elgins *Native Tongue* Trilogie." *Frauen in Kultur und Gesellschaft: Beiträge zur 2. Fachtagung Frauen-/Gender-Forschung in Rheinland-Pfalz*. Ed. Renate von Bardeleben. Tübingen: Stauffenburg, 2000a, 335–347.
_____. "The Profession of Science Fiction, 53: Towards a Society of Non-Violence." Interview with Suzette Haden Elgin. *Foundation* 79 (2000c), 15–34.
_____. Rev. of: "*Contemporary Feminist Utopianism*, by Lucy Sargisson." *AAA—Arbeiten aus Anglistik und Amerikanistik* 24:1 (1999a), 117–121.

_____. "The Split Self in Margaret Atwood's Female Dystopia *The Handmaid's Tale*." *Selbst und Andere/s oder Von Begegnungen und Grenzziehungen*. Eds. Christina Strobel and Doris Eibl. Augsburg: Wißner, 1998, 110–123.

_____. "'We Are All Cyborgs': Cyberfeminism and the Cyborg as Transgressive Metaphor of the Future in Marge Piercy's *He, She and It*." *Wie natürlich ist Geschlecht? Gender und die Konstruktion von Natur und Technik*. Eds. Ursula Pasero and Anja Gottburgsen. Wiesbaden: Westdeutscher, 2002, 306–318.

Moi, Toril. *Sexual/Textual Politics: Feminist Literary Theory*. 1985. London: Routledge, 1995.

_____. *What Is a Woman? And Other Essays*. Oxford: Oxford University Press, 1999.

Morton, A.L. *The English Utopia*. London: Lawrence & Wishart, 1952.

Moskowitz, Sam. *Strange Horizons: The Spectrum of Science Fiction*. New York: Scribner's, 1976.

Moylan, Tom. *Demand the Impossible: Science Fiction and the Utopian Imagination*. New York: Methuen, 1986.

_____. *Scraps of the Untainted Sky: Science Fiction, Utopia, Dystopia*. Boulder: Westview, 2000.

Mumford, Lewis. *The Story of Utopias*. New York: Viking, 1962.

_____. "Utopia, the City and the Machine." *Utopias and Utopian Thought*. Ed. Frank E. Manuel. Boston: Houghton Mifflin, 1966, 3–24.

Murphy, M. Lynne. Introduction. "Women and Linguistic Innovation: An Annotated Bibliography." *Women and Language* 15:1 (1992), 3–5.

Murphy, Patrick D. "Reducing the Dystopian Distance; Pseudo-Documentary Framing in Near-Future Fiction." *Science-Fiction Studies* 17:1 (1990), 25–40.

Mycak, Sonia. *In Search of the Split Subject: Psychoanalysis, Phenomenology, and the Novels of Margaret Atwood*. Toronto: ECW, 1996.

Nischik, Reingard M. *Mentalstilistik: Ein Beitrag zur Stiltheorie und Narrativik. Dargestellt am Erzählwerk Margaret Atwoods*. Tübingen: Narr, 1991.

Nixon, Nicola. "Cyberpunk: Preparing the Ground for Revolution or Keeping the Boys Satisfied?" *Science-Fiction Studies* 19:3 (1992), 219–235.

Norris, Christopher. *Deconstruction: Theory and Practice*. London: Methuen, 1982.

Oates, Joyce Carol. "Dancing on the Edge of the Precipice." *Margaret Atwood: Conversations*. Ed. Earl G. Ingersoll. Willowdale: Firefly, 1990, 74–85.

Orwell, George. *The Collected Essays, Journalism and Letters of George Orwell*. 1968. Eds. Sonia Orwell and Ian Angus. Harmondsworth: Penguin, 1970.

Pache, Walter. "Canadian Literature in English: A Retrospective and Retrogressive Survey." *Aus der Werkstatt der Augsburger Kanadistik: Analysen—Berichte—Dokumentationen*. Ed. Rainer-Olaf Schultze. Bochum: Brockmeyer, 1996, 3–20.

Parry, Benita. "Signs of Our Times: Discussion of Homi Bhaba's *The Location of Culture*." *Third Text* 28/29 (1994), 5–24.

Patai, Daphne. "Beyond Defensiveness: Feminist Research Strategies." *Women and Utopia: Critical Interpretations*. Eds. Marleen Barr and Nicholas D. Smith. Lanham, MD: University Press of America, 1983, 148–169.

Pearson, Jacqueline. "Where No Man Has Gone Before: Sexual Politics and Women's Science Fiction." *Science Fiction, Social Conflict, and War*. Ed. Philip John Davies. Manchester: Manchester University Press, 1990, 8–25.

Penelope, Julia. *Speaking Freely: Unlearning the Lies of the Father's Tongues*. New York: Pergamon, 1990.

Penn, Julia M. *Linguistic Relativity Versus Innate Idea: The Origins of the Sapir-Whorf-Hypothesis in German Thought*. Den Haag: Mouton, 1972.

Pfaelzer, Jean. "The Changing of the Avant-Garde: The Feminist Utopia." *Science-Fiction Studies* 15:3 (1988), 282–294.

———. "A State of One's Own: Feminism as Ideology in American Utopias 1880–1915." *Extrapolation* 24:4 (1983), 311–326.

———. "What Happened to History?" *Feminism, Utopia, and Narrative*. Eds. Libby Falk Jones and Sarah Webster Goodwin. Knoxville: University of Tennessee Press, 1990, 191–200.

Pfister, Manfred. *Alternative Welten*. München: Fink, 1982.

Pratt, Mary Louise. *Imperial Eyes: Travel Writing and Transculturation*. London: Routledge, 1992.

Priebe, Dagmar. *Kommunikation und Massenmedien in englischen und amerikanischen Utopien des 20. Jahrhunderts*. Frankfurt: Lang, 1998.

Rabkin, Eric S. "Atavism and Utopia." *No Place Else: Explorations in Utopian and Dystopian Fiction*. Eds. Eric S. Rabkin, Martin H. Greenberg, and Joseph D. Olander. Carbondale: Southern Illinois University Press, 1983, 1–10.

———. *The Fantastic in Literature*. Princeton, NJ: Princeton University Press, 1976.

Rao, Eleonora. *Strategies for Identity: The Fiction of Margaret Atwood*. New York: Lang, 1993.

Reesman, Jeanne Campbell. "Dark Knowledge in *The Handmaid's Tale*." *The CEA Critic* 53:3 (1991), 6–22.

Rich, Adrienne. "Compulsory Heterosexuality and Lesbian Experience." *Signs* 5 (1980), 631–660.

———. *Of Woman Born: Motherhood as Experience and Institution*. New York: Norton, 1976.

Roberts, Robin. "The Female Alien: Pulp Science Fiction's Legacy to Feminists." *Journal of Popular Culture* 21:2 (1987), 33–52.

———. *A New Species: Gender and Science in Science Fiction*. Urbana: University of Illinois Press, 1993.

———. "Post-Modernism and Feminist Science Fiction." *Science-Fiction Studies* 17:2 (1990) 136–152.

Roemer, Kenneth M. "Defining America as Utopia." *America as Utopia*. Ed. Kenneth M. Roemer. New York: Burt Franklin, 1981, 1–15.

———. *The Obsolete Necessity: America in Utopian Writings, 1888–1900*. Kent, OH: Kent State University Press, 1976.

———. "Utopian Studies: A Fiction with Notes Appended." *Extrapolation* 25:4 (1984), 318–334.

Rohrlich, Ruby, and Elaine Hoffman Baruch (eds.). *Women in Search of Utopia, Mavericks and Mythmakers*. New York: Schocken, 1984.

Rooke, Constance. *Fear of the Open Heart: Essays on Contemporary Canadian Writing*. Toronto: Coach House, 1989.

Rosinsky, Nathalie M. *Feminist Futures: Contemporary Women's Speculative Fiction*. Ann Arbor: UMI, 1984.

Rubenstein, Roberta. "Nature and Nurture in Dystopia: *The Handmaid's Tale*." *Margaret Atwood: Vision and Forms*. Eds. Kathryn VanSpanckern and Jan Garden Casto. Carbondale: Southern Illinois University Press, 1988, 101–112.

Russ, Joanna. "*Amor Vincit Foeminam*: The Battle of the Sexes in Science Fiction." *Science-Fiction Studies* 7:1 (1980b), 2–15.

———. "The Image of Women in Science Fiction." *Images of Women in Fiction: Feminist Perspectives*. Ed. Susan Koppelman Cornillon. Rev. ed. OH: Bowling Green State University Popular Press, 1973a, 79–94.

_____. "Recent Feminist Utopias." *Future Females: A Critical Anthology.* Ed. Marleen S. Barr. Bowling Green, OH: Bowling Green State University Popular Press, 1981, 71–85.

_____. "What Can a Heroine Do? Or Why Women Can't Write." *Images of Women in Fiction: Feminist Perspectives.* Ed. Susan Koppelman Cornillon. Rev. ed. OH: Bowling Green State University Popular Press, 1973b, 3–20.

Sage, Lorna. *Women in the House of Fiction: Post-War Women Novelists.* New York: Routledge, 1992.

Salvaggio, Ruth. "Octavia Butler and the Black Science-Fiction Heroine." *Black American Literature Forum* 18:2 (1984), 78–81.

Samuelson, David N. "Delany as Postmodern Icon." *Science-Fiction Studies* 24:1 (1997), 150–153.

Sanders, Scott. "Woman as Nature in Science Fiction." *Future Females: A Critical Anthology.* Ed. Marleen S. Barr. Bowling Green, OH: Bowling Green State University Popular Press, 1981, 42–59.

Sandler, Linda. "A Question of Metamorphosis." *Margaret Atwood: Conversations.* Ed. Earl G. Ingersoll. Willowdale: Firefly, 1990, 40–57.

Sapir, Edward. *Language: An Introduction to the Study of Speech.* New York: Harcourt, 1921.

Sargent, Lyman Tower. *British and American Utopian Literature, 1516–1985: An Annotated, Chronological Bibliography.* London: Garland, 1988.

_____. "The Three Faces of Utopianism Revisited." *Utopian Studies* 15:1 (1994), 1–38.

_____. "Utopia: The Problem of Definition." *Extrapolation* 16:2 (1975), 137–158.

Sargisson, Lucy. *Contemporary Feminist Utopianism.* London: Routledge, 1996.

Scholes, Robert. *The Fabulators.* New York: Oxford University Press, 1967.

_____. *Protocols of Reading.* New Haven: Yale University Press, 1989.

_____. *Structural Fabulation: An Essay on the Fiction of the Future.* Notre Dame, IN: University of Notre Dame Press, 1975.

_____, and Eric S. Rabkin. *Science Fiction: History, Science, Vision.* New York: Oxford University Press, 1977.

Schreiber, Le Anne. "Female Troubles: An Interview." *Vogue* January 1986, 209.

Scott, Joan. "Deconstructing Equality-versus-Difference." *Conflicts in Feminism.* Eds. Marianne Hirsch and Evelyn Fox Keller. London: Routledge, 1990, 134–148.

Shinn, Thelma J. "Worlds of Words and Swords: Suzette Haden Elgin and Joanna Russ at Work." *Women World-Walkers: New Dimensions of SF and Fantasy.* Ed. Jane B. Weedman. Lubbock, TX: Texas Tech, 1985, 207–222.

Shklar, Judith N. "What Is the Use of Utopia?" *Heterotopia: Postmodern Utopia and the Body Politic.* Ed. Tobin Siebers. Ann Arbor: University of Michigan Press, 1994, 40–56.

Showalter, Elaine. "Feminist Criticism in the Wilderness." *The New Feminist Criticism: Essays on Women, Literature, and Theory.* Ed. Elaine Showalter. New York: Pantheon, 1985, 243–270.

Siebers, Tobin (ed.). *Heterotopia: Postmodern Utopia and the Body Politic.* Ann Arbor: University of Michigan Press, 1994.

Sisk, David W. *Transformations of Languages in Modern Dystopias.* Westport, CT: Greenwood, 1997.

Slobin, D.I. *Psycholinguistics.* London: Scott & Foresman, 1971.

Snodgrass, Mary Ellen. *Encyclopedia of Utopian Literature.* Santa Barbara: ABC-Clio, 1995.

Soyinka, Wole. *The Burden of Memory, the Muse of Forgiveness.* Oxford: Oxford University Press, 1999.
Spelman, Elisabeth V. *Inessential Woman: Problems of Exclusion in Feminist Thought.* London: Women's, 1990.
Spender, Dale. *Man Made Language.* London: Routledge, 1980.
Spivak, Gayatri Chakravorty. "Can the Subaltern Speak?" *Colonial Discourse and Post-Colonial Theory.* Harvester Wheatsheaf: Hemel Hempstead, 1993, 66–111.
Springer, Claudia. *Electronic Eros: Bodies and Desire in the Postindustrial Age.* London: Athlone, 1996.
Staels, Hilde. *Margaret Atwood's Novels: A Study of Narrative Discourse.* Tübingen: Francke, 1995.
Stein, Karen F. "Margaret Atwood's Modest Proposal *The Handmaid's Tale.*" *Canadian Literature* 148 (1996), 57–73.
_____. "Margaret Atwood's *The Handmaid's Tale*: Scheherazade in Dystopia." *University of Toronto Quarterly* 61:2 (1991/1992), 269–279.
Stimpson, Catharine R. "Feminisms and Utopia." *Utopian Studies III.* Eds. Michael S. Cummings and Nicholas D. Smith. Lanham, MD: University Press of America, 1991.
Suleri, Sara. "Woman Skin Deep: Feminism and the Postcolonial Condition." *The Post-Colonial Studies Reader.* Eds. Bill Ashcroft, Gareth Griffiths, and Helen Tiffin. London: Routledge, 1995, 273–280.
Suvin, Darko. "Defining the Literary Genre of Utopia: Some Historical Semantics, Some Genealogy, A Proposal and a Plea." *Studies in the Literary Imagination* 6 (1973), 112–140).
_____. *Metamorphoses of Science Fiction: On the Poetics and History of a Literary Genre.* New Haven: Yale University Press, 1979.
Tannen, Deborah. *You Just Don't Understand: Women and Men in Conversation.* New York: Morrow, 1990.
Thomas, Sheree R. (ed.). *Dark Matter: A Century of Speculative Fiction from the African Diaspora.* New York: Warner, 2000.
Tillich, Paul. "Critique and Justification of Utopia." *Utopias and Utopian Thought.* Ed. Frank E. Manuel. Boston: Houghton Mifflin, 1966, 296–309.
Todorov, Tzvetan. *The Fantastic: A Structural Approach to a Literary Genre.* Trans. Richard Howard. Cleveland: Case Western Reserve University Press, 1973.
Tomc, Sandra. "'The Missionary Position': Feminism and Nationalism in Margaret Atwood's *The Handmaid's Tale.*" *Canadian Literature* 138/139 (1993), 73–90.
Tompkins, Jane P. "The Reader in History: The Changing Shape of Literary Response." *Reader-Response Criticism: From Formalism to Post-Structuralism.* Ed. Jane P. Tompkins. Baltimore: John Hopkins University Press, 1980, 201–32.
Vasey, Anne. "Handling Monsters: Suzy McKee Charnas and Her Modest Proposal." Unpublished paper, given at the ICFA 17–22nd March 1999, Fort Lauderdale.
Vattimo, Gianni. *Transparent Society.* Baltimore: John Hopkins University Press, 1992.
Walsh, Chad. *From Utopia to Nightmare.* New York: Harper and Row, 1962.
Weinbaum, Batya. *Islands of Women and Amazons: Representations and Realities.* Austin: University of Texas Press, 1999.
Wells, Kim. "Suzette Haden Elgin: An Interview." Internet 3. August 1999. http://www.kimsbridalpa.ges.com/editorials/hadenelgin.htm [Accessed: 13.8.1999].

Westfahl, Gary. "'A Convenient Analog System': John W. Campbell, Jr.'s Theory of Science Fiction." *Foundation* 54:1 (1992), 52–69.
Whorf, Benjamin Lee. *Language, Thought and Reality: Selected Writings of Benjamin Lee Whorf.* Ed. John B. Carroll. Cambridge, MA: MIT, 1956.
Wiemer, Annegret J. "Foreign L(anguish), Mother Tongue: Concepts of Language in Contemporary Feminist Science Fiction." *Women's Studies* 14 (1987), 163–173.
Wilson, Sharon Rose. *Margaret Atwood's Fairy-Tale Sexual Politics.* Jackson: University Press of Mississippi, 1993.
Wolfe, Gary K. *Critical Terms for Science Fiction and Fantasy: A Glossary and Guide to Scholarship.* New York: Greenwood, 1986.
Wolmark, Jenny. *Aliens and Others: Science Fiction, Feminism and Postmodernism.* Hemel Hempstead: Harvester Wheatsheaf, 1994.
_____. "The Postmodern Romances of Feminist Science Fiction." *Cybersexualities: A Reader on Feminist Theory, Cyborgs and Cyberspace.* Ed. Jenny Wolmark. Edinburgh: Edinburgh University Press, 1999, 230–238.
_____, ed. *Cybersexualities: A Reader on Feminist Theory, Cyborgs and Cyberspace.* Edinburgh: Edinburgh University Press, 1999.
Wood, Diane S. "Bradbury and Atwood: Exile as Rational Decision." *The Literature of Emigration and Exile.* Eds. James Whitlark and Wendell Aycok. Lubbock: Texas Tech, 1992, 131–142.
Workman, Nancy V. "Sufi Mysticism in Margaret Atwood's *The Handmaid's Tale.*" *Studies in Canadian Literature* 14:2 (1989), 10–26.
Wu, Dingbo. "Understanding Utopian Literature." *Extrapolation* 34:3 (1993), 230–244.
Young, Robert. *Colonial Desire: Hybridity in Theory, Culture and Race.* London: Routledge, 1995.
Zaki, Hoda M. *Phoenix Renewed: The Survival and Mutation of Utopian Thought in North American Science Fiction, 1965–1982.* Mercer Island: Starmont, 1988.
Zimmermann, Bonnie. *The Safe Sea of Women: Lesbian Fiction 1969–1989.* Boston: Beacon, 1990.
_____. "What Has Never Been: An Overview of Lesbian Feminist Literary Criticism." *Feminist Studies* 7 (1981), 451–475.

Index

Aaron (biblical, OT) 102
Abbott, Edwin A. 41
Albinski, Nan Bowman 2, 25
Aldiss, Brian 43, 129
Alexander, Thea Plym 26
Alice in Wonderland 181
Alice's Adventures in Wonderland 85, 219
Alridge, Alexandra 29, 30
Always Coming Home 24
Amazing Stories 41
L'An 2440 19
Anatomy of Criticism 240
And Chaos Died 75
Anderson, Kristine 127, 128
Anderson, Poul 74, 75
Ang, Li 231
Anthem 34
Apocrypha 108
Aquinas, Thomas 101
Ardener, Edwin 176
Ardener, Shirley 176
Argos 24
Aristotle 1
Armitt, Lucie 80, 127
"The Artist of the Beautiful" 42
Ashcroft, Bill 64
Asimov, Isaac 30, 42
Astounding Science-Fiction 41
Astounding Stories 41
Attebery, Brian 27, 153
Atwood, Margaret 1, 4, 5, 7, 8, 11, 33, 35, 37, 46, 50, 67, 80, 196, 215, 229–269, 270–272, 274–277, 281
Auerbach, Nina 87
Austen, Jane 244
L'autre Monde ou les Etats et Empires de la Lune 19

Babel-17 131

Baccolini, Raffaella 52, 53, 54, 232
Backlash 35
Bacon, Francis 19
Bagemihl, Bruce 195
Bailey, Richard W. 127
Ballard, J.G. 43
Bammer, Angelika 25, 52
Banerjee, Chinmoy 240, 263
Banks, Ian M. 76
Barker, Wendy 268
Barnes, Myra Edwards 127
Barnouw, Dagmar 25
Barr, Marleen S. 2, 25, 40, 48, 154, 156, 196
Bartkowski, Frances 2, 23, 25, 187, 212, 255
Baruch, Elaine Hoffman 25
Bek, Eykar 159
"The Bell-Tower" 42
Bellamy, Edward 14, 18, 20, 22, 29
Benefits 36
Berghahn, Klaus L. 13
Bergmann, Harriet 238
Bersianik, Louky 25–26, 231
Bethke, Bruce 47
Beyond This Horizon 42
Bhabha, Homi K. 6, 64, 65, 66, 132, 146
Biesterfeld, Wolfgang 13
"The Birthmark" 42
Bishop, Michael 76
"Black Destroyer" 76
Black Skin, White Masks 64, 188, 208
Blake, William 103
Bleich, David 12
The Blind Assassin 11, 229, 230, 257, 265
Bloch, Ernst 16, 17
Blunt, Alison 89
Body of Glass 48

Index

The Body-Snatchers 44, 75
Booker, M. Keith 129, 130, 141
Brackett, Leigh 43
Bradbury, Ray 33, 231
Bradley, Marion Zimmer 26, 75
The Brain-Stealers 44
Brave New World 28, 32, 33, 34
Bray, Mary Kay 127
Broderick, Damien 3
Bronfen, Elisabeth 45
The Brothers Karamazov 32
Brunner, John 43
Bryant, Dorothy 26
Bulwer-Lytton, Edward 29
Burdekin, Katharine 34
Burgess, Anthony 30, 32
Burroughs, Edgar Rice 74
Burroughs, William S. 47
The Butcher's Wife 231
Butler, Judith 60
Butler, Octavia 26, 27, 50, 53, 76, 79
Butler, Samuel 20, 29

Cabet, Etienne 13
Cadigan, Pat 48
Cadora, Karen 48
Callenbach, Ernest 25
Caminero-Santangelo, Maria 259
Campanella, Tommaso 19
Campbell, John W., Jr. 38, 41, 74, 76
"Can the Subaltern Speak?" 65
Canopus 24
Carroll, Lewis 85, 181, 219
Carter, Angela 4, 35, 36, 37, 50
The Caves of Steel 42
Césaire, Aimé 207
Chandler, Raymond 47
Charnas, Suzy McKee 1, 4, 6, 7, 26, 35, 36, 37, 50, 60, 64, 66, 145–228, 230, 238, 239, 245, 270–278, 281–286
Chaucer, Geoffrey 236
Cherryh, C.J. 46, 74, 76
Childhood's End 75
Chodorow, Nancy 193, 194
Chomsky, Noam 109
The Circle Game 229
"The Circle Game" 263
La Città del Sole 19
Cixous, Hélène 6, 61, 62, 63, 125, 133, 275
Clarke, Arthur C. 42, 75
Clemente, Bill 224
A Clockwork Orange 30, 32

Clute, John 44, 75
Colonialism/Postcolonialism 64
Colossus 31
The Coming Race 29
The Concept of Utopias 51
A Connecticut Yankee in King Arthur's Court 21
The Conqueror's Child 4, 25, 145–148, 151, 154–159, 161, 163, 165, 167, 176, 182, 183, 191, 193, 206, 208, 213, 214, 224, 225, 227, 277, 281, 282
Conrad, Joseph 218
Contact 76
Contemporary Feminist Utopianism 3, 53
Cooper, Edmund 44
Cooper, Parley J. 44
Copernicus 19
Count Zero 47
Cranny-Francis, Anne 154
Critical Terms for Science Fiction and Fantasy 38
Crucible Island 31
Culture 76
"Cyberpunk" 47
Cybersexualities: A Reader on Feminist Theory, Cyborgs and Cyberspace 210

Daly, Mary 57, 58, 165, 166
Damasio, Antonio 49
Dance the Eagle to Sleep 35
Darkover 75
Darwin, Charles 23, 187
Davey, Frank 240
de Beauvoir, Simone 62
De Bergerac, Cyrano 19
Deconstruction: Theory and Practice 61
Defoe, Daniel 83, 184
de la Concha, Angelas 58, 98
Delaney, Samuel R. 3, 27, 41, 45, 51, 127, 131
de Lauretis, Teresa 59, 280
De le terre à la lune 41
de l'Isle-Adam, Villiers 42
Demand the Impossible: Science Fiction and the Utopian Imagination 51
De optimo reipublicae statu, deque nova insula Utopia 18
De Pizan, Christine 21
Derrida, Jacques 61, 62, 113, 131
De Saussure, Ferdinand 61
Devine, Maureen 25
Dialectic of Sex 57
Dick, Philip K. 41, 43
Dickinson, Emily 268

Index

Disch, Thomas M. 74
Discipline and Punish 246
The Dispossessed 27, 116, 121
d Layo, Servan 159
Donawerth, Jane L. 4, 25, 85, 86, 104
A Door Into Ocean 26, 46, 76, 126
Dopp, Jamie 256
Dorsey, Candas Jane 48
Dostoevsky 32
Dow, C.H. 108
Downward to the Earth 76
The Drowned World 43
DuBois, W.E.B. 27
Dunaway, Faye 229
Duvall, Robert 229

Earthsong 4, 71–144, 272
Ecotopia 25
Ecotopia Emerging 25
The Edible Woman 241
Elgin, Suzette Haden 1, 4, 6, 25, 33, 37, 50, 64, 67, 71–144, 146, 153, 172, 177, 215, 230, 237, 238, 239, 266, 270–274, 276–277, 281, 285
Elliott, Robert C. 12
The End of Utopia 2
Engels, Friederich 16, 20
Die Entwicklung des Socialismus von der Utopia zur wissenschaft 20
Erewhon 20, 29
Erewhon Revisited 20
The Eugélionne 26, 231
Evans, Mark 237
L'Ève future 42
Exodus 102
The Eye of the Heron 160

Fahrenheit 451 33, 34, 231, 235, 261
Faludi, Susan 35, 277, 278
Fanon, Frantz 64, 188, 208, 210
Farley, Tucker 258
Farmer, Philip José 44
Fehlner, Gert 73
The Female Man 4, 24, 26, 27, 87, 154, 155
The Feminine Mystique 57
The Feminists 44
Ferns, Chris 2, 17, 18, 52
The Fifth Head of Cerberus 75
Findley, Timothey 231
Finnell, Susanna 240, 241
Finney, Jack 44, 75
Firestone, Shulamith 57
The First Men in the Moon 41

Fitting, Peter 129, 141, 191
Five to Twelve 44
Flatland 41
Flesh 44
Florence, Penny 76, 127, 141
Footfall 75
Forster, E.M. 31
Foucault, Michel 55, 246
The Four Gated City 35
Fourier, Charles 13
Frankenstein, or The Modern Prometheus 30, 42, 231
Freud, Sigmund 187
Friedan, Betty 57
Frye, Northrop 14, 240
Fuller, Margaret 22
The Furies 4, 64, 145–148, 150–151, 153, 156–159, 163, 166, 186, 187, 203, 204, 210, 211, 213, 220, 227, 281, 282, 284
Futurist Manifesto 29
The Futurological Congress 131

Galileo 19
The Gate to Women's Country 26, 46, 154
Gearhart, Sally Miller 23, 25, 146, 154, 199
Gender Genocide 44
The Genocides 74
Gernsback, Hugo 38, 41
Ghandi 130
Gibbon's Decline and Fall 26
Gibson, William 47
Gilbert, Sandra 133
Gilman, Charlotte Perkins 22, 23, 25, 26, 85, 154
The Girls from Planet 5 44
Givner, Jessie 231
Gnüg, Hiltrud 13
Gödel 129, 130
Gödel, Escher, Bach 128
Godwin, Francis 19
Gold Coast 53
Goodwin, Sarah Webster 25
Gordimer, Nadine 231
Gordon, Joan 4
Gotlieb, Phyllis 43
"A Gourdful of Glory" 231
Grace, George W. 131
Grace, Sherrill E. 231, 256
Graves, Robert 172
"The Great Inquisitor" 32
Griffin, Susan 122

Griffiths, Gareth 64
Grosz, Elizabeth 59
Gubar, Susan 133, 252
Les Guérillères 24, 126, 146
Gulliver's Travels 29, 218, 222
Gyn/Ecology 58, 166

Hamilton, Edmond 74
Hammer, Stephanie Barbé 240
Hammett, Dashiell 47
The Handmaid's Tale 1, 4, 5, 7, 8, 33, 34, 35, 36, 37, 80, 196, 209, 229–269, 270–272, 274, 277, 284
Hansard Commons 28
Haraway, Donna J. 48, 56, 146, 171
Hardwired 47
Harper, Mary 48
Haschak, Paul G. 2
Hawthorne, Nathaniel 42
He, She and It 4, 48, 53
Head, Bessie 224
Heart of Darkness 218
Heinlein, Robert A. 27, 41, 42, 44, 74, 75, 153
Heller, Arno 13, 263
"The Helping Hand" 74
Heorides 240
Herland 22, 23, 25, 26, 86, 154
Heroes and Villains 4, 35, 36, 37
Heuermann, Hartmut 13
Hillegas, Mark R. 30
Hockett 130
Hoffmann, E.T.A 30
Hofstadter, Douglas 128
Hölbling, Walter 13
Holdfast 1, 5, 35, 37, 64, 145–228, 230, 241, 242, 246, 270–271, 273–274, 276–278, 281
Holland-Cunz, Barbara 25
Homer 152
hooks, bell 58
Hopkinson, Nalo 27
"Houston, Houston, Do You Read?" 26, 47, 154
Howells, Coral Ann 231, 261
Hubbard, L. Ron 74
Hudson 130
Huggan, Graham 91
Hutcheon, Linda 256
Huxley, Aldous 25, 28, 32

Idoru 47
Iliad 152
Implosion 44

"Interlunar" 268
Invaders from Earth 74
The Invisible Man 42
Irigaray, Luce 6, 59, 135
The Iron Heel 31
Island 25
The Island of Dr. Moreau 29, 42
Islands in the Net 47

Jackson, Rosemary 39
Jacoby, Russell 2
Jameson, Frederic 47, 74
JanMohamed, Abdul 77
Jesus 101–103, 136, 137
Jones, D.F. 31, 44
Jones, Dorothy 240
Jones, E.D. 108
Jones, Gwyneth 1, 4, 46, 76
Jones, Libby Falk 25
Joseph (biblical, NT) 102
The Judas Rose 4, 71–144
July's People 231
Juniper Time 270

Kaler, Anne K. 240, 244
Kanneh, Kadiatu 95
Das Kapital 20
Kateb, George 12
Kauffman, Linda 240
Keinhorst, Annette 25
Ketterer, David 231, 238, 244, 266
The Kin of Ata Are Waiting for You 26
King, Martin Luther 130
King, Maureen 221
Klarer, Mario 25, 132, 133
Knight, Damon 45
Kolmerten, Carol 25
Kornbluth, C.M. 43
Kramarae, Cheris 72, 128, 129
Kristeva, Julia 6, 132, 133, 266, 267
Kumar, Krishan 12, 14, 15

Lacan, Jacques 132, 133
Lacombe, Michele 240, 261
Lane, Mary Bradley 22
Lange, Bernd-Peter 13
Languages of Pao 131
Larson, Janet 239
Last and First Men 41
Laurence, Margaret 231
LeBihan, Jill 264
Leblanc, Lauraine 48

Index

Lecker, Robert 231, 240
Lefanu, Sarah 2, 25, 39, 45, 52, 148, 154, 155, 156
The Left Hand of Darkness 4, 76, 126
Le Guin, Ursula K. 4, 5, 24, 27, 39, 44, 50, 51, 76, 116, 121, 126, 160
Leibniz, Gottfried 134
Leinster, Murray 44
Lem, Stanislaw 131
Le Queux, William 31
Lessing, Doris 24, 35, 37, 46
Lévi-Strauss, Claude 62
Levinas, Emmanuel 61
Levitas, Ruth 12, 16, 17, 51
Limbo 30
Le Livre de la Cité des Dames 22
London, Jack 31
The Lonesome Node 127
Looking Backward 14, 29
Looking Backward 2000-1887 20
Loomba, Ania 64, 66, 172
The Lord of the Rings 134
Lorde, Audre 58
Luhmann, Niklas 80, 132
Lyotard, Jean-François 61, 131

Maccabeus 108
Macdonald, Ross 47
Machiavelli 32
"The Machine Stops" 31
Malak, Amin 253
The Man in the Moone 19
"A Manifesto for Cyborgs" 48
Mannheim, Karl 16
Manuel, Frank E. 12, 14
Manuel, Fritzie P. 12, 14
Marx, Karl 16, 20
McCaffrey, Anne 75
McCarthy, Mary 240, 266
McHale, Brian 27, 47
McIntyre, Vonda N. 46
Mead, Margaret 13
The Measure of Miranda 231
Melville, Herman 42
The Memoirs of a Survivor 35, 37
Men Like Gods 41
Mercier, Louis Sébastien 19
Merril, Judith 27, 41, 43
Meyers, Walter E. 127
Micromégas 19
Mill, John Stuart 28
Miller, Perry 236, 237
Miner, Madonne 240
Minh-ha, Trinh T. 100

Miriam (biblical, OT) 102
Mirkham, Beryl 182
Mixon, Laura J. 48
Mizora: A Prophecy 22
A Modern Utopia 20, 22, 23, 25
A Modest Proposal 209, 237
Moffett, Judith 45, 86
Moi, Toril 62
Mona Lisa Overdrive 47
"The Monster" 76
The Moon Is a Harsh Mistress 44
Moore, C.L. 43
More, Thomas 11, 14, 15, 18, 19, 22
Morris, William 16, 20, 22
Morton, A.L. 14
Morton, Arthur 12
Moses (biblical, OT) 102
Mosley, Walter 27
Motherlines 4, 25, 26, 145–147, 149–156, 158–159, 161, 166, 168, 192, 201, 207, 210, 211, 212, 220, 272
Moylan, Tom 2, 12, 40, 50, 51, 52, 53, 54, 55, 60, 232
Mumford, Lewis 12
Murphy, M. Lynne 127
Murphy, Patrick D. 231
Murphy, Sarah 231
Mycak, Sonia 7, 256

Narrating Utopia 17
Native Tongue 4, 5, 6, 25, 33, 36, 37, 64, 71–144, 156, 158, 177, 230, 241, 266, 270–273, 277, 285
Negley, Glenn 28
Neuromancer 47
New Atlantis 19
News from Nowhere 20, 22
The Next Generation 76
Nicholls, Peter 44, 75
Nietzsche 30
1984 28, 32, 33, 34, 120, 131, 261
Niven, Larry 75
Nixon, Nicola 48
Norris, Christopher 61
North, Andrew 43
Norton, Andre 43
Not Wanted on the Voyage 231

Of Woman Born 58
On Strike Against God 279
Ore, Rebecca 48
Orlando 42
Orwell, George 28, 31, 131, 231

Ovid 240
Owen, Robert 13
The Ozark Trilogy 80

Pallen, Condé B. 31
Parable of the Sower 53
Parry, Benita 132
The Passion of New Eve 4, 35
Patrick, J. Max 28
Patternist 26, 76
Pearson, Carol 56
Penelope, Julia 128, 134, 135
Pern 75
Pfaelzer, Jean 11
Pfister, Manfred 13
Phillpotts, Eden 76
Piercy, Marge 4, 25, 26, 35, 46, 48, 50, 51, 53, 126, 231
Pinter, Harold 229
Plato 14, 18
Player Piano 30
Poe, Edgar Allan 42, 262
Poetics 1
Pohl, Frederik 43
The Post-Colonial Studies Reader 64
Pournelle, Jerry 75
Pratt, Marie Louise 7, 65, 216
Pride and Prejudice 244
Priebe, Dagmar 4, 80, 120, 129, 131
The Prince 32
The Principle of Hope 16
The Puppet Masters 75

Quest for Utopia 28

Rabkin, Eric S. 39
Rand, Ayn 34
Rao, Eleonora 7, 232, 239, 255, 263, 265
"Rappaccini's Daughter" 42
"The Raven" 262
Reesman, Campbell 267–268
Report on Probability A 43
The Reproduction of Mothering 193
The Republic 18
Return to Tomorrow 74
Rich, Adrienne 58
Richardson, Natasha 229
Roberts, Robin 45
Robinson, Kim Stanley 53
Robinson Crusoe 83, 184
Roemer, Kenneth M. 12, 15, 16
Rohrlich, Ruby 25
Rooke, Constance 238

Rose, Gillian 89
Rubenstein, Roberta 265
The Ruins of Isis 26
Russ, Joanna 4, 24, 26, 27, 44, 45, 50, 51, 75, 86, 87, 153, 154, 155, 279

Sagan, Carl 76
Sage, Lorna 260
Said, Edward 65
Samuelson, David N. 3
The Sands of Mars 42, 75
Sapir, Edward 130
Sargent, Lyman Tower 2, 12, 15, 16, 17, 50, 53, 54
Sargent, Pamela 46, 75, 155
Sargisson, Lucy 3, 4, 5, 50, 53, 54, 56, 57, 59–66, 68, 118, 165, 170, 187, 195, 196, 281
Saunders, Charles 27
Saurus 76
Schlöndorff, Volker 229
Scholes, Robert 40, 160
Science Fiction Studies 2
Scott, Joan 59
Scott, Melissa 46
Scraps of the Untainted Sky 2, 51
The Second Sex 62
The Second Stage 57
Seeber, Hans Ulrich 13
Sexual/Textual Politics 62
Shakespeare, William 49
Sheldon, Alice 26, 43
Shelley, Mary 30, 42, 231
Shinn, Thelma 80, 81, 118
Shklar, Judith N. 55
Shockley, Evie 27
The Shore of Women 46, 155
Showalter, Elaine 176
"The Sick Rose" 103
Siebers, Tobin 55
Le Silence de la Cité 48
Silverberg, Robert 74, 76
Singer, Daniel 279
Sisk, David 4, 29, 80, 81, 127, 143, 264
Sister/Outsider 58
Skinner, B.F. 25
Slonczewski, Joan 26, 46, 76, 126
Smith, Winston 261
Snodgrass, Mary Ellen 2
Sorel 16
Soyinka, Wole 159, 161
Space Cadet 153
Spelman, Elisabeth 60
Spender, Dale 176

Spivak, Gayatri 58, 65
Spretnak, Charlene 122
Springer, Claudia 48
Staels, Hilde 255, 266
Stand on Zanzibar 43
Stein, Karen 237, 259
Sterling, Bruce 47
Stiffed 277
Stimpson, Catherine 241
Stovel, Nora Foster 255
Sturgeon 44, 45
Suleri, Sara 58
Surfacing 7, 241
Survival 243
"Surviving" 45, 86
Suvin, Darko 12, 15, 40, 41
Swastika Night 34
Swift, Jonathan 29, 209, 218, 222, 237

Tannen, Deborah 73
Tepper, Sheri S. 26, 46, 154
The Terminal Beach 43
Thomas, Sheree R. 27
Tiffin, Helen 64
Tillich, Paul 16
Time Enough for Love 74
The Time Machine 13, 21, 29, 41
Tiptree, James, Jr. 26, 43, 46, 47, 86, 145, 154
Todorov, Tzvetan 39
Tolkien, J.R.R. 39, 134
Tomc, Sandra 237, 240, 242, 243, 252
Totem and Taboo 187
Twain, Mark 21
2150 A.D. 26
The Two of Them 153

The Unknown Tomorrow 31
Utopia 19, 22

The Vampire Tapestry 220
Vance, Jack 76, 131
van Vogt, A.E. 42, 76
Vattimo, Gianni 55
Venus of Dreams 75
Venus of Shadows 75
Verne, Jules 41
A Vindication of the Rights of Women 22
Vinge, Joan D. 46
Vingt mille lieues sous les mers 41
Virgin Mary 101–102
Virgin Planet 75
Virtual Light 47

Voltaire 19
Vonarburg, Elizabeth 48
Vonnegut, Kurt 30
Voyage au centre de la terre 41

Walden Two 25
Walk to the End of the World 4, 35, 145–147, 149, 152, 153, 155–159, 175, 177, 186, 187, 201, 207, 209, 210, 213, 217, 221, 225, 272, 284
Walker, Alice 58
Walsh, Chad 30
The Wanderground: Stories of the Hill Women 25, 26, 146, 154
The War of the Worlds 41, 75
The Waste Land 164
We 28, 32, 41
Webster, Mary 236, 237
Weinbaum, Batya 171
Weldon, Fay 46
Wells, H.G. 13, 20, 21, 22, 23, 25, 29, 41, 75, 231
West with the Night 182
Westfahl, Gary 38
"What Happened to History" 11
What Is a Woman 62
"What Is the Use of Utopia?" 55
"When It Changed" 45, 86
When the Sleeper Wakes 29
White Queen 76
"Who Goes There?" 76
Whorf, Benjamin Lee 130
Wilhelm, Kate 270
William, Walter Jon 47
Wilson, Richard 44
Wilson, Sharon Rose 241
With Her in Our Land 22, 23
Wittig, Monique 24, 60, 126, 146, 199
Wolfe, Bernard 30
Wolfe, Gary K. 2, 38
Wollstonecraft, Mary 22
Wolmark, Jenny 2, 48, 196, 207, 210
Woman in the Nineteenth Century 22
Woman on the Edge of Time 4, 25, 26, 126, 231
Women and Men Speaking 72
"The Women Men Don't See" 46, 86
Woolf, Virginia 42, 45
The Word for World Is Forest 76
Workman, Nancy V. 237
Wu, Dingbo 15
Wylie, Philip 44
Wyndham, John 42

Xenogenesis 26, 79

You Just Don't Understand 73

Zacharasiewicz, Waldemar 13

Zaki, Hoda M. 25
Zamenhof, L.L. 134
Zamyatin, Yevgeny 28, 33, 41
Zimmermann, Bonnie 58, 82